Victorian Gaslighting

SUNY series, Studies in the Long Nineteenth Century

Pamela K. Gilbert, editor

Victorian Gaslighting

Genealogy of an Injustice

Edited by Diana Bellonby, Nora Gilbert,

and Tara MacDonald

Cover credit: Ingrid Bergman in *Gaslight* (1944; dir. George Cukor). MGM/Photofest.
Published by State University of New York Press, Albany

Printed in the United States of America

EU GPSR Authorised Representative:
Logos Europe, 9 rue Nicolas Poussin, 17000, La Rochelle, France
contact@logoseurope.eu

For information, contact State University of New York Press, Albany, NY
www.sunypress.edu

Library of Congress Cataloging-in-Publication Data

Names: Bellonby, Diana E. editor | Gilbert, Nora editor | MacDonald, Tara editor
Title: Victorian gaslighting : genealogy of an injustice / edited by Diana Bellonby, Nora Gilbert, and Tara MacDonald.
Description: Albany : State University of New York Press, 2026. | Series: SUNY series, studies in the long nineteenth century | Includes bibliographical references and index.
Identifiers: LCCN 2025034343 | ISBN 9798855805918 (hardcover) | ISBN 9798855807110 (epub) | ISBN 9798855805932 (PDF)
Subjects: LCSH: English literature—19th century—History and criticism | Manipulative behavior in literature | Manipulative behavior—Great Britain—History—19th century | Feminist theory | LCGFT: Literary criticism | Essays
Classification: LCC PR468.M37 V53 2026
LC record available at https://lccn.loc.gov/2025034343

Contents

Illustrations

Acknowledgments

We are happy to have the opportunity to thank everyone who has supported this project over the last three years. This book began as a panel at the North American Victorian Studies Association in October 2022 called "Genealogy of an Injustice: Case Studies in Victorian Gaslighting." The coeditors — and contributor Elizabeth Womack — all participated on the panel, and the feedback we received made it clear that tracing this concept through the nineteenth century would be a valuable endeavor both in and beyond Victorian studies. We continued discussions with excellent audiences at an MLA (Modern Language Association) roundtable in Philadelphia in January 2024 and a VISAWUS (Victorian Interdisciplinary Studies Association of the Western United States) online roundtable in September 2024.

In addition to our receptive and helpful audiences, we would like to acknowledge the generosity of the special collections librarians at the Margaret Herrick Library in Los Angeles, the Harry Ransom Center at the University of Texas at Austin, Boston University, and the British Library for helping us track down archival materials, as well as the University of North Texas and the University of Idaho for their financial support.

It was at the NAVSA 2022 book exhibit that we first met and began discussing the book idea with our editor, Rebecca Colesworthy, who has thoughtfully guided us through the different phases of the process, from proposal to submission to publication; we couldn't be more grateful for her ongoing enthusiasm and responsiveness. We were also enormously lucky to receive detailed, insightful feedback from our three anonymous readers, and we would like to express our gratitude to each of them. We're thrilled to have this book appear in Pamela Gilbert's "Studies in the Long Nineteenth Century" series at SUNY, and we appreciate Pamela's generous support of the project.

But our biggest thanks go to our superb contributors, who trusted us with their ideas and who wrote such moving, groundbreaking chapters drawn from an impressive range of expertise. It was a pleasure to work with all of you.

Diana would also like to thank Diana Maltz for sharing her wisdom about Vernon Lee, Zinnia Piotrowski for generously assisting her research, and Deanna Kreisel and Elizabeth Meadows for providing emotional support when she needed it most. She will always be deeply grateful to her coeditors for giving her the gift of a wonderful first book experience. Finally, to her loving husband Matt and beloved children, Aria and Adrian, thank you for listening, believing, and giving her so many reasons to feel hopeful.

Nora would additionally like to thank all the students who took her "Gaslighting: Sex, Gender, and Mental Illness in Victorian and Neo-Victorian Literature and Film" classes in 2019 and 2023 for sharing their perspectives on and insights about Victorian gaslighting with her, as well as Andrea Kaston Tange and the members of her Midwest Victorian Studies Association 2023 Summer Seminar workshopping group — Zarena Aslami, Renate Dohmen,

Melissa McLeod, and Ashley Miller — for the feedback they provided on an early draft of her *Trilby/Dracula/Gaslight* chapter. She was also delighted to share this work with the Friends of the Dickens Project under the auspices of a Friends Faculty Fellowship in the spring of 2024. On a personal level, she would like to thank her three wonderful and always-supportive sons, Grady, Quinn, and Keaton, and, especially, her wonderful, always-supportive husband Josh, for not being *anything like* the husband in *Gaslight*.

Tara would like to thank the audience at the NAVSA 2024 Seattle hub, who gave useful feedback on her chapter, and her coeditors, who encouraged her to explore obstetric gaslighting. She was eight months pregnant at the NAVSA 2022, and she is grateful to her husband, Chad, for his encouragement and support these past few years, and to her now-toddler, Lucas, for being such a delightful and happy distraction.

Finally, we wish to thank one another! This was truly a collaborative effort that involved countless emails, text messages, and Zoom calls across time zones. Working with other feminist scholars gave each of us much-needed solidarity and joy during strange, challenging, and increasingly anti-feminist times.

Introduction

Gaslighting Before *Gaslight*

Diana Bellonby, Nora Gilbert, and Tara MacDonald

The term "gaslighting" has reentered the popular lexicon with a vengeance over the past decade, appearing in countless news stories, books, and articles about sex, race, politics, medicine, and emotional control. Such accounts often note that the term derives from a particular twentieth-century source text: the 1944 film *Gaslight*, based on Patrick Hamilton's 1938 play of the same name, which tells the story of a sadistic husband who manipulates his wife into believing she's losing her mind. Rarely emphasized, however, is the fact that Hamilton pointedly set his play in Victorian London. Far from incidental, this Victorian setting — and plot, characters, and themes — provides an evocative guide to the nineteenth-century social, political, and cultural developments that cohered to fuel the type of abuse *Gaslight* captures so harrowingly, recognizably well.

To understand "gaslighting," we argue, one must understand *Gaslight* — both the story and its formative Victorian history. The thirteen essays gathered in this collection explore examples of gaslighting in novels, novellas, poems, journals, autobiographies, letters, newspaper articles, literary reviews, domestic manuals, and medical reports written throughout the nineteenth century and throughout the British empire. Building on recent studies of contemporary gaslighting by philosophers, sociologists, and political scientists, we seek to demonstrate the urgent value of historicizing a form of violence that is fundamentally tied to misogynist and white supremacist systems of oppression and the ways in which those systems were narrated, defended, effaced, suppressed, and distorted in Victorian literature and culture.

Though it is difficult to pinpoint precisely when "gaslight" began to circulate as a verb in everyday speech, we do know when Hamilton's story was first used to name a real-life problem that demanded clinical attention.[1] In a 1969 issue of the medical journal *The Lancet*, British psychiatrists Russell Barton and J. A. Whitehead recognized "the Gas-Light Phenomenon" by comparing Hamilton's fictional plot of a husband scheming "to get rid of his wife by driving her into a lunatic asylum" to several cases of family members trying to do the same to their "unwanted and restricting relative[s]."[2] Over the course of the 1970s and 1980s, more and more psychiatrists took to using the word "gaslighting" to describe the emotional and behavioral patterns that accompanied relationships like the one fictionalized in *Gaslight*. Psychoanalysts Victor Calef and Edward Weinshel, for example, conceived of gaslighting as a matter of projection and introjection, while family therapists Gertrude Gass and William Nichols classified it as a "marital syndrome."[3] It was also during this period that the term first made its way into the kind of critical feminist discourse we spotlight (and model) in this volume. For instance, in Adrienne Rich's iconic speech-turned-polemical-pamphlet from the mid-1970s, "Women and Honor: Some Notes on Lying," she insisted that "Women have been driven mad, 'gaslighted,' for centuries by the refutation of our experience and our instincts in a culture which validates only male experience. The truth of our bodies and minds has been mystified to us. We therefore have a primary obligation to each other: not to undermine each other's sense of reality for the sake of expediency; not to gaslight each other."[4]

In the mid-2010s, the subject began to receive sustained scholarly attention outside the disciplines of psychiatry and applied psychology. In her much-cited 2014 article, "Turning Up the Lights on Gaslighting," philosopher Kate Abramson provided the first in-depth examination of the phenomenon's moral harms and gendered structure. She observed that, while not always or necessarily sexist, gaslighting overwhelmingly affects women, and perpetrators "frequently rely on the target's internalization of sexist norms."[5] In 2019, in a similarly foundational article, Paige Sweet proposed a sociological definition based on extensive interviews with domestic abuse survivors, whose testimony supports her argument that gender inequality is a condition of possibility for gaslighting. Sweet heard the phrase "crazy bitch" so often during her fieldwork that she came to consider it "the literal discourse of gaslighting."[6] Since then, a wave of feminist philosophers have theorized gaslighting primarily as a form of "epistemic injustice" that harms people in their capacity as knowers.[7] Others have constructed philosophical definitions based on affective or moral approaches, such as Kate Manne, who highlights cases in which the gaslighter weaponizes norms of morality, rather than sanity; the latter epithet in "crazy bitch," she contends, is just as important as the former.[8]

In recent years, too, as "gaslighting" has reached ever-higher heights of popular currency, more critics have begun to stress that it can be structural, not just interpersonal; that is, whole groups of people can be manipulated in this way. Philosopher Elena Ruíz, for example, identifies "crazy"-making mechanisms built into settler colonial cultures. For Ruíz, gaslighting can "refer to the effort of one *culture* to undermine another *culture's* confidence and stability by causing the victim-*ized collective* to doubt [its] own sense and beliefs."[9] Innumerable journalists, pundits, and other scholars, meanwhile, have insisted that politicians can gaslight constituencies, even national populations—that, to name the most obvious and influential example of the past decade, "Donald Trump Is Gaslighting America," as Lauren Duca put it in her viral 2016 article.[10] And in 2022, when Merriam-Webster announced gaslighting as its Word of the Year, they underscored patterns of deception in global communication systems: "In this age of misinformation — of 'fake news,' conspiracy theories, Twitter trolls, and deep fakes — gaslighting has emerged as a word for our time."[11] Abramson's latest book, *On Gaslighting* (2024), however, pushes back against such expansions of the term, especially via the category of structural gaslighting, which she dismisses as a conflation of different forms of oppression.

This volume, which marks the first investigation of gaslighting's nineteenth-century British roots, employs a capacious, yet historically grounded approach to defining past and present forms, including structural ones. Among the most valuable critical concepts engaged in this book are those that name the connection between gaslighting and resistance. In 2019, political scientists Angelique M. Davis and Rose Ernst coined the indispensable term "racial gaslighting" to describe "the political, social, economic and cultural process that perpetuates and normalizes a white supremacist reality through pathologizing those who resist."[12] Jeff Engelhardt recently posited the related notion of "normative gaslighting" to denote instances in which "some person(s) report systemic injustice, and then multiple others raise unwarranted doubts about that report and/or reporter."[13] Alongside Davis, Ernst, and Engelhardt, Veronica Ivy [Rachel McKinnon], Paul-Mikhail Catapang Podosky, and others have observed that gaslighting typically occurs in response to a person's report of injustice, especially sexist and/or racist injustice.

It is no accident that today gaslighting often happens in response to feminist and/or anti-racist resistance for, as we argue in the remainder of this introduction, the Victorian history of gaslighting represents a genealogy of challenges to the interlocking institutions of patriarchy, slavery, and colonialism. To resist is to confront society-wide myths insofar as these institutions rely on chronically reinforced master narratives that authorize falsehoods about the mental, moral, and emotional natures of women, racialized others, and colonized subjects, thereby damaging their ability to articulate, validate, and even believe their own lived experiences. Three of the leading master narratives examined in this collection include the medical myth that women's reproductive bodies render them naturally susceptible to insanity, the pseudoscientific lie that nonwhite people are naturally prone to irrationality and emotional excess, and the organizing illusion underpinning the enterprise of British colonization itself, wherein Englishmen move into a space that is not their own and attempt to "civilize" its native inhabitants by convincing them that everything they think to be true — their religious beliefs, their cultural practices, their sense of national or regional identity and autonomy — is in fact wrongheaded, misguided, foolish, "crazy."

Gaslighting can be many different things: misogynist, racist, homophobic, transphobic, xenophobic, economic, religious, medical, institutional, and so forth. But in any manifestation, it is always *narrative* insofar as gaslighting depends on the power to propagate a false story that negates another person's reality. Yet, none of the leading ways in which this type of emotional abuse has been defined — as a scheme to hospitalize a sane person, as an intimate partner's act of projection, as a common feature of men's domestic violence against women, as a problem of knowledge and credibility, or as a political crisis in the age of fake news — accounts for the essential role of storytelling. *Victorian Gaslighting* not only offers new insights, such as a concrete historical framework for abstract concepts, an inaugural record of key voices, and an introduction to modes not named in existing literature (such as abolitionist gaslighting and capitalist gaslighting), but also elucidates a bewilderingly variegated phenomenon by harnessing the explanatory power of the story that still best captures the term's meaning.

Though there were multiple versions of *Gaslight* produced for the stage and screen in the 1930s and 1940s whose plots differed in ways that will be discussed in the next section, the storyline that remains constant through all of them is this: Sometime in the latter part of the nineteenth century,[14] a man attempts to steal some rare, famous jewels from an older woman in her London townhome, but he cannot find the jewels in question and winds up murdering her instead. Years later, the man — now living under a pseudonym and married to a young woman who knows nothing about his violent past — moves into the same townhome in order to continue searching for the jewels. After a while, the man grows tired of having to conduct his search surreptitiously at night to keep it secret from his wife and decides to convince both her and their two household servants that she is losing her grip on reality so that he has the legal right to consign her to an insane asylum. The way he does this is by moving around small household objects (a brooch, a pocket watch, a little picture hanging on the wall) and then telling her that *she* is the one who must have moved or stolen them — and that, if she doesn't remember doing so, it's further proof of her insanity. The scheme is horrifically successful, and the man is on the verge of having the woman committed when a detective who has taken interest in the case arrives on the scene, affirms the woman's sense that she is "slowly, methodically, systematically being *driven* out of [her] mind,"[15] works with the woman to piece together the plot, and has the man arrested for murder.

Also in every version of *Gaslight*, the husband emotionally abuses his wife through a combination of structural conditions, rhetorical maneuvers, and interpersonal tactics. He marries her in order to take advantage of the patriarchal laws of coverture. He uses his authority to exert control over every member of the household. He stirs up antagonism between his wife and the servants, publicly humiliating her in front of them. He labels her "hysterical," "highly strung," "anxious," "fanciful," "absent-minded," "ridiculous," "silly," "insane," "crazy," and "mad." He discourages and prevents her from leaving the house. He withholds affection and social connection. He blames, scolds, dismisses, shames, mocks, and silences her. Above all, he rejects her experience of reality and isolates her from any person likely to confirm its validity. This nexus of social, political, and psychological harms may be familiar enough to seem ahistorical, but it corresponds to real-life threats and historical developments that uniquely crystallized in nineteenth-century Britain. While its component parts all existed before the Victorian period, gaslighting reached the level of a recognizable paradigm only during a century when the concept of "madness" was debated, misused, policed, and medicalized like never before.

Not One but Many *Gaslights*

Even though many recent articles, books, and news stories on the subject of gaslighting do make an at least cursory nod to the term's textual origin, the text to which they almost always allude is the Hollywood film version of *Gaslight* from 1944, when, in fact, that film was the fourth successful iteration of the "Gaslight" narrative to be produced in the United Kingdom and the United States within six years. (For a chart outlining the key differences between these four versions, see Table I.1.) The story of how the plot of *Gaslight* was revised and reshaped over the course of those four productions is both more complex than most people realize and more reflective of the gendered cultural tendencies that our collection highlights: the tendency to underestimate and devalue a woman's intellectual and analytical capabilities; the tendency to suppress and silence a woman's thoughts and speech; the tendency to relegate the woman to the role of helpless victim who must rely on the aid of male detectives, family members, suitors, et al. So pervasive and abiding are these cultural tendencies that they even fuel misreadings of the plot of *Gaslight* in critical discussions of "gaslighting" today.

It is especially egregious when such discussions make no mention of the 1938 play by Patrick Hamilton, since it is Hamilton who must be credited with conceiving of the story that gave rise to the term. Hamilton is best known today for his two hit plays that were made into Hollywood movies — *Gas Light* (two words, in the original title) and *Rope* (1929) — though he, along with many critics of his day, considered his novels (*The Midnight Bell*, *Hangover Square*, *The Slaves of Solitude*) to be his greater artistic achievements. Critical acclaim on multiple fronts notwithstanding, Hamilton never achieved the same kind of name recognition that many of his equally lauded contemporaries did; indeed, in the words of one of his biographers, he continues to be something of an "eerie non-presence in modern British literary history."[16] *Gas Light* is, it should be noted, somewhat of an outlier in Hamilton's oeuvre insofar as its primary sympathies lie with a suffering woman. In his novels, it is typically "an innocent young man" who is being "driven to a breakdown or even to murder by a calculating, attractive young woman who doesn't return his infatuation," as Miranda Miller has summarized.[17] The semi-autobiographical nature of these novels is widely acknowledged, with Nigel Jones even going so far as to say that "it is fortunate that Patrick Hamilton had the talent to sublimate his darker desires, and transmute them into some of the 20th century's most highly regarded dramas and fiction. If he had not, he himself could have become one of the criminals, con artists and murderers who people his works."[18]

But Jones also points out another clear biographical referent for the violent male characters of Hamilton's fictional cosmos, especially *Gas Light*: "[Jack] Manningham's abuse of Bella has become emblematic for feminists of patriarchy within the family. Patrick Hamilton knew whereof he wrote since he sprang from just such a family. His father, Bernard Hamilton, a pretentious novelist known in the family as the Old Devil, was a bullying alcoholic who held his

Table I.1. Chart outlining the key differences between the four major stage and screen versions of *Gaslight* produced in the 1930s and 1940s. *Source*: Created by Nora Gilbert.

Title:	Format:	Location:	Premiere date:	Names of major characters:
Gas Light	Stage play	London	December 1938	**The husband:** Jack Manningham (a.k.a. Sydney Power) **The wife:** Bella Manningham **The detective:** Sergeant Rough **The murder victim:** Alice Barlow
Gaslight	Film	London	June 1940	**The husband:** Paul Mallen (a.k.a. Louis Bauer) **The wife:** Bella Mallen **The detective:** Sergeant Rough **The murder victim:** Alice Barlow
Angel Street	Stage play	New York	December 1941	**The husband:** Jack Manningham (a.k.a. Sydney Power) **The wife:** Bella Manningham **The detective:** Sergeant Rough **The murder victim:** Alice Barlow
Gaslight	Film	Los Angeles	May 1944	**The husband:** Gregory Anton (a.k.a. Sergius Bauer) **The wife:** Paula Alquist/Anton **The detective:** Brian Cameron **The murder victim:** Alice Alquist

wife Nellie and their children in thrall with pseudo-military discipline."[19] In *Gas Light*, however, Hamilton didn't choose to write about patriarchal domestic abuse from a young son's (read: his own) point of view; he chose to write about it from the vantage point of a bullied, sadistically disciplined wife. And it was this vantage point — this *woman's story* — that resonated so strongly with audiences on both sides of the Atlantic in the four major productions of *Gaslight* that were staged and filmed over the course of World War II.

The first production of *Gas Light* (subtitled, not insignificantly, *A Victorian Thriller in Three Acts*) premiered at the Richmond Theatre in London on

December 5, 1938, and went on to enjoy an initial West End run of 141 performances. Within a year, the first film adaptation of the play had been commissioned, written, and produced. Directed by Thorold Dickinson and starring Diana Wynyard as "Bella" and Anton Walbrook as her husband "Paul Mallen," *Gaslight* (now one word instead of two) was released by British National Films on June 25, 1940 (fig. I.1). The British film opened up the play in the way that cinematic adaptations tend to do: where *Gas Light* had all taken place in one room in the space of two consecutive hours, the film shows Bella gradually being gaslit over the course of several months, includes many scenes set outside the parameters of the home, and introduces the character of Bella's paternalistic male cousin from Devonshire who comes to London to save her from her husband's nefarious grip (in conjunction with the play's primary paternalistic savior-figure, retired police detective "Sergeant Rough").

Next came the American adaptations: first, a short-lived Los Angeles stage production in the spring of 1941 that was seen by an impressed Vincent Price, who immediately went about securing the rights so that he could star in a Broadway production (renamed *Angel Street*) by the end of the same year. In spite of this production's initial unlucky timing — with Pearl Harbor Day decimating the public's desire for theatrical entertainment just two days after

Figure I.1. Paul Mallen (Anton Walbrook) gaslights Bella (Diana Wynyard) in the British National film adaptation of *Gaslight* (1940). *Source*: *Gaslight* (Thorold Dickinson, 1940).

its premiere on December 5 — *Angel Street* soon rebounded and wound up becoming one of the longest-running non-musical Broadway plays of all time, logging a total of 1,295 performances before its closing night on December 30, 1944. Though the first edition of *Angel Street* that was published by Samuel French in 1942 implicitly suggests that the only difference between *Gas Light* and *Angel Street* is the title, there are in fact a plethora of small but sometimes significant differences between the dialogue and stage directions of the Samuel French edition of *Angel Street* and the first edition of *Gas Light* that was published by Constable and Company in 1939. One example of such a difference can be seen in the stage directions on the last page of each play, right after Jack Manningham has been taken off to jail by the police. In *Gas Light*, we are simply told that "MRS. MANNINGHAM *buries her head on* ROUGH's *shoulder*,"[20] whereas in *Angel Street*, things get violent: "MRS. MANNINGHAM *stands apart, trembling with homicidal rage.* ROUGH *takes her by the shoulders sternly. She struggles to get away. He slaps her across the face. She is momentarily stunned.*"[21] It is unclear who added this new interaction between Rough and Bella to the Samuel French script of the Broadway play (along with its many other tweaks, additions, omissions, and revisions). What does seem clear, however, is that the gender politics of *Gas Light* and *Angel Street* are not identical and should not be conflated.

Impressed by the critical and popular successes of *Gas Light*, *Gaslight*, and *Angel Street*, Hollywood soon came calling, with its largest and most prestigious studio, Metro-Goldwyn-Mayer, purchasing the remake rights from British National in 1942. The MGM film opens up the play even more, with additional scenes set in Italy, the Tower of London, et cetera, and a new backstory that recasts the murdered woman as a professional opera singer and the heroine as her niece who hopes to follow in the same footsteps, until her voice is muted when she meets and marries a gaslighter. But the biggest change in the Hollywoodized version is the transformation of the detective character from the avuncular "Sergeant Rough" to the potential love interest "Brian Cameron." The only way for a woman to successfully escape from domestic violence, this version strongly implies, is by replacing her psychotic husband with another, gentler man. Directed by George Cukor and starring Ingrid Bergman as "Paula Alquist" and Charles Boyer as "Gregory Anton," the MGM film premiered on May 4, 1944, and became the most decorated version of them all: nominated for seven Academy Awards, it won for Best Actress and Best Art Direction and continues to be considered one of the greatest psychological thrillers in American film history (fig. I.2).[22]

While it is by no means unusual for a Hollywood adaptation or remake to outperform or overshadow its precursor(s), MGM executives seem to have gone to greater lengths than usual to make sure such outperforming would happen in this particular case: they included in their rights-acquisition contract with British National a clause that authorized the destruction of all existing prints of the earlier film. In relating the story of this incident, one recent critic even described it as MGM's attempt "to gaslight audiences by pretending that the British movie never existed."[23] Fortunately for posterity, at least one copy of the British print did survive, and today the Wynyard/Walbrook version of the film is as easy to access and view as its Bergman/Boyer counterpart.

Less easy to access, however, is the version of Hamilton's play that appears to be the one he originally wrote for the London stage. The primary pieces of evidence we have come across in our archival research that suggest the existence of a lost original script are two documents in the MGM *Gaslight* production files at the Margaret Herrick Library in Los Angeles, both of which appear to be synopses written up for MGM executives who were considering adapting Hamilton's *Gas Light* for the screen. One of them, written in April 1942 by an unnamed reader, lays out the major plot differences between "GASLIGHT (English play)," "ANGEL STREET (New York play)," and "MOVIE VERSION" (meaning, at that point, the 1940 British film).[24] In this document's first sentence, it is noted that "the most obvious point of difference" between the three versions is the way they end; namely, in both the "New York play" and the British National "movie version," "the climax belongs to Rough, the hero-detective," whereas in the "original English play," the climax "belongs to Bella."[25] Though the author of this comparative document doesn't go into too

Figure I.2. Gregory Anton (Charles Boyer) gaslights Paula (Ingrid Bergman) in the MGM film adaptation of *Gaslight* (1944). *Source: Gaslight* (George Cukor, 1944).

much detail about what takes place in the original, Bella-"owned" climax, the author of another synopsis filed away in the same MGM archive does.

This second synopsis — whose author is identified to be Blythe Parsons, and which appears to have been commissioned by a different MGM executive in the late 1930s shortly after the initial run of Hamilton's play — provides a far more detailed précis of the "original English play's" storyline. The climactic scene Parsons describes at the end of this précis does indeed differ radically from the endings of both *Angel Street* and the British film version of *Gaslight* in just the ways that the unsigned 1942 document suggests it does, but it also differs radically from the climactic scene that appears at the end of every published and archival copy of *Gas Light* we have encountered: the first edition of *Gas Light* released by Constable and Company in 1939, the "Lord Chamberlin's Plays" copy of *Gas Light* held by the British Library, the handwritten draft of *Gas Light* housed in Boston University's Patrick Hamilton Collection, and other early printed copies of the play that are also stored in MGM's *Gaslight* production files at the Herrick Library. The original ending of Hamilton's play to which both of the MGM synopsis documents allude is, in other words, something of an "eerie non-presence" in gaslighting's dramaturgical history.

The key difference between the endings is this: In all of the accessible copies of *Gas Light*, Bella has been so effectively gaslit by Jack Manningham that she believes him when he tells her she has merely "dreamed" her visit and conversations with Sergeant Rough — until, that is, Rough strides in and says, "Was I any part of this curious dream of yours, Mrs. Manningham? Perhaps my presence here will help you to recall it."[26] Rough then proceeds to narrate, for Jack, the tale of how Alice Barlow came to be murdered twenty years ago in the very room where they are now standing. Rough frames his narrative as a ghost story that he has been perceptive enough to "see" and "imagine" for himself ("What things I imagine!", "Remarkably clear, Sir, I see it!") and names the heroic role that he considers himself to have played in it ("For justice has waited too, and here she is, in my person, to exact her due!").[27] In all of the accessible versions of *Gas Light*, then, Rough presumptuously casts himself as both Jack's accuser and Bella's rescuer.

In the version recapped by Blythe Parsons in her MGM synopsis, on the other hand, the person who does the accusing (and the *self*-rescuing, via storytelling) is not Rough, but Bella. As Parsons puts it:

> [Jack] shouts at [Bella], saying that he knows everything she has been up to, and for a moment he forces her back into her former mental state, making her think she has been dreaming. But she suddenly says: "Surely I have not dreamed . . . if the light is going down . . ." He pays no attention to this, and she offers to tell him her dream. She is bolder now because the light has told her that the police are in the house. She tells him that she dreamed that she was an old woman and once lived in this house. The furniture then was a little different. The old woman

> was undressing and putting away her jewels when a tall young man entered. Manningham says: "You interest me Bella. Go on." She adds: "That man was you. Twenty years ago. You see the mad things I dream. I screamed when I saw you. You cut my throat open with a knife. I lay dead on the floor of this house. But somehow I lived. I lived and watched you all through the night as you ransacked this house, hour after hour, ripping everything up, turning everything out, madly seeking the thing you could not find." He says: "What's the game Bella – eh? What's the game?" She says: "I'm telling you my mad dream, my sane husband." And she goes on to describe the detective who came to see her. She adds that they found what he could not find. As she speaks the door opens and Rough enters with others of the police. She is showing her husband the brooch he gave her, and the secret compartment which held the Barlow diamonds. She adds that the last thing she saw in her dream was a rope around his neck, but she continues: "I am mad, am I not?"[28] At this moment Rough advances.

We cite this section of Parsons's MGM synopsis in full to help restore this iteration of the play's climax to the literary record. In it, Bella explicitly reclaims the perceptual, investigative, and oratory powers Jack has so violently wrenched away from her — and she does so by telling the story of another violently wronged woman from a place of radical (even transcorporeal) solidarity and empathy. Far more than in any of the editions of Hamilton's play to which we now have access, Bella is, in this version, able to combat the false narrative Jack has been foisting upon her with a defiant, rhetorically powerful narrative of her own.

This is not to say that the various stage and screen versions of *Gaslight* that we can still read and watch divest their heroine of defiance and rhetorical power altogether. All of them do, for instance, contain a memorable scene near the end in which Bella/Paula asks to have a moment alone with her husband (after he has been captured and tied up in a chair by the police) and then insists that she is too "mad" to help him escape when he begins begging her to do so: "If I were not mad I could have helped you," she replies with vengeful relish, "but because I am mad I have hated you, and because I am mad I have betrayed you, and because I am mad, I am rejoicing in my heart — without a shred of pity — without a shred of regret — watching you go with glory in my heart!"[29]

But there is also another part of the *Gaslight* narrative, in all its incarnations, that emphasizes the strength and resilience of the gaslit heroine to a degree that often goes unacknowledged or misrepresented in contemporary discussions of gaslighting. A case in point can be seen in Kate Abramson's *On Gaslighting*, when she cites the following as a prime example of how the husband in the MGM film version of *Gaslight* (Hamilton's play does not get mentioned) goes about driving his wife insane:

> The title of the movie is drawn from the following manipulative move. Gregory regularly searches for Paula's jewels in the attic, and when he does so, his turning on the lights there has the effect of dimming the gaslights elsewhere in the house. Every time this happens Paula asks him why the gaslights have dimmed. And every time Gregory denies that any such thing has happened, insists Paula is imagining things, and suggests that this too is a sign of her growing mental illness.[30]

While Abramson is correct in her description of the lights dimming in the lower part of the house when Gregory turns them on in the attic, the rest of what she details simply does not take place, in the MGM film or in any other stage or screen version of *Gaslight*. Paula/Bella never once asks Gregory/Paul/Jack "why the gaslights have dimmed" — or even lets on to him that she has noticed their dimming — which means that Gregory/Paul/Jack never once "denies that any such thing has happened" or uses the fact of the dimming to further his gaslighting goals.[31]

In the MGM film, Paula only discusses the dimming of the lights with her two housemaids, Nancy and Elizabeth, to ask whether they have turned the lights up in another room to cause the dimming to happen, and with Brian Cameron, who witnesses the dimming himself and is able to corroborate what she has been experiencing. ("You saw that too? . . . Oh, then it really happens; I thought I imagined it!" she sighs in relief.) In *Gas Light* and *Angel Street*, Sergeant Rough doesn't play a corroborative role so much as an appreciative one; when Bella shares with him her observation that the gas lights always go down after her husband leaves and come back up shortly before he arrives home — making her suspect that "somehow *he* had come back and that it was *he* who was walking about up there"[32] — Rough fully acknowledges the role that her skills of discernment are playing in solving the mystery and catching a murderer:

> ROUGH. You know, Mrs. Manningham, you should have been a policeman.
> MRS. MANNINGHAM. Are you laughing at me? Do you think I imagine everything, too?
> ROUGH. Oh no! I was merely praising the keenness of your observation. I not only think you are right in your suppositions, I think you have made a very remarkable discovery, and one which may have very far-reaching consequences.[33]

Instead of serving as yet another example of scheming manipulation on the husband's part, then, the dimming of the titular gas lights in fact represents *a way out* of the gaslighting abyss for the wife who — in spite of all her husband's efforts to blur and blight her sense of her surroundings — is sharp-witted and sharp-sighted enough to realize it's happening.

Viewed from this angle, it is a bit ironic that "gaslighting" has come to be the term used to describe the kind of psychological abuse depicted in the narrative; it would really be more apt to say that someone has been "brooched," or "pocket-watched," or "little pictured," since those are in fact the objects that the gaslighting husband hides and moves around in order to rattle the gaslit wife's mind. Yet, from another angle, the term feels just right, encompassing as it does *both* the threat of disorientation and self-doubt that can be brought on by nefarious external forces *and* the path to resistance, overcoming, and escape. And this is what the essays in this collection will highlight again and again: the relationship between acts of gaslighting and acts of resistance in Victorian literature and culture.

Gaslighting in an Era of Activism and Backlash

In her autobiography, Charlotte Perkins Gilman laments a misconception that persists today: "The nineteenth century, now so contemptuously discredited as 'Victorian,'" and thus hopelessly conservative, in fact witnessed a "world . . . of 'Movements'" for radical change.[34] During the same period in which the British empire was expanding its colonizing, white supremacist grip across the globe, Victorians were waging a staggering array of campaigns for social justice. The era's reform efforts included, among others, movements to abolish slavery, expand suffrage, transform education, secure women's rights, and reform the laws and medical theories governing the intertwined threats at the heart of gaslighting: wrongful accusations of insanity and wrongful confinement within a lunatic asylum. The kinds of gaslighting narratives we explore in this collection emerged, that is, during an era of activism marked by a uniquely medicalized collision course between white heteropatriarchal conventions and personal and social resistance. In this "world of movements," writers variously staked political positions, voiced nonconforming realities, and propelled or debated lunacy controversies using both nonfictional and fictional genres. Out of this confluence of forces, gaslighting became a fundamental feature of Victorian political discourse, popular culture, and everyday life.

The initial use of "the Gas-Light Phenomenon" as a clinical term by twentieth-century psychiatrists Russell Barton and J. A. Whitehead referred not to a form of emotional manipulation, but to the kind of malicious yet legal asylum committals that dated back to the late 1700s. In 1774, parliament passed Britain's first legislative attempt to control the unregulated madhouse industry: the Act for the Regulation of Private Madhouses. This law stipulated that a person could only be confined to an asylum with the signed certificate of a doctor; no certificate was required for persons confined within their own homes. The solution proved disastrous, for it granted outsized authority to medical men, while enabling lucrative "arrangements" between doctors, family members, and asylum proprietors. Most wrongfully detained patients, like the victim in

Gaslight, were targeted for their property, making committals part of a so-called mad-business. Efforts to pass new legislation failed until 1828 when the Act to Regulate the Care and Treatment of Insane Persons in England (known as the Madhouse Act) was created to protect patients from abuse and to protect the sane from institutionalization. The Madhouse Act required *two* certificates of lunacy for private patients, each signed by a different physician following a separate interview.[35] Every version of *Gaslight* cites this historical detail: in the stage and British film versions, the husband threatens to have his wife examined by "more than one doctor,"[36] while the husband in the MGM film even more pointedly threatens to bring in "two. I believe *two* is the required number."

By the late 1820s, as Hannah Augstein explains, "the practice of confinement had become highly controversial, culminating in a scandal which involved the well-known alienist [psychiatrist specializing in insanity] George Man Burrows who had issued certificates without even personally inspecting the alleged patients."[37] The Lunacy Act of 1845 imposed a new set of government controls through the establishment of a Lunacy Commission and a mandate that every English county operate an asylum. Predictably, the 1845 Act saw the number of persons committed to asylums increase, especially the number of women, along with a parallel decrease in women caring for inmates as proprietors.[38] Far from preventing wrongful confinement, Victorian lunacy laws concentrated power ever more tightly within the ranks of male commissioners, magistrates, and "mad-doctors." As Joan Busfield, Sarah Wise, and others have noted, nearly as many men as women were wrongfully confined in British lunatic asylums.[39] What, then, made gaslighting, in contrast to malicious incarceration, such a gendered and racialized phenomenon?

The answer lies in the dynamic interplay between medico-cultural master narratives of insanity and white patriarchal beliefs, laws, and customs, which gave gaslighting a different set of conditions — and a different calculus of risk — depending on one's embodied identity. The nineteenth-century expansion of psychiatric medicine generated a profusion of conjectures about the anatomical and social signs of madness, which purportedly applied to all bodies. In 1828, for example, George Man Burrows claimed he could smell a crazy person: "I consider the maniacal odour a pathognomonic symptom so unerring, that if I detected it in any person, I should not hesitate to pronounce him insane."[40] In application and interpretation, however, Victorian psychiatry's teeming grab bag of medical concepts divided along gendered lines. Typologies associated with men included, among others, the mad genius, the criminal lunatic, and the masturbatory lunatic — types supposedly exhibiting excessive energy or even excessive acumen, but not a loss of one's basic sense of reality. In contrast, feminine types — hysterical, maternal, and hereditary — struck at the core of a person's social standing as an independent moral agent. These are the diagnostic labels deployed by the villain in *Gaslight*.

In the theatrical versions of *Gaslight*, references to Bella as "hysterical" appear only in the stage directions ("*She screams hysterically,*" "*She is completely hysterical,*" and so on[41]), but in the MGM film, Gregory tells Paula, point-blank, to "stop being hysterical." In each case, *Gaslight* is invoking medical dogma according to which insanity stems from women's naturally diseased reproductive bodies. The ancient fictional disorder of "hysteria," from the Greek *hystéra* (or womb), signified a wandering uterus, a disobedient organ that needed to be returned to its proper place through marriage, sex with a man, or smelling salts.[42] Steeped in longstanding beliefs about the link between madness and the maternal body, while faced with a preponderance of poverty-stricken mothers in English asylums, Victorian doctors invented theories such as that of "lactational insanity," or the supposed "delirium of poor mothers who nursed their babies for long periods in order to save money and to prevent conception."[43] Over the course of the nineteenth century, alienists increasingly accepted the nosological definition of madness as a hereditary disease passed down through the mother — again, tethering insanity to innate reproductive womanhood. It is this prevailing myth that the husband in *Gaslight* exploits, shouting, "You're stark gibbering mad — like your wretched mother before you!" in the play and, with even more cruelty and specificity in the MGM film, "Your mother was mad. She died in an asylum when you were a year old. . . . It began with her imagining things, that she heard noises, footsteps, voices, and then the voices began to speak to her, and in the end she died in an asylum with no brain at all!"[44]

A deadly case of medical gaslighting from the 1840s helps illustrate how these overlapping legal, medical, and cultural developments operated historically. In his "Observations on the Connexion of Insanity with Diseases in the Organs of Physical Life" (1844), James C. Prichard uses the example of a thirty-five-year-old woman dubbed "A. B." to support his concept of "moral insanity," which he had defined in 1835 as "a morbid perversion of the natural feelings, affections, inclinations, temper, habits, moral dispositions, and natural impulses, without any remarkable disorder or defect of the intellect."[45] In 1844, he wanted to prove that this psychopathology derives not just from the brain, but from other body parts too. He tells the story of A. B., "a lady highly accomplished, and of great mental endowments, pious, affectionate, and sincere," who suddenly refused to eat, complained of acute abdominal pain, and became "low-spirited and hypochondriacal."[46] Prichard interprets her behavioral change as a deterioration from (sane) self-denial to (insane) selfishness: "Formerly devoted to her duties, and to works of benevolence to others, she now thought only of herself, and her complaints."[47] Her loved ones consigned her to an asylum, where she was force-fed, despite constantly protesting that eating caused excruciating pain. After several years of medical gaslighting while trapped in a madhouse, she died. The dissection of her corpse revealed ulcers and lesions covering her entire intestinal canal. Prichard admits, the "dissection afforded proof that the perpetual complaints made by the patient . . . were not unreal, as it had been sometimes suspected," but he nevertheless interprets her ulcers and lesions as evidence of moral insanity: the "disease in the intestinal canal had been coëval with the mental disorder"; "this case furnishes, on this view, an example of insanity mainly dependent on a diseased state of organs very remote from the brain."[48] In other words, a Victorian woman's attention to her own bodily needs over the needs of others was perceived not only as immoral but as insanely so. Even when no one doubted a woman's reason, when she was not harming anyone, and when her property was not at stake, she could still be institutionalized as a "moral" lunatic, her testimony disbelieved, and her pain fatally ignored.

Mary Wollstonecraft presaged the institutionally sanctioned rise of wrongful madness allegations against women, while articulating the first theory of gaslighting *avant la lettre*, in her groundbreaking *Vindication of the Rights of Woman* (1792). She argues that patriarchy relies on a systematic program of gaslighting — of making women believe the lie that they are mentally unfit for autonomous lives as rational beings. Speaking mainly to middle-class white women, Wollstonecraft calls for "a revolution in female manners," by which she means a transformation in the way women are educated and socialized, so they can utilize — rather than sabotage — their God-given power of reason.[49] She laments the chronic social habit whereby men assert women's mental "inferiority till women are almost sunk below the standard of rational creatures," and she names Jean-Jacques Rousseau as the Enlightenment gaslighter responsible for popularizing the most pernicious myths about women's natural irrationality, childishness, and coquettishness.[50] Wollstonecraft bluntly declares that women's "minds are not in a healthy state," not owing to innate weakness, but to their psychologically debilitating miseducation.[51]

Canonical histories of British abolitionism have credited Wollstonecraft and other white women, such as Hannah More and Elizabeth Heyrick, with bolstering the male-dominated, transnational movement that came of age in England during the 1780s. Heyrick, a prolific second-wave British abolitionist, for example, published three influential pamphlets that fueled the 1820s turn toward immediatism, including her defense of the slave rebels in the British colony of Demerara and her landmark *Immediate not Gradual Abolition* (1824). Recently, however, historian Manisha Sinha and other scholars of abolitionism have shown that, in fact, the personal testimonies, legal petitions, and rebellions of enslaved or formerly enslaved Africans, rather than the efforts of white abolitionists, constituted the most powerful acts of resistance.[52] The West Indian insurrection that, more than anything else, precipitated Britain's Slavery Abolition Act of 1833 was Samuel Sharpe's 1831 Rebellion, the largest slave revolt in the history of the British colonies. Carried out by nearly 60,000 enslaved Jamaicans, Sharpe's Rebellion, Sinha explains, "was preceded by a wave of slave resistance and free black activism in the West Indies."[53] While militant protests proved crucial to achieving abolition of the trade (in 1807) and of slavery throughout the empire (in 1833), Black testimony inflamed as it challenged the interwoven economic and ideological threads of racism, racial slavery, and racial gaslighting. The infusion of African voices in British culture, such as Olaudah Equiano's bestselling 1789 autobiography, sparked gaslighting counterattacks, which maligned these writers' basic reasoning capacity and emotional control. Rising myths classifying non-white bodies as irrevocably inferior functioned as a wellspring of racial gaslighting. In other words, nineteenth-century racial gaslighters did not just pathologize those who dared to resist slavery and racism, but they also constructed a foundational meaning-making structure that distorted the spoken and unspoken realities of Black British life. As bell hooks put it, "White supremacy has always relied upon a structure of deceit."[54]

Nineteenth-century Britain's racial "structure of deceit" operated very differently for Black men and women. Whereas Black male abolitionists, such as Equiano, Ottobah Cugoano, and other self-proclaimed "Sons of Africa," published their own writings and spoke as influential representatives of a global cause beginning in the eighteenth century, the first Black woman's public account of her life in Britain did not appear until the year of Sharpe's Rebellion with *The History of Mary Prince, A West Indian Slave* (1831). As Doreen Thierauf details in this volume's eleventh chapter, Prince's words were mediated by white activists who recorded, edited, and appended her story with their own strategic filters, practicing what Thierauf terms "abolitionist gaslighting." Black Atlantic women like Prince were systematically gaslit via rhetorical maneuvers that erased their voices, spoke for them, projected onto them, disbelieved them, attacked their credibility, and positioned them in harmful competition with white women. Together, patriarchy, colonial slavery, and the ideological orders invented to rationalize them brought the weight of multiple gaslighting programs to bear on women of color. It wasn't until the late 1850s that British audiences got to hear directly from a Black female abolitionist in her own voice. From 1859 to 1867, Sarah Parker Remond fought racial, misogynoirist, and abolitionist gaslighting by giving speeches to packed audiences across the British Isles. Speaking to "promiscuous" (gender-mixed) and cross-class crowds, Remond rejected conventional antislavery appeals that elided graphic truths, instead calling out enslaved women's sexual vulnerability: "In the open market place," she told her listeners, "women are exposed for sale — their persons not always covered. Yes, I can tell you English men and women, that women are sold into slavery with cheeks like the lily and the rose, as well as those that might compare with the wing of the raven."[55] For the first time, unmediated public testimony by a Black woman broadcast the ubiquity of sexual violence, forced sex work, and forced childbearing under slavery. In the wake of the 1833 Abolition Act, however, British antislavery campaigns had dwindled, becoming largely defunct by the 1850s.[56] This evaporation of organized activism caused a devastating continuation of silence, mythmaking, and what Charles Mills has termed "white ignorance" about racism and racist violence in the Black Atlantic, feeding yet new forms of racial gaslighting.[57]

The British press also fed into the silence and misinformation underwriting colonial and racial gaslighting in the period. For instance, English readers heard reports from a distant outpost of the British empire about the Indian Rebellion of 1857, one of the largest challenges to British imperial rule in the nineteenth century. This rebellion began on May 10, 1857, when Hindu and Muslim sepoys (soldiers) in Meerut were required to bite off the ends of rifle cartridges greased with pork and beef fat, counter to their religious beliefs. The sensationalized British reports of the widespread Indian uprisings that followed — reports that were rife, as Andrea Kaston Tange has put it, with the "exaggerated," the "uncorroborated," and the "fabricated" — collectively justified colonial "order" by "disregarding [the] oppressive colonial systems that provoked the uprisings and instead deploying melodramatic conventions to construct an absolute, irredeemable villain."[58] These narratives, too, functioned as a form of epistemic gaslighting, perpetrated on a geopolitical scale.

In Hamilton's *Gas Light*, the only explicit mention of a colonized region of the British empire occurs when Sergeant Rough informs Bella that Jack Manningham "spent five years . . . on the Continent of Australia," where his first wife presumably "lives still."[59] But in both film adaptations, the subject of British imperialism joins the narrative fold in more thematically significant ways. In the British National film, the jewels for which Alice Barlow has been murdered are given a very specific backstory, which we learn about through a newspaper article that briefly flashes across the screen right after we see her being strangled to death: "The famous Barlow Rubies," the article reads, "reputed to be worth Twenty Thousand Pounds, *which were brought back from the Punjab by the late Mr. Charles Barlow*, are believed by the Police to be the motive for the horrible murder of his relict, Mrs. Alice Barlow" (emphasis added). In this version, an Englishman's casual arrogation of precious Indian jewels serves as the animating force that sets the entire plot into motion. In the MGM version, meanwhile, though we are told that the jewels for which Alice Alquist was killed are the "crown jewels" of "another country," a tie to *British* imperialism in particular is also hinted at during the scene that takes place at the Tower of London. There, we see Gregory admiring — to put it mildly — both "the Imperial State Crown" that "was made for the coronation of Queen Victoria" (containing, as he lists off all too knowledgeably, "the Ruby of the Black Prince," "the Stuart Sapphire," and "the diamonds and pearls from the earrings of Queen Elizabeth") and the gemstone that appears to be his favorite, "the Koh-i-Noor . . . the most famous diamond in the world" (which, crucially, made its way into the clutches of the British empire at the end of the Second Anglo-Sikh War in 1849, along with the rest of the annexed Punjab). The MGM version, then, implicitly links the gaslighting husband's monomaniacal obsession with foreign jewels that he wants to possess at all costs to the long, bloody history of colonization.

During this period of national aggression and anti-colonial rebellion, British feminists began campaigning to reform the legal, economic, and social centerpiece of patriarchal oppression at home: marriage. In the 1850s and 1860s, without the power of political representation, they took to the press to debunk the programmatic myths that gaslit women into believing in their mental incapacities and "naturally" dependent, domestic lives, especially in relation to work and sex. Victorian marital ideals held that women did not need rights to their own bodies, property, or children — nor did they need formal education or paying jobs — because their husbands would protect them through coverture, the law that subsumes a wife's legal identity within her husband's. As one

Saturday Review author put it in 1859, "Married life is woman's profession and to this her life training — that of dependence — is modelled."[60] In the courtship scenes added to the beginning of MGM's *Gaslight*, Gregory achieves this patriarchal fantasy by convincing Paula to give up her professional singing aspirations to marry him, thereby consigning her to a subordinate, housebound life devoid of meaningful work. Harriet Martineau (whose autobiographical and economic writings are discussed at length in Lana Dalley's chapter of this volume) attempted to dismantle the compound myths that middle-class women do not work, do not *want* to work, and do not *need* to work. In "Female Industry" (1859), for example, she bluntly observed that "a very large proportion of the women of England earn their own bread."[61] Contrary to the imaginary, manipulative ideals codified by law, British women denied access to training and jobs outside the home labored without pay inside the home, while thousands of poor women were forced into sex work and/or indigence, surviving only at the mercy of asylums. In 1860, another influential feminist, Emily Davies, called out "false notions of propriety" that convince women that their work is not work; "that indolence is feminine and refined"; and "that if a lady may, in certain cases, be permitted to work, her labour must at any rate be unpaid."[62]

One Victorian woman fatefully battled the sex-shaming stigma attached to working women in her effort to create a place for women in the male-dominated medical profession. In 1852, young Florence Nightingale penned a rageful feminist manifesto, "Cassandra,"[63] in which she laments the wasted lives — and brains — of women who want to think independently and work professionally but remain trapped in family homes, expected to dedicate every waking hour to mind-numbingly trivial tasks and to treat marriage as their only vocational outlet. "The accumulation of nervous energy" brought on by this claustrophobic lifestyle, Nightingale despairs, "makes [women] feel every night, when they go to bed, as if they were going mad."[64] In *Gaslight*, a significant portion of the wife's misery results from her suffocating stasis and prolonged inactivity; the husband refuses to allow her to perform even small chores like adding coal to the fire, instead insisting she call one of the housemaids to do such tasks for her. Nightingale condemned precisely this kind of forced idleness, and she managed to escape from a life of domestic drudgery via the profession of nursing — a profession that she revolutionized during her years on the frontlines of the Crimean War and beyond.

As much as Nightingale's successful nursing career must be credited with opening doors for certain working women and making important medical breakthroughs, it also helped enshrine the godlike power of white male doctors and the subservient role of white female nurses, while excluding care workers of color, thereby exacerbating the structural inequities that fostered (and continue to foster) racialized medical gaslighting. The best-known example of a woman of color who wished to join Nightingale's team but was repeatedly rebuffed is Jamaican nurse, entrepreneur, and memoirist Mary Seacole. In her 1857 autobiography, Seacole describes the looks of "curiosity and surprise" she received from several of Nightingale's staff members, as well as the "impatience" to be rid of her she sensed in Nightingale's own body language, by way of "a slight, perhaps unwitting motion of the firmly planted right foot."[65] The reason why Nightingale and her colleagues remained so reluctant to welcome Seacole into the nursing fold, the subtext makes clear, was their presumption that she possessed "less reason, logic, and rationality" because of her race, as Alisha Walters has put it.[66] And it is "Seacole's narrative" itself (meaning: her autobiography), Walters argues, that so powerfully "intervenes against the negative associations attributed to the emotional, brown, and female Creole body."[67]

In the 1860s, Victorian feminists confronted a major setback in the form of a new legal mechanism whereby men could institutionalize, stigmatize, and sexually assault women in the name of preventative medical "care": the Contagious Diseases Acts. These laws were instituted by Parliament in 1864, 1866, and 1869 to control the spread of venereal disease among the armed forces. The first act was introduced in Parliament late at night without public or Parliamentary debate.[68] Under the acts, any woman in a port or garrison town suspected of being a sex worker could be forced to undergo medical examination, and if doctors found her to be infected, she could be confined to a Lock Hospital against her will for three months; the maximum stay increased to nine months in 1869.[69] In effect, these laws provided political backing for the sexual double standard. The Royal Commission on the CDA states this matter-of-factly: "There is no comparison to be made between prostitutes and the men who consort with them. With the one sex the offence is committed as a matter of gain; with the other it is an irregular indulgence of a natural impulse."[70] The Acts functioned as another type of institutional gaslighting in which women could be falsely labeled — in this instance, as "prostitutes" rather than "lunatics" — and confined against their will. The activists who sought to repeal the Acts, particularly Josephine Butler and Elizabeth Wolstenholme, argued that Victorian society at large was being gaslit into believing that it was female sexuality that needed controlling when, in fact, supposedly "natural" *male* "impulses" were responsible for the spread of disease.

Upholding patriarchal myths about marriage, labor, and mental and sexual disease was the phenomenon we now call rape culture, or the systemic cultural practices and beliefs that normalize men's sexual violence against women, excuse predators, and blame victims. Victorian rape culture fostered a gaslighting culture in that the censorship of public speech about sex — combined with the legal sanction of marital rape, the chronic symbolic distortion of rape into romance, and the lack of either basic sex education or a vocabulary for sexual harm — enabled the society-wide erasure of girls' and women's *actual* sexual experiences.[71] For their "protection," girls and women were kept ignorant of their own bodily functions, the process of reproduction, and sexual expectations in marriage. Denied a language with which to understand or name their physical and mental realities, women could more easily be manipulated into doubting them. One late-Victorian commentator sarcastically fumed about the fact that "it is not indelicate to train up daughters to catch eligible husbands. . . . But give them a sound practical knowledge of their own physiology? . . . Shocking!

Most improper!'"[72] Leading anti-CDA activist Elizabeth Wolstenholme would become the first British woman to publicly call out marital rape; despite being maligned, censured, and even deemed insane for speaking openly about sex, she also became the first to publish a sex education textbook for children. Like Wollstonecraft, Wolstenholme realized that Britain's legal and medical system not only facilitated the sexual assault and wrongful confinement of women but also lured them into obliviousness and confusion about their health. Rape culture's foundational role in the intersecting regimes of patriarchy, class hierarchy, enslavement, and colonization meant that the thickest layers of epistemic effacement shrouded the sexual lives of poor women and women of color. For example, in late-Victorian South Africa, white officials expressed anxiety about what they called "the Black Peril," the fear that Black men were raping innocent white women; in contrast, feminists like Olive Schreiner recognized that this controversy should more accurately be termed "the White Peril," since Black women were far more at risk of rape by white men in colonial South Africa.

Some Victorian women sought an alternative to male-dominated medicine in the form of Spiritualism, a set of religio-medical beliefs that became popular in the 1870s. Characterized by domestic séances, hypnotic demonstrations, and inspirational speeches, Spiritualism subverted the patriarchal hierarchy of knowledge and power by placing women in a privileged position as mediums, discerning vessels for the channeling of other spirits. Often the same women who publicly experimented with Spiritualism were accused of insanity and/or institutionalized. Spiritualists Louisa Lowe and Georgina Weldon, for example, narrated their experiences of malicious detention and gaslighting in personal, reform-oriented accounts: Lowe's *The Bastilles of England, or The Lunacy Laws at Work* (1883) and Weldon's *The History of My Orphanage: Or, the Outpourings of an Alleged Lunatic* (1878) and *How I Escaped the Mad Doctors* (1882). Other Victorian women who wanted to pursue their Spiritualist beliefs and escape from patriarchal British gaslighting found refuge in travel and even emigration to non-Western countries such as India, as Narin Hassan discusses in her contribution to this collection.

By the 1880s and 1890s, the period in which *Gaslight* is set, Victorian culture's spotlight on madness shifted from lunacy scandals to hysteria panics that ensnared not only women and racialized others, but also an expanding array of nonconforming bodies, especially Jews, feminized white men, and members of the LGBTQ+ community. In the 1870s, acclaimed French neurologist Jean-Martin Charcot had legitimized the medical concept of hysteria, reclassifying this "womanly" disorder as a universal disease of the nervous system, not the uterus. Men, not just women, could be hysterics too. But the stigma of irrational femininity stuck to the word and its uses by the most influential late-Victorian doctors. In 1892, for example, the Charcot-trained German physician Max Nordau unleashed an explosive book, *Degeneration*, in which he applied the hybrid concept of "hysterical degeneracy" to avant-garde artists, especially sexually subversive poets such as Oscar Wilde. Just four years later, Charcot's most famous student, Sigmund Freud, proclaimed that he had discovered the cause of hysteria: childhood sexual abuse. Within fewer than ten years, however, Freud recanted his trauma theory and replaced it with a theory of dreams that authorizes a core myth of Victorian gaslighting: the idea that a woman merely *dreams* her real traumas and actual pain and suffering. Far from improving mental health outcomes, Charcot's, Nordau's, and Freud's attempts to modernize a misogynistic medical fiction made more and more people — from radical poets to people whom sexologist Havelock Ellis labeled sexual "inverts" to child rape survivors — newly vulnerable to gaslighting or additional layers of trauma inflicted by their doctors.

The anti-feminist, white-supremacist, "degeneration"-phobic cultural backlash that permeated the fin de siècle also owed much of its epistemological power to the scientific theories of Charles Darwin, especially those he propounded in *The Descent of Man* (1871). Darwin's purportedly "science"-based arguments about the evolutionary superiority of both the male sex and the white race were gobbled up by those who feared losing their patriarchal, imperial dominance over others and, in turn, fueled the eugenicist movement and other forms of scientific racism and social Darwinism.[73] "To this day," as anthropologist Agustín Fuentes has recently emphasized, "nationalist/separatist idealogues [continue to] use Darwin's words and general arguments as basis for their erroneous and intentionally hurtful and hateful positions and actions"[74] — including positions and actions that, following Davis and Ernst, we would now call racial gaslighting.

This, of course, is just one example among many of the ongoing, reverberating effects of the Victorian history we have been tracing. Victorian gaslighting is still very much with us: in our medical practices, in our institutions, in our cultural and gender biases. But the work performed by nineteenth-century activists to expose and oppose the forces of gaslighting remains very much with us, too. Though we have been focusing thus far on reformers who approached this work by speaking and writing in didactic and/or deeply personal forms, this era also witnessed a proliferation of popular fictions that told stories of both gaslighting and resistance to gaslighting. Some of these stories were overt and unequivocal in their political messaging, while others laid themselves open to multiple interpretations and contributed to public conversations about social and political issues in complex, even self-contradictory ways. What they all had in common was their ability to reach significantly wider audiences than did most other forms of speech and writing in the period. The fact that women authored so much of the period's most trenchant gaslighting fiction underscores the importance of fiction-writing and storytelling for people, both then and now, whose voices are chronically marginalized or erased in science, medicine, politics, and the law.

Victorian Gaslighting Narratives

A number of popular fiction genres that emerged just before or during the Victorian era showed a particularly strong interest in the themes of mental illness, involuntary confinement, and domestic abuse that lie at the heart of the *Gaslight* plot: genres such as Gothic fiction, sensation fiction, and New Woman fiction. For example, in her final years of life, Mary Wollstonecraft turned from describing and decrying patriarchal gaslighting tactics in political treatises like the *Rights of Woman* to describing and decrying them in her take on the Gothic novel, *Maria; or, the Wrongs of Woman* (1798). In telling the proto-gaslighting story of a woman who is wrongfully consigned to an insane asylum by an abusive husband who wishes to control her fortune and pursue extramarital affairs, *Maria* combines Wollstonecraft's unique brand of feminist polemics with the emotional intensity of the "female Gothic" tradition that had recently been initiated by Ann Radcliffe. Half a century later, Charlotte Brontë would write another pivotal female Gothic novel — *Jane Eyre* (1847) — that similarly features a wife whose husband labels her "mad" and locks her up. But this time the wife (Bertha Mason) is imprisoned in the home instead of an asylum, and this time she is so marginalized, dismissed, and denigrated within the narrative (due, in no small part, to her West Indian, Creole identity) that we do not get to hear any of her story in her own voice. We do get to hear the story of the husband's bigamist courtship of the novel's eponymous heroine, however — a story that is rife with manipulation, deceit, head games, and other forms of interpersonal gaslighting.

At the start of the 1860s, a new genre was born that brought some of the more sensational plot elements of novels like *Maria* and *Jane Eyre* to the narrative fore: the genre aptly dubbed sensation fiction. Two of sensation fiction's foundational texts, Wilkie Collins's *The Woman in White* (1859–1860) and Mary Elizabeth Braddon's *Lady Audley's Secret* (1861–1862), capitalized on the public interest in midcentury wrongful committal scandals (most famously, those of Louisa Nottidge and Rosina Bulwer-Lytton[75]) by telling stories that emphasized the susceptibility of the asylum system to manipulation and abuse. *The Woman in White* shows multiple innocent female characters being wrongfully confined by scheming male villains, while *Lady Audley's Secret* depicts a cat-and-mouse game between its titular antiheroine and her nephew-by-bigamist-marriage in which they each declare the other to be "mad" and deserving of institutional committal; in the end, not surprisingly, it is the nephew who manages to bend the will of medical authority to his side. A few decades later, "New Woman" writers like Mona Caird, Sarah Grand, Ella Hepworth Dixon, and Olive Schreiner also contributed to the fight against patriarchal gaslighting by penning stories that described or fictionalized their own traumatic experiences. The best-known example of this kind of New Woman narrative is Charlotte Perkins Gilman's "The Yellow Wallpaper" (1892), which serves as a scathing indictment of Silas Weir Mitchell's "rest cure" for women that prescribed homebound, bedridden stasis, with lots of milk and meat but no exercise or social or intellectual stimulation. In Gilman's account, the postpartum wife who is forced to follow this treatment protocol by her doctor-husband is medically gaslit into losing her mind.[76]

Maria, *Jane Eyre*, *The Woman in White*, "The Yellow Wallpaper": these are some of the texts that might first spring to mind for contemporary readers who are trying to think of "gaslighting" narratives that came before *Gaslight*. In the thirteen chapters assembled in this volume, our contributors focus on narratives with somewhat less obvious, though no less significant, relationships to gaslighting. The narratives discussed here are fictional and nonfictional, canonical and noncanonical, set in locations across the British empire — the English metropole, the Caribbean, India, South Africa, America when it was still a British colony — as well as other European locales such as France, Greece, Italy, and Transylvania. Each chapter historicizes gaslighting within a specific nineteenth-century context while also attending to the fact that we are engaging with these texts from our own varied, twenty-first-century perspectives, with some essays even making explicit connections to contemporary figures, laws, or social practices.

The opening two sections of the book focus on some of the chief thematic concerns of the *Gaslight* plays and films: illness, abuse, marriage, and property. The first section, "The Gaslit Mind and Body," uses a medical humanities approach to examine Victorian narratives that perversely blur the lines between treatment, diagnosis, and cause of mental and physical illness, while also exploring the lengths to which some gaslit victims will go to reclaim their psychological and bodily autonomy. First, Nora Gilbert draws connections between gaslighting and a form of medicalized mind control that loomed large in the nineteenth-century cultural imagination: mesmerism/hypnotism. By putting two late-Victorian tales featuring nefarious, foreign hypnotists (*Trilby* and *Dracula*) into conversation with the 1940 and 1944 film adaptations of *Gaslight* (in each of which the gaslighting husband is played by a non-English actor), Gilbert reads the cinematized gaslighting plot through the lens of xenophobia and other Victorian fears and prejudices. Next, Narin Hassan traces the colonial legacies of gaslighting, specifically examining white Victorian women's infatuation with yoga and meditation. While Hassan argues that the mind/body practices of yoga and spiritual movements such as Theosophy provided such women relief from psychologically abusive marriages and Western medical discourses, she also attends to the ways in which Indian women were marginalized by such movements. Finally, Tara MacDonald investigates obstetric gaslighting as a specific form of male, medicalized abuse in Olive Schreiner's posthumously published *From Man to Man* (1926), a novel that is unusually candid about the embodied experiences of pregnancy and pregnancy loss. Schreiner's novel, she argues, critiques the ways in which marital, obstetric, and colonial gaslighting are insidiously interconnected in late-Victorian South Africa.

The essays in the second section, "Marital and Monetary Manipulations," consider a variety of nineteenth-century literary texts that cast the marriage market and the nuptial state itself in a mentally destabilizing, economically exploitative light — as well as the real-life marriage of one famous Victorian couple that has recently been viewed through the lens of gaslighting. Jill Rappoport emphasizes the centrality of Victorian women's property to the plot of Hamilton's *Gas Light* and reads it against women's stifled abilities to exercise their economic rights in a range of Victorian novels. Her analysis of economic gaslighting shows that women's property rights are just as vital an aspect of the genealogy of gaslighting as is emotional abuse. Rosetta Young then reads the courtship experiences of two very different mixed-race Black heiresses, Olivia Fairfield in the anonymously authored *The Woman of Colour* (1808) and Rhoda Swartz in William Makepeace Thackeray's *Vanity Fair* (1847–1848), as forms of racial gaslighting. More specifically, Young identifies what these women endure at the hands of other characters (and, in the case of *Vanity Fair*, the narrator/author) to be misogynoirist gaslighting. Katherine Kim turns to a historical example in her reading of Charles Dickens as gaslighter. She explores the ways in which Dickens gaslit both his wife Catherine and the lesser-known author Catherine Crowe by vindictively manipulating public perceptions of their mental fitness. Sarah Kersh, too, examines the connections between courtship, marriage, and gaslighting, though her focus is on Victorian women's poetry. She argues that Elizabeth Barrett Browning's *Aurora Leigh* (1856) and Amy Levy's "Xantippe" (1881) depict forms of normative gaslighting that insist women must abandon their intellectual and creative pursuits in favor of marriage and heteronormative "happiness"; yet the female voices in these poems fight back against such cultural misperceptions.

The next section, "Case Studies in Institutional Gaslighting," analyzes gaslit communities manipulated by those who exploit the authority of larger institutions. Grace Franklin takes the subject of our volume literally by examining the tactics of Britain's coal-gas industry as its leaders tried to assuage (by dismissing and belittling) concerns about the domestic harms of gas and soot. She labels such maneuvers capitalist gaslighting and shows both how Charlotte Elizabeth Tonna's *The Wrongs of Woman* (1843–1844) exposes and critiques such gaslighting and how housekeeping manuals from the period alternately reinforced and resisted it. Lana Dalley then discusses epistemic gaslighting in the context of Victorian women's exclusion from the field of political economy. She traces this across a range of texts but focuses especially on the sexist attacks that Harriet Martineau endured upon the publication of her *Illustrations of Political Economy* (1832), as discussed in her autobiography. Finally, Shalyn Claggett explores religious gaslighting in Elizabeth Gaskell's short story "Lois the Witch" (1861), the title character of which becomes a victim of the Salem witchcraft trials. While Claggett focuses on the patriarchal religious culture of fundamentalist Puritanism, she also calls attention to the fact that the women in Lois's family are the ones who accuse her of being a witch — an accusation that they nearly gaslight Lois into believing — and how this plot point highlights the degree to which patriarchal institutions promote and rely on women betraying one another.

The final section, "Rape Culture and Rhetorical Control," establishes fundamental intersections between sexual, linguistic, and psychological violence in works by women writers who either endured or perpetuated symbolic distortions of rape. Doreen Thierauf discusses *The History of Mary Prince, A West Indian Slave; Related by Herself* (1831) and the ways in which this text and its paratexts enacted a form of racialized testimonial injustice that she terms abolitionist gaslighting. While the abolitionists responsible for transcribing and editing Mary Prince's story acknowledged the cruelties of slavery, they also, as Thierauf shows, reinforced nineteenth-century rape culture by denying the realities of sexual violence under slavery. Elizabeth Coggin Womack examines Margaret Oliphant's novel, *The Perpetual Curate* (1864), in which a minister is on trial for raping a teenage girl. Although Oliphant references actual, well-publicized clerical abuse from the period, in finding the clergyman innocent and implying that those who suspected him were silly gossipers, she undermines the reader's sense that they should question clergymen about the realities of sexual abuse; Oliphant, Womack suggests, thus gaslights her readers. Diana Bellonby moves to late-Victorian aesthetic fiction, interpreting lesbian art critic Vernon Lee's *Miss Brown* (1884) as a radical protest against rape culture in London's art world. Bellonby argues that critics of Lee's novel, including her mentor Henry James, gaslit her, and that the psychological and intellectual crises she recorded in her journal, letters, and later writings offer a window into late-Victorian hysteria panics and the forms of gaslighting endured by queer intellectuals like Lee and Oscar Wilde.

The essays collected in this volume simultaneously show what we can learn about Victorian culture by reading it through the lens of gaslighting and what we can learn about contemporary forms of gaslighting by sharpening our understanding of their historical antecedents. This history teaches us that challenging an injustice that is as social as it is personal — and as narrative as it is psychological — requires more than simply combatting false accusations of madness; it also requires giving voice to the histories of systemically gaslit people. Only by building a humanistic culture, story by story, can we heed, rather than police and deny, all of our physical and psychological truths.

Notes

1. The *OED* identifies the earliest-known written denominalization of the term to be anthropologist Anthony F. C. Wallace's 1961 discussion of the "popular belie[f]" that one can "'gaslight' a perfectly healthy person into psychosis by interpreting his own behavior to him as symptomatic of serious mental illness" (Wallace, *Culture and Personality*, 228).
2. Barton and Whitehead, "Gas-Light Phenomenon," 1258.
3. Calef and Weinshel, "Some Clinical Consequences"; Gass and Nichols, "Gaslighting: A Marital Syndrome."
4. Rich, "Women and Honor," 191. Rich first read these "notes" in a speech given at a women writers' workshop in Oneonta, New York, in 1975, then published them in pamphlet form in 1977 and in *On Lies, Secrets, and Silence: Selected Prose 1966–1978* in 1979. Another important text in this vein is Joanna Russ's recently republished classic, *How to Suppress Women's Writing* (1983).
5. Abramson, "Turning Up the Lights on Gaslighting," 3.
6. Sweet, "The Sociology of Gaslighting," 861.
7. Miranda Fricker developed this concept in *Epistemic Injustice: Power and the Ethics of Knowing* (2007). Alison Bailey, Nora Berenstain, Kristie Dotson, Veronica Ivy [Rachel McKinnon], Gaile Pohlhaus, Jr., and Cynthia Stark, among others, have published influential accounts of epistemic oppression and epistemic gaslighting.
8. Manne, "Moral Gaslighting," 122.
9. Ruíz, "Cultural Gaslighting," 689.
10. For a small sampling of popular and academic works that have discussed gaslighting in the first and second Trump administrations, see Amanda Carpenter's *Gaslighting America: Why We Love It When Trump Lies to Us* (2018); G. Alex Sinha's "Lies, Gaslighting and Propaganda" (2020); Bonnie Honig's *Shell-Shocked: Feminist Criticism After Trump* (especially chapter 2: "*Gaslight* and the Shock Politics Two-Step") (2021); Aurora Donzelli's "On Metapragmatic Gaslighting: Truth and Trump's Epistemic Tactics in a Plague Year" (2025); and the Center for Racial and Disability Justice's "Manufactured Confusion: Gaslighting as a Tool of Power in the Trump Administration" (2025).
11. Cabral, "Gaslighting," par. 4.
12. Davis and Ernst, "Racial Gaslighting," 763. See also Elaine Frantz's piece on racial gaslighting published in *Vox* the same year, "America's Long, Rich History of Pretending Systemic Racism Doesn't Exist," and Heston Tobias and Ameil Joseph's "Sustaining Systemic Racism Through Psychological Gaslighting" (2020).
13. Engelhardt, "Some Reflections," 8. They specify that "normative gaslighting is common because it is produced systematically by dominant epistemic systems."

14. The various stage and screen versions of *Gaslight* are all dated slightly differently: the year is specified to be 1880 in *Angel Street*, 1885 in both film adaptations, 1893 in certain editions of *Gas Light*, and "sometime in the latter part of the last century" in others.
15. Hamilton, *Gas Light*, 42.
16. French, *Patrick Hamilton*, 2.
17. Miller, "The Man Who Invented Gaslighting," par. 2.
18. Jones, "The Man Who Invented Gaslighting," par. 10.
19. Jones, "The Man Who Invented Gaslighting," par. 6.
20. Hamilton, *Gas Light*, 83.
21. Hamilton, *Angel Street*, 107.
22. For example, MGM's *Gaslight* ranks 78th on the AFI's "100 Most Thrilling American Films" list.
23. Hoberman, "Why 'Gaslight' Hasn't Lost Its Glow," par. 9. To make textual history matters even more complicated, the MGM version was released in the UK as *The Murder in Thornton Square* so that it wouldn't be confused with the British National film version, which, in turn, was referred to as *Angel Street* when it finally reached screens in the US.
24. Anonymous, "Gaslight . . . Angel Street," 1-2.
25. Anonymous, "Gaslight . . . Angel Street," 1-2.
26. Hamilton, *Gas Light*, 76.
27. Hamilton, *Gas Light*, 78, 79.
28. Parsons, "Synopsis for Mr. Knopf," 10.
29. Hamilton, *Gas Light*, 82–83. These lines are more or less identical in the MGM film, *Gas Light*, and *Angel Street*. They are slightly different in the British National film, though the underlying "I'm too 'mad' to help you escape" sentiment remains the same.
30. Abramson, *On Gaslighting*, 2–3.
31. Abramson is certainly not alone in her misdescription of this plot point in *Gaslight*. Other examples include Calef and Weinshel's "Some Clinical Consequences," Cawthra et al.'s "'Imposed Psychosis,'" Dorpat's "On the Double Whammy and Gaslighting," Stern's *Gaslight Effect*, Yagoda's "How Old Is 'Gaslighting'?," Sweet's "Sociology of Galighting," Cabral's "Gaslighting," Jamison's "So You Think You've Been Gaslit," and Cynthia Stark's "Varieties of Gaslighting," as well as both Merriam-Webster's and Wikipedia's entries on the word. The only critic we have encountered who also explicitly calls out this common error in gaslighting criticism is Kelly Oliver, who correctly notes that "it is the gaslights that reassure the wife that she is *not* going mad" and that "the irony of the gaslights saving her rather than condemning her is further intensified by the fact that several scholars who cite the film to support their theories of gaslighting do so by *erroneously* claiming that the husband uses the gaslights to drive his wife crazy" ("Affective Gaslighting," 135). It is thus all the more ironic that in the introduction to the essay collection in which "Affective Gaslighting" appears — *Gaslighting: Philosophical*

Approaches, which is coedited by Oliver — the same descriptive error is again repeated: "Paula, quite naturally, notices the dimming lights, but when she questions Gregory about them, he turns her observation into merely another symptom" (Gunn and Longair, 3).

32. Hamilton, *Gas Light*, 32–33.
33. Hamilton, *Gas Light*, 33.
34. Gilman, *Living of Charlotte Perkins Gilman*, 234.
35. Wise, *Inconvenient People*, xx–xxi.
36. Hamilton, *Gas Light*, 24.
37. Augstein, "J C Prichard's Concept," 337.
38. While male lunatics had previously outnumbered women, by the 1850s, more women filled England's public institutions. By 1897, according to a Special Report of the Commissioners in Lunacy on the Alleged Increase in Insanity, a 55:45 ratio of female to male inmates populated the country's asylums (Busfield, "Female Malady?," 265). On the decrease in female asylum proprietors, see Showalter, *Female Malady*, 54.
39. Wise, *Inconvenient People*, xvii–xix. See also endnote 43.
40. Burrows, *Commentaries*, 297.
41. Hamilton, *Gas Light*, 24, 83.
42. For an overview of the medical history of hysteria, see Tasca et al., "Women and Hysteria."
43. Showalter, *Female Malady*, 54.
44. Hamilton, *Gas Light*, 21.
45. Prichard, *Treatise on Insanity*, 6.
46. Prichard, "Observations," 324.
47. Prichard, "Observations," 324.
48. Prichard, "Observations," 324.
49. Wollstonecraft, *Vindication*, 113.
50. Wollstonecraft, *Vindication*, 101. She quotes widely from Rousseau's *Emile; or, On Education* (1762): "All the ideas of women," he claims, "should be directed to the study of men, and to the attainment of those agreeable accomplishments which have taste for their object; for as to works of genius, they are beyond [women's] capacity" (quoted in Wollstonecraft, *Vindication*, 106).
51. Wollstonecraft, *Vindication*, 71.
52. See, for example, Sinha, *Slave's Cause*, 129.
53. Sinha, *Slave's Cause*, 213.
54. hooks, *Sisters of the Yam*, 12.
55. Remond, *Black Abolitionist Papers*, 438. Teresa Zackodnik notes that Remond "was successfully appealing to a developing woman's rights and feminist political culture" in Britain (*Press, Platform, Pulpit*, 80).
56. Blackett, "African Americans," 55.
57. Mills, "White Ignorance," 13.
58. Tange, "Picturing the Villain," 200, 201.
59. Hamilton, *Gas Light*, 43.

60. Anonymous, "Queen Bees or Working Bees?," 672.
61. Martineau, "Female Industry," 294.
62. Davies, *Voice of Toil*, 682.
63. Nightingale's title alludes to the Greek myth of Cassandra, who was cursed by Apollo to speak true prophecies but never to be believed.
64. Nightingale, *Cassandra*, 43.
65. Seacole, *Wonderful Adventures*, 81, 82.
66. Walters, "Tears I could not repress," par. 16.
67. Walters, "Tears I could not repress," par. 16.
68. McHugh, *Prostitution and Victorian Social Reform*, 37.
69. Walkowitz, *Prostitution and Victorian Society*, 76, 86.
70. Quoted in Rover, *Love, Morals, and the Feminists*, 75.
71. The marital rape exemption in English law, based on a code authored by Matthew Hale (1609–1676), meant that a wife had no right to her own body. This exemption was not removed until 1994.
72. Cameron, "How We Marry," 690.
73. See, for example, such sexist and racist assertions as "The chief distinction in the intellectual powers of the two sexes is shewn by man's attaining to a higher eminence, in whatever he takes up, than can woman" and "Their [meaning "various races'"] mental characteristics are likewise very distinct; chiefly as it would appear in their emotional, but partly in their intellectual, faculties." Darwin, *Descent of Man*, 858, 260.
74. Fuentes, "'On the Races of Man,'" 161.
75. For more on the Louisa Nottidge and Rosina Bulwer-Lytton wrongful consignment cases — as well as the related case of Charles Dickens's failed attempt to have his own wife committed — see Katherine Kim's chapter in this collection.
76. For more on "The Yellow Wallpaper" and its connection to another New Woman narrative that portrays the same type of gaslighting, see Tara MacDonald's chapter in this collection.

Bibliography

Abramson, Kate. *On Gaslighting.* Princeton University Press, 2024.

———. "Turning Up the Lights on Gaslighting." *Philosophical Perspectives* 28 (2014): 1–30.

Anonymous. "Gaslight . . . Angel Street . . . Movie Version." MGM production files for *Gaslight*, Margaret Herrick Library, Los Angeles.

Anonymous. *The Anti-Jacobin Review and Magazine, or Monthly Political and Literary Censor* 5 (1800): 25.

Augstein, Hannah Franziska. "J C Prichard's Concept of Moral Insanity—a Medical Theory of the Corruption of Human Nature." *Medical History* 40 (1996): 311–43.

Bailey, Alison. "On Gaslighting and Epistemic Injustice: Editor's Introduction." *Hypatia* 35 (2020): 667–73.
Barton, Russell and J. A. Whitehead. "The Gas-Light Phenomenon." *The Lancet* 1, no. 7608 (1969): 1258–60.
Berenstain, Nora. "White Feminist Gaslighting." *Hypatia* 35 (2020): 733–58.
Blackett, Richard J. M. "African Americans, the British Working Class and the American Civil War." *Slavery and Abolition* 17, no. 2 (1996): 51–67.
Bland, Lucy. *Banishing the Beast: Feminism, Sex and Morality*. Tauris Parke, 2002.
Bradshaw, David J., and Suzanne Ozment, eds. *The Voice of Toil: Nineteenth-Century British Writings about Work*. Ohio University Press, 2000.
Busfield, Joan. "The Female Malady? Men, Women, and Madness in Nineteenth Century Britain." *Sociology* 28, no. 1 (1994): 259–77.
Burrows, George Man. *Commentaries on the Causes, Forms, Symptoms and Treatment, Moral and Medical, of Insanity*. Thomas and George Underwood, 1828.
Cabral, Sam. "Gaslighting: Merriam-Webster Picks Its Word of the Year." *BBC News*. November 29, 2022.
Calef, Victor, and Edward Weinshel. "Some Clinical Consequences of Introjection: Gaslighting." *The Psychoanalytic Quarterly* 50 (1981): 44–66.
Cameron, Laura B. "How We Marry." *Westminster Review* 145 (1896): 690–94.
Carpenter, Amanda. *Gaslighting America: Why We Love It When Trump Lies to Us*. Broadside Books, 2018.
Cawthra, R., G. O'Brien, and F. Hassanyeh. "'Imposed Psychosis': A Case Variant of the Gaslight Phenomenon." *British Journal of Psychiatry* 150 (1987): 553–56.
Center for Racial and Disability Justice. "Manufactured Confusion: Gaslighting as a Tool of Power in the Trump Administration." *Medium*. April 4, 2025. https://nlawcrdj.medium.com/manufactured-confusion-gaslighting-as-a-tool-of-power-in-the-trump-administration-cac5dfed1475
Cukor, George, dir. *Gaslight*. Metro-Goldwyn-Mayer, 1944.
Darwin, Charles. *The Descent of Man and Selection in Relation to Sex*. John Murray, 1901.
Davis, Angelique M., and Rose Ernst. "Racial Gaslighting." *Politics, Groups, and Identities* 7, no. 4 (2019): 761–74.
Dickinson, Thorold, dir. *Gaslight*. British National Films, 1940.
Donzelli, Aurora. "On Metapragmatic Gaslighting: Truth and Trump's Epistemic Tactics in a Plague Year." *Signs and Society* 11, no. 2 (2025): 173–200.
Dorpat, Theodore L. "On the Double Whammy and Gaslighting." *Psychoanalysis & Psychotherapy* 11, no. 1 (1994): 91–96.
Duca, Lauren. "Donald Trump Is Gaslighting America." *Teen Vogue*. December 10, 2016. https://www.teenvogue.com/story/donald-trump-is-gaslighting-america.

Engelhardt, Jeffrey. "Some Reflections on Gaslighting and Language Games." *Feminist Philosophy Quarterly* 9, no. 3 (2023): 1–25.

Frantz, Elaine. "America's Long, Rich History of Pretending Systemic Racism Doesn't Exist." *Vox*. May 16, 2019. https://www.vox.com/first-person/2019/5/16/18627753/racism-kkk-police-brutality-sandra-bland.

French, Sean. *Patrick Hamilton: A Life*. Faber and Faber, 1993.

Fuentes, Agustín. "'On the Races of Man': Race, Racism, Science, and Hope." In *A Most Interesting Problem: What Darwin's* Descent of Man *Got Right and Wrong about Human Evolution*, edited by Jeremy DeSilva and Janet Browne, 144–61. Princeton University Press, 2021.

Gass, Gertrude Zemon, and William C. Nichols. "Gaslighting: A Marital Syndrome." *Contemporary Family Therapy* 10, no. 1 (1988): 3–15.

Gilman, Charlotte Perkins. *The Living of Charlotte Perkins Gilman: An Autobiography*. University of Wisconsin Press, 1990.

Gunn, Hanna Kiri, and Holly Longair. Introduction to *Gaslighting: Philosophical Approaches*, edited by Kelly Oliver, Hanna Kiri Gunn, and Holly Longair, 1–22. SUNY Press, 2025.

Hamilton, Patrick. *Angel Street: A Victorian Thriller in Three Acts (Acting Edition)*. Samuel French, 1942.

———. *Gas Light: A Victorian Thriller in Three Acts*. Constable and Company, 1939.

Hoberman, J. "Why 'Gaslight' Hasn't Lost Its Glow." *The New York Times*. August 21, 2019. https://www.nytimes.com/2019/08/21/arts/gaslight-movie-afterlife.html.

Honig, Bonnie. *Shell-Shocked: Feminist Criticism After Trump*. Fordham University Press, 2021.

hooks, bell. *Sisters of the Yam: Black Women and Self-Recovery*. South End Press, 2005.

Ivy, Veronica. [Rachel McKinnon]. "Allies Behaving Badly: Gaslighting as Epistemic Injustice." In *Gaslighting: Philosophical Approaches*, edited by Kelly Oliver, Hanna Kiri Gunn, and Holly Longair, 177–91. SUNY Press, 2025.

Jackson, Jenn M. *Black Women Taught Us: An Intimate History of Black Feminism*. Random House, 2024.

Jamison, Leslie. "So You Think You've Been Gaslit." *The New Yorker*. April 1, 2024. https://www.newyorker.com/magazine/2024/04/08/so-you-think-youve-been-gaslit.

Jones, Nigel. "The Man Who Invented Gaslighting." *The Critic Magazine*. June 19, 2020. https://thecritic.co.uk/the-man-who-invented-gaslighting.

Kutcher, S. P. "The Gaslight Syndrome." *Canadian Journal of Psychiatry* 27 (1982): 224–27.

Manne, Kate. *Down Girl: The Logic of Misogyny*. Oxford University Press, 2017.

———. *Entitled: How Male Privilege Hurts Women*. Penguin, 2020.

———. "Moral Gaslighting." In *Gaslighting: Philosophical Approaches*, edited by Kelly Oliver, Hanna Kiri Gunn, and Holly Longair, 103–26. SUNY Press, 2025.

Martineau, Harriet. "Female Industry." *The Edinburgh Review* 109 (1859): 293–336.

McHugh, Paul. *Prostitution and Victorian Social Reform*. Croom Helm, 1980.

Mills, Charles W. "White Ignorance." In *Race and Epistemologies of Ignorance*, edited by Shannon Sullivan and Nancy Tuana, 13–38. SUNY Press, 2007.

Miller, Miranda. "The Man Who Invented Gaslighting." Royal Literary Fund. September 24, 2018. https://www.rlf.org.uk/showcase/the-man-who-invented-gaslighting/

Oliver, Kelly. "Affective Gaslighting." In *Gaslighting: Philosophical Approaches*, edited by Kelly Oliver, Hanna Kiri Gunn, and Holly Longair, 127–45. SUNY Press, 2025.

Parsons, Blythe. "Synopsis for Mr. Knopf," MGM production files for *Gaslight*, Margaret Herrick Library, Los Angeles.

Podosky, Paul-Mikhail Catapang. "Gaslighting, First- and Second-Order." *Hypatia* 36 (2021): 207–27.

Pohlhaus, Jr., Gaile. "Gaslighting and Echoing, or Why Collective Epistemic Resistance is not a 'Witch Hunt.'" *Hypatia* 35 (2020): 674–86.

Prichard, James Cowles. *A Treatise on Insanity, and Other Disorders Affecting the Mind*. Sherwood, Gilbert, and Piper, 1835.

———. "Observations on the Connexion of Insanity with Diseases in the Organs of Physical Life." *Provincial Medical Journal* 174 (1844): 323–24.

Rich, Adrienne. "Women and Honor: Some Notes on Lying." In *On Lies, Secrets, and Silence: Selected Prose 1966-1978*, 185–94. W. W. Norton & Company, 1979.

Ripley, C. Peter, ed. *The Black Abolitionist Papers Vol. I: The British Isles, 1830–1865*. University of North Carolina Press, 2015.

Rover, Constance. *Love, Morals and the Feminists*. Routledge, 1970.

Ruíz, Elena. "Cultural Gaslighting." *Hypatia* 35 (2020): 687–713.

Russ, Joanna. *How to Suppress Women's Writing*. University of Texas Press, 2018.

Seacole, Mary. *Wonderful Adventures of Mrs Seacole in Many Lands*. Edited by Sara Salih. Penguin, 2005.

Showalter, Elaine. *The Female Malady: Women, Madness, and English Culture, 1830–1980*. Pantheon Books, 1985.

Sinha, G. Alex. "Lies, Gaslighting and Propaganda." *Buffalo Law Review* 68, no. 4 (2020): 1037–16.

Sinha, Manisha. *The Slave's Cause: A History of Abolition*. Yale University Press, 2016.

Stark, Cynthia. "Gaslighting, Misogyny, and Psychological Oppression." *The Monist* 102 (2019): 221–35.

———. "Varieties of Gaslighting." In *Gaslighting: Philosophical Approaches*, edited by Kelly Oliver, Hanna Kiri Gunn, and Holly Longair, 213–29. SUNY Press, 2025.

Stern, Robin. *The Gaslight Effect: How to Spot and Survive the Hidden Manipulation Others Use to Control Your Life*. Harmony, 2007.

Sweet, Paige L. "The Sociology of Gaslighting." *American Sociological Review* 84, no. 5 (2019): 851–75.

Tasca, Cecilia, Mariangela Rapetti, Mauro Giovanni Carta, and Bianca Fadda. "Women and Hysteria in the History of Mental Health." *Clinical Practice & Epidemiology in Mental Health* 8 (2012): 110–19.

Tange, Andrea Kaston. "Picturing the Villain: Image-Making and the Indian Uprising." *Victorian Studies* 63, no. 2 (2021): 193–223.

Tobias, Heston, and Ameil Joseph. "Sustaining Systemic Racism Through Psychological Gaslighting: Denials of Racial Profiling and Justifications of Carding by Police Utilizing Local News Media." *Race and Justice* 10, no. 4 (2020): 424–55.

Walkowitz, Judith. *Prostitution and Victorian Society: Women, Class and the State*. Cambridge University Press, 1980.

Wallace, Anthony F. C. *Culture and Personality*. Random House, 1961.

Walters, Alisha. "'The tears I could not repress, rolling down my brown cheeks': Mary Seacole, Feeling, and the Imperial Body." *Nineteenth-Century Gender Studies* 16, no. 1 (2020).

Wise, Sarah. *Inconvenient People: Lunacy, Liberty, and the Mad-Doctors in England*. Counterpoint, 2012.

Wollstonecraft, Mary. *A Vindication of the Rights of Men* and *A Vindication of the Rights of Woman*. Edited by Janet Todd. Oxford University Press, 1993.

Yagoda, Ben. "How Old Is 'Gaslighting'?" *The Chronicle of Higher Education*. January 12, 2017. https://www.chronicle.com/blogs/linguafranca/how-old-is-gaslight.

Zackodnik, Teresa. *Press, Platform, Pulpit: Black Feminist Publics in the Era of Reform*. University of Tennessee Press, 2011.

Part I

The Gaslit Mind and Body

It is perhaps not surprising that "medical gaslighting" has become an identifiable subvariant of the form of abuse we are historicizing in this collection, given the centrality of physical and mental illness to the *Gaslight* plot. All three of the chapters in our first section consider the role that gaslighting played in specific medical, pseudo-medical, and therapeutic practices of the Victorian era, from hypnotism to yoga to obstetric care. In particular, each chapter examines the interrelations between the bodily and psychological harms inflicted upon gaslit victims (usually women) by dubious Victorian practitioners of healing (usually men), but also the ways in which many such victims engaged in corporal and cerebral acts of resistance, retaliation, and resilience.

1

"Strange Intonations"

The Foreign Accents of Disabling Mind Control in *Trilby*, *Dracula*, and the Two Film Versions of *Gaslight*

Nora Gilbert

One of the deepest, darkest fears Patrick Hamilton taps into with his harrowing tale of psychological abuse is the fear that our mental health (and, along with it, our physical health) is inherently *violable* — that another person can, in other words, cause us to become mentally and/or physically ill simply by proclaiming us to be so. This fear loomed especially large for the Victorians, thanks to certain medical theories about nervous suggestibility and neuromimesis that were gaining traction throughout the period.[1] For while some doctors touted their ability to harness the "power of suggestion" for salutary purposes by engaging in the emerging medical practice of hypnotherapy, others warned of the grave harm such power could do to "susceptible," "impressionable" patients. In the 1890s — the decade during which Hamilton's gaslighting plot is set — two bestselling British novels depicted the dangerous, deleterious side of mind control by pointedly (and xenophobically) casting a foreign character in the role of the nefarious mesmerist: George du Maurier's *Trilby* (1894) and Bram Stoker's *Dracula* (1897). In this chapter, I read du Maurier's Svengali and Stoker's titular vampire as key genealogical precursors to the conspicuously un-English husband figures in the two film versions of *Gaslight*, played by Austrian actor Anton Walbrook in British National's 1940 production and by French actor Charles Boyer in Metro-Goldwyn-Mayer's 1944 remake. Like *Trilby* and *Dracula* before them, both cinematic adaptations of Hamilton's play emphasize the interconnections between fear, foreignness, forcefulness, and psychosomatic violability.

To understand how those interconnections came to be so deeply entrenched in the British cultural imagination by the last decade of the nineteenth century, we need to bear in mind where the majority of developments in the field of medicalized mind control had been taking place in the century leading up to it; namely, not in England. The first major such development, for example, involved the controversial experimentations of Franz Anton Mesmer. Born in Germany but best known for the treatments he performed in Vienna from 1768 to 1777 and in Paris from 1778 to 1784, Mesmer believed he could cure his patients' physical ailments by enlisting the forces of "animal magnetism" — that is, by touching his patients' bodies at their "poles" with either magnets or his bare hands until the patients' bodily fluids had been "relocated" enough for them to feel better. The practice became so popular so quickly that, in 1784, King Louis XVI commissioned two different scientific studies (one led by Antoine Lavoisier, one by Benjamin Franklin) to determine whether or not Mesmer's procedure was actually doing his patients any good. Both studies determined that it was not Mesmer's magnets or hand movements that were alleviating his patients' physical ailments, but rather their *belief* that his treatments could do so. Thus, as Jessica Riskin helpfully synopsizes: "It was not Mesmer, then, but his investigators who made mesmerism into the source of a new psychology, a nascent theory of the unconscious that credited the mind with startling powers over the body. Writing on the eve of the Revolution, the commissioners cautioned that the imagination could be manipulated to intoxicate crowds, provoke riots, spur fanaticism. The imagination was, they warned, an 'active and terrible power.'"[2]

In spite of this dire warning, mesmeric healing practices continued to proliferate well into the nineteenth century. About halfway through that century, an important change occurred when James Braid coined the term "neurohypnotism" (soon shortened to "hypnotism") to describe the sleeplike, highly impressionable state he was able to induce in his patients by getting them to focus hard on an external object or light source, with no manual or magnetic contact required. But even though it was Scottish-born, Manchester-based Braid who made this important breakthrough, his work "ignited few sparks of curiosity among his [British] compatriots in the medical profession," as historian Janet Oppenheim has noted; instead, "the interesting studies of hypnotism were proceeding elsewhere, in Germany, Holland, Switzerland, Italy, the United States, and, especially, France."[3] Two French medical facilities in particular became the most influential hubs of hypnotherapy experimentation in the 1870s and 1880s — the Salpêtrière Hospital in Paris (led by Jean-Martin Charcot) and the Nancy School of Hypnosis in Nancy (led by Ambroise-Auguste Liébeault and Hippolyte Bernheim). The main difference between the two schools' views on hypnosis had to do with the question of pathology: where Charcot believed that only "hysterical," mentally disordered patients could be hypnotized, Liébeault and Bernheim believed that the vast majority of people were "suggestible" and that hypnosis was a "natural" rather than a "neurotic" mental state. One thing both schools agreed upon, though, was the sheer magnitude of the power that the hypnotizer wielded over the hypnotee. Charcot acknowledged that "our [meaning hypnotists'] power does not encounter any limits in this domain, for we can extend our influence almost toward the infinite,"[4] while Bernheim described the hypnotized subject as "an automaton directed by a foreign will."[5] Even, then, by the time hypnotism (née mesmerism) had been embraced by well-respected medical professionals like Charcot, Liébeault, and Bernheim, it continued to be associated with the same kind of "active and terrible power" that Louis XVI's scientific advisors had warned of a century before.

The question of which patients were most susceptible to this "terrible power" was frequently answered in gendered terms; Charcot's insistence on the constitutive link between hypnosis and "hysteria," for example, inherently suggested that women were more at risk than men.[6] Within the British medical establishment in particular, Oppenheim explains, ongoing resistance to hypnotic practices stemmed at least in part from male physicians' paternalistic concerns for the safety of their wives and daughters — those "defenseless women, who might, while under hypnosis, be subjected to sexual advances of which they were subsequently unaware."[7] But there were also some male physicians from this period who began to apply the principles of "influence" and "suggestibility" to their treatment of female patients even when they weren't practicing hypnotism per se. In American physician Silas Weir Mitchell's *Lectures on Diseases of the Nervous System, Especially in Women* (1881), for instance, he mentions that "if you cause such hysteric women as these to believe that you can cure them, you enlist on your side their own troops, for as you can create symptoms, so can you also create absence of symptoms. There is in all this something like the so-called magnetizing of which we used to hear and see so much."[8] Athena Vrettos has limned this counsel of Mitchell's in terms that are especially apropos for this chapter: "*A kind of medical Svengali*, Mitchell advocated the physician's ability to manipulate patients out of their neuroses through sheer force of personality."[9] But I also want to call attention to the fact that Mitchell acknowledges, in this counsel, that doctors can use their "magnetizing" powers of persuasion to *create* symptoms in female patients just as easily as they can use them to *alleviate* symptoms. All it takes to do either one, he tells the doctors to whom his lectures are directed, is convince the "hysteric woman" in question to trust and believe you. This, I would argue, is an early, overt example of gendered medical gaslighting.

Women were not the only subset of patients who were believed to be more easily suggestible and hypnotizable because more prone to hysteria, neurasthenia, and other mental disorders, however. Another group that was frequently targeted in nineteenth-century European medical discourse in this way was the Jewish population. One of the most vocal contributors to such discourse was Jean-Martin Charcot, who, as Daniel Pick has highlighted, "often pointed to the idea of an innate Jewish nervousness; he developed various accounts of peculiar racial conditions and declared Jews to be the finest subjects for the study of nervous disease."[10] On the flip side of the coin, by the end of the nineteenth century Jews were also starting to be associated with the role of the hypno-*tizer* more and more as well, thanks to the high-profile contributions to the study and praxis of hypnotherapy made by such Jewish physicians as Hippolyte Bernheim in France, Albert Moll in Germany, and Josef Breuer and (before he turned from hypnosis to psychoanalysis as his primary medical approach) Breuer's protégé, Sigmund Freud, in Austria. By the end of the century, in other words, fears about the potentially nefarious power of the unscrupulous hypnotist were being grafted onto longstanding — but also historically specific[11] — fears about the "surreptitiously invasi[ve]," "successfully insinuating Jew," to again use Pick's phrasing; in the "literature, journalism and political thought on both sides of the Channel" of the 1890s, Pick reminds us, "Jews were often depicted as contaminating the mind and body of gentiles, as well as controlling everything from the stock market to public taste in art."[12]

Pick's purpose in sketching out the history of the relationship between antisemitism and anti-mesmerism is to contextualize his book-length discussion of one 1890s text in particular: George du Maurier's *Trilby*. But knowing a bit about this history can illuminate aspects of *Dracula* and the two film versions of *Gaslight* as well. Some critics have already recognized this to be true of *Dracula*, thanks to its direct engagement with both hypnotism and the fear of the foreign Other.[13] It is perhaps somewhat less easy to see the relevance of this history to *Gaslight*, since what the husband does to the wife in that narrative is not technically mesmerism or hypnotism, and since the issue of "foreignness" does not factor into Patrick Hamilton's original gaslighting plot in any way. And yet, what the husband does to the wife in *Gaslight* is a form of manipulative, perfidious mind control (just as mesmerism and hypnotism are portrayed to be in *Trilby* and *Dracula*), and both of the 1940s film adaptations do insert the issue of foreignness into the gaslighting proceedings by way of their casting choices. Reading *Trilby*'s and *Dracula*'s hypnotism plots as antecedents to the cinematized *Gaslight* plot allows us to think more carefully and critically about the films' underlying messaging with respect to villainy, abuse, and the (perceived) threat of foreign influence.

Monstrous Mesmerism in *Trilby* and *Dracula*

It has by now become something of a critical commonplace to put du Maurier's Svengali and Stoker's Dracula into literary-historical conversation with one another, often by triangulating them with a third symbolic figure. Nina Auerbach, for example, considers a defining "tableau" of the fin de siècle imaginary to be that of "three men lean[ing] hungrily over three mesmerized and apparently characterless women, whose wills are suspended by those of the magus/masters. The looming men are Svengali, Dracula, and Freud; the lushly hapless women are Trilby O'Ferrall, Lucy Westenra, and (as Freud calls her) 'Frau Emmy von N., age 40, from Livonia.'"[14] According to Jules Zanger, meanwhile, a more illuminating comparison can be drawn between Svengali, Dracula, and Jack the Ripper, the three "horrific personalities" that "terrorized and titillated" the English public "in the last decades of the nineteenth century,"[15] while Lois Cucullu finds an earlier interlocutor in Edgar Allan Poe's "The Man in the Crowd," arguing that both *Trilby* and *Dracula* "evince the same modern disquiet over the allure and sprawl of the city as did Poe's earlier tale," but with the added xenophobic ingredient of "a tyrannical, impure, and manic Oriental figure" who "orchestrates events," "menace[s] Western rule," and "exercise[s] dominion over the weak."[16] For the purposes of this chapter, I am interested in all three of the shared qualities of Svengali and Dracula that Auerbach, Zanger, and Cucullu spotlight in these summaries: their "mesmeric" persuasiveness, their "titillating" monstrousness, their "menacing" foreignness. But I am also specifically interested in the ways those qualities intersect with each of the texts' depictions of mental and physical health versus mental and physical illness.

In *Trilby*, of course, Svengali is "foreign" in a very particular way, as the novel repeatedly reminds us: he is an "Oriental Israelite Hebrew Jew" with Austrian and Polish familial roots who speaks "fluent French" that sounds "much more ghastly" because it's "pronounced with a Hebrew-German accent, and uttered in his hoarse, rasping, nasal, throaty rook's caw, his big yellow teeth baring themselves in a mongrel canine snarl, his heavy upper eyelids drooping over his insolent black eyes."[17] As Dirk Delabastita notes of this passage and others like it, "Svengali's linguistic, articulatory and physical imperfections are inextricably linked with each other — and with his moral depravity — to produce an image of subhuman racial inferiority."[18] The raging antisemitism of du Maurier's depiction of Svengali — "tawdry and dirty," "grossly impertinent," "about as bad as they make 'em" (*Trilby* 41–42) — is certainly reflective of widespread xenophobic responses to the influx of Jewish migrants to Western Europe during the last decades of the nineteenth century, but it is also reflective of widespread British attitudes toward mesmerism, hypnotism, and other forms of psychiatric manipulation that were attributed to foreign (often Jewish) outsiders.

For although Svengali first attempts to "charm" Trilby O'Ferrall (a working-class artist's model of Irish, Scottish, and English descent living in 1850s Paris[19]) with his "divine" piano-playing skills (12), he is in fact frustrated by how very little his musical enchantment trick works on her: "she didn't even look his way," the narrator tells us (17). But where musical mesmerism fails, medicinal mesmerism succeeds. Months later, when Trilby is suffering from "maddening" pain related to "neuralgia in her eyes," Svengali reveals that even though he is a musician by trade, he happens to be skilled in the field of hypnotherapy as well:

> Svengali told her to sit down on the divan, and sat opposite to her, and bade her look him well in the white of the eyes.
>
> "Recartez-moi pien tans le planc tes yeux." [*Look at me right in the white of the eyes.*[20]]
>
> Then he made little passes and counterpasses on her forehead and temples and down her cheek and neck. Soon her eyes closed and her face grew placid. After a while, a quarter of an hour perhaps, he asked her if she suffered still.
>
> "Oh! presque plus du tout, monsieur — c'est le ciel." [*Oh! almost not at all anymore, sir — it's like heaven.*] (49)

At this point, Svengali switches from speaking in French to speaking in German, so that he can describe to "the Laird" (a Scottish character who speaks a little German, which Trilby does not) the complete control he has over Trilby's mind and body in her hypnotized state. Trilby is, as Svengali proudly demonstrates, unable to open her eyes, open her mouth, or move her body in any way while she is thus "spellbound" by him (49).

Thrilled as Trilby is when she awakens from her trance to find that Svengali has successfully "taken all [her] pain away," the Laird vehemently discourages her from ever agreeing to this kind of medical intervention again: "I'd sooner have any pain than have it cured in that unnatural way, and by such a man as that! He's a bad fellow, Svengali — I'm sure of it! He mesmerized you; that's what it is — mesmerism! I've often heard of it, but never seen it done before. They get you into their power, and just make you do any blessed thing they please — lie, murder, steal — anything! and kill yourself into the bargain when they've done with you!" (52). In this speech, the Laird explicitly accuses Svengali of being the kind of corrupt, unscrupulous charlatan that so many members of the nineteenth-century British medical establishment considered foreign (and, especially, Jewish) mesmerists and hypnotists to be. The "unnaturalness" of the act of mesmerism is directly linked, in the Laird's eyes, to the "bad"-ness of Svengali himself — which is linked, throughout the novel, to Svengali's foreignness (and, especially, his Jewishness) over and over again.

The Laird also correctly presages in this passage where the therapeutic-mesmerism plot of the novel will, eventually, go: years later, after Trilby has been guilt-tripped into leaving the man she loves and has lost her beloved younger brother to scarlet fever — when, as she puts it, "I was mad with grief, and pain in my eyes, and wanted to kill myself" (256) — she turns once more to Svengali for psychosomatic aid. Although Svengali does manage to "cure [her] almost directly" and promises to "always cure [her] and take care of [her]" moving forward (257), even within Trilby's naïvely sugarcoated narration of the events it becomes clear that Svengali's mesmeric "cure" is doing far more physical harm than good: "As soon as I felt uneasy about things, or had any pain, he would say, 'Dors, ma mignonne!' [*'Sleep, my darling!'*] and I would sleep at once — for hours, I think — and wake up, oh, so tired! and find him kneeling by me, always so anxious and kind — and Marta and Gecko! — and sometimes we had the doctor, and I was ill in bed" (258; see fig. 1.1). Precisely as the Laird had feared, as soon as Svengali "gets" Trilby "into his power," he makes her do "any blessed thing he pleases" (namely, he makes her become "the greatest [opera] singer in all the world" [271]) in such an exhausting, disabling, destructive way that it does ultimately result in her "killing herself" shortly after Svengali — due to his own sudden demise — is "done with her." Medicinal mind control proves, in *Trilby*, to be deadly.

Figure 1.1. Svengali hypnotizes Trilby as his aunt Marta helps to get her dressed for a performance in *Trilby* (1894). Illustration by George du Maurier. *Source*: *Trilby*. Harper & Brothers, 1894.

The Laird is not the only one to correctly anticipate this turn that the narrative takes, however. Right after Svengali successfully hypnotizes Trilby for the first time, he himself tells her in no uncertain terms what he plans to do with his mesmeric powers in the future: "When your pain arrives, then shall you come once more to Svengali, and he shall take it away from you, and keep it himself for a soufenir of you when you are gone. And when you have it no more, he shall play you the 'Rosemonde' of Schubert, all alone for you. . . . *And you shall see nothing, hear nothing, think of nothing but Svengali, Svengali, Svengali!*" (52). These words of Svengali's (spoken, as the spelling of "soufenir" reminds us, in his "Hebrew-German accent") are not simply prophetic; they're performative. Because Trilby has, the narrator tells us, "a singularly impressionable nature, as was shown by her quick and ready susceptibility to Svengali's hypnotic influence," her brain soon starts doing precisely what Svengali has told it to: "'Svengali, Svengali, Svengali!' went ringing in her head and ears till it became an obsession, a dirge, a knell, an unendurable burden, almost as hard to bear as the pain in her eyes" (53). What is most proto-*Gaslight*ian about du

Maurier's sinister tale of mental manipulation, then, is the fact that Svengali uses his powers of persuasion to convince Trilby that she is chronically ill and in constant need of his therapeutic services — which, he insists, he can administer most effectively if she stays put in their shared home, "never going out or seeing anyone" (257).

The fact that Trilby moves in with Svengali from the time she becomes "mad with grief" after the death of her brother strongly suggests, too, that there is a sexual component to the hypnotic power he wields over her. For even though Svengali can't marry Trilby because he's "got a wife [still] living" in Prussia, and even though Trilby makes clear to Svengali that she isn't remotely attracted to him, sexually or romantically ("Poor Svengali! . . . He was always very kind! But I never could be fond of him in the way he wished — never! It made me sick even to think of!" [257]), the other characters in the novel all clearly believe that opera-singing isn't the only thing Svengali forces Trilby to do without her knowledge or consent while she is under his hypnotic spell. The novel thus directly plays into the Victorian fears about the sexual threat of hypnotic practices that I outlined earlier in this chapter — including, importantly, the xenophobic dynamic of many such fears. According to the racial logic of the novel, "sweet" and "innocent" Irish/Scottish/English women like Trilby O'Ferrall are the ones who are "singularly" vulnerable to the predatory pseudo-medical ploys of Austrian/Polish/German/Hebrew interlopers like Svengali.

***

Several years after the enormous — indeed, unprecedented[21] — popularity of *Trilby* showed how very open audiences on both sides of the Atlantic were to reading and embracing this racial logic, another novel burst onto the literary scene that followed, in certain ways, quite clearly in *Trilby*'s footsteps. In the early 1990s, Jules Zanger was the first to argue that because both Svengali and Dracula are portrayed within their respective narratives as "aliens among us" who move from the "mysterious," "poisonous" East to the "innocent" West "on missions of corruption"; because both possess "what appear to be supernatural powers of control"; because both "are repeatedly linked literally or metaphorically to non-human creatures," we can and should read Dracula not only as closely connected to Svengali, but also to a "generalized," deeply antisemitic "stereotype of the Jew."[22] But whether we read Dracula's sinister foreignness as a gesture toward antisemitism or toward broader xenophobic fears of the late Victorian period (the fear of "reverse colonization," for example, as Stephen Arata has famously phrased it[23]), what's clear is that *Dracula* imbues its monstrously foreign eponymous vampire with the same insidious mesmeric power that *Trilby* had bequeathed to its monstrously foreign Svengali.

Though the first character we get to see being "calmed" and "soothed" into a trancelike state in Stoker's novel is Jonathan Harker ("I was becoming hypnotized!" he retrospectively writes in his journal of his close-call encounter with the "three ghostly women" in Castle Dracula[24]), the two main characters that the Count entrances himself are both — like Trilby O'Ferrall — white, British young women. Lucy Westenra's vampiric metamorphosis via hypnosis occurs next in the story, though we don't get to witness it firsthand since it is related to us almost entirely through the journal entries of her friend Mina Harker and her suitor Dr. Seward. But when Dracula moves on to Mina, we do get to hear her meticulous recounting of what it's like to fall under the vampire's hypnotic spell. She describes, for example, the way a "leaden lethargy seemed to chain my limbs and even my will" (in much the same way that Svengali's trance made it impossible for Trilby to open her eyes or her mouth, or move *her* limbs) and the way the "gas-light which I had left lit for Jonathan" started "shining like a red eye" just before "things began to whirl through my brain" and "all became black darkness" (241) — a counterpart, to be sure, to the "white" of Svengali's "eye" he had commanded Trilby to gaze into just before she slipped into the "spellbound" state.

But it isn't until Dracula's third visit to Mina's room that he first materializes into corporeal form and begins to talk the Svengalian talk, echoing and even superseding Svengali in his assertion of mental and physical possession and control: "You," he gloatingly informs Mina, "are now to me flesh of my flesh; blood of my blood; kin of my kin; my bountiful wine-press for a while; and shall be later on my companion and my helper. . . . You have aided in thwarting me; now you shall come to my call. When my brain says 'Come!' to you, you shall cross land or sea to do my bidding" (267–68). And even though Mina Harker could hardly be said to possess the "singularly impressionable nature" of Trilby O'Ferrall, she does seem to experience the same "quick and ready susceptibility" to Dracula's "hypnotic influence" that Trilby had experienced at the hands (literally) of Svengali. This influence is also, again, clearly coded as sexually violent in nature, first when Mina finds herself unable (and "not" even "want[ing]") to hinder Dracula from "plac[ing] his reeking lips upon [her] throat" and drinking her blood (267), and then when, as she recalls the following day with horror, "he pulled open his shirt," "opened a vein in his breast," and "seized my neck and pressed my mouth to the wound" so that she is forced to drink *his* blood in return (268). In contrast to *Trilby*, where it is strongly implied but never shown that Svengali sexually assaults Trilby while she is hypnotized, in *Dracula* the brutality and carnality of what Dracula does to Mina is drawn for us in lurid detail.

It should be noted, too, that while nothing in Dracula's "flesh of my flesh" speech is phonetically marked as foreign-accented in the same way that "soufenir" and so many of Svengali's other words and phrases are in *Trilby*, Jonathan does observe when he first meets Dracula that he speaks "excellent English, *but with a strange intonation*" (18; emphasis mine). As Delabastita has pointed out, the fact that Dracula doesn't "butcher" the English language "as a linguistic badge of his foreignness and depraved behavior" (à la Svengali) can be explained easily enough: "Dracula has honed his linguistic skills as a speaker of English as a strategy of camouflage and infiltration. Linguistic assimilation enables him to get behind the frontline and blend in. This makes him doubly dangerous."[25] There is, however, one character in *Dracula* who does "butcher" the English language in more or less all of his quoted dialogue: the Dutch Dr. Van Helsing. Van Helsing is not painted in the same nefariously foreign light that Dracula and Svengali are, but he is linked to both of them through his un-English accent and through his un-English embrace of the practice of hypnosis. For even if Dr. Seward (the novel's symbolic representative of the British medical establishment) is willing to concede that hypnotism does have some scientific validity because, in his words, "Charcot has proved that pretty well" (178), it is Van Helsing who performs hypnosis on Mina over and over again in order to track Dracula's plans and movements. In a way, then, the last fifth of the novel can be read as a sort of cerebral tug-of-war, with the benevolent hypnotism of the "good" foreigner (Christian, Western European, human Van Helsing) pulling Mina's mind in one direction, and the malevolent hypnotism of the "bad" foreigner (non-Christian, Eastern European, vampiric Dracula) pulling it in the other.

But there is also a way, as Jordan Kistler has recently argued, that the cerebral tug-of-war can be read as a battle not between Dracula and Van Helsing, but between Dracula and Mina herself. In Kistler's view, even though the character Van Helsing "subscribe[s] to the typical gothic narrative of the powerful hypnotist and the vulnerable female subject," the novel as a whole "presents mesmerism as a means of empowerment for its female subject" because it shows Mina actively *choosing* to be hypnotized by Van Helsing ("'I want you to hypnotize me!' she said. 'Do it before the dawn, for I feel that then I can speak, and speak freely!" [Stoker 289]) so that she can "form a mesmeric *rapport*" with Dracula and gain "access to his mind."[26] In so doing, Kistler contends, the novel "reverses the popular worry that hypnotism could lead to rape, to instead present it as a force that can be manipulated by Mina to regain her agency and autonomy *after* an explicit sexual assault."[27] But while I agree with Kistler that the hypnotism plot in *Dracula* provocatively counters the gendered power dynamic between male hypnotizer and female hypnotee seen in *Trilby* and so many other late-nineteenth-century mesmerism narratives, I also think it problematically reinforces the racialized power dynamic between villainous foreign hypnotizer and victimized British hypnotee seen in the same.

***

Because *Trilby* and *Dracula* were two of the most widely read and culturally influential novels of the late nineteenth century, they played a not insignificant role in shaping the way fin de siècle Victorians thought about mesmerism, monstrousness, and certain kinds of foreignness. Over the course of the next few decades, moreover, both novels were reprinted and adapted for the stage and screen so regularly that audiences of the 1930s and 1940s (meaning: the audiences who went to see the original theatrical and film productions of *Gaslight*) would still have known their stories well. In the section that follows, I will show how the two film adaptions of *Gaslight* draw on the literary traditions of *Trilby* and *Dracula* by similarly scapegoating foreign men for quintessentially British forms of patriarchal violence — how, in other words, the two film adaptations cast a xenophobic pall over Hamilton's intended critique of homegrown British gaslighting.

Gaslight (1940) and *Gaslight* (1944): Sleeping with the Foreign Enemy

There are only five characters in the cast of Patrick Hamilton's 1938 play *Gas Light*, all of whom are (presumably) English: Bella Manningham is the suffering protagonist, Elizabeth and Nancy are the two maidservants employed in her London townhome, Sergeant Rough is the retired Scotland Yard detective who comes to her aid, and Jack Manningham is the man to whom she has been married for five years — or, at least, that's what she thinks his name is, until he is later revealed to be Sydney Power, a distant cousin (and the psychopathic murderer) of an elderly Englishwoman named Alice Barlow. When performed by actors with English accents all around, the plot of *Gas Light* is painted as a pointedly internal, domestic (by which I mean both contained within the home and contained within the nation) affair. But this is not the case in either of the film adaptations that were made within the first few years of the play's original run, *Gaslight* (dir. Thorold Dickinson, British National Films, 1940) or *Gaslight* (dir. George Cukor, MGM, 1944). In both film versions, the idea of "foreignness" is inextricably linked to the narrative's portrayal of psychological abuse, manipulation, and depravity.

The reason for this has entirely to do with casting. In the British National version, there was just one non-English actor who was cast in one of the play's five main roles: Austrian-born Anton Walbrook was chosen to play the role of the gaslighting husband. Walbrook had, in fact, only been "Anton Walbrook" for a few years prior to making the film — up until that point, he had forged a successful Austrian and German film acting career using his birth name, Adolf Wohlbrück. His motivation for the name change certainly stemmed from the 1933 rise to power of another Austrian-born Adolf from whom he wanted to distance himself, though it is important to point out that Wohlbrück remained in Germany for significantly longer than did most other artists fleeing from the Third Reich; it wasn't until October 1936 that he arrived in Hollywood (and from there relocated to England a few months later). The three years that Wohlbrück had chosen to remain in Nazi Germany and star in some of its most acclaimed films caused the Joint Boycott Council of the American Jewish Congress and the Jewish Labor Committee to object to his participation in his first US film, *The Soldier and the Lady* (dir. George Nichols, RKO, 1937), and to call for its boycott — a call that was only rescinded after RKO publicly "produc[ed] an affidavit of the actor's 'non-Aryan' status."[28] For the truth Wohlbrück had tried to keep secret until the threatened boycott was that his mother's side of the family was Jewish. By the time "Anton Walbrook" received top billing in the British National film version of *Gaslight* in 1940, then, it was publicly well known both that the actor was part-Jewish and that he had been content to remain in Nazi Germany for what seemed, to many, to be disturbingly long. Walbrook was in the unique position, that is, of being the target of both antisemitic prejudice and anti-Nazi anger at one and the same time.

When Patrick Hamilton first heard about the casting choice of Walbrook, he was opposed to it for a very specific reason; as the film's director, Thorold Dickinson, later recounted, "When I asked for Mr. Hamilton I was told he would have nothing to do with the production, as he objected to the part of Manningham being played by a German. I myself had changed the name of the character to 'Mallen' to make it less English."[29] But Hamilton's objection may not have been based on his WWII-related antipathy toward Germans alone — it may also have stemmed from his reluctance to outsource the crime of "gaslighting" to a foreign foe. The kind of sadistic psychological violence that Hamilton had, in *Gas Light*, specifically meant to be inflicted by a "suave and authoritative" Victorian Englishman upon a "haggard, wan, frightened" English wife[30] was now suddenly going to be infused into yet another wartime film in which, as James Down has put it, "the concept of foreign nationality and 'otherness'" was used "to accentuate the sense of threat."[31] Or, put another way, "gaslighting" was about to become a foreign rather than a domestic affair.

In addition to the name change that Dickinson had come up with (Jack Manningham aka Sydney Power becomes Paul Mallen aka Louis Bauer), there are several moments in the film that call attention to the character's newly assumed foreignness. Most obviously, there is a scene early on wherein Paul and Bella (Diana Wynyard), who have recently moved into the London townhouse where Alice Barlow was murdered twenty years before, are being stared at and gossiped about as they make their way out of their new neighborhood's church one Sunday. Among the whispered remarks that we're actually able to hear are these:

> MAN #1: Those are the Mallens, from Number Twelve.
> WOMAN #1: Yes, I thought we might call on them.
> MAN #1: Not in London, it wouldn't be correct.
> WOMAN #1: Oh, but . . .
> MAN #1: My dear, I said *no*.
> . . .
> MAN #2 (*sounding disdainful*): I hear he's a foreigner.
> WOMAN #2 (*sounding surprised*): But he looks most respectable!

As these comments make clear, Paul's "foreignness" is presumed to preclude his "respectability" from the outset — a xenophobic presumption that the plot of the film is all too happy to substantiate, as it gradually reveals the mysterious foreigner Paul Mallen/Louis Bauer to be not just socially un-"respectable" but also sadistically, sociopathically unhinged. The decision to have this initial questioning of Paul's "respectability" take place as he and his neighbors are filing out of a Christian church ("St. Mary's Pimlico Square," a sign tells us it is called) is, I think, suggestive of the idea that his religious bona fides are being questioned by his neighbors as well. Audience members who were aware of Walbrook's Jewish heritage might, indeed, have been particularly likely to read the scene in this way.

Another way that the film emphasizes Paul's foreignness/otherness is by adding a new character to the cast who serves as a Very English competitor for Bella's trust and affection: her cousin from Devonshire, Vincent Ullswater (Robert Newton). Vincent and the rest of Bella's relations had, we are told, objected to her marriage to Paul from the start and become estranged from her as a result, for reasons that are left unsaid but that are intimated to stem from the fact that they don't consider him to be "one of them" — in terms of class, nationality, perhaps (again) even religion. When Vincent travels to London to check on Bella and invite her to come stay in Devonshire with his sister and him, a scene ensues in which we see (and, more importantly, *hear*) a representative of Bella's loving, respectable, Very English family go toe to toe with her unloving, un-"respectable," foreign husband. Vincent speaks in a clipped, upper-crust English accent about how therapeutic a visit to Devonshire would be for his cousin's health ("the air always used to do her so much good down there"), while Paul speaks in an exaggeratedly sinister and sibilant Austrian accent about how little he is interested in Vincent's medical advice or assistance ("*I'm* the best guardian of my wife's health!"). In the end, Vincent cannot bring himself to use the "physical force" that Paul insists will be "required" if he wants to see Bella. The farthest Vincent is willing to go is to say to Paul, with a Very English frown, "I don't think I like your *tone*, Mallen" — to which Mallen, without changing his tone in the slightest, replies, "You are under no obligation to listen to it, Mr. Ullswater" (see fig. 1.2).

The viewer of the 1940 film version of *Gaslight*, however, *is* obligated to listen to Mallen's un-"like"able tone (his "strange intonation," as Jonathan Harker might have called it) for the duration of the movie. For every word that Paul Mallen/Louis Bauer speaks in his efforts to convince Bella that she has moved a picture from a wall for no apparent reason, that she has lost her brooch, that she has lost his pocket watch, that she is too ill to leave the house, that she is too ill to receive visitors, that she is losing her mind, that she has lost her mind — every word he speaks in his efforts to undermine her sense of self and of reality, to turn her into "an automaton directed by a foreign will,"[32] to *gaslight her* — is spoken in an inescapably foreign accent.

The same, of course, can be said of all the words spoken by Charles Boyer in the MGM film version of *Gaslight* that came out just four years later. The role that foreignness plays in MGM's *Gaslight* is more complicated than in British National's, because it is not just the husband but all three of the play's leading roles that are given to non-English actors in the Hollywoodized version: Swedish Ingrid Bergman plays the wife (whose name is changed to Paula Alquist), American Joseph Cotten plays the detective (whose name becomes Brian Cameron), and Frenchman Charles Boyer plays the husband (whose

Figure 1.2. Austrian-accented Paul Mallen (Anton Walbrook) and English-accented Vincent Ullswater (Robert Newton) face off in the British National adaptation of *Gaslight* (1940). *Source*: *Gaslight* (Thorold Dickinson, 1940).

name keeps changing in the early MGM screenplay drafts, from Ivan Petroff to Gregory Chernov to Gregory Anton). But the nationalities of Bergman, Cotten, and Boyer do not graft neatly onto our sense of the Englishness or non-Englishness of their respective characters within the film, as is the case in the British National version. For example, although Joseph Cotten doesn't even attempt to make his accent sound British instead of American, the film makes no reference to his Americanness; he is an employee of Scotland Yard who has a niece and a nephew with strong English accents, and it is implied that he has lived in London himself since he was a young boy (when he saw Alice Alquist perform at Covent Garden and was "overcome with admiration"). And even though Paula's last name does suggest her Swedishness, we also know that the London townhouse in Thornton Square where the majority of the film's action takes place is where she was "brought up" until the murder of her aunt caused her to relocate to Italy. In one early draft of the MGM screenplay, a description line mentions that even though the heroine is a "cosmopolitan" woman whose nationality is unclear, "when she speaks, she speaks pure English."[33]

Boyer's character, on the other hand, is certainly meant to seem "impurely" foreign, though not in a French way — his real name turns out to be non-Gallic-sounding Sergius Bauer, and even though Paula meets him in Italy, it is revealed near the end that her aunt had met him years before when "he was a young pianist who played for her in Prague." The same screenplay draft that mentions the "pureness" of Paula's English speaking voice, moreover, also gets more specific about Gregory/Sergius's national heritage in its description line about him: "An accompanist (Boyer), Polish and fortyish, is accompanying Bella at the piano," it reads.[34] What's clear from this early MGM script is that even after Boyer — "the French lover," as he was known throughout his Hollywood career — had been cast in the role of the gaslighting husband, the filmmaking powers that be wanted his character to retain some of the more Central European mystique with which Anton Walbrook had imbued it in the British film adaptation. Perhaps this is even why they wound up changing the character's last name from Petroff to Chernov to Anton: to subtly allude back to Walbrook.

After seeing an early cut of the film, David O. Selznick (who had loaned out Ingrid Bergman and Joseph Cotten to MGM for the production and was therefore invested in its success) made clear which particular Austrian/Polish/German/Hebrew figure he thought Boyer's character should be evoking in audiences' minds: "The picture is desperately in need," Selznick opined in a lengthy letter to L. B. Mayer, "of at least two more scenes . . . in which we see the husband as a lover; in which we see both his tenderness and also the Svengali-like sex hold that he has on her. Boyer is at his best in such scenes."[35] The rave reviews Boyer wound up receiving for his performance in the final cut of the film prove the acuity of Selznick's recommendation: reviewers in both the *New York Times* and *Daily Variety* specifically praised Boyer for his "hypnotic" performance, while more recent critics have specifically noted its "Svengalian" flair.[36]

The main scenes that were added to the Hollywood adaptation to give Boyer more "husband-as-lover" screentime are the ones that take place in Italy at the start of the film. These scenes provide substantially more sexual/romantic exposition than we're given either in Hamilton's play (the entirety of which takes place over the course of one evening, seven years into the Manninghams' marriage) or in Dickinson's film (which begins with the murder of Alice Barlow in 1865 and then jumps ahead twenty years to the day the Mallens move into the London townhome where she had once resided). In the MGM version, we first see Paula and Gregory together when he is accompanying her on the piano as she sings an aria from Donizetti's 1835 opera, *Lucia di Lammermoor* (itself an adaptation of Scott's 1819 novel *The Bride of Lammermoor* — a novel that is, not coincidentally, centrally about a woman who is driven mad via a manipulative marriage plot). But instead of using the "Svengali-like sex hold" he has over Paula to fashion her into "the greatest singer in all the world" as Svengali does to Trilby, Gregory does the opposite: he causes her to fall so madly in love with him that she loses her interest in singing, and even her ability to sing well. "Paula, you are not concentrating," her Italian singing teacher chides her; "Your mind's not on your singing. All these years you've worked so hard, and now — what's come over you?" The answer, of course, is that Gregory Anton has come over her, and used his powers of sexual persuasion to convince her to focus all of her mental energy on *him* instead of her singing career.

During the singing lesson scene, Gregory and Paula avoid making eye contact with one another so as to keep their relationship secret from the Maestro, but in the scene that takes place outside the singing studio — the scene in which Gregory pressures Paula to marry him right away, even though, as she demurs, they've "only known each other two weeks" — Gregory doesn't look away from Paula's face for so much as a second and keeps forcibly bringing her eyes back into contact with his own. ("*Look at me right in the white of the eyes*," we might well imagine him saying to her.) Though Paula does resist Gregory's "Svengali-like sex hold" a bit longer by insisting on taking a trip to Lake Como to mull his marriage proposal over, Gregory is waiting for her at the Como train station when she arrives and, in one of the more physicalized power moves in the film, we see his hand grab her from behind and turn her to face him (fig. 1.3) so that she is forced to gaze into his "hypnotic" eyes once more (fig. 1.4), this time with more successfully spellbinding results: the film cuts directly from this shot to Gregory and Paula's honeymoon scene.

Figure 1.3. Gregory Anton (Charles Boyer) manhandles Paula Alquist (Ingrid Bergman) in the MGM adaptation of *Gaslight* (1944). *Source*: *Gaslight* (George Cukor, 1944).

But as sexually satisfied and happy with her decision to marry Gregory as Paula appears to be while they are honeymooning at Lake Como, her eventual realization that "Gregory" is in fact "Sergius Bauer" (and, even more painfully, that "Sergius Bauer has a wife living in Prague now," as she ultimately learns from Brian) casts a retroactive pall over her sexual interactions with him throughout the film and recategorizes those interactions as nonconsensual and abusive in nature — a recategorization that aligns them with the nonconsensual sexual abuses that Trilby and Mina are subjected to while under the hypnotic influences of Svengali and Dracula, respectively.

By the end of the Italian honeymoon scene, it becomes evident that Gregory's motivation for wedding and bedding Paula has nothing to do with his sexual attraction to her; what he really wants access to is the London townhome she has inherited from her aunt. This part of the plot is more reminiscent of *Dracula* than *Trilby*, in that it too stokes fear by depicting a mysterious outsider from Central/Eastern Europe manipulating a woman's mind in order to infiltrate London for nefarious purposes. Gregory, in fact, nefariously infiltrates London not once but twice: when he gets Paula to agree to marry him and move with him into her London townhouse, but also years earlier, when he breaks into the

Figure 1.4. Gregory's hypnotic gaze succeeds in winning Paula over in *Gaslight* (1944). *Source*: *Gaslight* (George Cukor, 1944).

same townhouse to try to steal the crown jewels that her aunt had been gifted by a royal admirer: "Dear Miss Alquist, I beg of you to see me just once more. I have followed you to London . . . " reads the beginning of the letter from Sergius Bauer to Alice Alquist that eventually proves his guilt. Hence, even though the MGM version doesn't question Gregory Anton's "respectability" on the basis of his "foreignness" as overtly as the British National version does, it certainly does paint him in darkly villainous hues for daring to puncture and penetrate the inner sanctum of upper-middle-class English life.

After moving into the upper-middle-class homestead of 9 Thornton Square, Gregory transitions from using his powers of persuasion to court and seduce Paula to using them to convince her that she's becoming more and more physically and mentally ill. This is where the "gaslighting" plot, as we now think of it, kicks into high gear. In both film versions, various cinematic elements contribute to the mesmeric/hypnotic feel of the gaslighting proceedings: elements such as camera angles, camera movements, music, set design, and, especially, lighting. The primary way lighting factors into the narrative, of course, is that Bella/Paula notices the flames of the gaslit fixtures in her home flickering and dimming shortly after Paul/Gregory goes out for the evening and then again shortly before he comes back; it is this keen observation on her part that ultimately helps to solve the mystery and put an end to her psychological abuse. (For more on the feminist implications of this plot element, see this collection's introduction.) But another, subtler way that gas lighting plays into the narrative's power dynamic is via Paul/Gregory's insistence that Bella/Paula never light any of the fixtures in the household herself. He either lights them himself or he forces her to sit by and watch as her nemesis, Nancy the parlormaid (Cathleen Cordell/Angela Lansbury), is tasked with lighting them for her, thereby reinforcing the false narrative of her helplessness and invalidism.

It is in the shadowy glow of this gas-powered lighting that we see Bella/Paula fall deeper and deeper into the chasm of Paul/Gregory's manipulative control. Though the "hypnotic" nature of this control is not mentioned by name anywhere in the dialogue of either film (or of Hamilton's play), the term is explicitly used once in the stage directions of the British National screenplay. After Paul has accused Bella of moving the infamous "little picture" on the wall and ordered her to go retrieve it from wherever she has hidden it, the action is described as follows: "MRS. MALLEN, her eyes still fixed on her husband, rises from her chair. He seems to be using some strange hypnotic influence over her but does not touch her, and yet we see the force that drives her to move backwards across the room towards the door, feeling with her hands behind her as she goes, protesting all the way."[37] In each film version, it is while under this same "strange hypnotic influence" — while under "the spell of [her husband's] mesmerism," as Bonnie Honig, too, has put it[38] — that the gaslit wife finds herself being slowly but surely "driven backwards" in terms of her physical and emotional health. Instead of the traditional hypnotist's injunction of "You are getting sleepy, very sleepy," in other words, here the implied injunction is "You are getting sick, very sick."

Significantly, though, the persecuted wife is not the only one who suffers from "sickness" in the *Gaslight* plot. By the end of the story, the persecuting husband is revealed to suffer from severe mental illness himself in the form of a monomaniacal jewel obsession — he turns out to be, as several critics have dubbed him, "the *madman* in the attic."[39] By simultaneously condemning the foreign husband for the "invasive" mental harm he does to a "weak" and "susceptible" woman *and* for being mentally "weak" and "susceptible" to "nervous disease" himself, the two film adaptations of *Gaslight* subtly hark back to the double-edged antisemitic fears and prejudices that were so prominent in late nineteenth-century Britain, in the ways that were outlined at the start of this chapter.

The "madness" of the gaslighting husband thus serves both as a clinical explanation for the depth and depravity of his spousal abuse and, in the final beat of each film, as something that the abused wife is able to exploit and weaponize for retaliatory purposes. After Paul/Gregory has been tied up by the police and is trying to convince Bella/Paula to cut him free with a knife so he can escape ("Come closer, Paula. Closer. Look into my eyes," Gregory even murmurs in the MGM version, more "Svengali-like" than ever), she turns the tables by playing mind games on *him*, pretending she is going to follow his instructions but then using the gaslighting techniques she has learned from him to do otherwise:

> Paula (*looking in the drawer to which Gregory has directed her*): There's no knife here.
> Gregory: Yes, I put it there; look for it!
> Paula: I don't see any knife.
> Gregory: I put it there tonight!
> Paula (*pulling a knife out of the drawer*): Well, it isn't here. You must have dreamed you put it there. (*She looks down at the knife, then back at Gregory.*) Are you suggesting that this is a knife I hold in my hand? Have you gone mad, my husband?[40]

Here, we feel a bit of the comeuppance politics that Jordan Kistler sees in *Dracula* when Mina "regains her agency and autonomy" by "manipulating" the powers of hypnosis the Count thinks he wields exclusively over her. And yet, just as Mina must rely on Dr. Van Helsing's paternalistic help to regain her "agency and autonomy" in the end (along with the help of Jonathan Harker, John Seward, Arthur Holmwood, and Quincey Morris), Bella must rely on the help of her cousin Vincent and Sergeant Rough, and Paula must rely on the help of Brian Cameron. This is deflating not only from a feminist-empowerment perspective, but also because it serves to underscore and magnify the films' xenophobic "us versus them" mentalities. At the end of *Dracula*, Mina may triumph over her mental and physical assaulter, but so too does a Dutch-Anglo-American band of vampire-hunters triumph over an Eastern European "invader." At the end of *Gaslight*, Bella/Paula may succeed in expelling an abusive, psychotic gaslighter from her life, but so too do the representatives of Scotland Yard who have come to her aid succeed in expelling an "undesirable" foreign influence from the middle-class English home.

***

In a dialogue exchange that appears in one of the early MGM screenplay drafts but didn't make it into the final cut of the film, the character who would come to be called Paula Alquist tells the character who would come to be called Brian Cameron that "it's impossible" for her to pursue a romantic relationship with him because of the "shame" she feels for having been duped into a bigamist marriage by the dastardly foreigner who would come to be called Gregory Anton. To comfort her (and to try to keep the chance of a romantic relationship with her alive), the Brian Cameron character replies: "Mesmerism. Animal magnetism. That's all it was. And that's that, and we'll never mention it again."[41] I hope in this chapter to have shown that, even without explicitly "mention[ing] it," both 1940s films bearing the name *Gaslight* quietly but troublingly played off of ingrained Victorian stereotypes about the mental and bodily harm that monstrous mesmerists of a certain foreign persuasion might do to impressionable young Englishwomen. It is important for us to recognize that this, too, is part of the ideological work that the *cinematic* gaslighting narrative performs, along with its hauntingly powerful indictment of psychosomatic brutality.

Notes

1. The term "neuromimesis" was coined in the 1870s to describe the "imitation of the symptoms of a physical disease by (a person with) a psychological disorder." *OED*, s.v. "neuromimesis (n.)."
2. Riskin, "Franz Anton Mesmer," par. 13.
3. Oppenheim, *Shattered Nerves*, 299.
4. This is Stefan Andriopoulos's translation of a sentence from Charcot's *Clinical Lectures on the Diseases of the Nervous System* (1889). Andriopoulos, "Sleeper Effect," 90.
5. Bernheim, *Suggestive Therapeutics*, 60.
6. For more on the relationship between gaslighting and medical diagnoses of "hysteria," see both this collection's introduction and Diana Bellonby's chapter, "Gaslighting Vernon Lee."
7. Oppenheim, *Shattered Nerves*, 300.
8. Mitchell, *Lectures on Diseases*, 60.
9. Vrettos, *Somatic Fictions*, 87 (emphasis mine). To get a sense of how Mitchell's most famous patient, Charlotte Perkins Gilman, felt about his "Svengalian" bedside manner, one need only read Gilman's "The Yellow Wallpaper" (1892) and "Why I Wrote The Yellow Wallpaper" (1913).
10. Pick, *Svengali's Web*, 143.
11. Antisemitic xenophobia was especially high-pitched in the late nineteenth and early twentieth centuries, when Russian pogroms caused an influx of Jewish immigrants to flee to England and other Western European countries.
12. Pick, *Svengali's Web*, 4.
13. See, for example, Zanger, "Sympathetic Vibration"; Halberstam, "Technologies of Monstrosity"; and Kistler, "Mesmeric Rapport."
14. Auerbach, "Magi and Maidens," 283.
15. Zanger, "Sympathetic Vibration," 33.
16. Cucullu, "Sleep Deprived," 305.
17. Du Maurier, *Trilby*, 244, 41, 170, 11, 92. Further references to *Trilby* will be cited parenthetically.
18. Delabastita, "Thrilled by Trilby," 36. For another essay that analyzes the relationship between Svengali's voice/accent and the novel's antisemitism, see Wald, "How Svengali Lost His Jewish Accent."
19. Though Trilby is born and raised in France, her father is an Irish gentleman and her mother is a barmaid whose ancestors hail from Scotland, English, and Ireland.
20. This sentence is a perfect example of du Maurier hinting at the "much more ghastly" sound of Svengali's French due to his "Hebrew-German accent" — the nonaccented way to say this instruction in French would be "*Regardez-moi bien dans le blanc des yeux.*" (I thank Deanna Kreisel for her help with this translation.)

21. As Elaine Showalter describes in her introduction to the novel, "*Trilby* became the first modern bestseller in American publishing" by selling "more than 200,000 copies in the first year," with the subsequent English editions proving to be "hugely successful as well." The novel also inspired a full-blown craze — "Trilby-mania" — that influenced everything from fashion to music to food products. *Trilby*, vii–viii.
22. Zanger, "Sympathetic Vibration," 35.
23. Arata, "Occidental Tourist," 621.
24. Stoker, *Dracula*, 44–45. Further references to *Dracula* will be cited parenthetically.
25. Delabastita, "Thrilled by Trilby," 30.
26. Kistler, "Mesmeric Rapport," 379.
27. Kistler, "Mesmeric Rapport," 378.
28. Downs, *Anton Walbrook*, 127.
29. Dickinson, quoted in Downs, *Anton Walbrook*, 168.
30. Hamilton, *Gas Light*, 7.
31. Downs, *Anton Walbrook*, 168.
32. This, again, is Bernheim. See note 5.
33. Balderston, Draft of *Gaslight*, January 5, 1943.
34. Balderston, Draft of *Gaslight*, January 5, 1943.
35. Selznick to Mayer, January 24, 1944, 4.
36. Crowther, Review of *Gaslight*, May 5, 1944; Anonymous, Review of *Gaslight*, May 8, 1944. For recent critical comparisons of Boyer's Gregory to Svengali, see Baxter, *Charles Boyer*, 148; and Davis, Review of "The Seventh Veil," par. 11.
37. Rawlinson and Boland, Draft of *Gaslight*, February 12, 1940.
38. Honig, *Shell-Shocked*, 23–24.
39. See, for example, Melville, "Madman in the Attic"; and Young, "Woman's Space," 68.
40. The lines are slightly different in the British National film version, but the thrust of the scene is the same.
41. Balderston, Draft of *Gaslight*, January 22, 1943. In this draft, "Paula" is still called "Bella," "Gregory" is called "Ivan," and "Brian" is called "Sir Roger."

Bibliography

Andriopoulos, Stefan. "The Sleeper Effect: Hypnotism, Mind Control, Terrorism." *Grey Room* 45 (2011): 88–105.

Anonymous. Review of *Gaslight*. *Daily Variety*, May 8, 1944.

Arata, Stephen D. "The Occidental Tourist: *Dracula* and the Anxiety of Reverse Colonization." *Victorian Studies* 33, no. 4 (1990): 621–45.

Auerbach, Nina. "Magi and Maidens: The Romance of the Victorian Freud." *Critical Inquiry* 8, no. 2 (1981): 281–300.

Balderston, John. Draft of *Gaslight* dated January 5, 1943. MGM *Gaslight* file, Margaret Herrick Library, Los Angeles.

Balderston, John. Draft of *Gaslight* dated January 22, 1943. MGM *Gaslight* file, Margaret Herrick Library, Los Angeles.

Baxter, John. *Charles Boyer: The French Lover.* University Press of Kentucky, 2021.

Bernheim, Hippolyte. *Suggestive Therapeutics: A Treatise on the Nature and Uses of Hypnotism*. Translated by Christian Herter. Thoemmes Press, 1998.

Crowther, Bosley. Review of *Gaslight*. *New York Times*, May 5, 1944.

Cucullu, Lois. "Sleep Deprived and Ultramodern: How Novels Turned Dream Girls into Insomniacs." *NOVEL: A Forum on Fiction* 42, no. 2 (2009): 304–10.

Cukor, George, dir. *Gaslight*. Metro-Goldwyn-Mayer, 1944.

Davis, Nick. Review of "The Seventh Veil." *Nick's Flick Picks*, February 2010. https://www.nicksflickpicks.com/7thveil.html.

Delabastita, Dirk. "Thrilled by *Trilby*? Dreading *Dracula*? Late-Victorian Thrillers and the Curse of the Foreign Tongue." In *The Voices of Suspense and Their Translation in Thrillers*, edited by Susanne Cadera and Anita Pavic Pintaric, 23–45. Rodopi, 2014.

Dickinson, Thorold, dir. *Gaslight*. British National Films, 1940.

Downs, James. *Anton Walbrook: A Life of Masks and Mirrors*. Peter Lang, 2021.

Du Maurier, George. *Trilby*. Edited by Dennis Denisoff and Elaine Showalter. Oxford University Press, 2009.

Halberstam, Jack. "Technologies of Monstrosity: Bram Stoker's *Dracula*." *Victorian Studies* 36, no. 3 (1993): 333–52.

Hamilton, Patrick. *Gas Light: A Victorian Thriller in Three Acts*. Constable and Company, 1939.

Honig, Bonnie. *Shell-Shocked: Feminist Criticism After Trump*. Fordham University Press, 2021.

Kistler, Jordan. "Mesmeric Rapport: The Power of Female Sympathy in Bram Stoker's *Dracula*." *Journal of Victorian Culture* 23, no. 3 (2018): 366–80.

Melville, David. "The Madman in the Attic: *Gaslight* and the 'Psycho Dandy.'" *Senses of Cinema* 75 (2015).

Mitchell, Silas Weir. *Lectures on Diseases of the Nervous System, Especially in Women*. Henry C. Lea's Son & Co., 1881.

Oppenheim, Janet. *Shattered Nerves: Doctors, Patients, and Depression in Victorian England*. Oxford University Press, 1991.

Pick, Daniel. *Svengali's Web: The Alien Enchanter in Modern Culture*. Yale University Press, 2000.

Rawlinson, A. R., and Bridget Boland. Draft of *Gaslight* (British National version) dated February 12, 1940. MGM *Gaslight* file, Margaret Herrick Library, Los Angeles.

Riskin, Jessica. "Franz Anton Mesmer (1734–1815)." *The Super-Enlightenment: A Digital Archive*. https://exhibits.stanford.edu/super-e/feature/franz-anton-mesmer-1734-1815.

Selznick, David O. to L. B. Mayer. January 24, 1944. MGM *Gaslight* file, Margaret Herrick Library, Los Angeles.

Stoker, Bram. *Dracula*. Edited by Roger Luckhurst. Oxford University Press, 2011.

Wald, Gayle. "How Svengali Lost His Jewish Accent." *Sounding Out!*, September 26, 2011.

Vrettos, Athena. *Somatic Fictions: Imagining Illness in Victorian Culture.* Stanford University Press, 1995.

Young, Kay. "A Woman's Space is in the Home: Architecture, Privacy, and Melodrama in *Pamela* and *Gaslight*." *Partial Answers* 2, no. 2 (2004): 51–74.

Zanger, Jules. "A Sympathetic Vibration: Dracula and the Jews." *English Literature in Transition 1880–1920* 34, no. 1 (1991): 33–44.

2

Spiritual Energies

Gaslighting, Yoga, and Cultures of Healing in Nineteenth-Century India

Narin Hassan

Some trauma therapists recommend mind-body practices to recuperate from gaslighting. Amelia Kelley, for example, includes yoga and meditation in the treatment options she outlines in *Gaslighting Recovery for Women* (2023), and she views yoga as a vital tool for regulating stress hormones, gaining self-awareness and confidence, and alleviating the pain that comes from this particular type of trauma.[1] Modern attention to mind-body practices in medical contexts coincides with the rise of yoga and meditation as popular self-care activities. Yet, while these modalities have been shown to act as a restorative balm for various stressors, their therapeutic value has the potential to be co-opted. For example, in a critique of International Yoga Day, a popular initiative proposed in 2014 by Indian Prime Minister Narendra Modi (and concurrently established as a global event by the United Nations), Roohi Narula describes the coercive use of yoga as a signpost for benevolence: "Modi's politics of yoga is a clear example of gaslighting allowing him to invisibilise the functioning of oppressive structures."[2] Narula refers to Modi's embrace of an intrinsically mystical India as cultural capital to improve the nation's global image and considers this a form of gaslighting rooted in colonial histories. In a similar critique, Sheena Sood uses the term "om-washing" to describe how yoga has been usurped to conceal supremacist ideologies through initiatives like International Yoga Day: "participating in such events legitimises Modi's attempts at om-washing. . . . It's time to reclaim yoga by rejecting Modi's appropriation of this ancient practice."[3]

Such examples show how healing cultural practices can be employed deceptively to create a false image of altruism and harmony; they function as a form of "cultural gaslighting," which, as Elena Ruíz claims, "diverts critical attention away from structural epistemic oppressions that continue to underwrite the colonial project."[4] While Ruíz analyzes medical gaslighting and its relationship to settler colonialism, her focus on structural forms of gaslighting may be applied to the ways that therapeutic systems like yoga intertwine with abusive regimes and practices. Yoga, like other effective mind-body modalities, can be manipulated to re-create the very problems it is designed to resist — reinforcing structural inequities and colonial legacies as well as reproducing psychic, emotional, and spiritual harm. In what follows, I track those very legacies, demonstrating how contemporary associations of yoga with health, well-being, and cultural politics began during the Victorian period.

Along with the increasing visibility of mind-body practices in contemporary politics and culture, yoga has its share of gaslighting stories — from the sexual abuse scandals in traditions including Bikram, Ashtanga, Anusara, and Iyengar, to the personal accounts of spiritual gaslighting that now filter through news media. These include physical assaults (like pressure toward extreme physical exertion) as well as mental mistreatments (such as psychic and hypnotic control, extreme cultish lifestyle expectations, and hierarchical organizational structures). Despite these accusations, yoga is a highly beneficial prescription for physical and emotional health, a guru culture continues to proliferate, and spiritual tourism is booming. Cities such as Rishikesh, India, flourish as yoga hubs, and yoga retreat centers are branded as sanctuaries that provide valuable physical and emotional support to visitors. While much can be said of the divergent political, medical, and cultural deployment of yoga, its global reach, and its connections to other "alternative" practices, my aim in this essay is to examine how the multivalent aspects of yoga as a spiritual pursuit have an enduring history that intersects with our investigation of gaslighting and its complex representations. I approach this topic as a literary scholar as well as a dedicated yoga practitioner and teacher interested in yoga history and its relationship to gender and colonialism. I consider how participation in evolving cultures of yoga aligned with women's travel encounters and spiritual explorations, offering therapeutic responses to what we now call gaslighting. Reading the growth of yoga through expanding spiritual movements in the nineteenth century gives us a way to analyze how these practices functioned as a respite from domestic confinement, appealed to women as self-care practices that offered a sense of control, and functioned as an alternative to increasingly institutionalized, masculine, Western medical discourses. It also illuminates how British and American women benefited from these pursuits and laid claim to Indian traditions in a way that provided them with the authority (sometimes at the expense of Indian women) to shape spiritual discourses and self-care practices.

I consider these topics through three key areas — first, by briefly referencing how spiritual activities appealed to women in the mid- to late nineteenth century and intersected with stories of marital gaslighting. Then, I link Swami Vivekananda's travels, which mark a pivotal moment in the global reception of yoga, to the appeal of Eastern spirituality for British and American women. Through speeches, writings, and collaborations, Vivekananda promoted the ideals of an ancient philosophy as a unifying force for the West in much the same way as Modi's International Yoga Day functions as a phenomenon with wide cultural appeal rooted in Hindu nationalism. Finally, I trace the convergence of Vivekananda's efforts with the rise of the Theosophical movement.

My focus in this section is on Annie Besant's leadership in this organization, her embrace of Eastern philosophy, and her depictions of yoga as therapeutic. These topics are framed by a complex gendered colonial history, which includes the impulse of white women to promote Eastern spiritual practices and responses by Indian feminists Pandita Ramabai and Cornelia Sorabji (whose concerns were often deflected); they critiqued the "guru worship" of Western women and argued that yogic spiritual beliefs were appropriated by them. Numerous scholars have discussed the appeal of spiritualism for British and American women in this period and the feminization of spiritualist spaces.[5] I argue that these women turned to esoteric experiences, particularly those based on Eastern philosophies, for healing and to challenge emerging scientific theories that limited them. Yoga and meditation practices — through their emphasis on cognitive expansion and access to astral planes, ancient histories, expanded geographies, and past lives — appealed to women who desired self-revision and social transformation. Women could turn to "fringe" spiritual practices to navigate difficulties in their domestic lives.[6] These practices — particularly those tied to ancient Indian philosophies and related to yoga and meditation — gave women the opportunity to manage their experiences of dismissal, abuse, and gaslighting by harnessing the powers of the mind. Yet, depictions of ancient Eastern spiritual practices also depended upon Orientalist representations and often supported idealized patriarchal histories. This chapter asks that we consider yoga and meditation within a patchwork of Victorian spiritualist practices in order to better understand evolving conceptions of the mind and body, as well as how those conceptions relate to gaslighting.

Gaslighting and Spiritualism: Marital Resistance, Psychology, and Eastern Philosophy

Women's participation in a plethora of spiritualist activities in the nineteenth century — ranging from mediumship to spiritualist societies to redefining and promoting meditation and yoga traditions — can be viewed in response to neurological theories and marital structures that were harmful to women. For example, through much of the Victorian period, spiritual practices were intertwined with accusations of mental instability and female lunacy. The most obvious cases, which have been carefully discussed by Judith Walkowitz, Roy Porter, Helen Nicholson, and others, are those of Georgina Weldon, Louisa Lowe, and Rosina Bulwer-Lytton. These women were victims of gaslighting and spiritual policing by their husbands and medical men who threatened to (or did) put them in asylums because of their engagement with spiritual activities. Walkowitz writes: "Medical men, alarmed by the growing popularity of spiritualism among the educated classes, had themselves instigated this larger conflict. They caricatured spiritualists as crazy women and feminized men engaged in superstitious, popular, and fraudulent practices."[7] Nicholson describes how "spiritualism provided a number of easy targets for unscrupulous husbands wishing to confine their wives."[8] In their writing, Weldon and Lowe were open about their activities as spiritualists. Their foray into these practices may have been prompted by marital gaslighting and the oppression they felt within their homes.[9]

Such lunacy trials occurred at a time when scientific progress and spiritual practices were often at odds with one another: the 1870s and 1880s were decades in which medical doctors, alienists, and psychologists were reshaping conceptions of sanity and grappling with the intersections of science and spiritualism.[10] In this period, psychology became institutionalized as a discipline: the American Neurological Association was established with the *Journal of Nervous and Mental Disease* as its official journal (this was soon after the first American textbook of neurology was published in 1871) and, in the same year, the Psychological Society of Great Britain was established.[11] These developments reflect the wide-ranging interest in psychology and brain science in Western medical contexts alongside the publication of numerous texts in the field of sexology that addressed topics such as hysteria and mediomania (that is, hysteria resulting from mediumship).[12] As Diana Bellonby discusses in her chapter in this volume, these discourses produced restrictive diagnoses for women; they existed in tension with practices of spiritual exploration that allowed for more flexible understandings of the mind and body.

Further, a plethora of practices related to Western spiritualism were intertwined with movements of yoga, mysticism, and Eastern philosophy. Two of the most sustained and organized of these were the establishment of the Theosophical Society in 1875, an esoteric organization based on Eastern religion and influenced by principles grounded in the occult, which was formed by Helena Petrova Blavatsky and Henry Olcott, and the spread of Vedantic knowledge, based on the ancient Sanskrit scriptures, precipitated by the journeys of Swami Vivekananda to the United States and Europe in the 1890s. These simultaneously occurring movements — one that expanded from Vivekananda's travel to the West and the other from the travels of Blavatksy and Besant to the East — participated in the formation of a guru culture and were tied to a burgeoning interest in the occult as well as yoga and meditation.

Again, these concurrent shifts appealed particularly to women as they provided an escape from the bounds of domesticity and offered them ways to expand their perceptions. Both practices touted the so-called universality and applicability of Eastern religions and philosophies beyond borders, while setting a foundation for many of the yoga, meditation, and "New Age" movements that became popularized in the twentieth century. Through references to Eastern traditions, these movements intellectualized spirituality and shifted its emphasis from the space of the séance to science. For example, the leaders of the Theosophical Society (many of whom were women) sought to promote the organization's activities in line with conceptions of science.[13] They also made the claim that Western psychology alone could not heal the deep wounds of trauma; instead, physical and mental practices — rooted in forms of meditation, self-reflection, and belief in systems such as reincarnation — could provide healing. Spiritualist philosophies such as Theosophy and practices of yoga and meditation connected women to other spaces — geographical and astral — and offered them a path to expand consciousness, escape the bounds of domesticity, and gain knowledge from ancient systems that were reconfigured as progressive and transformational.

Guru Cultures: Spiritual Gaslighting, Gender, and the Lure of Yoga

In "The Heathen Invasion," an article published in 1911 in *Hampton-Columbian Magazine* (a monthly magazine based in New York), Mabel Potter Daggett sensationalizes the expansion of yoga by suggesting its hypnotic influence on women besotted by Indian gurus: "From the moment that the guru has whispered to his pupil the mantra or secret formula to reveal which would invite the anger of the gods there is formed between the two a tie the most indissoluble of any on earth WOMEN TAKEN FROM HOME AND FAMILY."[14] Daggett's essay hearkens to the fin de siècle moment when Indian yogis such as Swami Vivekananda introduced yoga to the Western world and promoted the practice for harmony and healing. Daggett critiques yoga practices as particularly dangerous for women: "Eve is eating the apple again. It is offered as a knowledge of the occult that shall solve the riddles of existence. Yoga, that eastern philosophy the emblem of which is the coiled serpent, is being widely disseminated here."[15] Daggett's Orientalist critique of this "invasion" and claim that women were "taken from home and family" through seductive foreign mantras alludes to the British and American women who left their homes to travel with the Swami and, in some cases, to move permanently to India to immerse themselves in the lifestyles that he and other gurus espoused. Sara Bull, Sarah Farmer, Josephine Macleod, Margaret Noble, and many others became Swami Vivekananda's disciples, spread his ideals, funded his travels, and organized speaking tours for him.[16]

Vivekananda and his rapidly expanding network of followers promoted the notion that ancient philosophies of India could be consolidated under the umbrella of yoga. Such practices of self-improvement and spirituality connected women and provided them with expanded notions of selfhood, new ways to imagine freedom, and alternative forms of care. Letters between the various figures engaged with Swami Vivekananda reveal the female-centered networks of communication and activity surrounding his visits and the efforts of women to spread his philosophies.[17] Yet, as noted in the beginning of this section, the collaborations of women with Swami Vivekananda and other Indian gurus also produced dramatic responses from critics. Elizabeth A. Reed, an American author who wrote numerous books related to religion and Oriental studies at the turn of the century, cautioned: "Let the white woman beware of the hypnotic influence of the East — let her remember that when her Guru or god-man, has once whispered his mystic syllables into her ear and she has sworn allegiance to him, she is forever helpless in his hands . . . The Swami, Gossain, or Guru is now quite at home in both Europe and America and many a desolate home lies in the trail of his silken robes."[18] Describing the case of a New England woman "having fallen under the hypnotic sway," she also noted, "can we wonder that she then went hopelessly insane and was for years in the asylum?"[19] Critical responses like this came at a time when, as Stephen Prothero has argued, yoga was intertwined with both Hinduphilia and Hinduphobia, and when white men also began to profit from its popularity. Pierre Bernard, also known as "Oom the Omnipotent," opened tantric yoga studios in San Francisco and New York and became the topic of legal and media scandals in 1910. As Prothero notes, "Newspapers investigating his reconstituted 'Oriental Sanctum' reported hearing 'wild Oriental music and women's cries, but not those of distress.' In 1910 Bernard was charged again by two young women who accused him of forcing them to serve as spiritual prostitutes. . . . Ultimately Bernard's accusers refused to testify, leaving the papers to speculate that he has exerted some irresistible psychic power over them."[20]

Critiques of yoga also came from Indian women writers, including Pandita Ramabai and Cornelia Sorabji, who were wary of the resurgence of Hindu patriarchal structures through the guise of yoga and found Western women to be gullible to the charms of Indian gurus. Swami Vivekananda grappled with the ways that Indian female intellectuals challenged his presentation of Indian yogic ideals as liberating and transformative. He describes Ramabai, a Hindu widow who traveled to the United States and eventually converted to Christianity, as a source of tension and resistance. In an 1896 letter to Sara Bull — often described as the "Mother" of Vivekananda's movement, as she helped to spread his mission in the United States and India — he writes, "I am astonished to hear the scandals the Ramabai circles are indulging in about me. Don't you see, Mrs. Bull, that however a man may conduct himself, there will always be persons who invent the blackest lies about him."[21] Kumari Jayawardena argues that while Vivekananda searched for a "true" woman leader in India, he overlooked Pandita Ramabai, who was a "courageous woman leader" but didn't receive acknowledgment for her feminist efforts at the time. Instead, he anointed his follower, Margaret Noble (who he named "Sister Nivedita" and described as "a true lioness" for the Indian cause) and prioritized white women as his collaborators.[22]

Sorabji, an Indian woman writer who was educated as a lawyer and who traveled extensively outside of India, speaks respectfully of Vivekananda but writes in 1932 that his "visit to the Chicago Parliament of Religions — about fifty years ago now — was perhaps the beginning of the swami influx into America."[23] She describes the proliferation of unregulated, oversimplified yoga practices as particularly dangerous to women vulnerable to the lure of swami men: "These swamis enter America. They tell Americans what they would like to hear, and prepare books for their women disciples peppered with 'karma' 'the pranic fluid' and 'reincarnation' 'Yoga' etc — all of which make the readers of these books feel learned and esoteric. The swamis do not tell them that the orthodox Hindu believes that his Karma may earn him rebirth as, say, a flea" (371). Sorabji critiques the modern development of yoga as a system that has been diluted and misinterpreted, and she suggests that the appropriation of the practice by white women is supported by the misguidance they receive from untrustworthy swamis. She writes: "I was lately at the Vedantic centre in Boston, where the swami in charge, dressed as an English cleric, serves an 'altar' on which were Easter lilies, and at the foot of which burned a red light in a tall brass Hindu property. His helpers are 'consecrated women' — Western women; those at the Los Angeles centre dress like nuns. One of them lectures on Hinduism. She told me she had spent three months in India!" (372). Sorabji describes the proliferation of new yoga centers led by swamis and Western women who assume spiritual authority without sufficient knowledge. She underscores how American women misrepresent traditional practices and participate in a process of cultural gaslighting as they are swayed by Indian men:

> There is no reason why people should not study Hinduism for themselves without the aid of pseudo-swamis. There are books and translations enough, made by scholars; and the practice of meditation, of going into silence, cannot fail to help us all. . . . I have seen a Western woman bend to and fro saying 'Ram-Ram-Hari-Ram' hundreds of times at a sitting. . . . The deluded one said she was practising Yoga as her *guru* had taught her, and that it was wonderfully uplifting. She did look a little disconcerted, I must say, when asked if she knew that the words she used represented the invocation for the dead, chanted by the carriers of the corpse to the Burning Ghat. (373)

But even as Sorabji calls out certain Western women for consuming Indian cultural practices without a true understanding of their purpose or meaning, she also recognizes that the pursuit of spiritual practices abroad reflects an unease at home: "Those who run after swamis and fancy religions," she writes, "are really feeling after something to ease their hearts, not having taken enough time to study what their own country has had to offer" (367).

Both Ramabai and Sorabji challenge Vivekananda's presentations of yoga as a path to global harmony and solidarity. For even though Vivekananda was, as Peter van der Veer notes, probably the "first major Indian advocate of a 'Hindu Spirituality'" and "first and foremost, interested in Hindu unity,"[24] women like Ramabai and Sorabji argued that unity was impossible within a history steeped in patriarchal oppression and gaslighting. While the white women who took on Vivekananda's mission often became anointed as public faces for his cause and some Indian women (such as Sarada Devi) held the position of "holy mothers," many Indian women were marginalized within or excluded from Vivekananda's spiritual movement. Feminist figures like Sorabji and Ramabai were, in particular, viewed as disruptors to his cause, largely because of their critique of his embrace of Hinduism via patriarchal authority.

Annie Besant, Theosophy, and the Promotion of Yoga as Transformation

The ideals Vivekananda shared coincided with the global growth of the Theosophical Society, which became increasingly focused on the comprehension of ancient Indian yogic texts and encouraged female leadership. I turn to the case of Annie Besant, arguably one of the most famous and active figures in the movement, who traveled to Adyar, India, where she immersed herself in a spiritual journey and produced texts about the power of yoga and Eastern philosophies. Besant is one of the more controversial women of the nineteenth century, known for her engagement in a variety of political activities (initially as a leader of the birth control movement and later in life as an expatriate who spoke for Indian independence), and is recognized as a writer, speaker, and spiritual leader. While the canon of Besant's writing is vast, my focus is on her representation of marriage in *An Autobiography* (1893), and her treatises on yoga. While Besant is guarded in sharing her matrimonial struggles, her memoir reveals how she was pressured into an oppressive marriage and how she gained liberation through her travels to India. I discuss how Besant presents yoga as a path to healing and truth-seeking, and I trace how she empowered herself by laying claim to these practices and making them available to broader audiences through the position she gained as a spiritual leader.

Besant begins *An Autobiography*, written after her immersion in Theosophy, with an image of her astrological chart and a reference to the metaphysical tendencies of her childhood, noting, "As a child I was mystical and imaginative religious to the very finger-tips, and with a certain faculty for seeing visions and dreaming dreams."[25] While her childhood was filled with imaginary play and sensitivity toward "psychic impressions" (27), she describes her relationship with the clergyman Frank Besant as a mistake that led to oppression. During a whirlwind trip, she felt like she was coerced into marrying him: "We were thrown together for a week, the only two young ones in a small party of holiday-makers, and in our walks, rides, and drives we were naturally companions; an hour or two before he left he asked me to marry him, taking my consent for granted as I had allowed him such full companionship" (69). Startled and unable to refuse his proposal, she describes how he "bound me over to silence till he could himself speak to my mother, urging authoritatively that it would be dishonourable of me to break his confidence . . . and then, out of sheer weakness and fear of inflicting pain I drifted into an engagement with a man I did not pretend to love" (69–70).

The Besants' marriage was, according to several biographers, rife with struggle and abuse.[26] Drawing evidence from documents in the Public Record

Office, for example, Arthur Nethercot relates the story of Besant giving birth to one of her children "somewhat prematurely in consequence of a shock" — a "shock" that, presumably, was the result of Walter "str[iking] her on the shoulder, while simultaneously suggesting that she leave him and go back home."[27] Further evidence shows that she frequently sought to leave her husband, whose aggression created mental and physical trauma: "Whenever she could no longer endure her husband's treatment, Annie took the train down to London to seek her mother's comfort. In June during a new altercation, Frank took her by the shoulders and 'shook her violently, striking her with his knee with violence several times and thus causing her to leave his house and to return to her mother's house.' Moreover, she asserted, he kept a loaded gun in his study and several times threatened to shoot her."[28] In 1873, following years of ill health — including "serious heart trouble" that she attributes to "the constant strain under which I lived" (117) — Annie Besant left her husband. In particular, she describes how her husband's domineering religious expectations contributed to her decision to flee: "At last, in July or August, 1873, the crisis came. I was told that I must conform to the outward observances of the Church, and attend the Communion; I refused. Then came the distinct alternative; conformity or exclusion from home — in other words, hypocrisy or expulsion. I chose the latter" (117). She then writes, "With a great price I had obtained my freedom, but — I was free. Home, friends, social position, were the price demanded and paid, and, being free, I wondered what to do with my freedom." (119). Besant presents the dual force of her abusive marriage and the religious pressure imposed upon her as gaslighting; she emphasizes how the pressure to conform resulted in psychological stress, along with the physical abuse she endured.

In sharp contrast, Besant describes Helena Petrova Blavatsky as a savior providing her with the tools to find freedom and clarity: "Thus was ushered in 1889, the to me never-to-be-forgotten year in which I found my way 'Home,' and had the priceless good fortune of meeting, and of becoming the pupil of H.P. Blavatsky. Ever more and more had been growing on me the feeling that something more than I had was needed for the cure of social ills" (338). Besant's introduction to Blavatsky and her ideas came when W. T. Stead asked her to review Blavatsky's *The Secret Doctrine* (1888). Reading the text left her "dazzled, blinded by the light in which disjointed facts were seen as parts of a mighty whole, and all my puzzles, riddles, problems, seemed to disappear . . . in that flash of illumination I knew that the weary search was over and the very Truth was found" (340). She asked Stead for an introduction to the writer and, soon after, Blavatsky asked her to join the Theosophical Society: "We rose to go, and for a moment the veil lifted, and two brilliant, piercing eyes met mine, and with a yearning throb in the voice: 'Oh, my dear Mrs. Besant, if you would only come among us!' I felt a well-nigh uncontrollable desire to bend down and kiss her, under the compulsion of that yearning voice, those compelling eyes" (341). Besant describes this encounter as mesmerizing; she represents Blavatsky as a powerful, larger-than-life figure who compels and attracts her toward Theosophy in a way that is both physically and spiritually captivating.

Blavatsky's theories reconfirmed her belief in psychic phenomena and encouraged her to publicize Theosophy more widely. While her reflections upon her marriage suggest both physical trauma and mental anguish, her immersion in Theosophy takes her "home" and provides opportunities for transformation. Besant is simultaneously hypnotized by Blavatsky's presence and energized by the opportunity to be her student. Besant's emphasis on the search for "truth" and her references to Blavatsky's psychic powers present Theosophy as a means of reclaiming her own intuitive power.

But Theosophy was itself a system mired in accusations of using false claims to attract practitioners. Blavatsky was accused of being a fake to promote herself as a conduit for knowledge;[29] yet, Besant focused her efforts upon emphasizing how Blavatsky and other leaders of the movement had access to ancient truths. Emphasizing her utmost devotion to Blavatsky and the cause of Theosophy, she writes, "I speak of her with the reverence due from a pupil to a teacher who never failed her. . . . This same path of knowledge that I am treading is open to all others who will pay the toll demanded at the gateway — and that toll is willingness to renounce everything for the sake of spiritual truth" (344). Diverting from Blavatsky's approach that Eastern philosophies contained classical truths and occult knowledge that should be protected from wide dissemination and saved only for chosen devotees, Besant's goal was to make this knowledge more widely available. Kurt Leland describes how she viewed the introspective practices as opportunities to expand spiritual consciousness and how she believed the goal of occult training "was to develop the bodies as vehicles of consciousness so that students could rise to the spiritual plane, where they might be further educated by the Masters."[30] Besant's reflections upon yoga and meditation publicized these elusive practices as universalized pathways to self-control that could be accessible to broader audiences and lead to enlightenment and healing.

In addition, Besant consistently emphasized the quest for truth and clarity as her highest aspiration. At the end of her tract "Why I Became a Theosophist," she writes, "I ask no other epitaph on my tomb but SHE TRIED TO FOLLOW TRUTH."[31] Besant expanded this process of truth-seeking to her study of yoga texts. Yoga, Besant argues, provides access to higher truths as well as higher planes of consciousness that prevent psychological disorders and psychic manipulations. She describes yoga as part of "the ordinary psychological science of India," which is thousands of years old and far surpasses Western science in its recognition and healing of disorders.[32] When she compares the theories of Maudsley and Lombroso on hysteria to Indian knowledge, she writes, "Now in India, where these things are studied, the science of Yoga is intended to prevent the dangers of hysteria in those who are coming into touch with the higher planes. It is therefore a science that works along two lines: a discipline and purification of the body, in order that the nerve cells may be able to vibrate in answer to the higher impacts without disturbance and without the causing of hysteria, and a training of the mind."[33] Besant's references to the benefits of yoga provide readers with an alternative mode through which to gain psychological healing.

Besant continues to reference the power of yoga as a transformative science in her *Introduction to Yoga* (1908), a series of lectures that were later published. In the forward to this text, she explains: "These lectures are intended to give an outline of Yoga, in order to prepare the student to take up, for practical purposes, the *Sutras of Patanjali*, the chief treatise on Yoga." In this guide, she describes yoga as "the unfolding of consciousness"[34] and "the last process of evolution" (13) and notes that "yoga is a science. . . . It takes up the laws of psychology, applicable to the unfolding of the whole consciousness of man on every plan, in every world, and applies those rationally in a particular case" (9). Through such references Besant suggests that yoga is a gateway to higher evolutionary consciousness that can challenge limiting scientific assertions of femininity; she presents yoga as a recovery modality that can produce clarity out of confusion. Further, Besant suggests that the mind and the body can be unified through "the two great forms of yoga — the Hatha yoga and the Raja yoga" (155) and establishes that these mind-body theories from the East can help Western women gain more mental and physical control: "Our senses are not really in the physical body but in the astral, and the centres of those senses are in the astral body. . . . The brain is merely like a telegraph wire along which the message goes; you see by the stimulation of these astral centres. That is the first thing to remember. But Hatha yoga includes much more than the stimulation of the senses. It includes a complete control over every part of the physical body" (160). Describing both the physical (Hatha) practice as well as the mental, meditative (Raja) practice, she emphasizes the balance between mind and body and suggests that unifying both through the refined systems of yogic knowledge can provide a control of the self — much in the same way that trauma therapists now emphasize physical awareness as a path to healing. Besant's Theosophical framework integrates yoga and presents it as a simultaneously mystical and scientific force that, when practiced correctly, can provide self-control, healing, and transformation.[35]

While Besant made the broad practices of yoga and meditation more available to Western audiences, the self-improvement methods she and others espoused could also contribute to spiritual gaslighting. The Theosophical Society, like other organizations, ran the risk of making false or diluted claims and deceiving believers. Further, Besant's Theosophical doctrines and spiritual pursuits, like the narratives created by Vivekananda's followers, often celebrated Hindu rites and rituals in ways that overshadowed arguments for reform produced by Indian feminists. As Kumari Jayawardena argues in her reading of Besant's gender politics, "She used the argument of cultural relativism and asserted that Western models were unsuitable for India. Limiting her feminism to the West, she advocated orthodoxy and traditional education for Indian women."[36] Indeed, figures like Sorabji, who were fighting for female education and reform, critiqued Besant's position as a British woman appropriating and misconstruing Indian spiritual practices. In a letter to the editor of *The Times* on June 3, 1914, Sorabji wrote that Besant's "great gift of oratorial language is so misleading that no one acquainted with facts, and belonging to India, and living and working in India, is entitled to keep silence if there is even one further word which can be said to minimize the inflammatory nature of her statements."[37] In another letter, addressed "To Everyone," she described Besant performing self-aggrandizing spiritual rituals:

> Mrs. Besant has a great following here. . . . But many English people are beginning to find her out. . . . It seems she has a hypnotic influence on 3 sisters, quite poor, who live here. Mrs. B. stayed with them and insisted on the floor of her room being lined with white flowers (!) and the poor things had to afford them. Then every morning, she appeared on the balcony dressed in white and they had to come and bow before her. It's such rubbish. To what religious persuasion do these rites belong, I wonder.[38]

Sorabji's depiction of Besant "dressed in white" and her reference to her "hypnotic influence" imply that her spiritual performances participated in a form of mind control. Sorabji's reference to her inauthentic religious "rites" also suggests a false or duplicitous form of appropriation. Finally, Sorabji indicates that Besant's spiritual leadership was an egotistical performance that made hierarchical gestures.

Thus, while Besant's references to yoga's capacity to provide psychological support are a call to embrace the practice as a form of freedom and resistance from psychic harm and oppression, her authoritative claims also participated in a process of self-promotion that depended on usurping traditional practices and producing new, marketable discourses and systems based upon ancient traditions. To turn to contemporary uses of the term "gaslighting" once again, feminist critics of color have argued that yoga has been whitewashed in ways that perform progressive politics and mask privilege. For example, Rumya Putcha criticizes contemporary, Americanized yoga for its engagement in the kind of hypocritical racial politics wherein "White people can claim they are free of prejudice by performing progressive, multicultural politics in public, while continuing to harbor and even voice deeply disturbing prejudices and resentments in private. . . . The social and psychological mechanism by which people deny reality and responsibility is known as gaslighting — a form of manipulation and abuse."[39] This process of cultural gaslighting, Putcha argues, is a colonization of yoga by white women that shields them from recognizing their own microaggressions and upholds white fragility. As I have shown, such a process can be seen historically as British and American women performed their spiritual leadership in the nineteenth century and made yoga part of their public discourses. Thus, analyzing women's quest for enlightenment in India allows us to deepen our understanding of the complex gendered and racial hierarchies at play within colonial contexts.[40]

While greater access to yoga and meditation practices provided individual and communal opportunities for healing, such growth also privileged the visibility of Western practitioners and emphasized the responsibility of the individual to lay claim to healthy experiences. In a similar vein, the proliferation of contemporary wellness practices has placed the responsibility to heal from societal stresses on the individual; wellness is equated with harmony, and yoga and meditation are marketed (largely to women) as commodities that reinforce hierarchies of privilege for those who have the means to access them within an increasingly corporatized and globalized wellness industry. Yoga and meditation were (and are) deeply powerful introspective well-being practices that have the capacity to provide relief from gaslighting and other forms of oppression — they encourage us to be self-aware, to be intuitive, and to care for ourselves. They also allow us to expand our focus and become more aware of manipulation by others. Yet the openness and fluidity of yoga discourses and practices can also allow for egoism, dependency, and confusion. A reading of women's call to yoga in the nineteenth century, like yoga itself, asks us to read closely between the lines — to consider how the practice could provide healing and transformation while also reproducing structural hierarchies in the pursuit of spiritual knowledge.

Notes

1. Kelley, *Gaslighting Recovery for Women*, 149.
2. Narula, "Yoga-tta Be Kidding Me."
3. Sood, "Om-washing."
4. Ruíz, "Cultural Gaslighting," 689.
5. See work by Dixon, Owen, Oppenheim, Galvan, Kontou, and others.
6. Here, I refer to Gauri Viswanathan's reading of Theosophy within the broader mystical contexts of nineteenth-century spirituality and its place as an experiential practice within broader spiritual "fringe" movements of the period (Viswananathan, "Ordinary Business of Occultism," 5). Miriam Wallraven, in her reading of Besant, writes about the "lunatic fringe" and ways that women's spiritual activities were assigned with this term ("Mere Instrument," 393).
7. Walkowitz, *City of Dreadful Delight*, 172.
8. Nicholson, "Introduction," 143.
9. Nicholson also notes: "On the surface, the Lowe household presented a perfect picture of domestic bliss and tranquility. However, after Louisa's incarceration, she began to reveal the truth about her unhappy, and at times, terrifying married life. Throughout her marriage Louisa Lowe had made regular and lengthy trips to the continent. Although these trips abroad appeared to be merely holidays to German spa towns, they were in fact attempts to escape from her unhappy marriage and cruel husband" ("Introduction," 140). Judith Walkowitz argues that spiritual activities created an escape from the burdens of marriage and domesticity: "Humble female mediums with marital problems frequently looked to the spiritualist lecture and séance circuit as a source of employment and refuge from unhappy homes. Before very long, Mrs. Weldon would herself appeal to spiritualists for collective protection and support against patriarchal plotting" (*City of Dreadful Delight*, 176).
10. As Edward Brown notes in his reading of neurology in the nineteenth century, spiritualist practices were thriving at the same moment that the medical specialization of neurology was becoming institutionalized: "If the 1870s was a period in which modern spiritualism was renewing its growth, it was also, for a variety of reasons, a period in which the profession of neurology was being born" ("Neurology and Spiritualism," 566).
11. S. E. D. Short notes how "the interest of physicians in spiritualism, as in the case of the general public, diminished after 1860 only to be revived in heightened form from 1870 to the mid-1880s. During this fifteen-year period a group of prominent Anglo-American medical men, whose major professional interest might conveniently be designated neuroscience, launched a polemical attack on spiritualism. Included in this group were the physiologist W. B. Carpenter, the neurologists William A. Hammond and George M. Beard, and the alienist Henry Maudsley" ("Physicians and Psychics," 344).

12. "Mediomania" became popularized after the publication of Dr. Frederick Rowland Marvin's book, *The Philosophy of Spiritualism and the Pathology and Treatment of Mediomania* (1874).
13. Along with Blavatsky, Annie Besant, Anna Kingsford, Alice Bailey, and others led the charge of expanding Theosophical ideas, arguing for how the system could be transformative for women as well as society.
14. Daggett, "Heathen Invasion," 399.
15. Daggett, "Heathen Invasion," 399.
16. For example, Kate Sanborn, who Vivekananda encountered on a train journey from Vancouver to Chicago, assisted with his formal registration in the Parliament of Religions and invited him to be a guest in her home. Sara Bull, whom I discuss below, also invited Swami Vivekananda to live in her home and developed a series of "Cambridge conferences" there that provided a forum to discuss comparative religions. For an overview of Vivekananda's influence and work with these women, see Harris, *Guru to the World*.
17. *The Letters of Sara Bull* and the sections of *Reminiscences of Swami Vivekananda* that feature the letters of Sister Nivedita (Margaret Noble) and Josephine Macleod contain numerous examples of the exchanges between women devotees of the Swami. For example, in a letter to Sara Bull, Josephine Macleod describes her experience of traveling with Vivekananda as a transformative and celestial experience: "If I weren't a great Yogini my heart would be sad at not having you here—but being one I must not write or think as mortals do but take you headlong into the heaven where I have been" (*Reminiscences of Swami Vivekananda*).
18. Reed, *Hinduism in Europe and America*, 131.
19. Reed, *Hinduism in Europe and America*, 129.
20. Prothero, "Hinduphobia and Hinduphilia," 18.
21. Vivekananda, *Letters*, 217.
22. Kumari Jayawardena also writes: "In some case white female spiritual figures attained more prominence than any of their Indian woman counterparts and were trained with great deference almost as saints and divine mothers and are commemorated even today" (*White Woman's Other Burden*, 176).
23. Sorabji, "Hindu Swamis and Women of the West," 366. Further references will be cited parenthetically.
24. Van der Veer, *Imperial Encounters*, 76.
25. Besant, *Autobiography*, 24. Further references will be cited parenthetically.
26. See, for example, Nethercot's *First Five Lives of Annie Besant* and Taylor's *Annie Besant: A Biography*.
27. Nethercot, *First Five Lives*, 35.
28. Nethercot, *First Five Lives*, 43.
29. Gauri Viswanathan writes: "Indeed, the Theosophical Society is more carnivalesque than Carmelite. Charles Leadbeater was accused of molesting

little boys, Besant of stealing young Brahmin men from their helpless fathers and turning them into messiahs, and Madame Blavatsky and her cofounder Colonel Olcott of perpetrating astral frauds. All the while these colorful figures concentrated their energies on securing the blessing and wisdom of elusive masters from the inner Tibetan reaches to help them build an institution consecrated to the preservation of Eastern mysteries" ("Ordinary Business of Occultism," 7).

30. Leland, *Invisible Worlds*, 2–3.
31. Besant, *Why I Became a Theosophist*, 30.
32. Besant, *Collection*, 155.
33. Besant, *Collection*, 112.
34. Besant, *Introduction to Yoga*, 6. Further references will be cited parenthetically.
35. Several scholars describe how Theosophy hovered between science and mysticism as it provided a space for female leadership. Elizabeth Carolyn Miller discusses "the odd combination of scientific materialism and mystical occultism that characterizes theosophy and spiritualism" ("Body, Spirit, Print," 256). Miriam Wallraven writes: "In contrast to the subservient role of women in traditional religions, the spiritualist movement was inconceivable without women, who constituted most of the mediums. Likewise, the Theosophical Society relied on the leadership and participation of women, and propagated gender equality and women's rights" ("Mere Instrument," 391).
36. Jayawardena, *White Woman's Other Burden*, 123.
37. Quoted in Vadgama, *Indian Portia*, 366.
38. Quoted in Vadgama, 418.
39. Putcha, "Yoga and the Maintenance."
40. For important critical background on the contexts of race and gender within imperial contexts, see the broad range of work by Antoinette Burton, Philippa Levine, Ann Stoler, and others.

Bibliography

Atmaprana, Pravrajika. *Western Women in the Footsteps of Swami Vivekananda.* Ramakrishna Mission, 2009.

Basham, Diana. *The Trial of Woman: Feminism and the Occult Sciences in Victorian Literature and Society*. New York University Press, 1992.

Besant, Annie. *An Autobiography*. T. Fisher Unwin, 1893.

———. *The Collection*, Volume 1. CreateSpace Publishing Platform, 2016.

———. *Introduction to Yoga*. Theosophical Publishing Society, 1908.

———. *Why I Became a Theosophist*. Freethought Publishing Company, 1889.

Brown, Edward M. "Neurology and Spiritualism in the 1870s." *Bulletin of the History of Medicine* 57, no. 4 (1983): 563–77.

Burke, Marie Louise. *Swami Vivekananda in the West, New Discoveries: His Prophetic Mission*. Advaita Ashrama, 1992.

Daggett, Mabel Potter. "The Heathen Invasion." *Hampton-Columbian Magazine* 27, no. 4 (1911): 399–411.

Deslippe, Philip. "The Swami Circuit: Mapping the Terrain of Early American Yoga." *Journal of Yoga Studies* 1 (2018): 5–44.

Dixon, Joy. *The Divine Feminine. Theosophy and Feminism in England*. Johns Hopkins Press, 2001.

Galvan, Jill. *The Sympathetic Medium. Feminine Channeling, The Occult, and Communication Technologies*. Cornell University Press, 2010.

Harris, Ruth. *Guru to the World: The Life and Legacy of Vivekananda*. Harvard University Press, 2022.

Kontou, Tatiana. *Women and the Victorian Occult*. Routledge, 2013.

Jayawardena, Kumari. *The White Woman's Other Burden: Western Women and South Asia During British Rule*. Routledge, 1995.

Kelley, Amelia. *Gaslighting Recovery for Women: The Complete Guide to Recognizing Manipulation and Achieving Freedom from Emotional Abuse*. Penguin Random House, 2023.

Leland, Kurt, ed. *Invisible Worlds: Annie Besant on Psychic and Spiritual Development*. Quest Books, 2013.

The Life of Swami Vivekananda, Vol. 1. Advaita Ashrama, 1979.

Marvin, Frederic Rowland. *The Philosophy of Spiritualism and the Pathology and Treatment of Mediomania*. Asa K. Butts and Co., 1874.

Miller, Elizabeth Carolyn. "Body, Spirit, Print: The Radical Autobiographies of Annie Besantand Helen and Olivia Rossetti." *Feminist Studies* 35, no. 2 (Summer 2009): 243–73.

Narula, Roohi. "Yoga-tta Be Kidding Me: Capitalism and Gaslighting in Modi's India." *Feminism in India.* July 26, 2018. https://feminisminindia.com/2018/07/26/yoga-capitalism-gaslighting-modi-india.

Nethercot, Arthur H. *The First Five Lives of Annie Besant*. University of Chicago Press, 1960.

Nicholson, Helen. "Introduction to the Writings of Louisa Lowe." In *Women, Madness and Spiritualism*, edited by Roy Porter, Helen Nicholson, and Bridget Bennett, 139–56. Routledge, 2004.

Oppenheim, Janet. *The Other World: Spiritualism and Psychical Research in England, 1850-1914*. Cambridge University Press, 1988.

Owen, Alex. *The Darkened Room: Women, Power, and Spiritualism in Late-Victorian England*. University of Pennsylvania Press, 1990.

Prabuddhaprana, Pravrajika. *Saint Sara: The Life of Sara Chapman Bull, the American Mother of Swami Vivekananda*. Sri Sarada Math, 2002.

Prothero, Steven. "Hinduphilia and Hinduphobia in US Culture." In *The Stranger's Religion: Fascination and Fear*, edited by Anna Lannstrom, 13–27. University of Notre Dame Press, 2004.

Putcha, Rumya. "Yoga and the Maintenance of White Womanhood." March 31, 2018. https://rumyaputcha.com/115-2.

Reed, Elizabeth Armstrong. *Hinduism in Europe and America.* GP Putnam's Sons, 1914.
Ruíz, Elena. "Cultural Gaslighting." *Hypatia.* 35, no. 4 (2020): 687–713.
Short, S. E. D., "Physicians and Psychics: The Anglo-American Medical Response to Spiritualism, 1870–1890." *Journal of the History of Medicine and Allied Sciences* 39, no. 3 (1984): 339–55.
Sood, Sheena. "'Om-washing': Why Modi's yoga day pose is deceptive." *Al Jazeera.* June 23, 2023. https://www.aljazeera.com/opinions/2023/6/22/om-washing-modis-yoga-day-pose-of-deception.
Sorabji, Cornelia. "Hindu Swamis and Women of the West." *The Nineteenth Century and After* 62, no. 9 (1932): 365–73.
Taylor, Anne. *Annie Besant: A Biography.* Oxford University Press, 1992.
Tweed, Thomas A., and Stephen R. Prothero. *Asian Religions in America: A Documentary History.* Oxford University Press, 1999.
Vadgama, Kusoon, ed. *An Indian Portia. Selected Writings of Cornelia Sorabji 1866–1954.* Blacker, 2011.
Van der Veer, Peter. *Imperial Encounters: Religion and Modernity in India and Britain.* Princeton University Press, 2001.
Viswanathan, Gauri. "In Search of Madame Blavatsky: Reading the Exoteric, Retrieving the Esoteric." *Representations* 141, no. 1 (2018): 67–94.
———. "The Ordinary Business of Occultism." *Critical Inquiry* 27, no.1 (2000): 1–20.
Vivekananda, Swami. *Reminiscences of Swami Vivekananda.* 3rd edition. Advaita Ashrama, 1983. https://www.ramakrishnavivekananda.info/reminiscences/reminiscences_of_sv.htm
———. *The Complete Works of Swami Vivekananda.* Vedanta Press, 1971.
Wallraven, Miriam. "'A Mere Instrument' or 'Proud as Lucifer'?: Self-Presentations in the Occult Autobiographies by Emma Hardinge Britton (1900) and Annie Besant (1893)." *Women's Writing.* 15, no. 3 (2008): 390–411.
Walkowitz, Judith. *City of Dreadful Delight: Narratives of Sexual Danger in Victorian London.* University of Chicago Press, 1992.

3

Obstetric Gaslighting in Olive Schreiner's *From Man to Man*

Tara MacDonald

Nineteenth-century scholars tend to think of Charlotte Perkins Gilman's "The Yellow Wallpaper" (1892) as the New Woman urtext about a postpartum woman being gaslit by her doctor-husband. Following the birth of her baby, the narrator's husband forbids her to write or have any engagement with the outside world, even though she senses that this proscription is the very opposite of what her recovering body and mind need: "I sometimes fancy that in my condition if I had less opposition and more society and stimulus — but John says the very worst thing I can do is to think about my condition."[1] The reason the narrator feels she can't contest John's recommended treatment, she makes clear, is that he has the full weight of medical and patriarchal authority behind him:

> John is a physician, and *perhaps* — (I would not say it to a living soul, of course, but this is dead paper and a great relief to my mind) — *perhaps* that is one reason I do not get well faster.
>
> You see he does not believe I am sick!
>
> And what can one do?
>
> If a physician of high standing, and one's own husband, assures friends and relatives that there is really nothing the matter with one but temporary nervous depression — a slight hysterical tendency — what is one to do?[2]

John's treatment results *not* in curing the narrator of her "hysterical tendency" but in driving her insane; she ends the story convinced that she has emerged from the room's wallpaper as she creeps around with other imagined women. "The Yellow Wallpaper," however, is not the only New Woman narrative featuring a husband who gaslights his postpartum wife. Olive Schreiner's *From Man to Man*, written in the 1870s and 1880s though not published until 1926, depicts a husband employing very similar tactics in order to manipulate his pregnant and postpartum wife. Even if the text wasn't accessible to those beyond her circle, Schreiner was telling a story much like Gilman's a decade earlier. In addition, its colonial South African setting means that the novel raises important questions about marital and maternal gaslighting in the context of race and empire.

While the husband in Schreiner's *From Man to Man* is not a medical professional, I argue that his gaslighting constitutes what would come to be called obstetric gaslighting. His behavior is the most consistent example of gaslighting in the text, but Schreiner also depicts doctors who misunderstand and misdiagnose the pregnant character, Rebekah. New Women writers like Schreiner were notoriously critical of the late-Victorian medical establishment. The repeal of the Contagious Diseases Acts, as discussed in this collection's introduction, registered a widespread antagonism between feminists and male doctors — an antagonism that was also articulated in the anti-vivisection campaign and in New Women's attempts to use birth control and become doctors themselves. At stake was their desire to control and safeguard their own bodies. In their fiction, New Women writers often depicted nefarious husbands colluding with doctors, or conflated the dangerous husband and the dangerous doctor, as in Gilman's story and Sarah Grand's novel *The Beth Book* (1897). In the latter, Beth gradually realizes that her husband is a doctor at a Lock Hospital involved in the quarantining of sex workers under the directives of the Contagious Diseases Acts. He is also a vivisectionist, an adulterer, and a domineering figure who reads Beth's mail, looks through her drawers, and accuses her of infidelity. As I have elsewhere argued, many late-Victorian feminists specifically resented the medical profession's desire to shield women from information about their own bodies and reproductive capacities, as well as evidence of their husbands' sexually transmitted diseases.[3]

Such misinformation and manipulation, from figures who consolidated both patriarchal and institutional power, could certainly result in what we now term medical gaslighting. Philosopher Elena Ruíz argues that medical gaslighting is just one example of structural gaslighting, calling it "the interpersonal phenomenon of having one's experience of illness marginalized (including having one's self-reported or presenting symptoms downplayed, silenced, or psychologically manipulated) by a clinical provider or healthcare professional."[4] Obstetric gaslighting, understood as a subset of medical gaslighting, has only recently been coined. In a 2022 article in *Social Science & Medicine*, Priya Fielding-Singh and Amelia Dmowska record that gaslighting operates "as an important, yet underexamined mechanism of obstetric violence, or the institutional and interpersonal violation of women's rights during pregnancy, childbirth, and postpartum."[5] They note that a key condition for obstetric gaslighting is the medicalization of childbirth, which in turn exists "within longstanding medical traditions of gender discrimination and a broader privileging of biomedical expertise over women's lived experiences."[6] This is an important observation; however, it is also worth noting that the denial of women's bodily knowledge and experience extends beyond the medical profession. Indeed, pregnant persons and new mothers are often recipients of advice about their bodies and babies from nondoctors, and such advice can be tantamount to gaslighting, as when others downplay women's claims of pain or discomfort or blame what they are feeling on "just hormones." So while obstetric gaslighting is an important and understudied subset of medical gaslighting, it extends beyond the strictly medical since pregnant and postpartum bodies and minds are so policed in patriarchal culture, as Schreiner's novel demonstrates.

Schreiner began writing both *The Story of an African Farm* (1883), her best-known novel, and *From Man to Man* in the 1870s while working as a governess in what is now the Eastern Cape province in South Africa. She traveled to London in 1881, found a publisher for *Story*, and quickly became a literary celebrity. She was part of Karl Pearson's Men's and Women's club and friends with figures such as Edward Carpenter, Havelock Ellis, and Eleanor Marx. In 1889, she returned to South Africa, where she remained an important public figure. While *Story* made a splash, Schreiner never found a publisher for *From Man to Man*: it was rejected by both Chapman and Hall and Macmillan in 1881. It is tempting to speculate that the novel's detailed descriptions of maternity and pregnancy loss made late-Victorian publishers uncomfortable, although there is plenty in this candid novel that could have concerned them. Schreiner continued to revise the novel at various points until her death in 1920, and her husband eventually published the incomplete manuscript in 1926. A new critical edition by Dorothy Driver in 2015 has led to some increased scholarship, but *From Man to Man* remains an underexplored text, despite its value to feminist literary criticism.[7]

The novel depicts the lives of two English sisters who grow up in South Africa, Rebekah and Bertie. As a young woman, Bertie is raped by her tutor, an event that impacts the rest of her life; while she hopes that a move to Cape Town will allow her to leave her past behind, gossip follows her from the remote family farm to the city. Schreiner's letters and notes suggest that she intended for Bertie to eventually become a sex worker in London. In contrast, Rebekah marries her cousin, Frank, whom she loves, but she gradually learns that he is unfaithful; she must then confront his dishonesty and the collapse of her ideals. Frank's treatment of Rebekah is the most pointed example of gaslighting in the novel. He insists on his innocence while being unfaithful with multiple women, including their mixed-race domestic worker. When Rebekah tries to confront him, he tells her that she is "acting like a mad woman" and blames her pregnant and nursing body: "Your condition makes you take these silly little fancies into your head!"[8] Frank insists that he knows more about her mental and physical well-being than she does, and he employs obstetric gaslighting by consistently calling attention to Rebekah's maternal body in attempts to control and condemn her behavior.

Rebekah is not the only pregnant person in the novel. Frank's abuse of their "coloured" domestic worker, Clartje, results in her pregnancy. While critics have referred to Frank's "sexual liaison" with Clartje, the power dynamics of their relationship mean that his actions must be read as rape.[9] Further, as I explain in more detail later, Schreiner intended for Clartje to be read as "coloured," not as Black, which impacts how her character should be understood within the context of colonial South Africa.[10] While Rebekah knows of

Frank's various infidelities, which she confesses in a lengthy letter to him, his rape of Clartje is what finally ends their marriage. Schreiner includes Rebekah's letter in chapter eight of the novel, and it is a candid record of Frank's cruelty and her growing realizations. I argue that it is through Rebekah's awakening consciousness and the recording of her pain that the novel most pointedly critiques Frank's gaslighting. However, I also suggest that the presence of Clartje complicates an easy reading of the white-woman-as-victim and raises questions about gender, power, and the regulation of racialized bodies in the novel. Such questions remain timely: I write this chapter in 2025, three years after Roe v. Wade was overturned in the United States, where women's sexual and reproductive health remains perilous in many states. Black women face not only targeted decreases in care but also higher maternal mortality rates than those for white and Hispanic women; similar inequalities exist in contemporary South Africa.[11] As Jennifer C. H. Sebring puts it, "Western medicine as we know it today is a colonial enterprise that upholds logic, reason and science above lived experience."[12] While Frank is no doctor, he abuses his status as a white colonial man in order to both manipulate his wife and violate their young servant. His character thus allows Schreiner to criticize marital, obstetric, and colonial gaslighting at once, as well as the ways in which they are insidiously intertwined.

Medical Knowledge, Embodied Knowledge

From Man to Man is a novel invested in the experiences of pregnancy, birth, and motherhood, as evidenced by its opening line — "The little mother lay in the agony of childbirth" (1) — and its dedication. Schreiner's only child, a daughter, was born in 1895 but died after just a few hours. She records this loss, as well as the loss of her sister, Ellie, in the opening pages of the novel. She dedicates *From Man to Man* to Ellie, "Who died, aged eighteen months, when I was nine years old," and to "My Only Daughter. Born on the 30th April, and died the 1st May" (lxii). Following the death of her one-day-old daughter, Schreiner suffered four miscarriages. Her letters, compiled in *The Olive Schreiner Letters Online*, include many that detail her experiences of pregnancy and pregnancy loss. When pregnant with her daughter, she asks her friend Mary Sauer in 1894 if she has "a good book giving the way a woman should treat herself while she is pregnant."[13] And she writes, in 1895, "I seem to be radiating heat all round. I wonder if everyone feels so when they are pregnant!"[14] In later letters, she is open about her losses. She tells editor W. T. Stead in 1896, "I've had three miscarriages since the birth of my last child, & at the last I nearly died; I am now pregnant again; but the doctors have ordered me to keep quite still avoiding especially all mental excitement or the evil will recur: I am not going to bring any more articles out for a couple of months till I am stronger."[15] To her sister-in-law, Frances, in the same year, she writes that she is anxious that Frances's illness "might be a miscarriage. It leaves one so tired – & seems such a loss. . . . I may be pregnant again but I don't like to tell any one about it till I am sure."[16] These letters show the importance, for Schreiner, of candidly sharing her experiences, and they also reveal her negotiation of her own health, her work, and the advice of medical professionals. Her doctors' advice that she remain "quite still" and not write is of course reminiscent of "The Yellow Wallpaper" — which was based on Gilman's experience with Dr. Silas Weir Mitchell[17] — and suggests that Schreiner might have published more if she'd received different medical advice or care.

In addition to her personal losses and her lifelong interest in maternity and motherhood, Schreiner was committed to obstetric medicine as a field of study. In fact, her dream was not to be a writer but a doctor. She wrote in 1881, "I am not yet beginning my medical studies as both my brothers think I had better get my books ready for publication before I begin. They think I ought to stick to literature, but I can't quite see it."[18] Schreiner thought that being a doctor would be "the most perfect of lives; it satisfies the craving to know, and also the craving to serve."[19] Yet all of her attempts to become a nurse or doctor were stalled by her own health issues. She became ill a few days after enrolling in nurse's training at the Edinburgh Royal Infirmary. She then spent the summer of 1881 preparing for medical school entrance exams but struggled, according to Joyce Avrech Berkman, due to her lack of a structured education, given the limited opportunities permitted to her as a young woman.[20] Finally, she tried to enroll in a midwifery program at the Women's Hospital in Endell Street, but a lung inflammation cut her time short. Despite these disappointments, she continued to read medical literature and attend lectures.[21] Berkman argues that Schreiner's desire to heal and serve transferred into her literary ambitions. This is a convincing claim, though it is also clear that Schreiner's interest in medicine and the body carried over into the content of her work as well.

Indeed, the sections of *From Man to Man* that focus on Rebekah's story are frank about her experiences of bearing four children and enduring multiple miscarriages. The chapters are either focalized through her, include her philosophizing, or feature descriptions of her physical discomforts, especially those endured during pregnancy: "She was to have another child in seven months, and her legs and the lower part of her body ached" (139). As Carolyn Burdett notes, Rebekah's narrative is "punctuated by reminders of her domestic existence" and by "her aching, [pregnant or] recently-pregnant body."[22] In this way, the novel is unusual in Victorian fiction. Livia Arndal Woods, in her recent *Pregnancy in the Victorian Novel*, points out that the description of pregnancy "as an embodied experience is — unsurprisingly — the exception rather than the rule" in Victorian novels, and that the bodies that *are* legibly pregnant tend to be those of "immodest characters who transgress gendered ideologies."[23] Rebekah is a clear exception, though the fact that the novel was not published until 1926 supports Woods's argument. Betraying her internalized misogyny, Schreiner complained in 1889, "The worst of this book of mine is that its [*sic*] so womanly. I think it's the most womanly book that ever was written, & God knows that I've willed it other wise!"[24] It is hard not to imagine that she was referring to the descriptions of Rebekah's pregnancy and the details of her nursing, darning socks, and making poultices for her sons' earaches. Yet it is the presence of these very elements that makes *From Man to Man* such an innovative Victorian text.

When Rebekah discovers that Frank has been sneaking into Clartje's quarters, she is pregnant with her fourth child. That night, she has been sleeping in the children's room because "she slept badly and moved from side to side when she was asleep and Frank said it disturbed him to have her in the same room" (203). Although she attempts to rest, "the sense of weight and physical discomfort would not let her" (203). She decides to visit Frank in their room but finds him gone; she looks outside to their veranda and sees him entering Clartje's quarters. Rebekah then stays up all night, writing Frank a letter outlining her feelings and their options moving forward — divorce, separation, or reconciliation with the promise of "no subterfuge or concealment" — but he refuses to read it (244). His unwillingness to even engage with her can itself be understood as a form of gaslighting, as it is a refusal to validate her experiences, but he then specifically calls out her behavior as irrational: "You've been so decent and sensible the last few years, I'd thought you'd given up this kind of thing. You, the mother of three children and on the point of having another, to go on in this nonsensical way!" (209). She pleads with him to read her letter, but Frank suspects that to read it would be to confront his adultery, and he is committed to his false narrative and to maintaining control.

When she refuses to concede, he shifts focus to Rebekah's maternal body and her role as a mother. Rebekah tells him that she stayed up all night to write the letter, and he criticizes her for not sleeping, saying, "You might at least think of your duty towards the child" (210). He continues, "You are not fit to be allowed to have children at all if you conduct yourself in this manner! . . . You're acting like a mad woman now!" (210). This is a change in tactic, and Schreiner includes descriptions that betray his strategizing, such as, "He looked down at her, doubtful just what line to pursue" (209). His focus on her unborn child is clearly an attempt to make her feel guilty for her (valid) feelings. Yet, his additional focus on her "fitness" to have future children betrays his medicalization and regulation of her body. Although Frank never reads Rebekah's lengthy letter, Schreiner includes it in its entirety for the reader. Rebekah writes that, in addition to Clartje, she caught him having an affair with their neighbor, Mrs Drummond, and with a young neighborhood girl of fourteen or fifteen. In all three cases, it is not until she literally sees Frank with another woman that she believes it. His gaslighting — his insistence that he is not cheating but, rather, that she is "a silly little woman . . . a little fool" — turns into her gaslighting of herself, as she tries, initially, to excuse his actions: "I had persuaded myself it was I who was wrong in not giving you a larger generous sympathy" (220, 230). Accepting that he will not read her letter, Rebekah then confronts Frank the next day with just two options: they can legally divorce, or they can live together but be effectively separated. Frank considers "bursting into a fit of rage such as had always silenced her; he would say he was shamefully treated, swear at her, and violently close the door," but he perceives that this would be futile (258). Instead, he returns to gaslighting her by focusing on her pregnant body: "You are a tired little woman. . . . Your condition makes you take these silly little fancies into your head! You need a good night's rest" (258). Frank consistently uses the word "little" in an attempt to infantilize Rebekah, and his insistence that her "condition" is to blame implies that she cannot think rationally while pregnant.

These instances of Frank gaslighting Rebekah by calling attention to her pregnancy are part of a broader pattern in which he also takes advantage of Rebekah's role as a mother with the goal of dismissing her and restricting her access to the outside world. For instance, when Rebekah, unaware of Frank's actions, complains that Clartje has been rude to her, Frank interrupts, "Isn't that the baby crying?" (193). Rebekah runs off to check, halting the discussion. Later, when she wants to join him at a party, he insists that she stay home because, in Rebekah's words, "it was damp and might rain so I must run no risks while I nursed" (216). This becomes part of his strategy, as she recognizes in her letter: "When you went for a day's fishing or to a dance or dinner and suggested it might be better for me not to go too because I had a baby coming, or afterwards had it to nurse, I never thought you did not want me" (213). Implied in his commands is that Frank knows what is best for Rebekah, and that her desires to leave the house or to write constitute irresponsible behavior as a mother. While Frank has a clear motive in not wanting Rebekah to discover his infidelity, his guidance is of course similar to that of the doctor-husband in "The Yellow Wallpaper," who forbids his wife from writing and having any society or stimulation.

Despite her threats that she would "go mad" if he refused to listen to her or read her letter, Rebekah does not descend into madness (209) — even if her letter does detail how she mistrusts and doubts herself. That said, her torment results in her having a miscarriage, becoming ill at various points, and giving birth to her last child early. So while Frank is not entirely successful in gaslighting Rebekah, his mistreatment has a profound impact on her. When Rebekah discovers Frank's affair with Mrs Drummond, she has a miscarriage: "The doctor said I was very ill, and when you came you only kissed me and went away. . . . They thought it was my body caused it, but it was my brain. I was in hell" (225). Later, when she falls ill while pregnant, her doctor warns her that she is "working too much" (229). Rebekah explains that he is wrong, in a passage that emphasizes the interconnectedness of her body and mind:

> Oh, it wasn't the childbearing or the work or the miscarriages; a woman can bear all and do all if the arms of a man are tight about her. I had loved so to bear for you and to work for you. Now nothing mattered; I couldn't read, I couldn't think! Oh, it isn't only the body of a woman that a man touches when he takes her in his hands; it's her brain, it's her intellect, it's her whole life! (229)

When she discovers Frank's abuse of Clartje, Rebekah nearly dies giving birth to a son at only seven months. These depictions of her psychologically influenced physical traumas might appear to give credibility to Frank's claims about her vulnerability. Instead, her lived experiences contrast with Frank's manipulative rhetoric as they suggest an embodied knowledge to which only Rebekah — not her husband, nor even her doctor — has access. ("*They* thought" it was this, but they were wrong.) She can, she maintains, endure pregnancy, pregnancy loss, childbirth, and her work, but she cannot endure the pain of a husband who does not love or respect her. It is Frank's manipulative cruelty that puts her at risk more than anything else in the novel.

Mother-Love and Female Suffering

Rebekah does not suffer the same fate as Gilman's narrator, who becomes victim to emotional distress and paranoia. Instead, Rebekah's mental strength and, perhaps more significantly, her financial and physical independence ultimately save her. As the passages above show, she insists upon her knowledge of her own body and refutes the notion that it is her childbearing, physical labor, or intellectual pursuits that cause her illnesses or depression. Further, Rebekah is able to achieve a degree of independence from Frank because she inherited money from her father when she married, and this allows her to buy a small wine garden and farm, which is her "hold on freedom and life" (239).[25] The children, she records, played "in the sun on the grass, and I worked" (238). The farm also permits her to have an independent income, which is key to her later separation from Frank. Her other "hold on freedom" is her study room, which gives her a space in which to write and think. As a child, she had dreamed of a room with a microscope and books lining the floor to the ceiling, and this room fulfills that fantasy; it also includes her fossils and insects. In it, Rebekah muses on natural science, evolution, the woman question, prostitution, crime, eugenics, racism, colonialism, and education. A number of critics have suggested that *From Man to Man* may even have been a source text for Virginia Woolf's "A Room of One's Own" (1929).[26]

The study is attached to her children's room so that she can easily attend to them, and her time in her room is punctuated by interruptions related to childcare and domestic tasks. These tasks sometimes impact her philosophizing: in one instance, she is recording notes about classical Greece when she stops to make a poultice for her son; when she returns, she "branche[s] off on a side line" (141). Moments like this have led scholars to adopt varying perspectives on the freedom that this space offers Rebekah. Ann Heilmann, for instance, calls attention to the small size of the room, its limited views, and its connection to the children's room, arguing that Rebekah's "creative space is colonized by [her] marital and maternal 'duties.'"[27] Heilmann, too, connects *From Man to Man* to "The Yellow Wallpaper," noting that the mark on the floor in Rebekah's study "running right round the desk" is "chillingly suggestive of the mark against which . . . the unnamed narrator presses her body when under the onslaught of her psychotic condition she creeps around her nursery-prison."[28] That said, Heilmann suggests that Rebekah's room, unlike the room in Gilman's story, permits Rebekah a degree of independent thought and scholarly output. Indeed, Rebekah herself frames the room as vital to her survival and not as a claustrophobic place of confinement. Its very existence brings her a sense of peace: "For days often, and sometimes for weeks, she did not come into this room; but she knew it was there; and there was always a quiet spot in her mind answering to it" (138).

I agree with Heilmann that Schreiner is at pains to note the daily tasks and duties that take up Rebekah's time and mental space, but I do not read her as an artistic failure. While Rebekah's intellectual life is often in tension with her children's needs, her experience of motherhood also informs her philosophical thought. As S. Pearl Brilmyer recently put it, in describing Rebekah's ideas alongside the material reality of her writing space and her aches during pregnancy, "the novel employs strategies of realist worldbuilding to bring philosophy back to the body and the world out of which it arises."[29] Her own experiences lead Rebekah to muse:

> Through all nature, life and growth and evolution are possible only because of mother-love. . . . Everywhere mother-love and the tender nurturing of the weak underlies life, and the higher the creature the larger the part it plays. Man individually and as a race is possible on earth only because, not for weeks or months but for years, love and the guardianship of the strong over the weak has existed. You may almost estimate the height of development in the creature by the amount of mother-love and care he stands for. (172)

"Mother-love" emerges as a philosophy of nurturing and tenderness, and a refutation of exploitation. It is, in effect, an anti-gaslighting philosophy as it emphasizes care and the alleviation of suffering. As an ethical practice, mother-love can also be adopted by men, as the pronoun "he" suggests. We can certainly extend Rebekah's — and Schreiner's — ideas regarding mother-love's ethics of care to the practice of medicine. Recall that Schreiner wanted to be a doctor because it satisfied her "craving to serve."[30] While Rebekah does not have such aspirations, she takes these ideas into her everyday life. Yet, her theories about suffering are put to the test when she confronts Clartje.

The novel doesn't supply us with enough details to know whether Frank is also gaslighting Clartje, but we learn that she, too, is pregnant. Frank's treatment of Clartje is what ultimately severs Rebekah and Frank's marriage, and she is thus a key character in the novel. In earlier published editions of *From Man to Man*, compiled by Schreiner's husband, she does not have a name. In Driver's introduction, she reveals that the character was named Clartje in Schreiner's 1886–1887 manuscript, and she adopts this name in her edition, as do I here. Clartje's status as "coloured" is significant, as Schreiner linked the "Cape Coloured" population — a recognized ethnic population today — to the laboring classes and to the legacy of slavery, explaining that they were comprised of "the first Dutch residents and their slaves."[31] Indeed, this mixed-race population included descendants of slaves from the Dutch East Indies, Indigenous Khoi, San, and Xhosa peoples, as well as European settlers. Burdett aptly suggests that Frank's "sexual liaison in the backyard thus evokes a past in which sexual, racial and class exploitation are bound together in the horror of slavery. It is this that Rebekah cannot bear."[32] Indeed, Frank's behavior, which I identify not as a "liaison" but as rape, represents the cruelty of white colonial masculinity. Schreiner's attention to white men's exploitation of Black and mixed-race women is evident in her other work, such as *Trooper Peter Halket of Mashonaland* (1897), in which she specifically calls attention to Black women's vulnerability to rape by white British troops.[33] In the early twentieth century, when South Africa was taken up with the "Black Peril," a moral panic in which white officials were anxious about the supposed sexual offenses being committed by Black men against white women, Schreiner recognized this as racial gaslighting.[34] Specifically, she saw it as a racist distraction from the real threat of sexual violence for women of color: "My feeling of course is that peril which has long over shadowed this country, is one which exists for all dark skinned women at the hands of white men."[35]

Rebekah may not connect all these dots, but she does attempt to speak with Clartje, in a striking scene that is focalized through her perspective. The day following her discovery, Rebekah finds herself walking outside, filled with despair, but she looks to Clartje's room and asks herself, "Because in your anguish you are alone and no hand comes to help you, can you put out your hand to none? Are you the only woman in the world who has suffered?" (254). Her mother-love compels her to reach out to Clartje — and this is consistent with her attempts to reach out to Mrs Drummond and the young woman with whom Frank had an affair. Yet, in all cases, the women reject Rebekah's attempts. Rebekah enters Clartje's room and finds her half-dressed in a "red striped flannel petticoat and a pair of crimson satin corsets, embroidered with white flowers" (255). As Lucy Valerie Graham writes, these details clearly raise the question of what the young woman has been given "in exchange for being sexually coerced by Rebekah's husband."[36] She also suggests that the "single bed" draws attention to the historical erasure of Black and "coloured" women's "sexual and family life in the migrant labour system of domestic employment."[37] Clartje looks at Rebekah with "a closed fist on each of her hips" (255). She then raises her chin and says, "Wat wil jij hê?" (255). Schreiner includes a footnote about the translation of this phrase; she thus clearly wanted readers to understand the significance of Clartje's speech: "Literally, 'What do you want?' But the pronoun '*jij*' is in Cape Dutch, the only language of the coloured people of the West, and is the most extreme insult when applied to a superior. It is used only to children or servants. Even equals avoid its use as much as possible" (255, footnote 22). Confronted with Clartje's physical and verbal boldness, Rebekah is silent and "all she had determined to say passed from her" (255). In response, "The girl threw back her head yet farther and burst into a laugh, intended to be defiant but with an undertone of fear; all her white teeth showing between her thick dark lips as she sat with her fists on her hips" (255). One antidote to gaslighting may be the sharing of suffering, but we do not have a moment of shared female suffering here. Instead, Schreiner emphasizes Clartje's racial difference ("her thick dark lips") but also her vulnerability. Clartje tries to be "defiant," but the "undertone of fear" is telling of her precarious social position. As Rebekah stares at Clartje, she has a realization that "it was with that girl even as it was with herself that day" (255). This ambiguous sentence could mean that Rebekah realizes that Clartje, too, is pregnant, or it may note that she witnesses the young woman's suffering, even if she does not know how to respond to it.

Clartje's laugh might recall, for some readers, Bertha Mason's "strange laugh" in *Jane Eyre* (1847) and the way that novel also focuses on the gaslighting of a white woman while giving the racialized woman little (to no) subjectivity.[38] Just as many readers have understood Bertha's laughter as a form of rebellion or resistance, I read Clartje's intent to be "defiant" as betraying her anger toward her white employer, a woman who did not notice her abuse at the hands of her husband. Audre Lorde's idea that such anger is "loaded with information and energy" is relevant here, as is Lorde's claim that anger is an appropriate response to a racist and problematic situation.[39] Lorde records speaking angrily at a conference and a white woman responding, "Tell me how you feel but don't say it too harshly or I cannot hear you."[40] In their confrontation, Rebekah seems unable to hear Clartje or to bear her pain. In response to the young woman's laughter, Rebekah leaves and closes the door behind her. Then, "on tiptoe, softly and quickly, she ran across the yard, like one who fears something that is following them and tries to escape" (255). A "hospitable, even generous, reading" of this scene, of the kind that Driver aims for in her edition of the novel, would note that Schreiner emphasizes the pain and anger of *both* women who suffer — if differently — in a patriarchal and racist environment that pits them against one another.[41] We might imagine, too, that Rebekah realizes that her attempt at empathy is perhaps impossible and even unethical since she cannot purport to truly understand Clartje's experience. A less "hospitable" reading, however, would call attention to Clartje's narrative erasure, as well as the fact that Rebekah seems to abandon a woman who is reliant on her financially.

Indeed, following this interaction, Clartje disappears from the room and from the novel. Readers can assume that Rebekah removes her, but Schreiner gives no details beyond the fact that Frank later goes to see Clartje and finds the room empty. Frank knows that the young woman is pregnant, and he shockingly reflects that he might be relieved from the situation by the baby's death, considering "the rate of infant mortality among the coloured population which he had seen in some paper" (260). Again, Frank is keen to employ his amateur medical knowledge in the service of his own desires and selfishness. Clartje, however, does give birth to Frank's baby, named Sartje, and the girl is raised by Rebekah. We are left merely to imagine the conversation between Rebekah and Clartje that leads to Rebekah adopting the child. Clartje's departure means both that she loses her means of employment and that she is free of her abusive employer. Yet, instead of exploring her future, Schreiner focuses on the aftermath for Rebekah. That Rebekah stays in the same house as Frank arguably suggests a failure on her part to live independently, but their agreement is nonetheless radical for a late-Victorian marriage. Rebekah tells him, "You will be free to lead your own life, to think your own thoughts, to form your own friendships; but you will understand that I also am equally free" (258). If to be gaslit is to have someone else dictate your reality, then Rebekah is indeed "free" from Frank's gaslighting by the end of the novel.

While Clartje and Rebekah do not have a moment of shared sympathy, Rebekah's healing energies become focused on raising Sartje and her own sons. She must contend with the fact that her sons, white British boys in colonial South Africa, are themselves part of the culture that permitted and even encouraged Frank's gaslighting and abuse of multiple women. Near the end of the novel, one of her boys complains that he does not want to be seen walking on the street with Sartje, which prompts Rebekah to narrate a lengthy allegory about racism. She ends by telling the boys:

> "You know, laddies," she said softly, "you are always talking of being *men*, and how fine it will be when you are grown up. It is a finer thing to be a 'man' than either of you can know now. But it's not being able to lift a great weight or strike a great blow or crush things beneath you that can ever make you that. The thing that really matters is this . . . that, if one should stand beside you and look down at you knowing all the story of your life, they should be able to say, 'This strong man's hand was always stretched out to cover those feebler; this great man's body never sought good or pleasure for itself at the price of something weaker.'" (381)

It is hard not to read this as a response to Frank's behavior. Her sons, she hopes, will be better men than their father. Along similar lines, in a letter to Havelock Ellis in 1884, Schreiner wrote that she hoped that *From Man to Man* "will help other people, it will help to make men more tender to women because they will understand them better; it will help to make some women more tender to others; it will comfort some women by showing them that others have felt as they do."[42] That Schreiner never finished or published the novel in her lifetime makes these sentiments bittersweet. Schreiner's sense that this novel would comfort women "by showing them that others have felt as they do" is a sign of the desperate need for a shared awareness and critique of obstetric gaslighting in this period. As Berkman argues, we can see the ways in which Schreiner's desire to heal was "transferred" into her own writing.

Yet Schreiner also supported her niece, Ursula, who underwent medical studies at Cambridge and was a nurse during World War I. One of the solutions to obstetric gaslighting for New Women like Schreiner was not only for women to be educated about their bodies and rights, but also for women to be trained as doctors. In a letter from 1896, Schreiner writes to her sister-in-law Frances that she has had a third "mishap" — miscarriage — since her daughter's birth. She writes:

> The first one I had hardly seemed to make me ill at all. I kept about my work, & was as strong as ever in a weeks time. The second one made me pretty weak, but this one seems quite to have prostrated me. It is a month now & I feel weaker than I did two days after the birth of my baby. Do you ever feel so weak, & have such pains in your legs & back after such a mishap? I do wish there were women doctors. I've had two doctors here [in Kimberley, South Africa], & neither of them have given me any consolation except to tell me I must lay on my back for six months if I ever want to have a live child — which of course I can't do. It would be so nice to have a woman doctor who had gone through everything herself.[43]

Schreiner does not record being explicitly gaslit by her doctors, but she does long for a woman OB-GYN who can combine both medical learning and embodied knowledge, one who has "gone through everything herself." Both her novel and her letters express the need for a shared discourse of maternal suffering and care — a need that is no less urgent today.

Notes

1. Gilman, "Yellow Wallpaper," 42.
2. Gilman, "Yellow Wallpaper," 41–42.
3. See Chapter Three, "Doctors, Dandies and New Man in New Woman Fiction," in MacDonald, *New Man, Masculinity, and Marriage*.
4. Ruíz, "Cultural Gaslighting," 689.
5. Fielding-Singh and Dmowska, "Obstetric Gaslighting," 2.
6. Fielding-Singh and Dmowska, "Obstetric Gaslighting," 3.
7. For instance, Sanja Nivesjö and Heidi Barends guest-edited a special issue of *The Journal of Commonweath Literature* in 2021 on *From Man to Man* in response to Driver's new edition of the novel. Driver's edition is currently only available in South Africa, which is likely why more criticism on the novel has not been published in North America and elsewhere. My thanks to Diana Maltz for lending me her copy.
8. Schreiner, *From Man to Man*, 210, 258. Further references to the novel will appear parenthetically.
9. Burdett, *Olive Schreiner and Progress*, 100.
10. In addition to the textual descriptions of her as "coloured," Lucy Valerie Graham points to Schreiner's footnote in which Clartje is described as speaking Cape Dutch, "the only language of the coloured people of the West" ("'Utterly Divided?'," 89).
11. Ruíz suggests that what can often get lost in individual accounts is the way that the harms of medical gaslighting are "consistently and unevenly distributed across specific populations, not by accident, but by design" ("Cultural Gaslighting," 689).
12. Sebring, "Towards a Sociological Understanding," 1957. Sebring also notes that women are not the only victims of medical-colonial gaslighting: "The same goes for other populations that do not fit the colonial image of the 'healthy' white male subject, although medicine has been slower to recognize the impact of epistemic invalidation on people of colour, and disabled, sick, Black, Indigenous, queer, intersex and transgender people, and especially those whose identity overlaps many of these categories" (1960).
13. *Olive Schreiner Letters Online*, https://www.oliveschreiner.org/vre?view=collections&colid=62&letterid=76.
14. *Olive Schreiner Letters Online*, https://www.oliveschreiner.org/vre?view=collections&colid=62&letterid=82.
15. *Olive Schreiner Letters Online*, https://www.oliveschreiner.org/vre?view=collections&colid=152&letterid=59.
16. *Olive Schreiner Letters Online*, https://www.oliveschreiner.org/vre?view=collections&colid=88&letterid=8.
17. Notoriously, Mitchell's treatment, dubbed the "rest cure," involved a "regimen of enforced bed rest, isolation, force-feeding, and massage" (Stiles, "The Rest Cure, 1873–1925.")

18. *Olive Schreiner Letters Online*, https://www.oliveschreiner.org/vre?view=collections&colid=137&letterid=19. Note from *Olive Schreiner Letters Online* regarding this letter: "This set of Cronwright-Schreiner extracts are of letters which appear in *The Letters of Olive Schreiner*, and regarding which there are typescripts made by him in the NLSA collections. They are included here for the sake of completeness. However, when surviving original letters can be compared, these show that Cronwright-Schreiner often changed or even bowdlerised in producing his versions. Considerable caution should therefore be used in referring to their content." Given what we know of Schreiner's life and what is recorded in other letters, however, I take the sentiments in this letter to be accurate.
19. *Olive Schreiner Letters Online*, https://www.oliveschreiner.org/vre?view=collections&colid=18&letterid=6.
20. Berkman, *Healing Imagination*, 26.
21. I rely, for these details, on Berkman, *Healing Imagination*, as well as Schreiner's letters.
22. Burdett, *Olive Schreiner and Progress*, 93.
23. Woods, *Pregnancy*, 1, 22.
24 *Olive Schreiner Letters Online*, https://www.oliveschreiner.org/vre?view=collections&colid=18&letterid=287.
25. Rebekah does point out, however, that the agent selling the farm "would not give me the deeds till he had seen [Frank] and [he] had given [his] consent, because I was a woman" (238).
26. Brilmyer, *Science of Character*, 184–85; Nivesjö and Barends, "Current Perspectives," 57. The latter is a suggestion by Jade Munslow Ong; the article includes interviews with Ong and other critics on the novel. Ong notes that Woolf reviewed Cronwright-Schreiner's edited collection of Schreiner's letters in 1925, although there is no documented evidence that she read *From Man to Man*.
27. Heilmann, *New Woman*, 152.
28. Heilmann, *New Woman*, 150.
29. Brilmyer, *Science of Character*, 183.
30. *Olive Schreiner Letters Online*, https://www.oliveschreiner.org/vre?view=collections&colid=18&letterid=6.
31. Schreiner, *Thoughts on South Africa*, 33.
32. Burdett, *Olive Schreiner and Progress*, 100.
33. See more on masculinity and *Trooper Peter Halket of Mashonaland* in chapter five of my book, *New Man, Masculinity, and Marriage*.
34. Angelique M. Davis and Rose Ernst define "racial gaslighting" as "*the political, social, economic and cultural process that perpetuates and normalizes a white supremacist reality through pathologizing those who resist*" ("Racial Gaslighting," 3).
35. *Olive Schreiner Letters Online*, https://www.oliveschreiner.org/vre?view=collections&colid=7&letterid=2.

36. Graham, "'Utterly Divided?'," 89.
37. Graham, "'Utterly Divided?'," 89.
38. Brontë, *Jane Eyre*, 149.
39. Lorde, "The Uses of Anger," 280.
40. Lorde, "The Uses of Anger," 278.
41. Driver, "Introduction," xlii.
42. *Olive Schreiner Letters Online*, https://www.oliveschreiner.org/vre?view=collections&colid=18&letterid=41.
43. *Olive Schreiner Letters Online*, https://www.oliveschreiner.org/vre?view=collections&colid=88&letterid=31.

Bibliography

Berkman, Joyce Avrech. *The Healing Imagination of Olive Schreiner: Beyond South African Colonialism*. University of Massachusetts Press, 1989.

Brilmyer, S. Pearl. *The Science of Character: Human Objecthood and the Ends of Victorian Realism*. University of Chicago Press, 2022.

Brontë, Charlotte. *Jane Eyre*. Edited by Margaret Smith. Oxford University Press, 2008.

Burdett, Carolyn. *Olive Schreiner and the Progress of Feminism: Evolution, Gender, Empire*. Palgrave, 2001.

Davis, Angelique, and Rose Ernst. "Racial Gaslighting." *Politics, Groups, and Identities* 7, no. 4 (2019): 761–74.

Driver, Dorothy. Introduction to *From Man to Man, or Perhaps Only —*, by Olive Schreiner, ix–xlvi. University of Cape Town Press, 2015.

Fielding-Singh, Priya and Amelia Dmowska. "Obstetric Gaslighting and the Denial of Mothers' Realities." *Social Science & Medicine* 301 (2022): 114938.

Gilman, Charlotte Perkins. *The Yellow Wallpaper*. Bedford Books, 1998.

Graham, Lucy Valerie. "'Utterly Divided'? The Feminist Perspectives of Lauretta Ngcobo and Olive Schreiner." *Scrunity2: Issues in English Studies in Southern Africa* 22, no. 1 (2017): 86–94.

Heilmann, Ann. *New Woman Strategies: Sarah Grand, Olive Schreiner, Mona Caird*. Manchester University Press, 2004.

Lorde, Audre. "The Uses of Anger." *Women's Studies Quarterly* 25, no. 1/2 (1997): 278–85.

MacDonald, Tara. *The New Man, Masculinity, and Marriage in the Victorian Novel*. Routledge, 2015.

Nivesjö, Sanja, and Heidi Barends. "Current Perspectives on Olive Schreiner's *From Man to Man or Perhaps Only —*." *The Journal of Commonweath Literature* 56, no. 1 (2021): 44–60.

Ruíz, Elena. "Cultural Gaslighting." *Hypatia* 35, no. 4 (2020): 687–713.

Schreiner, Olive. *From Man to Man, or Perhaps Only —*. Edited by Dorothy Driver. University of Cape Town Press, 2015.

———. *Thoughts on South Africa*. T. Fisher Unwin Ltd., 1923.

———. *The Olive Schreiner Letters Online*. Edited by Liz Stanley, David Shepherd, Helen Dampier, et al. (2012). https://www.oliveschreiner.org.

Sebring, Jennifer C. H. "Towards a Sociological Understanding of Medical Gaslighting in Western Health Care." *Sociology of Health and Illness* 43, no. 9 (2021): 1951–64.

Stiles, Anne. "The Rest Cure, 1873–1925." *BRANCH: Britain, Representation, and Nineteenth-Century History.* October 2012. https://branchcollective.org/?ps_articles=anne-stiles-the-rest-cure-1873-1925.

Woods, Livia Arndal. *Pregnancy in the Victorian Novel*. Ohio State University Press, 2023.

Part II

Marital and Monetary Manipulations

Gaslight is, at its heart, the story of an abusive marriage. This section discusses fictional and real examples of marriage in the Victorian period and how this fraught institution can become a site of trauma, manipulation, and coercion. These four chapters highlight specific marital, property, divorce, and inheritance laws, as well as the ways in which such legal restrictions and injunctions impacted both cultural practices and individual relationships. They explore women's economic agency, the figure of the mixed-race heiress, real-life marital gaslighter Charles Dickens, and how women's literary and artistic desires were often at odds with romantic and nuptial expectations, as depicted in novels and poetry of the period.

4

Whose Property Is It Anyway?

Economic Gaslighting in the Victorian Novel

Jill Rappoport

Gaslighting was about money from the start. In Patrick Hamilton's 1938 play *Gas Light: A Victorian Thriller in Three Acts*, this notorious form of psychological manipulation is inspired and enabled by Victorian women's property. Pursuit of a wealthy woman's jewels leads the antagonist (Jack Manningham) to murder her and, years later, in a plot to finally find and steal those jewels, to set up his marital home in the murdered woman's house. Once installed there, with no further need of the wife (Bella Manningham), whose presence now slows his continued hunt for the jewels, Jack tries to convince Bella of her own insanity; or, as the former police detective who gets involved in the case (Sergeant Rough) puts it, he tries to "slowly, methodically, systematically . . . *drive* [her] out of [her] mind."[1] That these efforts are resolutely economic at base appears in their motives and their methods: the wife's increasingly alienated relationship to property signals this gaslighting, even as the recovery of property eventually indicates her return to mental health and material freedom.

Proof of Bella's purportedly failing mental health in Hamilton's play consists of the disappearance of her personal property (a watch, a brooch, a grocery bill) and the reappearance of her husband's missing items (rings, keys, pencils, handkerchiefs) in her workbox, despite her anguished insistence that she doesn't remember moving or hiding any of them. Not only does her "remov[al]" of items from their "proper place" (19) mark her as unfit to manage a household (since poor domestic management was considered a clear sign of insanity for Victorian wives), but these actions are also framed as delinquent, the "wicked" behavior (52) of one who "lyingly and purposely conceal[s]" (24) and even "steal[s]" (21) both her own and her husband's property. Though accusing her of stealing her own possessions may seem paradoxical, it was not unusual; as I'll discuss, such accusations were common forms of economic gaslighting for women in Victorian fiction.

Ultimately, Bella proves her sanity — and her husband's deception — when she reclaims, from a desk that Rough initially sees as "bare," the grocer's bill she has been accused of misplacing, along with some of her other possessions:

> MRS. MANNINGHAM. What else is there? . . . Yes, look, my watch! And my brooch — my brooch. Look at these! My God, look at these! (*She pulls out drawer and takes it to table*).
> ROUGH. These are your property also, then?
> MRS. MANNINGHAM. Yes. Both of them. This watch I lost a week ago — my brooch has been missing three months. And he said he would give me no more gifts because I lost them. He said that in my wickedness I hid them away. (56)

In the genealogy of gaslighting, then, ideas of women's property must join those of men's emotional abuse. It is no coincidence that gaslighting comes into its own here, in a drama set in the late nineteenth century and dealing with women's property. The Victorian period saw gaslighting's methods of manipulation abound not only in the generalized gender-based oppression of the patriarchal domestic ideology that underlaid most intimate relationships, but also in the related, reality-challenging experiences that regularly undercut women's economic choices and their confidence in making them.[2] Victorian women's abilities to exercise their legal economic rights — new and longstanding alike — were frequently contested, sometimes directly but sometimes, as this chapter will demonstrate, through the less obvious undermining of perception and agency that we now associate with gaslighting. As we will see, the jewels that motivate this gaslighting function as symbols of those economic rights, as well as cultural assumptions and anxieties about women's property.

My shift in focus between the experience of one wife, whose husband uses property to intentionally "driv[e her] mad" (43), and Victorian women's larger economic experiences acknowledges differences of both intent and impact; the nineteenth-century cases of cultural gaslighting that interest me have pernicious but more subtle consequences. Yet, Hamilton's emphasis on a single, victimized woman's experience with her property may be seen to stand in for the more systemic misogyny of a culture whose property laws and economic structures regularly downplay women's abilities, choices, and rights to such a point that even these women begin to doubt that they have them. And this, too, is gaslighting. Scholars today distinguish between "*individual* and *collective* gaslighting,"[3] allowing us to consider a broader category such as middle- and upper-class Victorian wives, whose experiences of undercut reality may look different from those of a single deceived spouse. They have also expanded our understanding of gaslighting from "an interpersonal abuse mechanism" in which "one person knowingly, intentionally, and consistently undermines the perceptions of another," to gaslighting as a more "structural phenomenon" that "produces asymmetric harms for different populations."[4] According to Gaile Pohlhaus Jr., "epistemic gaslighting" works "to put out of circulation a particular way of understanding the world"; this form of gaslighting "occurs when a person, practice, image, or institution exerts unwarranted pressure on epistemic agents to doubt their own perceptions."[5] Such systemic, structural forms, I argue, manifest in Victorian fiction about women's property in specific ways that I refer to as economic gaslighting. Even as women's legal rights to property improved dramatically in the 1870s and 1880s, their access to it was systematically denied as ideologies of coverture, separate spheres, and familial obligation continued to hold sway. In numerous representations, Victorian women are made to feel bad about their wealth and to perceive their use of it as illicit; they frequently face demands to see their money as rightfully belonging to others, typically male members of their family. Though Hamilton's play condenses these widespread concerns into the extreme case of a single, disempowered figure, it nevertheless registers the economic roots of what we now understand as gaslighting and allows us to see how the offshoots continue to bear upon women's relationships with property today.

The four major play and film versions of *Gaslight* produced in the 1930s and 1940s all tell slightly different stories about the relationship between women's property and gaslighting. This chapter will focus on the 1939 Constable and Company edition, which is the earliest, most proximate version to Hamilton's original that is currently in print.[6] In this version, we are simply told that Jack Manningham "took th[e] house" that belonged to his murder victim, Alice Barlow, when it became available (29); in subsequent versions, his wife either purchases or inherits the house herself and is therefore more directly responsible for giving him access to it.[7] The Constable edition interests me partly because it sets the stage for this textual development: as both the object of the search and the vehicle that enables it, women's property is linked to the work of gaslighting in ways that the later versions expand upon. At the same time, I find it important that, unlike those later versions, the Constable edition makes no attempt to use the house or other property to supply an economic rationale for the Manninghams' marriage or justify "why," as Rough puts it, Jack "should employ this mad, secretive, circuitous way of getting at what he wants" (43). Economic gaslighting, as Hamilton originally conceived it and as it often figures throughout the nineteenth century, seems equally likely whether the woman in question has significant wealth (a house, financial assets) or merely a few "trinket[s]" (60). Its "mad . . . circuitous" operations deal in superfluity, with mind games and manipulation in excess of any justifiable words or actions. In this way, economic gaslighting distorts women's perceptions and possession of their property even as it calls attention to the limits of the (so-called) rational, masculine economic behavior that so frequently opposed it.

Economic Gaslighting

Like *Gas Light*'s Alice Barlow, the "old lady of great wealth" whose inherited rubies motivate the murder and attempted theft of Hamilton's play (36), Victorian women had far more money than previous generations of scholars have acknowledged. They financed government projects, supported family businesses, and passed down significant legacies.[8] England's common-law doctrine of coverture divested wives of their legal right to property upon marriage under the fiction that spouses were "one person,"[9] but specialized settlements and trusts created legal mechanisms to ensure that married women could earn, inherit, possess, and transfer their own property, though fewer than ten percent of marriages benefited from these expensive legal devices.[10] The movement to reform married women's property law, which argued in part for greater consistency in laws for the rich and the poor,[11] would eventually make those rights available to all wives in the Married Women's Property Acts of 1870 and 1882. Even before then, unmarried women had rights to their property, and control over household earnings and items was less stable in lived practice than in legal theory. Women participated in an expanding commercial sphere through production, shopkeeping, and purchases.[12] As Margot Finn and others have shown, strategic uses of credit and legal practices such as the law of necessaries (which required men to provide their wives with the items appropriate for their station in life) absolved women of their husbands' debts, giving wives both authority and a degree of impunity as consumers.[13] These strategies afforded opportunities for economic activity and also provided one way for working women to resist the limitations of coverture.

Increasingly, Victorian law proclaimed that women could and indeed did have economic rights. Yet fiction consistently showed the difficulty of asserting these rights. *Gas Light*'s Bella is unable to make minor purchases without trepidation, as we see when she buys muffins for tea "furtively" (7), with money from her own purse. When her husband asks her, "Why are you so apprehensive, Bella? I was not about to reproach you," her "nervous" response speaks to a history of abusive "reproach[es]" (8). The tension between women's having economic rights but being unable to use them appears most explicitly in Victorian sensation fiction, where husbands might imprison their wives for refusing to sign over their property. In Wilkie Collins's *The Woman in White* (1859–1860), heiress Lady Glyde (née Laura Fairlie) experiences physical cruelty from her husband, Sir Percival, when she refuses to consent to financial documents she has not read;[14] he later feigns her death and incarcerates her in a mental asylum to steal her wealth. *Gas Light*'s Jack, in pursuit of Alice Barlow's "great wealth" (36),[15] similarly turns to brutality with his wife — "if you utter another sound I'll knock you down and take you to your room and lock you in darkness for a week" (24) — and implies that he will place her in an insane asylum when he threatens to bring "more than one doctor" to evaluate her, since involuntary psychiatric commitment required signatures from two medical examiners (24).[16] On the other end of the class spectrum, as the 1856 Petition for Reform of the Married Women's Property Law insisted, meager earnings were "wrested from" starving working women by abusive husbands legally entitled to their income.[17]

While overt violence prevented women's exercise of their economic rights in the most sensational ways, women's economic agency faced related but more subtle threats in the deceptively benign forms of compassion, love, and duty. Charles Dickens, in *Little Dorrit* (1855–1857), gives voice to the difficulty of "'tying up' money" for the "tender-hearted," acknowledging the impossibility of preserving the legal property rights of women from greedy relatives.[18]

Manipulation of "tender-hearted" women for their fortunes proliferates in Victorian fiction, with characters such as Helen Huntingdon in Anne Brontë's *Tenant of Wildfell Hall* (1848) ruefully acknowledging that "by my own desire, nearly the whole of the income of my fortune is devoted . . . to the paying off of [my husband's] debts."[19] Even women accustomed to earning and spending their own money were skeptical about improving married women's property rights through legal means. Despite signing the 1856 Married Women's Property Law petition, Elizabeth Gaskell noted, "a husband can coax, wheedle, beat or tyrannize his wife out of something and no law whatever will help this."[20] Margaret Oliphant agreed: "If the man is a brute, he may *take* his wife's money. . . . If he does it lovingly, all the laws in the world . . . will not save a woman's fortune."[21]

Joining with the explicit violence and more subtle persuasion that undercut individual Victorian women's agency and property rights were discourses that called into question women's collective legal rights and capacity for economic thought. Novels from this period repeatedly give voice to views of women as financially incompetent. Along these lines, George Eliot's *Middlemarch* (1871-2) shows Mr. Brooke's disdainful response to his niece's suggestions for improving his land. Despite his own financial blundering, he dismisses her ideas categorically: "'Young ladies don't understand political economy, you know.'"[22] In Oliphant's *Hester* (1883), Mrs. John, a wife kept in ignorance of her late husband's ruined financial affairs, is disparaged as a "Poor little thing!" whose ideas about their money are "muddled altogether."[23] As Lana L. Dalley shows in her contribution to this volume, such gaslighting impacted the discipline of political economy by trivializing women's contributions in an effort to keep them out of the field. In *Gas Light*, the initial attempt to steal Alice Barlow's jewels occurs because of the related assumption that a woman wouldn't know how to care for extensive property: "it was well known that she kept them, without any proper precautions, in her bedroom," Rough tells Bella (36). The detective's ability to discover the murderer's present plot comes in part because of his revelation that a woman *might* take precautions about her possessions after all: "What if she had *not* been so careless? What if she had got those jewels hidden away in some inconceivably cunning place, in the walls, floored down, bricked in, maybe?" (37). Whether by directly negating their abilities, by naming and then treating such inconceivable "cunning" as the only alternative to "carelessness," or by suggesting that women operate in a different sphere of action, Victorian novels frequently practice economic gaslighting, suggesting that women's economic knowledge is both rare and, even when shown to be significant, still "not what a man wants."[24] Many people came to believe in this supposedly "feminine" incapacity, weakening the agency women may have exerted with respect to their own property, producing gendered financial inequalities, and creating opportunities for white-collar crimes by financial advisors.[25]

Such economic gaslighting caused many disempowered subjects to doubt their own perceptions and abilities. Though Mr. Brooke's remarks do not immediately extinguish his niece's ardent ideas, and assumptions about Alice

Barlow's carelessness do not lead her murderer to the jewels, the women in question nevertheless experience indirect but high costs from the social pressure to view them as incompetent economic subjects. Others, such as *Hester*'s Mrs. John, are more directly gaslit, internalizing the belief that the financial ignorance attributed to and encouraged in women is actually a form of reverence. Defending the spouse who betrayed his family's bank and then left her in debt with a young child, Mrs. John recalls that "he always had too much respect for me to mix me up with business."[26]

In addition to showcasing the systematic downplaying of women's intelligence and abilities,[27] Victorian fiction chipped away at women's exercise of their economic rights and understanding of their legal reality in two further ways that *Gas Light* calls attention to and that the rest of this chapter will discuss. One method of economic gaslighting entailed identifying women's legitimate possession as robbery — language that, as we will see, appears in novels by Eliot and Anthony Trollope and is in some cases even echoed by the women accused of such acts. The other, related method entailed defining women's wishes as secondary or even antagonistic to family interests in which they were not included. Fictional scenarios regarding marital money thus led many female characters to see the legal protections of their property as meaningless or injurious in the face of other familial claims.

"If I Steal Your Things"

As Jack encourages Bella to feel that she is losing not only her watch and brooch but also her mind, it is not enough for items to appear taken "from [their] place," subject to the "meaningless mischiefs" (21) for which he attempts to publicly "shame" her (18). Instead, he insists that she has "lyingly and purposely concealed" them (24) and attempts to persuade her that she intentionally acts as his "enem[y]" by doing so (25). He appears to discover evidence of her transgressions "lying hidden at the bottom of [her] work-box" (33), proof of the thefts that she comes to acknowledge as she attempts to make sense of her memory, mismatched with her material world. "I may be going mad," she says, but "before God — I never lie to you knowingly. . . . Jack, if I steal your things — your rings — your keys — your pencils and your handkerchiefs, and you find them later at the bottom of my box, as indeed you do, then I do not know that I have done it" (21). Despite calling her "half-witted" (18) and "stark, gibbering mad" (21) at a time when insanity pleas had begun to impact legal sentencing,[28] Jack emphasizes her guilt for these criminalized actions, "steal[ing]" both *his* things and, apparently, her own (*her* brooch, *her* watch). These latter accusations call into question not only her state of mind but also her right to do as she pleases with her personal property.

Jack's relocation of the objects, his lies, and his performances of anger at his (staged) discoveries are obvious forms of manipulation.[29] Less obvious is the way that he leads Bella to feel guilt and shame over her handling of her property — equating the misplaced brooch and household items such as bills and pictures with the theft of his own rings and handkerchiefs. Even if we set aside, for a moment, that his wife has moved *none* of these objects, it is important for us to recognize that she is held equally liable in both scenarios: stealing her husband's property and secreting away items of her own. The implication is that, despite what her legal rights may be, she is not free to act with respect to even her own personal property.

Accusing female characters of stealing both their own and others' property in order to diminish their agency emerges as a surprisingly common form of economic gaslighting in Victorian fiction written during the era of married women's property rights reform. In George Eliot's *Daniel Deronda* (1876), for example, the family diamonds that Gwendolen Grandcourt receives are framed as a robbery of her husband's former mistress's son.[30] Though Gwendolen feels momentary pleasure at the thought of having "her own diamonds," her domineering husband controls her adornment, and his former mistress's insistence that Gwendolen's possession is wrongful overpowers Gwendolen's own thoughts about her new possessions: "What a privilege this is, to have robbed another woman of!"[31] Gwendolen ultimately disregards that other woman but echoes the larger novel in treating her own hold on property as illicit in comparison with the illegitimate child's potential inheritance of his father's estate.[32] By the time her husband dies and leaves his estates and wealth to that son, Gwendolen and her friends are relieved that she is "saved from robbing others."[33] Representing marital property as a conflict between a wife's rights and those of a son, Eliot reiterates popular opinion that endowing wives with property meant stealing from children — no minor point in 1876, midway between the passage of the first and second Married Women's Property Acts in 1870 and 1882. Eliot's novel shows how this view influences a fictional wife's perceptions of "her own" wealth, despite a legal reality of ownership; such renderings also reinforce the gaslit perceptions of a culture intent on chipping away at women's ability to exercise property rights with confidence or pleasure.

Anthony Trollope similarly explores the labeling of women's claims to property as theft. In *The Eustace Diamonds* (1873), Lizzie Eustace's hold on the valuable diamond necklace her late husband presented to her is considered robbery; the narrator, along with the social world she inhabits, accuses her of "endeavouring to steal" the jewels.[34] Lengthy legal debates about gifts, heirlooms, and paraphernalia ultimately suggest that, despite her penchant for lies, Lizzie is correct when she insists that they are her own diamonds and refuses to give them to her brother-in-law or his lawyer to protect for her son, the heir.[35] Unlike Gwendolen in the previous case, Lizzie rejects the worldview that would undermine her ownership; she does not internalize the belief that her possession is illicit. Nonetheless, opinion is strongly against her, labeling her a "greedy, blood-sucking harp[y]."[36] Her refusal to concede leads to romantic trouble and isolation; she is a warning to those women who would claim property rights. In its widespread efforts to devalue her perspective, her economic agency, and her character, Trollope's novel itself enacts forms of economic gaslighting. We might see the many Victorian critics who have echoed its claims of Lizzie's theft as among the unconscious gaslighters, as well as the gaslit.

In contrast to "greedy" Lizzie Eustace, Trollope's Lady Laura, from *Phineas Finn* (1869) and *Phineas Redux* (1873), is "generous as the sun,"[37] using her fortune of £40,000 to discharge her brother's debts. Yet she, too, is accused of stealing her own property; though her brother repays her, his doing so after her marriage means that it cannot be preserved: "'if it had been paid in the usual way at my marriage, settlements would have been required that it should come back to the family after Mr Kennedy's death in the event of my having no child. But, as it is now, the money would go to his estate after my death.'"[38] Though Laura wonders "'what use would it be . . . to have a sum of money to leave behind me,'" her father's anger that this arrangement "'has robbed us all'"[39] reminds us that a woman's independent fortune was not necessarily considered her own. Whereas Laura's focus on "use" privileges her present ability to spend, invest, or donate her wealth, her father privileges descendants' future financial rights. Her "robbe[ry]" amounts to the mistaken sense that her legal fortune was her own to use — albeit to benefit a male family member! — rather than the property of her family, intended for future generations. Here, again, the novels suggest that Laura has been culpable and punish her accordingly, leaving her "withered, an old woman before her time."[40] Like Lizzie Eustace, she serves as a warning to the social world she inhabits, which accedes to her father's vision of her personal property rights and economic agency. Together, these examples showcase a form of economic gaslighting that systemically negated women's legal control over their own wealth by treating their possessions as illicit.

Many of these cases feature expensive jewels: diamonds worth £10,000 in *The Eustace Diamonds*; the Grandcourt marital diamonds in *Daniel Deronda*; and similarly valuable jewels in other novels subject to wives' "theft," such as the breathtakingly beautiful pearls in *Hester.* As a form of portable property typically appearing on women and counted among their legal possessions even when they could not claim other assets such as land, jewels are signs of the great wealth that some women had. Yet, their association with women's adornment also underplayed their potential as property. These depictions of women's supposed theft limit the understanding of women's property to possession, ignoring other strategic uses of these expensive items or the wealth they represent, such as selling or investing. Although *Gas Light*'s case differs — Jack displacing his attempted theft of rubies worth "[t]welve thousand pounds" (60) onto the feigned theft of a brooch by his frantic wife — here, too, a wife's theft stands in for her husband's illicit actions, anxieties about her property rights, and desire to conceal his own wrongdoing by projecting it onto her.[41]

Bella's brooch, unbeknownst to the criminal mastermind, actually holds the long-sought-after rubies — "beads . . . all loose and falling out" (59). Significantly, the jewels have been there all along, in the secondhand piece of jewelry Jack gave to Bella, his "common theft" of a "common trinket [Alice Barlow] wore all the day" (61, 60).[42] That the rubies are hidden in plain sight alongside other items of presumably little worth should remind us that common objects — whether personal ornaments, apparel, or household items — were often women's most valued possessions, items they bequeathed to others, notwithstanding laws against married women's wills. In Eliot's *Mill on the Floss*, Mrs. Tulliver weeps over the teapot and tablecloths she can no longer bequeath to her children when her husband's debts necessitate the sale of her "treasures."[43] *Gas Light*'s Bella holds her personal property in similar esteem, exclaiming, at the discovery of her brooch and watch, "Oh, Inspector, you have indeed found treasure to-night" (56). Though Rough is skeptical — "Not very much at present I'm afraid" (56) — such portable property frequently carried larger economic and emotional significance for women, safeguarding some wealth along with some financial choices regarding its use, concealment, or transfer. Though, as these examples show, women's grip on such items could be precarious, they nevertheless gave some women room to maneuver against the widespread economic gaslighting that attempted to strip them of more evident or large-scale financial agency. Even as Jack orchestrates the economic gaslighting that attempts to hold this property against his wife, he cannot perceive its true value.

"Great Wealth, and Decided Eccentricities"

False accusations of robbery depended on systemically undermining women's conception that they could lay claims to their own property. The language of theft in these examples from Victorian fiction and *Gas Light* may seem extreme, but it reinforces cultural expectations for women's property: that a woman's wealth should benefit, and even belong to, her larger family. Historically, a wife's marital settlement or separate estate was rarely intended for her use. Instead, it "allowed a father to preserve family property . . . for future male heirs."[44] Women might receive a life interest in property they inherited so that they could convey wealth to the next generation.[45] Women's wealth also served their families during their lifetimes. As Leonore Davidoff and Catherine Hall have shown, women's financial "involvement" in family businesses was "widespread" and instrumental to their successes.[46] A woman's assertion of her own property rights clashed with these expectations. Though in some cases, as we have seen, she might be ostracized as a thief, in others she is simply persuaded that her individual choices do not matter, that she owes this property to her family. In Oliphant's *Hester*, for example, Catherine Vernon's aunt, wishing her to marry a cousin, argues "that it would be almost dishonest to enrich another family with money which the Vernons had toiled for" (6). Although Catherine stays silent about her feelings and her (maternal, not Vernon) fortune, she never marries. Her choice to devote this personal fortune to the Vernons' bank (twice, during two separate crises) suggests that her aunt's sense of extreme, familial obligation has shaped Catherine's understanding as well. Her aunt serves as the mouthpiece for a broader economic gaslighting of Catherine's property rights and agency in favor of her perceived duties to her father's legacy. The novel's juxtaposition of these women with two generations of male cousins, who mismanage and steal family money, suggests that prioritizing the larger family's wealth in this way was a specifically gendered expectation.

Along similar lines, Hamilton's play challenges women's economic choices and capabilities in its depiction of Alice Barlow, "an old lady of great wealth, and decided eccentricities" (36). Rough notes that "her principal mania in life was the protection of cabmen. You may think that an extraordinary hobby, but in her odd way she did a lot of good" (36). Here, a woman's significant philanthropic economic agency is dismissed as a "mania" or "hobby." Part of what makes Alice's provisions for cabmen eccentric or odd (rather than generous or charitable) is that they direct wealth along unconventional lines — outside of the patrilineal structures of inheritance that pit a son's wealth against a wife's in *Daniel Deronda*, that lead Lady Laura's father to accuse her of "robb[ing] us all" in *Phineas Redux*, and that give pause when Lizzie Eustace professes delight at presenting the diamonds to her son's future wife, a transaction that would replace primogeniture with matrilineage.

Gas Light's Alice Barlow lacks heirs, which means that the rediscovered Barlow Rubies will "go to the Queen" (60).[47] Though the play grants great wealth to an older woman who has lived an unconventional life and whose wealth follows an unconventional pathway, the cost to her is shown to be high: death by murder. Fiction from the period of reform redoubles its emphasis on the importance of male heirs and punishes women who sought different ends for their wealth. Through these and other forms of economic gaslighting, Victorian fiction frequently trains women to see their own wealth as belonging to their larger families and to understand any lapses or eccentricities in women's financial choices as connected to and even culpable for tragic results.

Gaslight's Diffusion

Made aware of her husband's economic gaslighting, a relatively empowered Bella reclaims her possessions — "Here is a bill. Here is a letter. Here is a watch. . . . I have found them at last, you see!" (82) — which she now perceives as her own, for her sole and separate benefit: "But they don't help you, do they?" (82). Property seemingly offers her confidence, agency, and sanity. It also appears to threaten her feelings of sympathy, as she taunts Jack — "How can a mad woman help her husband to escape?" (82) — and watches his arrest "without a shred of pity — without a shred of regret — . . . with glory in my heart!" (83). Along these lines, Victorian commentators feared that women's economic rights would come at the expense of traditional femininity and, by extension, traditional marriages. Yet the play clearly attributes Bella's now-"pitiless" stance to her gaslighting: "If I were not mad I could have helped you — if I were not mad, whatever you had done, I could have pitied and protected you!" (82–83). In such a case, even the staunchest opponents of reform might have excused a wife's "hat[red]" and "rejoicing" (83).

Advancements in property rights did not, generally speaking, strip wives of sympathy for their husbands, nor did they offer immediate empowerment. Unlike Bella, real and fictional women from the nineteenth century onward continued to exercise their newfound financial agency to benefit families rather than their personal interests. In this and other ways, legal changes alone cannot undo the larger, patriarchal systems of economic gaslighting that continue to coerce Bella, even in such seemingly more benign forms as protection. For the aptly named Sergeant "Rough" who arrives to save the day serves as another source of manipulation. Asserting his right to Bella's home and its contents, he offers muted but nonetheless disturbing echoes of her marriage in his disregard for her feelings or possessions. He too has returned to the scene of the crime to continue his search: "if my theory is right the jewels *must* still be where she hid them" (37–38). He too uses Bella: "You have got to give me the evidence or help me find it" (44). Pushing his way into her presence, "keep[ing her] in the dark" (30), and bullying her into compliance — "You're working with me, aren't you — not against me?"(45) — Rough rummages through desks and bureaus as he wishes, "*splitting wood*" in his "violent methods" (58) and ignoring her when she begs him three times to "stop" his search (46). Rough, like the protective social force he embodies, cares little for Bella's own claims to property or personal comfort. For even though, in contrast to Jack, Rough wishes to convince Bella of her sanity and restore her belongings to her, these intentions do not preclude him from playing power games of his own, presenting himself as her savior ("I have come here to save you" [43]) while simultaneously infantilizing and belittling her (by calling her "my child" [83] and commanding her to "stop making a fool of [her]self" [62]). Finally, Rough's claims to Bella's personal property coincide with claims to her body. To calm her down and make her more amenable to his requests, he all but forces her to drink the "exceptional medicine" (meaning: whiskey) that he pours for her (34); after discovering the long-lost rubies, he "*kisses her*" (60). Undermining her bodily autonomy and psychological stability along with her economic rights in his efforts to crack the case, Rough contributes to creating the conditions that reduce Bella to that most feminized ailment of nineteenth-century medical gaslighting: according to the stage directions on the very final page of the play, "*she is completely hysterical*" (83).[48] *Gas Light* uncovers the manipulation behind a woman's marriage and money but cannot free her from — indeed, normalizes — the patriarchal power structures that supported her economic gaslighting in the first place. Like Bella, many Victorian women would find that even reforming married women's property law could not protect their rights from a culture intent on keeping its women in the dark and treating them like "children" or "fools" in need of "salvation."

Cultural ideologies that perpetuate economic gaslighting continue to be prevalent today, even as women's primary sources of wealth have shifted from inheritance to income.[49] Women are still disproportionately expected to sacrifice their careers to the larger need — whether through domestic caregiving or with excessive "office housework" and "altruistic citizenship behavior" at work

— with material impact on their economic status, particularly for women of color.[50] We see this in unequal pay and in the systems that keep women uncompensated for invisible labor at home or in the workplace[51] and that continue to punish women who attempt to make their own economic claims.[52]

Gas Light reminds us of the significance of women's property within discourses of marriage, both Victorian and contemporary, and suggests that the brutal crime at its core is less an outlier than we might hope. Countless women have been convinced that taking money from their own purses requires their husbands' assent, that any private use of their property amounts to theft, that they are fools whose money requires expert and even violent management. Economic gaslighting takes many forms today, and while fewer may be about marriage, many are still about property, or the power differentials that benefit those able to control the possession, use, and transmission of wealth. As we consider the Victorian roots of this now-popular but historically situated term, we illuminate how women's rights were obscured in the past, not only to give nuance to the narratives of the nineteenth century, but also to look with fresh vision on today's systemic injustices so that we may be better equipped to fight for those rights still to come.

Notes

1. Hamilton, *Gas Light*, 42. Further references will be cited parenthetically.
2. Paul-Mikhail Catapang Podosky distinguishes "getting people to believe that their understanding is mistaken" from "caus[ing] people to doubt their interpretive abilities." Podosky, "Gaslighting," 209.
3. Podosky, "Gaslighting," 207.
4. Ruíz, "Cultural Gaslighting," 688; Berenstain, "White Feminist Gaslighting," 733. For "racial" and "white feminist" structural gaslighting, see Ruíz, 693–95; Berenstain, 734. Podosky distinguishes "gaslighting as one-off events" from its "system of oppressive patterned behavior *over time*" (212).
5. Pohlhaus, "Gaslighting and Echoing," 676, 677, 679.
6. For an overview of some of the major differences between the four stage and screen versions of *Gaslight*, see this collection's introduction.
7. In the Broadway production of *Gas Light* (retitled *Angel Street*), Bella is endowed with "a bit of money" that allows her to make the real estate purchase that her husband has recommended to her as an "excellent investment" (Hamilton, *Angel Street*, 31); in the British National film version, Bella points out to her husband that "it was my money that allowed you to buy [the house]" and asks him, point-blank, "Is that why you married me, Paul?"; in the MGM film version, the murdered woman's niece (whose name is changed from Bella to Paula) inherits the house from her aunt and agrees, at her husband's request, to give up her own career in order to go live in it.
8. These and related points appear in Rappoport, *Imagining Women's Property*, especially 3–4 and 10–12.
9. Shanley, *Feminism, Marriage, and the Law*, 8; Staves, *Married Women's Separate Property*, 27–36, 129–30, 217; and Owens, "Property, Gender and the Life Course," 312.
10. Holcombe, *Wives and Property*, 46; Staves, *Married Women's Separate Property*, 59; Rutterford and Maltby, "Frank Must Marry Money," 185.
11. Holcombe, *Wives and Property*, 15, 16.
12. See Rappaport, *Shopping for Pleasure*; and Lysack, *Come Buy, Come Buy*.
13. Finn, "Women, Consumption and Coverture in England, c. 1760–1860," 706, 707; Finn, "Working-Class Women," 145; Rappaport, *Shopping*, 50–65; Bailey, "Favoured or Oppressed?," 353; Erickson, *Women and Property*, 150, 224; Staves, *Married Women's Separate Property*, 131.
14. Collins, *Woman in White*, 247–50, 304–5. See also Godfrey, "'Absolutely Miss Fairlie's Own,'" 166–71.
15. In *Angel Street* and the two film versions of *Gaslight*, he also pursues his wife's own property. See note 7.
16. For the 1828 Act to Regulate the Care and Treatment of Insane Persons in England, see Wise, *Inconvenient People*, xxi, xiv; McCandless, "Liberty

and Lunacy," 339, 345–46. For financial motivations behind wrongful confinement, see McCandless, 343–44. (I thank Lesley Hall from VICTORIA-l and Lewis Bentley from the Wellcome Library for recommending these sources.)

17. "Petition," quoted in Holcombe, *Wives and Property*, 237–38.
18. Dickens, *Little Dorrit*, 85–86.
19. Brontë, *Tenant of Wildfell Hall*, 208–9.
20. Gaskell, *Letters*, 379.
21. Oliphant, "Laws Concerning Women," 385. See also Oliphant, *Hester*, 28.
22. Eliot, *Middlemarch*, 17.
23. Oliphant, *Hester*, 244.
24. Oliphant, *Hester*, 370.
25. See Robb, *White-Collar*, 29–30, 184–85; and Robb, *Ladies*, 22.
26. Oliphant, *Hester*, 374.
27. For a discussion of this as a "credibility deficit," see Lana Dalley's contribution to this volume.
28. The 1843 McNaughtan Rules (sometimes M'Naghten or M'Naughten) provide legal criteria for insanity pleas. See Eigen, *Unconscious Crime*, 6; Smith, "Boundary Between," 366, 367. Interestingly, the actor in the play that Jack pretends he's going to take Bella to go see is "MacNaughton" (*Gas Light*, 12).
29. We are told that Jack had "ambition to be an actor" (*Gas Light*, 16).
30. Eliot, *Daniel Deronda*, 359. My discussion of several of the Victorian novels addressed in this chapter is reframed and condensed from a larger argument in my *Imagining Women's Property*.
31. Eliot, *Daniel Deronda*, 358, 427.
32. Wynne, *Women and Personal Property*, 116. For Victorian analogies between mistress and wife, see Shanley, *Feminism*, 61; Gallagher, "George Eliot and *Daniel Deronda*," 51–52.
33. Eliot, *Daniel Deronda*, 699.
34. Trollope, *Eustace Diamonds*, I:55.
35. See Ben-Yishai, *Common Precedents*, 119, 123; R. D. McMaster, *Trollope and the Law*, 78–84; Roth, "He Thought He Was Right (But Wasn't)," 890–91, 894; and Miller, *Novel and the Police*, 11. See also Blackstone, *Commentaries on the Laws of England*, quoted in McMaster, 80–81. As Kathy Psomiades notes, public opinion takes precedence over law; see Psomiades, "Heterosexual Exchange," 102.
36. Trollope, *Eustace Diamonds*, I:254.
37. Trollope, *Phineas Finn*, 409.
38. Trollope, *Phineas Redux*, 140.
39. Trollope, *Phineas Redux*, 141.
40. Trollope, *Phineas Finn*, 29; Trollope, *Phineas Redux*, 360.
41. Calef and Weinshel, who define gaslighting as "an effort to . . . manage greed" (64), prefer "introjection," noting that "while projection is . . . an

intrapsychic phenomenon, gaslighting . . . involves two people" (62). Describing victims, they note that "such individuals have a tendency to incorporate and to assimilate what others externalize and project onto them" (52). See Calef and Weinshel, "Some Clinical Consequences."

42. The MGM film adaptation similarly places the valuable jewels in a common and visible place: as Aviva Briefel has noted, the brooch, which in the film masquerades as a family heirloom, "has its double in" opera singer Alice Alquist's "precious gems [which] are embroidered alongside worthless paste on the dress that Alice used to wear" in her performances. While, as Briefel suggests, this "combin[ation of] priceless and cheap jewelry" encourages "misread[ing]," it might also indicate the value that this famous singer attributes to her income-producing role. See Briefel, *The Deceivers*, 171.
43. Eliot, *Mill on the Floss*, 213. For Victorian women's wills, see Combs, "A Measure," 1039.
44. Hoeckley, "Anomalous Ownership," 149; Staves, *Married Women's Separate Property*, 4, 84. See also Owens, "Property," 310; and Anonymous, "Lady and Her Marriage Settlement," 208.
45. Green, "To do the Right Thing," 140, 142; Owens, "Property, Gender and the Life Course," 305–6. See also Davidoff and Hall, *Family Fortunes*, 209.
46. Davidoff and Hall, *Family Fortunes*, 279. See also Nenadic, "Small Family Firm," 101, 103; Rose, "Family Firm," 67.
47. In the MGM film, the murdered woman, Alice Alquist, similarly has no children; her estate stays within the family but, by going to her niece, falls outside of traditional patrilineal descent as well. Victorian women did often choose other women for bequests; see Frank, *Law, Literature, and the Transmission of Culture*, 58.
48. For a discussion of nineteenth-century uses of "hysteria," see this collection's introduction and Diana Bellonby's chapter in it. In the MGM film version, the "elderly" Sergeant Rough softens into Joseph Cotten's much younger Inspector Cameron, a potential love interest for the newly single Paula. The transformation from rough to romance underscores the violence inherent in structures of legal "salvation" as well as Hollywood's confidence that women desire neither autonomy nor property but husbands who will take control over both.
49. We see the beginnings of this shift in the MGM film, with Alice Alquist's operatic career and the niece who attempts to follow in her professional footsteps but gives up those aspirations for the sake of marriage. For more on this aspect of the gaslighting plot, see Sarah Kersh's chapter in this collection.
50. See also Pew Research Center, "Raising Kids," 3, 7, 9–10; Cullinan, "In Collaborative Cultures," 2; Williams and Dempsey, *What Works for Women*, 68–70, 110–16; and Gutiérrez y Muhs, Flores Niemann, González, and Harris, eds., *Presumed Incompetent*.

51. Goldin, Kerr, Olivetti, and Barth, "Expanding Gender Earnings Gap," 113, 114. See also American Association of University Women (AAUW), "Simple Truth About the Gender Pay Gap."
52. See Small, Gelfand, Babcock, and Gettman, "Who Goes to the Bargaining Table?," 601, 604; Bowles, Babcock, and Lai, "Social Incentives," 85, 91; Bowles, Babcock, and McGinn, "Constraints and Triggers," 953.

Bibliography

American Association of University Women (AAUW). "The Simple Truth About the Gender Pay Gap." Fall 2018 Edition, 1–32, www.aauw.org.

Anonymous. "The Lady and Her Marriage Settlement." *Englishwoman's Domestic Magazine*, March 1, 1864.

Bailey, Joanne. "Favoured or Oppressed? Married Women, Property, and 'Coverture' in England, 1660-1800." *Continuity and Change* 17, no. 3 (2002): 351–72.

Ben-Yishai, Ayelet. *Common Precedents: The Presentness of the Past in Victorian Law and Fiction*. Oxford University Press, 2013.

Berenstain, Nora. "White Feminist Gaslighting." *Hypatia* 35 (2020): 733–58.

Bowles, Hannah Riley, Linda Babcock, and Kathleen L. McGinn. "Constraints and Triggers: Situational Mechanics of Gender in Negotiation." *Journal of Personality and Social Psychology* 89, no. 6 (2005): 951–65.

Bowles, Hannah Riley, Linda Babcock, and Lei Lai. "Social Incentives for Gender Differences in the Propensity to Initiate Negotiations: Sometimes it Does Hurt to Ask." *Organizational Behavior and Human Decision Processes* 103 (2007): 84–103.

Briefel, Aviva. *The Deceivers: Art Forgery and Identity in the Nineteenth Century*. Cornell University Press, 2006.

Brontë, Anne. *The Tenant of Wildfell Hall.* Edited by Herbert Rosengarten and Josephine McDonagh. Oxford University Press, 2008.

Calef, Victor, and Edward Weinshel. "Some Clinical Consequences of Introjection: Gaslighting." *The Psychoanalytic Quarterly* 50 (1981): 44-66.

Collins, Wilkie. *The Woman in White*. Edited by John Sutherland. Oxford University Press, 1996.

Combs, Mary Beth. "'A Measure of Legal Independence': The 1870 Married Women's Property Act and the Portfolio Allocations of British Wives." *The Journal of Economic History* 65, no. 4 (2005): 1028–57.

Cullinan, Renee. "In Collaborative Cultures, Women Carry More of the Weight." *Harvard Business Review*, July 24, 2018.

Davidoff, Leonore and Catherine Hall, *Family Fortunes: Men and Women of the English Middle Class, 1780–1850*. Routledge, 2002.

Dickens, Charles. *Little Dorrit*. Edited by Stephen Wall and Helen Small. Penguin, 1998.

Dolin, Tim. *Mistress of the House: Women of Property in the Victorian Novel.* Routledge, 2016.

Eigen, Joel Peter. *Unconscious Crime: Mental Absence and Criminal Responsibility in Victorian London.* Johns Hopkins University Press, 2003.

Eliot, George. *Daniel Deronda.* Edited by Terence Cave. Penguin, 1995.

———. *Middlemarch.* Edited by Rosemary Ashton. Penguin, 1994.

———. *The Mill on the Floss.* Edited by A. S. Byatt. Penguin, 2003.

Erickson, Amy Louise. *Women and Property in Early Modern England.* Routledge, 1993.

Finn, Margot. "Women, Consumption and Coverture in England, c. 1760–1860." *The Historical Journal* 39, no. 3 (1996): 703–22.

Finn, Margot. "Working-Class Women and the Contest for Consumer Control in Victorian County Courts." *Past and Present* 161 (1998): 116–54.

Frank, Cathrine O. *Law, Literature, and the Transmission of Culture in England, 1837–1925.* Routledge, 2016.

Gallagher, Catherine. "George Eliot and *Daniel Deronda*: The Prostitute and the Jewish Question." In *Sex, Politics, and Science in the Nineteenth-Century Novel: Selected Papers from the English Institute, 1983–84, New Series, No. 10*, edited by Ruth Bernard Yeazell, 39–62. Johns Hopkins University Press, 1986.

Gaskell, Elizabeth. *The Letters of Mrs. Gaskell.* Edited by J. A. V. and A. Pollard. Harvard University Press, 1967.

Godfrey, Esther. "'Absolutely Miss Fairlie's Own': Emasculating Economics in *The Woman in White.*" In *Economic Women: Essays on Desire and Dispossession in Nineteenth-Century British Culture*, edited by Lana L. Daley and Jill Rappoport, 162–75. Ohio State University Press, 2013.

Goldin, Claudia, and Sari Pekkala Kerr, Claudia Olivetti, and Erling Barth. "The Expanding Gender Earnings Gap: Evidence from the LEHD-2000 Census." *American Economic Review: Papers & Proceedings* 107, no. 5 (2017): 110–14.

Green, David R. "To do the Right Thing: Gender, Wealth, Inheritance and the London Middle Class." In *Women and their Money, 1700–1950: Essays on Women and Finance*, edited by Anne Laurence, Josephine Maltby, and Janette Rutterford, 133–50. Routledge, 2009.

Gutiérrez y Muhs, Gabriella, Yolanda Flores Niemann, Carmen G. González, and Angela P. Harris, eds. *Presumed Incompetent: The Intersections of Race and Class for Women in Academia.* University Press of Colorado, 2012.

Hamilton, Patrick. *Angel Street. A Victorian Thriller in Three Acts.* Samuel French, 1942.

———. *Gas Light: A Victorian Thriller in Three Acts.* Constable and Company, 1939.

Hoeckley, Cheri Larsen. "Anomalous Ownership: Copyright, Coverture, and *Aurora Leigh.*" *Victorian Poetry* 35, no. 2 (1998): 135–61.

Holcombe, Lee. *Wives and Property: Reform of the Married Women's Property Law in Nineteenth-Century England.* University of Toronto Press, 1983.
Lysack, Krista. *Come Buy, Come Buy: Shopping and the Culture of Consumption in Victorian Women's Writing*. Ohio University Press, 2008.
McCandless, Peter. "Liberty and Lunacy: The Victorians and Wrongful Confinement." In *Madhouses, Mad-Doctors, and Madmen: The Social History of Psychiatry in the Victorian Era*, edited by Andrew Scull, 339–62. University of Pennsylvania Press, 1981.
McMaster, R. D. *Trollope and the Law*. Macmillan, 1986.
Miller, D. A. *The Novel and the Police*. University of California Press, 1988.
Nenadic, Stana. "The Small Family Firm in Victorian Britain." *Business History* 35 (1993): 86–114.
Oliphant, Margaret. *Hester*. Edited by Philip Davis and Brian Nellist. Oxford University Press, 2003.
———. "The Laws Concerning Women." *Blackwood's Edinburgh Magazine* 486, no. 79 (1856): 379–87.
Owens, Alastair. "Property, Gender and the Life Course: Inheritance and Family Welfare Provision in Early Nineteenth-Century England." *Social History* 26, no. 3 (2001): 299–317.
Pew Research Center. "Raising Kids and Running a Household: How Working Parents Share the Load." Pew Research Center, 2015.
Podosky, Paul-Mikhail Catapang. "Gaslighting, First- and Second-Order." *Hypatia* 36 (2021): 207–27.
Pohlhaus, Jr., Gaile. "Gaslighting and Echoing, or Why Collective Epistemic Resistance is Not a 'Witch Hunt.'" *Hypatia* 35 (2020): 674–86.
Psomiades, Kathy Alexis. "Heterosexual Exchange and Other Victorian Fictions: *The Eustace Diamonds* and Victorian Anthropology." *NOVEL: A Forum on Fiction* 33, no. 1 (1999): 93–118.
Rappaport, Erika Diane. *Shopping for Pleasure: Women in the Making of London's West End.* Princeton University Press, 2000.
Rappoport, Jill. *Imagining Women's Property in Victorian Fiction.* Oxford University Press, 2023.
Robb, George. *Ladies of the Ticker: Women and Wall Street from the Gilded Age to the Great Depression*. University of Illinois Press, 2017.
———. *White-Collar Crime in Modern England: Financial Fraud and Business Morality, 1845–1929*. Cambridge University Press, 1992.
Rose, Mary. "The Family Firm in British Business, 1780-1914." In *Business Enterprise inModern Britain: From the Eighteenth to the Twentieth Century*, edited by Maurice W. Kirby and Mary B. Rose, 61–87. Routledge, 1994.
Roth, Alan. "He Thought He Was Right (But Wasn't): Property Law in Anthony Trollope's *The Eustace Diamonds.*" *Stanford Law Review* 44, no. 4 (1992): 879–97.
Ruíz, Elena. "Cultural Gaslighting." *Hypatia* 35 (2020): 687–713.

Rutterford, Janette, and Josephine Maltby. "Frank Must Marry Money: Men, Women, and Property in Trollope's Novels." *The Accounting Historians Journal* 33, no. 2 (2006): 169–99.
Shanley, Mary Lyndon. *Feminism, Marriage, and the Law in Victorian England.* Princeton University Press, 1989.
Small, Deborah A., Michele Gelfand, Linda Babcock, and Hilary Gettman. "Who Goes to the Bargaining Table? The Influence of Gender and Framing on the Initiation of Negotiation." *Journal of Personality and Social Psychology* 93, no. 4 (2007): 600–13.
Smith, Roger. "The Boundary Between Insanity and Criminal Responsibility in Nineteenth-Century England." *Madhouses, Mad-Doctors, and Madmen: The Social History of Psychiatry in the Victorian Era*, edited by Andrew Scull, 363–84. University of Pennsylvania Press, 1981.
Staves, Susan. *Married Women's Separate Property in England, 1660–1833.* Harvard University Press, 1990.
Trollope, Anthony. *The Eustace Diamonds.* Edited by W. J. McCormack. Oxford University Press, 2008.
———. *Phineas Finn.* Edited by Simon Dentith. Oxford University Press, 2011.
———. *Phineas Redux.* Edited by John Bowen. Oxford University Press, 2011.
Williams, Joan C., and Rachel Dempsey. *What Works for Women at Work: Four Patterns Working Women Need to Know.* New York University Press, 2018.
Wise, Sarah. *Inconvenient People: Lunacy, Liberty and the Mad-Doctors in Victorian England.* Bodley Head, 2012.
Wynne, Deborah. *Women and Personal Property in the Victorian Novel.* Routledge, 2016.

Rutherford, [illegible], and [illegible]. "[illegible] Money, Money: [illegible] and Property in Trollope's Novels." [illegible] (20[illegible]): [illegible].

[illegible]

5

Gaslighting, Misogynoir, and the Mixed-Race Heiress in *The Woman of Colour* and *Vanity Fair*

Rosetta Young

In the sixth episode of the Netflix docuseries *Harry & Meghan* (2022), Prince Harry critiques the members of the British royal family for how they have treated his wife, Meghan, and himself: "To see this institutional gaslighting that happens is — it is extraordinary. And that's why everything that's happened to us was always going to happen to us. Because if you speak truth to power, that's how they respond."[1] As Harry's phrasing here reveals, gaslighting is central to how the couple describes their experiences in the royal family over more than six hours of interviews, video diaries, and personal photographs. Throughout the series, the couple details how the British tabloids have enacted a campaign of racist and sexist abuse against Meghan that was (and is) often fueled by the press offices of other members of the royal family. While the British press has targeted Meghan for supposed transgressions large and small, the docuseries suggests that this animosity was built, first and foremost, on racism: the tabloids used Meghan's mixed-race identity — her mother is Black and her father is white — to generate vitriol among readers, painting her as a conniving, "exotic" outsider scamming her way into the highest ranks of British society. The royal family, meanwhile, has maintained that this racist abuse was not, in fact, racist at all, but rather just another iteration of what the white wives and girlfriends of royal men have had to contend with in the past. "This is not the same," Meghan insisted in the interview with Oprah Winfrey that the couple did prior to the release of *Harry & Meghan*. "And if a member of this family will comfortably say we've all had to deal with things that are rude — rude and racist are not the same."[2] What Meghan calls out here is a clear case of what political scientists Angelique M. Davis and Rose Ernst have termed "racial gaslighting," or "the political, social, economic, and cultural process that perpetuates and normalizes a white supremacist reality through pathologizing those who resist."[3] Davis and Ernst argue that "racial gaslighting . . . relies on the production of particular narratives"; namely, "*narratives that obfuscate the existence of a white supremacist state power structure*."[4] The narratives about Meghan that have been forwarded by both the British media and the royal family itself do just this: they gaslight her by suggesting that her experience of racism is merely a product of her own flawed perception.

In this essay, I locate a throughline between Meghan's experience of racial gaslighting over the past decade and the depiction of two wealthy, mixed-race Black women emigrant characters featured in nineteenth-century British fiction: Olivia Fairfield in the anonymously authored 1808 novel *The Woman of Colour* and Rhoda Swartz in William Makepeace Thackeray's *Vanity Fair* (1847–1848).[5] In these novels, the characters of Olivia and Rhoda find in England plenty of racism and misogyny, but perhaps the most insidious instances of discrimination come from the Britons they encounter who deny the existence of misogynoir even as they perpetuate it. Recent theoretical explorations of both "misogynoir" and "gaslighting" undergird my readings of these novels, since Olivia and Rhoda encounter gaslighting not just as a sexist or racist attack but as an intersectional assault within these texts. Davis and Ernst make clear that the "resistance" that provokes racial gaslighting need not be formal activism on the part of people of color; instead, "the survival, existence, resilience, and/or success of People of Color is an act of resistance on both macro and micro levels that results in racial gaslighting."[6] Following this logic, I show how, in their respective texts, Olivia's and Rhoda's mere presence in the British upper class is read by themselves, other characters, or both as an act of resistance in and of itself, even as they largely try to assimilate and conform. Ultimately, examining the narratives in which Olivia and Rhoda find themselves gaslit by white British characters helps to make visible the particular conditions of misogynoir — what Moya Bailey defines as "the uniquely co-constitutive racialized and sexist violence that befalls Black women as a result of their simultaneous and interlocking oppression at the intersection of racial and gender marginalization"[7] — that wealthy, mixed-race Black women emigrating to England faced in the first half of the nineteenth century (and beyond). These white characters fetishize and pathologize Olivia and Rhoda while insisting that misogynoir is not present in their culture or within themselves. While Olivia and Rhoda are both fictional, their renderings nevertheless provide valuable insights into the dynamics and conditions of misogynoirist gaslighting, albeit from different vantage points.

In literary history, Olivia and Rhoda both belong to a larger trend in late eighteenth- and early nineteenth-century fiction.[8] Based on historical instances of mixed-race heiresses emigrating from the colonies to the metropole, stories featuring such women became a commonplace of the period. In these stories, the mixed-race heiress typically enters the country with a large fortune and the goal of assimilating into the upper class through marriage. Both Olivia and Rhoda conform to this archetype, but their respective novels represent their experiences from radically different perspectives. An epistolary novel, *The Woman of Colour* is narrated through letters that the heroine, Olivia Fairfield, writes to her former governess, Mrs. Milbanke, detailing her emigration to England. The daughter of a white British planter and an enslaved African woman, Olivia has grown up in Jamaica as the illegitimate but beloved child of her wealthy father. Her father has recently died and, in his will, has left his £60,000 fortune to his nephew and her first cousin, Augustus Merton, on the condition that the young man marry Olivia; if he does not consent to marry her, she will become the ward of Augustus's married brother, Mr. George Merton. When she arrives in England, Augustus agrees to the union. Olivia falls in love with Augustus quickly, but even as he expresses admiration for her, she suspects that he is not happy about their looming nuptials. Once they are married, her doubts linger, despite the apparent harmony of their life together. This uneasy yet peaceful period does not last for long. In a gothic twist, Augustus's evil sister-in-law, Mrs. George Merton, reveals that Augustus is not Olivia's husband at all: he is already married to another woman, the innocent, gentle, white Angelina. Three years prior, Mrs. George Merton had tricked Augustus into thinking that Angelina had died during his absence from London — and now his sister-in-law reveals her deception so that she and her husband can claim Olivia's inheritance. By the end of the novel, Augustus has joyously reunited with Angelina and their young son, and Olivia returns to Jamaica with her inheritance now firmly in her possession (thanks to the deathbed guilt of Augustus's father); her attempt at assimilation into British society has been a failure, but the novel indicates that she is not spiritually broken by this turn of events. She resolves, for example, to commit her life to "ameliorating the situation, in instructing the minds — in mending the morals of our poor blacks."[9] Through this simultaneously sympathetic and condescending declaration, Olivia subtly aligns herself with the elite mixed-race population of Jamaica whom the white-dominated government increasingly came to see as inevitable coleaders of the country in the first half of the nineteenth century.[10] This emotionally liberatory yet politically complicated ending for Olivia — along with her position as narrator of *The Woman of Colour* — has caused critics to speculate that the novel itself may have been written by an author who shared her biography. As Lyndon J. Dominique writes in his introduction to the Broadview edition of the novel, "it seems most plausible to propose that a woman of color wrote *The Woman of Colour*."[11]

Meanwhile, instead of serving as narrator and ethical compass of *Vanity Fair*, Rhoda Swartz is a minor character in Thackeray's novel who flits in and out of frame. She appears in the very first chapter as the classmate of the novel's two protagonists, Amelia Sedley and Becky Sharp, with Thackeray describing her as "the rich woolly-haired mulatto from St. Kitt's"; later in the narrative, we learn that "her father was a German Jew — a slave-owner they say — connected with the Cannibal Islands in some way or other."[12] It is, thus, implied but not confirmed that her mother was an enslaved African woman; further, this description of her father reveals how antisemitism also conditions the racism that Rhoda experiences in the text and how her multiethnic identity marks her as an outsider to the British upper class twice over. In later chapters, Rhoda plays her biggest role in *Vanity Fair* when she enters the story as a potential wife for George Osborne. Mr. Osborne, George's father, wants his son to ditch his longtime fiancée, Amelia, in favor of Rhoda, who has a £200,000 dowry. George refuses to marry Rhoda and weds Amelia instead, severing his relationship with his father before his untimely death at the Battle of Waterloo. His reasons for rejecting Rhoda are explicitly racial: as he tells his father, "I don't like the colour, sir. . . . *I'm* not going to marry a Hottentot Venus" (214). After being jilted by George, Rhoda marries "a young sprig of Scottish nobility" and reemerges at the end of the narrative to pay a visit to Amelia, seemingly as content, prosperous, and selfish as all the other members of Thackeray's titular Vanity Fair (424). While Rhoda has not always received sustained attention from critics — many scholars of Thackeray skim over her portrayal — Jennifer DeVere Brody has argued that it is precisely Rhoda's "marginality that makes her significant."[13] Brody considers Rhoda to be "'socially marginal but symbolically significant'" and actively works to "redress[] readings of her as merely minor" by showing how "Miss Swartz . . . *ironically* sustains the dominant structures of the society that created her."[14] Brody also points out that while Rhoda's consciousness is far from the narrative center, her role in the plot is crucial; it is George's rejection of "the doubly debased" Rhoda that propels him to finally marry Amelia.[15] Here, Brody provides a rationale for why Rhoda deserves the same close attention that Olivia does, even though their narratives situate them so differently. Similarly, I use Rhoda's treatment at the hands of the characters and the narrator of *Vanity Fair* to show how dominant, white British society viewed women of color and, specifically, mixed-race Black heiresses. When turning to the phenomenon of gaslighting, it becomes clear that Rhoda exists at the same nexus of class, race, gender, and sexuality that Olivia does, but *Vanity Fair* views her from the very perspective that the earlier novel critiques. If *The Woman of Colour* shows the reader what it feels like to experience misogynoirist gaslighting, *Vanity Fair* reveals the interiority of the misogynoirist gaslighters themselves.

A key scene between Olivia and her uncle, Mr. Merton, provides an illustrative example of how misogynoirist gaslighting functions in both *The Woman of Colour* and *Vanity Fair*. After arriving in England and meeting Augustus, Olivia reveals to his father, her uncle by marriage, her fears that racism might inhibit her cousin's romantic feelings for her: "I am aware of my own person — I know that I am little less than a disgusting object to an Englishman — I know that your son (supposing for a moment that he could get over his own prejudices as to colour) would have to encounter all the sarcastic innuendoes and jeering remarks of his companions" (90). In response, her uncle dismisses her concerns and suggests that she is imagining problems that do not exist: "My beloved Miss Fairfield, you are voluntarily raising up bugbears to disturb your happiness; the chimeras of your own imagination affright you, and hurt your peace of mind!" (90). When Olivia repeats her suspicions about Augustus's true feelings, Mr. Merton tells her that she is becoming hysterical: "Again let me entreat you to calm your emotions, my dear young lady, and to see things in a different point of view" (90). Olivia insists upon the validity of her own perspective: "I see them as they are sir," she retorts (90). Nevertheless, her uncle continues to claim that she is overreacting and turns the charge of prejudice back on her and away from his son and his society: "Not so, believe me, — through a prejudiced medium you now look — I am confident that my son admires and esteems you" (90). Mr. Merton dismisses Olivia's concerns, despite having witnessed her treatment at the hands of Mrs. George Merton, who directs a constant flow of racist commentary toward Olivia throughout the beginning of the book. In doing so, Mr. Merton refuses to acknowledge the existence of white supremacy as a central structure of his upper-class British world. Indeed, in calling Olivia "prejudiced," he uses a rhetorical strategy that presages twenty-first-century "reverse racism" accusations: he suggests that it is, in fact, his family and himself who are being discriminated against by *her*. At the same time, Mr. Merton employs one of the classic rhetorical maneuvers of the gaslighter: calling a woman, as Kate Abramson puts it, "crazy, paranoid, or oversensitive."[16]

Here, Mr. Merton shows how sexism and racism overlap to create the misogynoirist gaslighting experienced by Olivia and Rhoda. Misogynoirist gaslighting enacts what Kimberlé Crenshaw has called "compound marginalization," which Black women often encounter in misogynistic, white supremacist cultures due to the intersection of racist and sexist structures.[17] For Olivia and Rhoda, their status as women on the marriage market collides with the stigmatization and fetishization of Blackness in nineteenth-century British culture; in this era and its fiction, heiresses of all races contend with fortune hunters, but Olivia and Rhoda find themselves even more precariously situated than their white peers. Further, whether Olivia and Rhoda overtly acknowledge this compound vulnerability or attempt to ignore it, their presence draws attention to the misogynoirist conditions of nineteenth-century British culture and constitutes a form of implicit protest. In order to stigmatize this resistance and deny the extent to which their culture oppresses Black women, key white characters in both novels insist that Olivia and Rhoda do not encounter misogynoir in England but rather open-hearted acceptance, despite the continual prejudice and gaslighting they face from society at large and from characters like the Mertons and the Osbornes themselves.

Olivia's "Rebellious and Repining Heart"

The Woman of Colour opens with a premise that, in the 200-plus years since its publication, has not lost any of its dramatic power. Onboard a ship to England, Olivia Fairfield knows that, upon landing, she must marry her cousin, Augustus, or risk losing all control of her £60,000 inheritance. Olivia questions the wisdom of her father's decision to provide for her in this manner: "I sometimes think, that had my dear parent left me a decent competence, I could have placed myself in some tranquil nook of my native island, and have been happily and usefully employed in meliorating the sorrows of the poor slaves who came within my reach. . . . But my father willed it otherwise — Lie still, then, rebellious and repining heart!" (55–56). Here, Olivia understands her father as exercising a patriarchal control over her life from beyond the grave. The laws dictating inheritance in Jamaica at this time might at first seem to complicate this interpretation, but closer examination ultimately supports Olivia's "repining" view of Mr. Fairfield's actions. As historian Daniel Livesay details, in 1761 the Jamaican government levied "an inheritance cap" that limited the amount of money that mixed-race and Black residents could receive from white parents.[18] The government instituted this cap because they saw the rising population of well-to-do, mixed-race Jamaicans as "threaten[ing] the racial divide that was so critical to keeping captives enslaved."[19] Therefore, at first glance, Mr. Fairfield seemingly has no legal way to leave Olivia his fortune, potentially making his peculiar will an elaborate means of working around a racial caste system. But the fact of the inheritance cap alone does not reveal the full historical picture. While the Jamaican government technically stopped a white father from leaving more than £2,000 to his Black child, very wealthy planters had established a pathway to evade this restriction. The government regularly heard "privilege" petitions on behalf of wealthy Jamaicans of color; these petitions were a type of application for additional rights that was prohibitively expensive for anyone but the most affluent residents of the island to file and which allowed the mixed-race children of wealthy planters to evade the inheritance cap.[20] Therefore, for mixed-race Jamaicans of Olivia's status, submitting such an application would have offered a way around the inheritance cap. Her father's failure to submit such a petition on Olivia's behalf suggests his disinclination to leave his entire fortune to his Black daughter.

This historical context shows how Olivia first experiences gaslighting in the novel at the hands of her father. With his will, he patronizingly (and falsely) suggests that an arranged marriage to Augustus is the best option for her, when a privilege petition would have given her more freedom and autonomy. Therefore, in multifaceted ways, by using his will to coerce Olivia into marrying Augustus, he attempts to invalidate her firsthand knowledge of white men and British culture. At the beginning of the novel, Olivia expresses to her fellow traveler, the English matron Mrs. Honeywood, her disgust at the situation in which she has been placed with respect to Augustus. Specifically, Olivia hates that her father's will aims to bribe Augustus into overlooking her Blackness in order to enrich himself; she worries that, if he does marry her, he will only do so for her fortune and despite his racial aversions. Mrs. Honeywood implicitly acknowledges the validity of this fear, which makes her one of the only white characters in the text to affirm Olivia's misgivings on this score. When Olivia informs the older woman that her father told her before his death that "in England, in his native country . . . a more liberal, a more distinguishing spirit had gone abroad" regarding race than in the West Indies, she recounts how "a sceptical expression overspread the marked countenance of Mrs. Honeywood" (58). Her father alludes here to the fact that the white planters of Jamaican high society refused to marry either the free women of color or the enslaved women with whom they frequently engaged in long-term, extramarital relationships — the latter of which necessarily, due to the power dynamics of slavery, constitute acts of rape. (For more on this subject, see Doreen Thierauf's chapter in this collection.) Moreover, as Olivia well knows, this group of racist, sexually abusive Jamaican planters also includes her father himself. When Olivia narrates the story of her own parents' relationship, she details how even deep love, admiration, and respect for her mother could not induce her father to marry her; she writes of their relationship: "[My father] loved [my mother] with fervour; but the pride of the man, the quick feeling of the European, the prejudices which he had imbibed in common with his countrymen, forbade his making this affectionate and heroic girl his wife" (55). To insist, first, that Olivia's white cousin will consent to marry her and, second, that such a union will bring her happiness defies everything that Olivia knows to be true about the intersection of sexuality, gender, race, and family in British imperial culture. Her father is, effectively, asking her to disregard her own understanding of the world and choose to believe, against all odds, that a wealthy white man like himself (one who, in fact, as Olivia notes, bears a "likeness to my dear father . . . so very striking" [67]) will gladly accept a Black woman as his wife. Her father is, in other words, using his last will and testament to gaslight Olivia regarding her own understanding of and lived experience within British colonial white supremacy, particularly the relationships between Black women and white men within this system.

This opening, paternal form of psychological manipulation sets the stage for Olivia's gaslighting at the hands of other members of her family as well. As I've described above, her uncle by marriage, Mr. Merton, picks up where her father leaves off by insisting that she has no reason to worry about the purity of Augustus's motives for marrying her. Once they agree to marry, however, it is Augustus himself who becomes Olivia's primary gaslighter. Much like her father before him, Augustus refuses to acknowledge that racism shapes his feelings for Olivia, even as she senses his hesitation to embrace her as his future wife. Upon their first meeting, she notes that he "stammered out some words of pleasure and happiness" but that "*he* seemed to have been examining me with scrutinizing attention. — Alas! I fear it was but a melancholy contemplation in a double sense; for I thought I distinguished a suppressed sigh" (72). Once Augustus consents to the marriage, Olivia still discerns reluctance beneath his congenial demeanor, even as she herself begins to fall in love with him. In one instance, she catches him with "his head almost rested on his breast . . . [looking] the very image of melancholy despondence" (76). Moments such as these cause her great consternation — they make her want "to fall on my knees before him, and to beseech him, not to make a sacrifice of his own and my happiness" — but then, at other times, "his whole countenance is illuminated by an expression of sweetness and placidity which makes me a sceptic to my preconceived opinion" (74). Finally, in the days before their marriage, Olivia confronts Augustus and urges him not to marry her if he does not think he can be happy with her. She references her race in this speech and how it might not be a feature of hers that he can accept, stating, "I am fully acquainted with the numerous disadvantages under which, as a stranger and a mulatto West Indian, I labour here" (92). She elaborates further on this point, assuming the nature of his objections: "The good qualities which I possess . . . are not to be discerned in my countenance" (92). Augustus rejects this characterization of his attitudes: "You surprise and painfully astonish me, my dearest Miss Fairfield! is it possible that you can for a moment suppose, that I feel no regard for you? Are you so insensible to your own numerous and unrivalled virtues and perfections? . . . Ingenuous, interesting Miss Fairfield! it is, at this moment, that I feel my utter unworthiness of this precious treasure. — Oh! may you never repent your goodness!" (92–93). Here, Augustus plays the lover and does not give any credence to Olivia's concerns about his apparent lack of romantic feelings for her or about his potential racial antipathy.

Despite — or perhaps, because of — these ardent assurances about her "numerous and unrivalled virtues and perfections," Olivia remains unconvinced of his sincerity. She writes to Mrs. Milbanke that "I am neither satisfied with myself nor with Augustus. I fancy that I . . . have now obtained from his principles and his pity, what he must have ever denied from a stronger feeling" (93). And, indeed, not long after their marriage and the above exchange, the novel includes a letter from Augustus to his friend, Lionel Monkland; in this letter, he admits to Monkland what he denied to Olivia: "I will confess to you, that the moment when my eyes were first cast on the person of my cousin, I started back with a momentary feeling nearly allied to disgust; for I beheld a skin approaching to the hue of a negro's, in the woman whom my father introduced to me as my intended wife!" (102). He then adversely compares Olivia's complexion to that of his late wife, Angelina: "*I* that had been used to contemplate a countenance, and a transparent skin of ivory" (102). The rest of the letter unfolds the truth of Augustus's emotional situation; while he admires Olivia for the strength of her spirit and her personal qualities, and even describes enjoying "the rich prize of her affections and her love," he also confesses that "my heart does not beat with the rapture of passion, — my soul is not overcome by soft emotions at her approach as heretofore" (103–4). He reveals that he has married Olivia because he esteems her and does not want her to suffer — as he is sure she will — as the ward of his brother and his wife. In short, he has not married Olivia for financial gain or from personal desire. Daniel Yu has pointed out that while Augustus claims he cannot love Olivia because he still adores his dead wife, his prizing of Angelina's fair skin and his initial reaction to Olivia reveals that this preference is, at heart, a racial one.[21] This insight supports my reading of Augustus's behavior as an instance of misogynoirist gaslighting. In the face of her suspicions, Augustus insists to Olivia that he has no racist objections to their union, even when he freely admits elsewhere that he does indeed harbor such prejudices.

Lastly, in a compelling connection to the original source of the term "gaslighting," both *The Woman of Colour* and Patrick Hamilton's *Gas Light* (1938) share bigamy plots. At the end of *Gas Light*, the heroine, Bella, discovers that her gaslighting husband has been married to someone else all along, a revelation that exposes another layer of his deception. In *The Woman of Colour*, Olivia suspects that her marriage to Augustus is somehow not whole: "I feel that I *am* not half his wife," she writes of their emotional disconnect before the reappearance of Angelina, "I am the partner of his bed — but not of his heart!" (120). These doubts function as a continuation of her previous misgivings about their marriage and presage her coming realization that she has not, in fact, escaped the concubinage to which white men in Jamaica relegate women of color. When it is revealed that Augustus already has a white wife whom he adores and that his marriage to Olivia was, indeed, never "real," it exposes another way in which he has been gaslighting her all along. He could have told her the truth about his previous marriage and his protective motivations for marrying her; he could have refused to consummate their union out of emotional and aesthetic loyalty to his dead wife — but he does no such thing. Whatever his personal reasons for consummating their marriage (whether they be lust, affection for Olivia, a desire to legally cement the marriage, et cetera), this action forms part of his gaslighting; by refusing to be honest with Olivia, he chooses to preserve the narrative, the "racial spectacle," that he and his society are free of prejudice. Therefore, in both *The Woman of Colour* and *Gas Light*, uncovered bigamy functions as the culminating example of a woman's invalidated misgivings turning out to be true. While emotionally painful, the exposure of bigamy in each narrative reveals the depth of the gaslighting to which the female protagonist has been subjected by her putative husband, and in Olivia's case, it reveals how her reading of Augustus as motivated by racist impulses was correct from the start.

Rhoda's "Perfect Contentment"

Much like *The Woman of Colour* before it, *Vanity Fair* presents a mixed-race Black heiress being gaslit by a white suitor and their family — in fact, another father-son duo takes center stage. Moving within a Regency-era society marked by intense racial awareness and prejudice, Rhoda Swartz nevertheless encounters white characters who insist to her face that they meet her with nothing but color-blind acceptance. The Osborne family implies to Rhoda that no thought of her race has ever crossed their minds, but they are, in fact, obsessed with her Blackness; they see it as the feature that makes her enormous fortune potentially attainable to them. The Misses Osbornes quickly befriend Rhoda with this aim in mind ("what a match for George she'd be" [207]), while Mr. Osborne asks her to dine with the family and insists upon his home as a particularly hospitable place for the young émigré: "You won't find…that splendour and rank to which you are accustomed at the West End, my dear Miss, at our humble mansion in Russell Square. . . . You'll find us . . . a plain table, a plain people, but a warm welcome, my dear Miss Rhoda — Rhoda, let me say, for my heart warms to you, it does really. I'm a frank man, and I like you" (206). Much as Augustus does with Olivia, Mr. Osborne plays the gallant to Rhoda's face but speaks differently behind her back. When she is not present, he not only fetishizes her mixed-race appearance and makes clear that he understands that her Blackness is the "price" that his family will have to pay to access her fortune, but he also suggests that Rhoda might even be willing to accept *him* — a man old enough to be her father — instead of his handsome young son. With a "knowing grin, and coarse laugh," he tells Will Dobbin, "'Gad, if Miss S. will have me, I'm her man. *I* aint particular about a shade or so of tawny" (229). Here, Mr. Osborne reveals his previously welcoming conduct to be an attempt to gaslight Rhoda into believing that she has entered a space in which her race has no bearing on her reception when, in fact, it conditions every aspect of her treatment.

The true object of Rhoda's interest, George, participates in the same kind of gaslighting that his father does, pretending to be unconscious of the racial dynamics of their relationship, even as, when she is absent, he mocks and stigmatizes her on that basis. Whereas his father treats Rhoda as his social superior and then makes clear privately that he thinks she is sexually available to any white British man willing to marry her, George acts as if he is courting her, but, to others, characterizes the potential connection as the ultimate degradation: "Marry that mulatto woman?" he snorts to his father; "I don't like the colour, sir. Ask the black that sweeps opposite Fleet Market, sir. *I'm* not going to marry a Hottentot Venus" (214). "The Hottentot Venus," as Moya Bailey explains, was "a young Khosian woman" named Sarah Baartman who "was displayed throughout Europe to paying white audiences as an example of the animalistic and inferior nature of the African woman" in the early nineteenth century.[22] Bailey specifically connects Baartman to the origins of misogynoir, arguing that she serves as a key example of how Black women have long borne the compound effects of "racist and sexualized violence."[23] Through this figuring of Rhoda as "a Hottentot Venus" who cannot compare to his white fiancée Amelia, George convinces himself to go through with his long-delayed marriage to the latter. Much like Olivia, Rhoda never really stands a chance with her white love interest because his biases predispose him toward the rival he perceives as the angelic English foil to her dark outsider. And much like Augustus, George hides his racial antipathy from Rhoda and reflexively manipulates her perception of reality. Although George and his father are at odds regarding Rhoda's role in their lives, they are united in their efforts to convince her that racism does not shape her reception in Russell Square, even when it absolutely does.

Nevertheless, the ironic, comic framing of Rhoda complicates any reading of her presentation; she is, for instance, both a device through which George Osborne's hypocritical racism is critiqued (we learn, for example, that despite his racial rejection of Rhoda, he had a "liaison" with "that beautiful quadroon girl, Miss Pye, at St Vincent's" [123]) and the vehicle through which Thackeray skewers Mr. Osborne's money-grubbing. The novel is clearly satirizing George and Mr. Osborne for the crudeness and hypocrisy that their treatment of Rhoda reveals; however, despite this critique of these characters, the narrator of *Vanity Fair* is complicit in the misogynoirist gaslighting of Rhoda as well. The narrator presents Rhoda as completely oblivious to the racism that surrounds her, suggesting that she is fooled by the machinations of people like the Osbornes. In one description after another, the narrator portrays Rhoda as overconfident in Russell Square due to her great wealth and as oblivious to the racist scorn of her "friends." In a marked contrast to Olivia's keen awareness of British prejudice, Rhoda, overdressed and overladen, is said to possess "perfect contentment" and to sit in their company "thinking herself charming," even when the narrator determines that she looks "about as elegantly decorated as a she chimney-sweep on May day" (209). The idea, of course, that Rhoda, as a Black woman in Regency England, could miss the racism of this society is absurd, as Olivia's experiences in *The Woman of Colour* and the historical record make clear (for instance, presumably Sarah Baartman would have been as culturally visible to Rhoda as she was to George, if not more so).

In this way, rather than revealing that the misogynoir of British society makes it difficult for a mixed-race heiress such as Rhoda to find security in its ranks, the narrator instead insists that she holds all the power in her relationship to it, even as, simultaneously, he depicts her as debased and debasing. As Brody writes, *Vanity Fair* presents Rhoda as "an object that is more abject than [the main characters'] corrupt values. They may be immoral, but she is hopelessly and permanently hybrid."[24] From the moment the narrator introduces Rhoda in chapter one, he hyperfixates on her phenotypically Black features, an impression reinforced by her name itself, which is a cognate for "schwarz," the German word for "black," suggesting that her Blackness is ultimately her defining attribute. He also associates her African ancestry with mental and emotional weakness; he designates her first as "woolly-haired," then as "woolly-headed," both derogatory descriptors Europeans applied to Black people since at least the eighteenth century.[25] In this scene, the narrator suggests that Rhoda is emotionally unstable and constitutionally hysterical: "and as for Miss Swartz . . . on the day Amelia went away, she was in such a passion of tears that they were obliged to send for Dr. Floss, and half tipsify her with salvolatile" (4–5). Later, the novel casts Rhoda as not only temperamental but also unintelligent. George Osborne points out that despite the extended time she has spent at Miss Pinkerton's, "you should see the hand she writes! Mrs. Colonel Haggistoun usually writes her letters, but in a moment of confidence, she put pen to paper for my sisters; she spelt satin satting, and Saint James's, Saint Jams'" (204). From this description, Amelia immediately recognizes her old classmate. This characterization suggests that the narrator's slip in chapter one from describing Rhoda as "woolly-haired" to "woolly-headed" is no accident; while "woolly-headed" was a synonym for "woolly-haired" in the early Victorian period, it was also emerging as a term for "dull-witted."[26] When it comes to George's marital prospects, the narrator indicates that clumsy, dim, indecently wealthy Rhoda embodies the worldly self-abasement demanded by Vanity Fair; in comparison, while Amelia may herself be silly and certainly no genius, at least she is pretty and white. Mr. Osborne insists that his son marry Rhoda; George refuses, rendering him, within the logic of the narration, briefly heroic due to his loyalty to Amelia, although it is a heroism undercut by the irony of Thackeray's tragicomedy and Rhoda's debased positioning. Through Rhoda's racialized lack of desirability, the narrator makes George's sacrifice for his long-suffering fiancée both noble and ridiculous: he is finally doing the right thing by Amelia, but he is only inspired to do so because of Rhoda's bathetic comparison.

Here, the narrator's complicity in the racial gaslighting of Rhoda begins to blend into one that Thackeray, as the author, ultimately also facilitates. At times, it is difficult to tell the difference not only between the racist views of the characters and those of the narrator, but between the narrator and the author as well. Take, for example, a scene in which George's racial disgust with Rhoda seems to mirror the narrator's own feelings about her character. When the narrator mocks Rhoda's appearance as she sits in the Osborne drawing room in Russell Square, his words lead straight into George's own strikingly similar reflections:

> Poor Swartz was seated in a place where Emmy had been accustomed to sit. Her bejewelled hands lay sprawling in her amber satin lap. Her tags and ear-rings twinkled, and her big eyes rolled about. She was doing nothing with perfect content-ment, and thinking herself charming. Anything so becoming as the satin the sisters had never seen.
>
> "Dammy," George said to a confidential friend, "she looked like a China doll, which has nothing to do all day but to grin and wag its head. By Jove, Will, it was all I could do to prevent myself from throwing the sofa-cushion at her." (209)

Here, George expresses real animus toward Rhoda's presence at Russell Square, suggesting that his racist rejection of her extends beyond his resistance to his father's matchmaking. With his use of the term "confidential friend" and the name "Will," Thackeray suggests a continuity between character, narrator, and author. While Thackeray could intend to indicate here that George is speaking to William Dobbin, his best friend, he also leaves open the possibility that George is speaking to himself, William Makepeace Thackeray. The conflation of Thackeray, the author, with *Vanity Fair*'s omniscient narrator is further supported by Thackeray's illustration of the narrator at the end of chapter nine, which scholars regard as a self-portrait (91n4). Through this alignment of narrator and author, the text suggests that not only does the narrator share George's racist sentiments and subsequent investment in gaslighting Rhoda, but that Thackeray himself does, too.

The paratext of the novel, particularly Thackeray's own caricatured illustrations of Rhoda, provides an even starker reinforcement of his sympathy with George's and the narrator's misogynoirist views (see figs. 5.1 and 5.2). Much like the narration, these images present Rhoda as buffoonish and inelegant, but they also show how this characterization ultimately stems from her authorial creator's racism. For instance, in the narration, Thackeray describes her to be ludicrously overladen with finery — she wears "turquoise-bracelets, countless rings, flowers, feathers, and all sorts of tags and gimcracks" (209). In the illustrations, however, she wears some jewelry — in the first image, a few bracelets, a necklace, and a headdress; in the second, you can also see a pair of earrings — but it is hardly the ludicrous mélange sketched by the narration (she appears, for instance, in no rings or flowers). Instead, in these two images, her physical attributes are exaggerated in ways that recall the anti-Black caricatures of the era, suggesting that what is really ridiculous to the author is not her dress, but rather her mere presence at Russell Square. The drawings also appear to covertly echo George's reference to Sarah Baartman and the silhouette, specifically her putatively large posterior, that inspired so many "comparison[s] between her body and that of the white women who viewed her."[27] Deborah Thomas has argued that the illustration of Miss Swartz "rehearsing for the drawing room" (fig. 5.1) invites the reader to compare the "artificial" bustle of Miss Osborne to "that of Miss Swartz," which "consists largely of herself" and "seems designed to direct a knowing reader's attention to the question of what lies beneath the 'polite' surface of Miss Swartz's dress."[28] The illustrations provide yet another racist vantage point from which Miss Swartz is viewed in *Vanity Fair*, this time belonging to the author/illustrator himself — ultimately, like George, Thackeray sees Rhoda as a "Hottentot Venus." In this way, Thackeray gaslights the reader, too; we are able to perceive the obvious misogynoir of Thackeray's characterization, even as he implicitly suggests that such prejudices do not taint his razor-sharp satire of Vanity Fair.

As these illustrations reinforce, when Rhoda is derided for her attire in *Vanity Fair*, it isn't actually her clothing or jewelry that is at issue — it is her Blackness. When George describes Rhoda's presentation at court to Amelia, this slippage between sartorial critique and racist commentary reveals itself baldly: "'You should have seen her dress for court, Emmy,' Osborne cried, laughing. . . . 'Diamonds and mahogany, my dear! think what an advantageous contrast — and the white feathers in her hair — *I mean in her wool*'" (204; emphasis mine). In this moment and others like it, Amelia rises higher in George's estimation by being positioned against her mixed-race alternative. Despite the Mertons' and Osbornes' repeated insistence that they are not racist, that Olivia's and Rhoda's Blackness does not serve to stigmatize or downgrade them in their eyes, the plot trajectory of each novel proves otherwise: neither Olivia Fairfield nor Rhoda Swartz is perceived by the racist characters around her to be anywhere near as "desirable" (meaning, in this context, as "marriageable") as her white English counterpart.

Therefore, in both texts, the romance between the white hero and his white wife is cast as the emotionally pure, economically disinterested relationship, the one pitted against a debased, interracial, mercenary union. It is perhaps here that we uncover a key motivation for these white characters' insistence on the absence of racism in their society. The misogynoirist gaslighting of Olivia and Rhoda sustains a narrative (even if, in *Vanity Fair*, one steeped in irony) in which the white couple's marriage represents the triumph of true affection over a corruptly capitalist society — a narrative that is harder to sustain if racism is acknowledged to be a key element drawing the couple together. However,

Figure 5.1. From chapter 21 of *Vanity Fair* (1847–1848), this image shows Rhoda Swartz attended by the Osborne sisters, who prepare her for an encounter with George in their drawing room. Illustration by W. M. Thackeray. *Source*: *Vanity Fair*. Bradbury and Evans, 1848.

Figure 5.2. In the second image of Rhoda from chapter 21 of *Vanity Fair*, Thackeray caricatures her piano performance. Illustration by W. M. Thackeray. *Source*: *Vanity Fair*. Bradbury and Evans, 1848.

whereas Olivia emerges from her text as an independent, self-actualized voice who has lived to tell the tale of her own encounter with a misogynoirist society, Rhoda is absorbed within that society's ranks, her "perfect contentment" undisrupted, unquestioned, and silent.

***

The reception histories and relative historical popularity of *A Woman of Colour* and *Vanity Fair* provide helpful context for why misogynoirist gaslighting remains so commonplace — both in Britain and in the United States, in the tabloids and in the lives of ordinary people. *Vanity Fair* was enormously popular from the beginning of its serialization in 1847 and has remained a canonical nineteenth-century novel and British cultural artifact; it has been adapted for film multiple times and has been regularly remade as a miniseries since the 1960s, including in 2018. *The Woman of Colour*, however, was neither widely read nor particularly culturally influential upon its publication; it has never been made into a movie or television series. The novel has become increasingly interesting to scholars — particularly as the contributions of eighteenth- and nineteenth-century authors of color to British literature have finally been given increased attention — but it is still far from having the canonical status of *Vanity Fair*. As a result, Thackeray's biased depiction of Rhoda Swartz has enjoyed far greater circulation than the nuanced portrayal of Olivia Fairfield's short-lived emigration to England. Given this reception history and the legacy of Thackeray's characterization of his mixed-race Black heiress in *Vanity Fair*, it is unsurprising that British culture (re)produced an analogous case of misogynoirist gaslighting in its treatment of Meghan, the Duchess of Sussex. While some might dismiss the tabloid depiction of Meghan as mere celebrity drama, George Osborne's use of the Victorian media portrayal of Sarah Baartman as "the Hottentot Venus" to denigrate Rhoda shows how racist depictions of famous Black women have long been used to forward misogynoir — and misogynoirist gaslighting — in everyday life.

Notes

1. *Harry & Meghan*, Episode 6. Meghan is widely known by her maiden name, Meghan Markle, but now prefers to go by her married name, Meghan Sussex (*With Love, Meghan*, Episode 2). For clarity, I call her "Meghan" in this essay.
2. *CBS Mornings*, "Harry and Meghan."
3. Davis and Ernst, "Racial Gaslighting," 761.
4. Davis and Ernst, "Racial Gaslighting," 763.
5. At different points in this chapter, I refer to Olivia and Rhoda as "Black," "mixed-race," and "Black mixed-race heiresses"; these racial identities overlap, intersect, and take prominence for Olivia and Rhoda at different moments in their texts. I have adopted Victoria Baugh's term "mixed-race heiress" from her article on this figure in early nineteenth-century novels and especially Jane Austen's *Sanditon* ("Mixed-Race Heiresses," 450). I use "mixed-race" and "Black mixed-race" because Olivia's and Rhoda's multiracial identities are highly salient to how they are depicted in these texts. For instance, "person of color" itself was an eighteenth- and nineteenth-century term in the Caribbean and Britain for people of both European and African ancestry; the choice by the author of *The Woman of Colour* to use this descriptor as the title of the novel indicates the importance placed on Olivia's mixed-race identity in the text. In both *The Woman of Colour* and *Vanity Fair*, Olivia and Rhoda conceptualize themselves and are received as mixed-race, and their cultural hybridity — which encompasses their Caribbean, British, African (and, in Rhoda's case, Jewish) roots — plays into how white British men gaslight them. Furthermore, Olivia's and Rhoda's presentations as mixed-race tap into Victorian-era fears about miscegenation and the moral and racial contagion presented by the colonies (Brody, *Impossible Purities*, 16; Reed, "Moving Fortunes," 513). That said, while their mixed-race identities are crucial to their characterizations, they are also very much perceived and experience the worlds of their novels as Black women. To this point, Olivia's story can be read within a broader transatlantic history of Black resistance and within the Black Radical Tradition, as Aljoe, Sinanan, and Wassif argue in the introduction to their recent cluster of essays on *The Woman of Colour* ("Introduction," 8).
6. Davis and Ernst, "Racial Gaslighting," 771.
7. Bailey, *Misogynoir Transformed*, 1.
8. For more on the figure of the mixed-race heiress in nineteenth-century fiction, see Baugh, "Mixed-Race Heiresses" and Dominique, introduction to *Woman of Colour*.
9. Anonymous, *Woman of Colour*, 188. Further references to this text will be cited parenthetically.
10. Livesay, *Children of Uncertain Fortune*, 349-50.

11. Dominique, "Introduction," 32.
12. Thackeray, *Vanity Fair*, 4, 204. Further references to this text will be cited parenthetically.
13. Brody, *Impossible Purities*, 27.
14. Brody, *Impossible Purities*, 27–28. Brody takes inspiration in her construction here of the "'socially marginal but symbolically significant'" from Peter Stallybrass and Allon White's *The Politics and Poetics of Transgression* and its thinking about social hierarchy, specifically their discussion of how "what is *socially* peripheral is so frequently *symbolically* central" (5).
15. Brody, *Impossible Purities*, 30.
16. Abramson, "Turning Up the Lights on Gaslighting," 13.
17. Crenshaw, "Mapping the Margins," 1282.
18. Livesay, *Children of Uncertain Fortune*, 69–70.
19. Livesay, *Children of Uncertain Fortune*, 69.
20. Livesay, *Children of Uncertain Fortune*, 15, 40–42, 87.
21. Yu, "August Disgust," 109–10.
22. Bailey, *Misogynoir Transformed*, xi.
23. Bailey, *Misogynoir Transformed*, xi.
24. Brody, *Impossible Purities*, 29.
25. *OED*, s.v. "woolly," (*adj.*), sense 3.b"; *OED*, s.v. "woolly-headed, adj., sense b."
26. *OED*, s.v. "woolly-headed, adj., sense c."
27. Bailey, *Misogynoir Transformed*, xi.
28. Thomas, "Miss Swartz," 3–5.

Bibliography

Abramson, Kate. "Turning Up the Lights on Gaslighting." *Philosophical Perspectives* 28 (2014): 1–30.

Aljoe, Nicole N., Kerry Sinanan, and Mariam Wassif. Introduction to "New Essays on *The Woman of Colour*." *Eighteenth-Century Fiction* 35, no. 1 (2023): 1–26.

Anonymous. *The Woman of Colour: A Tale*. Edited by Lyndon J. Dominique. Broadview Press, 2008.

Bailey, Moya. *Misogynoir Transformed: Black Women's Digital Resistance*. New York University Press, 2021.

Baugh, Victoria. "Mixed-Race Heiresses in Early-Nineteenth-Century Literature: *Sanditon*'s Miss Lambe in Context." *European Romantic Review* 29, no. 4 (2018): 449–58.

Brody, Jennifer DeVere. *Impossible Purities: Blackness, Femininity, and Victorian Culture*. Duke University Press, 1998.

CBS Mornings. "Harry and Meghan on how race factored into their U.K. press coverage." March 8, 2021. https://www.youtube.com/watch?v=Tl9KT9RwiGc.

Crenshaw, Kimberlé. "Mapping the Margins: Intersectionality, Identity Politics, and Violence against Women of Color." *Stanford Law Review* 43, no. 6 (1991): 1241–99.

Davis, Angelique M., and Rose Ernst. "Racial Gaslighting." *Politics, Groups, and Identities* 7, no. 4 (2019): 761–74.

Dominique, Lyndon J. "Introduction" to *The Woman of Colour: A Tale*. Broadview Press, 2008.

Harry & Meghan, 1, 6, "Episode 6," aired December 15, 2022, *Netflix*.

Livesay, Daniel. *Children of Uncertain Fortune: Mixed-Race Jamaicans in Britain and the Atlantic Family, 1733–1833*. University of North Carolina Press, 2018.

Oxford English Dictionary. "woolly (*adj*,), sense 3.b." March 2025. https://doi.org/10.1093/OED/6569999787.

Oxford English Dictionary. "woolly-headed (*adj*.), sense b." September 2024. https://doi.org/10.1093/OED/1558932763.

Reed, Jennifer. "Moving Fortunes: Caribbean Women's Marriage, Mobility, and Money in the Novel of Sentiment." *Eighteenth-Century Fiction* 31, no. 3 (2019): 509–28.

Stallybrass, Peter, and Allon White. *The Politics and Poetics of Transgression*. Cornell University Press, 1986.

Thackeray, William Makepeace. *Vanity Fair*. Edited by Peter Shillingsburg. Norton, 1994.

Thomas, Deborah A. "Miss Swartz and the Hottentot Venus Revisited." *Thackeray Newsletter* 36 (1992): 3–5.

With Love, Meghan, 2, "Welcome to the Party," aired March 4, 2025, *Netflix*.

Yu, Daniel. "August Disgust: Distinction, Disinterest, and Race in *The Woman of Colour*." *Eighteenth-Century Fiction* 35, no. 1 (2023): 103–11.

6

Charles Dickens as Gaslighter

A Tale of Two Catherines

Katherine J. Kim

In 2019, John Bowen published new archival research that detailed how Charles Dickens tried to commit his wife Catherine to an insane asylum. Various news organizations and websites around the world pounced on the story, several of which ascribed a particular term to the attempted (though foiled) plot: both Lila Thulin in *Smithsonian Magazine* and Kartikeya Shankar in the *Times of India* proclaimed it to be an example of Dickens "actually gaslighting" his wife, while Catherine Bennet went so far as to title her article on the subject in *The Observer* "'Barking Mad' . . . How Dickens Led to Our Modern Gaslighting Men."[1] Dickens, the renowned and revered author of novels such as *Oliver Twist* (1837–1839), *Great Expectations* (1860–1861), and *A Tale of Two Cities* (1859), was also now publicly declared a gaslighter.

While Dickens may not have been trying to make Catherine feel as if she were losing her mind in the same way that Jack Manningham does to his wife Bella in Patrick Hamilton's 1938 play *Gas Light*, his efforts are nonetheless linked to gaslighting in that he tried to make *others* believe she was insane. This type of gaslighting was first discussed in a 1969 article by Russell Barton and J. A. Whitehead, who coined the phrase "Gas-Light Phenomenon" — derived, they acknowledge, from Hamilton's "classic piece of 20th century victoriana [*sic*]" — to describe real-life "plots to remove an unwanted and restricting relative by securing admission to a mental hospital."[2] In the same vein, Dickens tried to rid himself of his "unwanted" wife via wrongful institutionalization; as a literary celebrity, his gaslighting "plot" involved weaponizing his cultural authority to manipulate public opinion.

It is worth noting that Dickens's attempt to consign his wife to an asylum, as well as his often-harmful treatment and discussions of women, are not recent discoveries. While the evidence Bowen presents (in the form of letters he found in the archives of Harvard University) reinforces prior assertions, information about Dickens's attempt has been known since the nineteenth century. Further, Dickens's actions in this case do not stand in stark contrast to his behaviors toward several other women in his personal and professional circles, including, as this chapter highlights, the once popular and respected author Catherine

Crowe. Yet the legal system, Dickens's position as an influential writer and publisher, his public persona as a philanthropist and an advocate for marginalized figures (including those in insane asylums), and the immense devotion of his readers over the years have contributed to the image of Dickens as a gaslighter being dismissed, refuted, and buried. The following analysis draws connections between Dickens's treatment of his wife and his treatment of Crowe, thus demonstrating a pattern of behavior that extends beyond his efforts to incarcerate his wife. The tale of these two Catherines — very different women with very different relationships to Dickens — shows how Dickens employed various gaslighting tactics in his attempts to publicly humiliate both women and dissociate himself from them. His actions against the two Catherines consequently reveal an image of Dickens that conflicts with the public one he crafted during his lifetime.

"Personal" and "Private": Dickens's Public Narrative about Catherine Dickens

Catherine Dickens's mother Georgina Hogarth and aunt Helen Thomson appear to have wanted Catherine to receive a judicial separation once her marriage fell apart irrevocably in 1858. In a letter that Thomson wrote to a close friend, she expresses outrage at Dickens's behavior and insists that Catherine would have "borne her trials," but once matters were "brought to an extremity," her family felt that she should agree to a separation.[3] While it is unclear if one specific event triggered Dickens's initiation of the separation, scholarly consensus holds that his infatuation with the teenage actress Ellen Ternan, whom he met in 1857, along with his growing distaste for Catherine's weight gain and fertility (they had ten children), was key.[4] However, Dickens's infidelity would not have been sufficient reason for a court-granted legal separation or divorce. The Matrimonial Causes Act of 1857 provided some women means to receive a secular (not ecclesiastical) separation or divorce, but as Robin Bolivar explains, the divorce standards were high, especially for women: "While a husband could obtain a divorce for mere adultery," a wife had to prove her husband to be guilty of either "incestuous adultery, bigamy combined with adultery, rape, sodomy, bestiality, adultery combined with cruelty, [or] adultery with two years' desertion."[5] A legal divorce request by Catherine would have led to embarrassment and public scrutiny of herself and her children. Consequently, she entered into unofficial separation negotiations.[6]

Yet, Dickens wanted to wield power over both the separation and its public appearance, and he did so by essentially holding his children, his funds, and the reputations of Catherine's family members ransom. Once rumors about Dickens having an affair with either Ternan or his sister-in-law Georgina Hogarth were circulating too much to ignore, Dickens turned to print to impose control. Dickens forced Catherine and her family to attach their names to public statements absolving Ternan of any wrongdoing by obliquely blaming themselves before he would continue separation negotiations. Indeed, Catherine's aunt records Dickens's insistence that he would only proceed if Catherine's "parents and sister Helen consented to sign their names to a paper he drew up" in which they would "acquit" him of having done "anything immoral" and deny "that any woman had anything to do with his separation."[7] They agreed to do so to move the separation along, but only after "many tears and sleepless nights"; ultimately, Catherine's family members' knowledge of "the stubborn and unyielding temper of her husband" caused them to "los[e] all hope of bringing things to a proper issue, unless concessions were made."[8] In addition, Dickens used his pulpit of *Household Words* to put forth a narrative of Catherine's lack of motherly and wifely abilities and her mental ailments.[9] His first statement, titled "Personal" and blazoned on the front of the June 12, 1858, issue (as well as earlier in *The Times* on the seventh), asserts "both in [his] own name and in [his] wife's name" that rumors about unnamed persons close to him (and thus implicitly him) were false.[10] Admitting to "domestic trouble" of "a sacredly private nature," Dickens writes that "this trouble has been made the occasion of misrepresentations, most grossly false, most monstrous, and most cruel — involving, not only me, but innocent persons dear to my heart."[11] Yet, for Dickens, the "innocent persons dear" to him do not include his wife of over two decades.

Even before publishing this statement, to which Catherine must have objected initially since she sent the copy Dickens gave her to a solicitor to prevent its publication, Dickens laid the groundwork for discrediting dissenting voices and generating doubts about his wife's wellness. On May 25, 1858, while their settlement was still being disputed, Dickens sent a letter to his readings manager, Arthur Smith, with instructions to show it to others. What Dickens called "the violated letter" then appeared in the *New York Daily Tribune* on August 16, 1858. In it, Dickens asserts that he and Catherine had "lived unhappily together for many years," had become "wonderfully unsuited to each other," and had relied on Catherine's sister Georgina Hogarth to raise their children and maintain their home.[12] While claiming to show "manly consideration" for his wife, he writes that a "peculiarity of [Catherine's] character has thrown all the children on someone else" and that "for some years past [she] has been in the habit of representing to me that it would be better for her to go away and live apart; that her always increasing estrangement was due to a mental disorder under which she sometimes labors — more, that she felt herself unfit for the life she had to lead as my wife, and that she would be better far away."[13] He then goes on to say that in spite of Catherine's desire to leave the home, until recently he had been insisting they remain together for the sake of their children, for whom she supposedly lacked maternal feeling. Furthermore, Dickens claims that the terms of the financial settlement he offered to Catherine were "as generous as if Mrs. Dickens were a lady of distinction, and I a man of fortune."[14] While pushing the false narrative of Catherine as mentally disturbed and as a bad housekeeper, wife, and mother, Dickens casts himself in a righteously "manly," financially "generous" light and blames Catherine for their marital breakdown.

Along with such public claims against the woman with whom he had long been happily married (as letters of his and his acquaintances' recollections attest), Dickens began attempting to rewrite history through personal letters.[15] In May 1858, for example, he wrote to their mutual friend Angela Burdett-Coutts:

> If the children loved her, or ever had loved her, this severance would have been a far easier thing than it is. But she has never attached one of them to herself, never played with them in their infancy, never attracted their confidence as they have grown older, never presented herself before them in the aspect of a mother. I have seen them fall off from her in a natural — not *un*natural — progress of estrangement, and at this moment I believe that Mary and Katey (whose dispositions are of the gentlest and most affectionate conceivable) harden into stone figures of girls when they can be got to go near her. . . . Her mind has, at times, been certainly confused besides.[16]

On both public and private fronts, then, Dickens was working hard in the late 1850s to paint Catherine as a distant, unattached, unloving, and mentally "confused" wife and mother.

In reality, Catherine never seems to have experienced serious mental illness at any point in her life and was, according to most (non-Dickens) accounts, an adept housekeeper and, more importantly, a loving and beloved mother; indeed, as John Sutherland has quipped, she "seems to have been remarkably sane."[17] One source of evidence that pointedly undermines Dickens's claims about Catherine is the series of interviews with their daughter, Kate Perugini, that Gladys Storey conducted and published in 1939. According to Kate:

> There came a day when, out of the combined efforts of [Catherine's] sister [Georgina Hogarth] and Mr. John Forster, to facilitate matters for the supposed comfort of Charles, a triangle evolved, in which Mrs. Dickens formed no part. So that incidents connected with the children and the home requiring consideration and adjustment were frequently settled by one or other of these two, in conference with the master of the house, without any reference to the mistress of it, who, in the natural sensitiveness of her refined nature, suffered exquisitely under this treatment; this led to many misunderstandings and muddles; and later to the accusation, by Miss Hogarth, that she threw the responsibility of her children upon others. An accusation as unkind as it was untrue.[18]

Kate presents a strikingly different portrait of life in the Dickens household than the one her father so vociferously described to friends and strangers around the time of his separation from her mother.

Dickens's endeavors to spread false rumors about Catherine succeeded to some extent. For instance, *Frank Leslie's Illustrated Newspaper* lamented that Dickens "endured his wife for twenty-five years" but could do so no longer, as Catherine was "constitutionally indolent and unintellectual" along with having "a tendency to corpulency, which is very disgusting to a man of elegant tastes, or one who has much company at home, since it materializes the head of his table, and converts the high priestess of the repast into the fattest joint on the board."[19] However, his actions also backfired. The *Liverpool Mercury* asserted that Dickens's language and disclosure of Catherine's possible mental and maternal failures showed the very opposite of the "manly consideration" he had boasted of: "If this is 'manly consideration' we should like to be favoured with a definition of unmanly selfishness and heartlessness."[20] An *Aberdeen Free Press* article declared "incompatibility" to be an insufficient reason for separation and Dickens's claims to the contrary to be "proof" of his "moral cowardice."[21] Private sympathy for Catherine existed as well. After the publication of "the violated letter," for example, Elizabeth Barrett Browning mentioned in a private letter, "What a dreadful letter that was! And what a crime for a man to use his genius as a cudgel . . . against the woman he promised to protect tenderly with life and heart — taking advantage of his hold with the public to turn public opinion against her."[22] Furthermore, the fact that Burdett-Coutts, according to Catherine's aunt Helen Thomson, invited Catherine to live with her "before matters were settled" — and after receiving Dickens's letter excoriating her — indicates that some people close to the couple who did not rely heavily on Dickens's power and influence over the public and the publishing world were willing to support Catherine.[23]

A letter from Helen Thomson to her friend Mrs. Stark reveals that Dickens went beyond merely asserting that Catherine suffered mentally: "I think it only right to contradict [Dickens's] statement, to such a friend as you; he did indeed endeavour to get the physician who attended her in illness, to sanction such a report, when he sternly refused, saying he considered Mrs. Dickens perfectly sound in mind, consequently he dared not in England assert anything of the kind."[24] Though Thomson's letter was copied and eventually circulated, Bowen explains that many people, including literary scholars, "dismissed it as fraudulent," with the exception of K. J. Fielding, who "showed in 1955 that it was not, and that we could give it authority as one of the fullest contemporary accounts of Dickens's behaviour."[25] Despite the existence of a letter describing Dickens's marital malfeasance written by someone intimately connected to the Dickenses, it was only after a male authority figure validated the letter's authenticity that resistance to viewing Dickens as a callous adulterer who falsely accused his wife of mental illness began to dissolve.

Perhaps, the thinking may have gone, Dickens deserved the same kind of sympathy that he asked his readers to feel for fictional characters in his novels like Stephen Blackpool, a factory worker who cannot divorce his mentally disturbed, alcoholic wife in *Hard Times* (1854). Whatever the reasoning, there is certainly a robust body of biographical scholarship that strives to read Dickens's treatment of Catherine in the most innocuous and sympathetic light possible. One case in point comes from John Sutherland, who concludes,

> [it] is extremely unlikely that Dickens intended to incarcerate Catherine. It is equally unlikely that he wanted to alienate her permanently from her children. What he may have intended was . . . to "show her the instruments." Give her and her mother a terrifying glimpse, that is, of what he might do, if she were to bring Ellen Ternan's name into play, or not join with him in putting down the outrageous allegations of incest with Georgina. . . . Within a few days, in early June, Catherine agreed to the terms of the separation.[26]

Hence, even though Helen Thomson's letter was (for the most part) not accepted as valid for nearly a century, Dickens's word, even while in the midst of contentious separation settlement negotiations, was (for the most part) considered truthful. This can be read as a secondary form of gaslighting, with scholars and other readers implicitly accusing Catherine of mental illness while seeing Dickens as a long-suffering husband.

It was only after Bowen released his newfound research in 2019 that a stronger belief in Dickens's attempt to commit Catherine developed. Such increased belief may partially have resulted from greater cultural awareness of the concept of "gaslighting" in the second decade of the twenty-first century. Bowen discovered that journalist Edward Dutton Cook, once Dickens's protégé and later Catherine's neighbor and close friend, wrote on January 7, 1879 to William Moy Thomas that Catherine "had outgrown [Dickens's] liking. She had borne ten children and had lost many of her good looks, was growing old, in fact. He even tried to shut her up in a lunatic asylum, poor thing! But bad as the law is in regard to proof of insanity he could not quite wrest it to his purpose."[27] Three days after Catherine's death on November 22, 1879, moreover, Cook admitted, "I feel that it was rather cowardly in me to shrink from writing about poor Mrs D. but the difficulty was great. I could not say what I thought just without offending the family. I made the attempt, as you will see by the enclosed. But I could not satisfy myself that it was wise to publish it: I withheld the little notice and consoled myself that I have been discreet if not valorous or upright."[28] Cook's enclosed statement has been lost;[29] however, Cook clearly felt conflicted about making information about Dickens's attempt public.

There were no laws governing a wife's madhouse committal before the 1774 Madhouse Act, but Robin Bolivar explains that in trying to regulate consignments, the act legitimized the "madhouse divorce" in which individuals could become virtually free of a spouse and take control of the couple's finances. The Insane Persons Act (1828) required "an Order and a Medical Certificate signed by two doctors who had examined the patient separately and personally. However, this procedure applied only to people who did not or could not hold property, such as married women" under the legal doctrine of coverture, which subsumed a wife's legal existence into her husband's.[30] After the passing of the 1845 Lunacy Act, physicians needed "to specify the factual underpinnings for the specific cases of certified insanity" rather than simply sign certificates.[31] Despite these amendments, by the time of the Dickenses' separation, a husband could relatively easily hide his wife in an asylum or a home acting as a private asylum. To release such a patient, the person who consigned her needed to request her release, or the Commissioners in Lunacy needed to confirm her sanity on two separate visits. However, such visits only occurred four times a year, meaning that a sane person could spend months wrongfully confined.[32] Additionally, some doctors failed to register single private patients, "[abusive] attendants blacklisted at asylums were often employed to guard wealthy single patients," and some patients were even "confined on the mere say-so of parents."[33] The threat of committal was more dangerous to women than men, as the "breadth of female behaviour considered insanity meant that it was an easy task to get the certification that the law required."[34] Frigidity, sexual desire, anger, aggression, and strong-mindedness could all be evidence for declaring a woman insane since they deviated from normative expectations for Victorian women.[35]

Due to the difficulty and expensiveness of acquiring a divorce, women's weak status in English law, and the relative ease of consigning someone to an insane asylum, there were many actual and fictional stories of committals for wrongful reasons that received wide attention. For instance, Louisa Nottidge, whose experience inspired Dickens's friend Wilkie Collins's *The Woman in White* (1859–1860), was committed in 1846 because she joined a millenarian sect of which her family disapproved. She was released in 1848 and famously succeeded in suing her brother and brother-in-law for the part they played in her confinement.[36] Georgina Weldon (who received Dickens's former residence, Tavistock House, in her marriage separation settlement) evaded capture by doctors sent by her husband and went on to expose lunacy law abuses.[37] Such real-life tales captivated the public because, as Joshua John Schwieso explains, "[wrongful] confinement had all the makings of a *cause célèbre*, combining, as it did, the themes of fraud perpetrated by family members who, of all people, should have been most caring, professional negligence or corruption on the part of the doctors who certified the victims, and horror at the thought of a sane person 'buried alive' amongst the insane."[38]

Dickens was hardly alone among his friends and peers when it came to weaponizing claims of insanity. One of the most infamous connections Dickens has to wrongful consignment stems from his friendship with Edward Bulwer-Lytton. Bulwer-Lytton had previously abused his wife Rosina and unsuccessfully tried to convince her to confess to adultery so they could divorce, even though he was the adulterer.[39] After their separation, he was frequently late with settlement payments; exercised his paternal right of custody over their children;

used his power and influence as an acclaimed writer, a baron, and a member of Parliament to undermine Rosina's literary career; and had Rosina spied on to collect evidence to commit her.[40] The enraged Rosina, who blamed Bulwer-Lytton for their daughter's death in a boardinghouse, did what she could to shame him privately and publicly.[41] She even threatened to interrupt a fund-raising event for his and Dickens's Guild of Literature and Art, which sought to create an "asylum" for poor artists. Dickens was so concerned that detectives stood at the doors in case Rosina appeared.[42]

On June 8, 1858, within a month of Dickens disseminating claims of Catherine's mental difficulties, Rosina interrupted an event during which Bulwer-Lytton was vying for reelection to Parliament. In response, Bulwer-Lytton, Dickens's intimate friend and biographer John Forster, and others conspired to have her kidnapped and committed. After public outcry, and due to the paperwork being questionable (she was not a drunk and her parents did not die insane, as the documents claimed), Bulwer-Lytton negotiated to have Rosina released and given an altered settlement in exchange for an end to her harassment of him. On July 17, 1858, Rosina was released. However, once Bulwer-Lytton began breaking their settlement terms again, Rosina resumed her verbal attacks.[43] Bulwer-Lytton denied Rosina's recounting of events, yet his denials were proven false through letters in Bulwer-Lytton's own handwriting verifying events such as his biting Rosina and threatening to "ruin" her.[44] Both Dickens and Bulwer-Lytton — two powerful, wealthy, and well-connected men — pushed unfounded claims of their wives' insanity due to their personal desires to be rid of them.

Furthermore, Dickens's attacks on his wife's reputation and mental well-being did not end once their settlement was signed. For instance, Dickens's daughter Kate Perugini revealed to Gladys Storey that Dickens purposely sent her and her sister to music lessons across the street from their mother's post-separation residence, where Catherine would see them from a distance and futilely wait for them to visit.[45] Expressing guilt for participating in the alienation Catherine felt from her children after they legally became Dickens's property and lived exclusively with him (except for the adult Charley, who sided and lived with Catherine), Kate ultimately declared Dickens to be "a wicked man" and admitted that "my poor mother was afraid of my father. She was never allowed to express an opinion — never allowed to say what she felt. . . . We were *all* very wicked not to take her part."[46] Through manipulation and influence, Dickens inflicted mental and emotional cruelty on Catherine. Or, as David K. Holbrook aptly put it, Dickens's "treatment of his wife seems determinedly governed by hatred and misrepresentation."[47]

"Stark mad — and stark naked": Catherine Crowe's Public Humiliation

During the same decade that his marriage with Catherine was dissolving, Dickens was also mistreating another woman in ways that could be called gaslighting: a little-examined author named Catherine Crowe. Situating Crowe alongside Catherine Dickens shows how Dickens's behavior toward his wife was part of a broader effort to gaslight women who challenged his virtuous public persona. Crowe was a popular mid-Victorian writer of novels, short stories, plays, children's literature, compilations, and translations whose popularity rose to the levels of Dickens and Thackeray.[48] In many ways, she was an unorthodox Victorian woman, fleeing from her husband at age forty-seven once her son began attending the Royal Military College. It was during the second half of her life that she began publishing to supplement the income she received after her father's death. By 1848, Dickens began publicly praising her, writing in an *Examiner* review of Crowe's *The Night-Side of Nature* (1848) that "the authoress of *Susan Hopley* and *Lilly Dawson* has established her title to a hearing whenever she chooses to claim one. She can never be read without pleasure or profit, and can never write otherwise than sensibly well."[49] Dickens published three works by Crowe in *Household Words* between 1850 and 1852: "Loaded Dice" (1850), "The Young Advocate" (1850), and "Esther Hammond's Wedding-Day" (1852). Although the two authors were at odds on the topic of Spiritualism (Dickens vocally rejecting it and Crowe keeping an open mind), they for a while were on friendly terms, dined and took walks together, and exchanged letters regarding copyright matters.[50] They also shared a penchant for championing social issues in their works, with Crowe writing about topics like animal cruelty, poverty, the need to abolish slavery, and women's education. Furthermore, Crowe was active in the art world, hosting artist gatherings and maintaining friendships with the likes of Harriet Martineau, the Sharples family, and Thomas De Quincey.[51]

Unfortunately, a medical incident appears to have disrupted both Crowe's career and Dickens's sentiments about her. On February 26, 1854, Crowe suffered an attack of "cerebral congestion," and rumors circulated that she was found roaming the streets of Edinburgh naked (though no firsthand account verifying the event exists). The supposedly hallucinating author was taken by lawyer and friend George Combe to John Conolly, a physician Dickens praised for his humane treatment of the mentally ill. Whatever happened to Crowe appears to have been an isolated occurrence, with Conolly noting that "[when Crowe] came here, her delusions had passed away like a dream."[52]

Although we do not know the exact information Dickens was told regarding Crowe's state, he quickly pounced on rumors about Crowe by circulating and likely embellishing them. On March 7, 1854, Dickens wrote to Reverend James White that Crowe

> has gone stark mad — and stark naked — on the spirit-rapping imposition. She was found t'other day in the street, clothed only in her chastity, a pocket-handkerchief and a visiting card. She had been informed, it appeared, by the spirits, that if she went out in that trim she would be invisible. She is now in a madhouse and, I fear, hopelessly insane. One of the curious manifestations of her disorder is that she can bear nothing black. There is a terrific business to be done, even when they are obliged to put coals on her fire.[53]

Dickens also wrote in a harsh, joking manner two days later to Emile de la Rue the following:

> There is a certain Mrs. Crowe . . . who wrote a book called the Night Side of Nature, and rather a clever story called Susan Hopley. She was a Medium, and an Ass, and I don't know what else. The other day she was discovered walking down her own street in Edinburgh, not only stark mad but stark naked too. She said the spirits had informed her that if she walked out with a card in her right hand and her pocket handkerchief in her left — and nothing else — she would be invisible. But she was not surprised (she added) to find herself visible, because she remembered that in opening the street door, she changed the card into the left hand and the pocket handkerchief into the right! She is now under restraint of course.[54]

In addition to spreading incorrect information (such as stating that Crowe was under restraint) and including details not mentioned in any other known references to the incident (such as Crowe not bearing anything black), Dickens may have either authored or informed a piece in the *Zoist*, a mesmerism and phrenology journal, titled "Another Person Insane through Spirit Fancies."[55] In this article, there appears the phrase "[she] has gone stark mad and stark naked on the spirit-rapping," a phrase suspiciously similar to ones seen in Dickens's letters.[56]

Crowe's popularity never again returned to the heights it reached before her health incident, and Dickens never again published her work. She was also forced to publicly defend herself, writing in the *Daily News*:

> I am very sorry to trouble the public about my private maladies or misfortunes, but since the press has made my late illness the subject of a paragraph, stating that I have gone mad on the subject of spirit rapping, I must beg leave to contradict the assertion. I have been for some time suffering from chronic gastric inflammation; and, after a journey to Edinburgh and a week of considerable fatigue and anxiety, I was taken ill on the 26th of

> February, and was certainly for five or six days — not more — in a state of unconsciousness. During this aberration, I talked of spirit rapping, and fancied spirits were directing me, because the phenomena, so called, have been engaging my attention, and I was writing on the subject; but I was not — and am not — mad about spirits or anything else, thank God! though very much out of health and exceedingly debilitated. I should feel greatly obliged by your insertion of this letter [and] if those journalists who have aided in spreading the erroneous impression will assist in disseminating this corrected statement, which I should have made earlier, but the paragraph did not meet my eye til to-day.[57]

Reading unflattering and false descriptions of her recent health crisis must have been an embarrassing shock. Yet, despite public humiliation, Crowe's friendships remained strong. In fact, researcher Geoffrey Larken notes that the only connection Crowe appears to have lost was her connection to Dickens.[58]

Though we cannot know for sure why Dickens chose to humiliate and gaslight Catherine Crowe, it may have stemmed from the lack of patience he was often seen to have with those whose thoughts or views differed from his own. For example, we know that Crowe became increasingly aligned with Spiritualism (despite calling more for openness to nonnormative ideas, rather than outright acceptance of such beliefs), while Dickens attacked it and favored mesmerism. Nowhere is his anti-Spiritualist vitriol clearer than in his 1866 piece, "Doubtfully Divine Missions": "As to the idle, silly, and credulous persons," he writes, "who are now abasing their intellects under the feet of that grossest of all the impostures — Spiritualism — we wish them no worse than that they may live long enough to see their names blazoned in the next edition of the 'History of Popular Delusions.'"[59] A well-known woman connected to Spiritualism who experienced hallucinations would have been evidence for Spiritualism's perilousness and speciousness in Dickens's mind and likely contributed to his desire to humiliate Catherine Crowe in the wake of her medical episode.

But Crowe may also have been threatening to Dickens due to her willingness to break with certain aspects of Victorian gender norms. In the only published book-length text on Crowe to date, Ruth Heholt deems Crowe radical in her "generic hybridity," pointing out Crowe's ability to combine and bend genres such as mystery and sensation fiction and the Newgate novel, while also providing criticism on topics such as poverty and women's rights.[60] Crowe's tendency to push boundaries socially, artistically, and professionally could have led others, including Dickens, to question her sanity since, as Marianne Camus observes, "it must have been rather easy to look odd, strange[,] or mad when behavioural norms were as strictly defined as they were for Victorian women, especially as women were generally thought to have a very fragile hold on reason."[61] Despite being a popular author who was admired by the likes of George Eliot and George Henry Lewes and who attended William Makepeace

Thackeray's renowned party for Charlotte Brontë, Crowe occasionally raised eyebrows, such as when she and another woman shocked Hans Christian Andersen by volunteering to inhale ether at a party.[62] Additionally, she was willing to face criticism for expressing her belief in a balance between science, religion, and the unknown. In *The Night-Side of Nature*, for example, Crowe asserts:

> Of nature's ordinary laws, we yet know but little; of their aberrations and perturbations, still less. How should we, when the world is a miracle and life a dream, of which we know neither the beginning nor the end! We do not even know that we see anything as it is. . . . We see things but as our visual organs represent them to us; and were those organs differently constructed, the aspect of the world would to us be changed. How, then, can we pretend to decide upon what is and what is not?[63]

In an age when women could easily be deemed insane (and even consigned to a mental institution) for actions or beliefs that challenged those of people in positions of power, Crowe spoke her mind. She did so not to assert authority over others and change their convictions, but rather to suggest possible alternative ways of thinking and seeing that ran counter to convention. Both her writings and her actions attest to Crowe's refusal to adhere to gender norms in the name of insulating herself from accusations of insanity.

***

On June 20, 1837, after the suicide of his illustrator Robert Seymour in 1836 and the sudden death of his beloved sister-in-law Mary Hogarth in March of 1837, Dickens printed an address to dispel rumors that *he* suffered from mental weakness or insanity. In response to questions about a delay in the release of part XV of *The Pickwick Papers* (1836–1837), he wrote:

> Its publication was interrupted by a severe domestic affliction of no ordinary kind; that this was the sole cause of the non-appearance of the present number in the usual course. . . . However superfluous this second notice may appear to many, it is rendered necessary by various idle speculations and absurdities which have been industriously propagated during the past month; which have reached the author's ears from many quarters, and have pained him exceedingly. By one set of intimate acquaintances, especially well informed, he has been killed outright; by another, driven mad; by a third, imprisoned for debt; by a fourth, sent per steamer to the United States; by a fifth, rendered incapable of any mental exertion for evermore — by

> all, in short, represented as doing anything but seeking in a few weeks' retirement the restoration of that cheerfulness and peace of which a sad bereavement had temporarily deprived him.[64]

Thus, Dickens had personal experience with the social stigma of rumors regarding his own sanity early on in his career. This experience may have impacted his depictions of mental illness and sanity in his later writings, including nonfiction works such as "A Curious Dance Round a Curious Tree" (1852) and "The Star of Bethlehem" (1857) — two articles supporting the better treatment and nonrestraint of insane asylum patients — and fictional works such as *Little Dorrit* (1855–1857) and *Our Mutual Friend* (1864–1865), in which the characters of Affery Flintwinch and Bella Wilfer, respectively, are effectively gaslit by male characters in the novels. Indeed, acknowledging and decrying social problems was and continues to be integral to Dickens's public image. During his life and long after his death, Dickens has been seen as a champion of the people, arguing for better care and increased compassion for those who desperately need but often do not receive it.

Despite his advocacy for many social improvements, Dickens's cruelly callous mistreatment of both his wife Catherine Dickens and his colleague Catherine Crowe reveals a contradictory character. As Holbrook has put it, although Dickens "believed consciously in love, charity, and forgiveness," "there was a deep division between art and life. . . . It is clear that in life he often behaved like one of his own villains rather than a hero."[65] Dickens's mockery of Crowe presents him as uncharitably lacking compassion for an elderly female acquaintance who may have suffered from an embarrassing and potentially stigmatizing mental affliction. Furthermore, that Dickens falsely accused his wife of having a mental disorder that made her an unfit wife and mother in order to improve his own public image during their separation is appalling enough. But the fact that knowledge of this false accusation was, for the most part, dismissed by critics and the general public until 2019 makes it all the more disturbing, if not surprising. Dickens's position as a famous novelist with power, wealth, popularity, and the means of disseminating his version of events in patriarchal Victorian England allowed him to wield authority over women in both his personal and professional circles, including in ways that we now call "gaslighting."

Notes

1. Thulin, "Trove of Letters"; Shankar, "Lost in Time"; Bennett, "Barking Mad."
2. Barton and Whitehead, "Gas-Light Phenomenon," 1258.
3. Thomson, quoted in Dickens, *Letters*, 8: 746.
4. For instance, see Nayder, *The Other Dickens.*
5. Bolivar, "Madhouse Divorce," 256n15.
6. Nayder, *Other Dickens*, 255.
7. Thomson, quoted in Dickens, *Letters*, 8: 746–47.
8. Thomson, quoted in Dickens, *Letters*, 8: 747.
9. Nayder, *Other Dickens*, 261–62.
10. Dickens, "Personal," 420.
11. Dickens, "Personal," 420. Nayder and others have noted the disingenuousness of Dickens widely publishing something he describes as "private" and "personal."
12. Dickens, *Letters*, 8: 740.
13. Dickens, *Letters*, 8: 740.
14. Dickens, *Letters*, 8: 741.
15. Many scholars have written about the falsity of Dickens's claims. For instance, see Nayder's *Other Dickens*.
16. Dickens, *Letters*, 8: 559–60.
17. Sutherland, *Victorian Fiction*, 79. For more on Catherine's sanity and good parenting, see Nayder, *Other Dickens*, 242–43, 273–77.
18. Storey, *Dickens and Daughter*, 23–24.
19. Anonymous, "Gossip of the World," 66.
20. Anonymous, quoted in Slater, *Great Charles Dickens Scandal*, 23.
21. Anonymous, quoted in Slater, 24.
22. Barrett Browning, quoted in Dickens, *Letters*, 8: 648–49, footnote 4.
23. Thomson, quoted in Dickens, *Letters*, 8: 565, footnote 3.
24. Bowen, "Madness," 7.
25. Bowen, "Madness," 7. Edward Guiliano has also recently noted that Dickens's probing the potential of committing Catherine was known to scholars before Bowen's research. Guilano, "Complex Women," 10.
26. Sutherland, *Victorian Fiction*, 80.
27. Bowen, "Madness," 13.
28. Bowen, "Madness," 35.
29. Bowen, "Query."
30. Bolivar, "Madhouse Divorce," 258.
31. Bolivar, "Madhouse Divorce," 260.
32. Bolivar, "Madhouse Divorce," 258, 260.
33. Wise, *Inconvenient People*, 196.
34. Bolivar, "Madhouse Divorce," 265.
35. Bolivar, "Madhouse Divorce," 263–64.
36. Schwieso, "Religious Fanaticism," 165.
37. Bolivar, "Madhouse Divorce," 254.

38. Schwieso, "Religious Fanaticism," 167.
39. Wise, *Inconvenient People*, 213–15.
40. Wise, *Inconvenient People*, 216–18.
41. Wise, *Inconvenient People*, 218–19.
42. Sutherland, *Victorian Fiction*, 70.
43. Wise, *Inconvenient People*, 224–43.
44. Wise, *Inconvenient People*, 213, 218.
45. Storey, *Dickens and Daughter*, 220.
46. Storey, *Dickens and Daughter*, 219.
47. Holbrook, *Charles Dickens*, 17.
48. Wilson, "Introduction," v.
49. Dickens, "Review," 131.
50. Geoffrey Larken's collection of research and documents related to Crowe is housed at the University of Kent's Templeman Library. The collection includes Larken's unpublished biography on Crowe, which serves as a resource for much of what is known about her.
51. For a more detailed account of Dickens's treatment of and feelings about Crowe, see Kim, "Catherine Crowe."
52. Conolly, Letter to George Combe.
53. Dickens, *Letters*, 7: 285–86.
54. Dickens, *Letters*, 7: 288. At one point, Dickens tried to cure Emile de la Rue's wife, Augusta, of anxiety, nightmares, delusions, and other ailments through mesmerism. Even during Dickens's lifetime, mesmerism was sometimes viewed as a tool of male dominance, as the mesmerizer was frequently a male who exerted control over a female subject. In contrast, Spiritualism was usually practiced by women as the conduit or source of control, and these women were often viewed by skeptics, including Dickens, as insane or fraudulent. For more information on the gender dynamics of mesmerism and spiritualism in the nineteenth century, see Kim, "Catherine Crowe."
55. Ruth Heholt claims that the piece was written by John Elliotson, the man who taught Dickens the technique of mesmerism that Dickens later used on Catherine, Auguste de la Rue's wife, and others. Heholt, *Catherine Crowe*, 14.
56. Anonymous, "Another Person Insane," 33.
57. Crowe, "Cruel Rumours," 2.
58. Larken's unpublished biography of Crowe and his research outline Crowe's personal and professional connections before and after the incident, finding that many of Crowe's friends remained so despite her public embarrassment.
59. Dickens, "Doubtfully Divine," 408.
60. Heholt, *Catherine Crowe*, 19.
61. Camus, *Gender and Madness*, 25.
62. Sussex, "Detective Maidservant," 59.
63. Crowe, *Night-Side*, 26.

64. Dickens, *Pickwick Papers*, 882. Also see Tambling, "Why Should I Call You Mad?" 62.
65. Holbrook, *Charles Dickens*, 172.

Bibliography

Ackroyd, Peter. *Dickens*. HarperCollins Publishers, 1990.

Anonymous. "Another Person Insane through Spirit Fancies. Second Postscript." *The Zoist: A Journal, or, Cerebral Physiology & Mesmerism, and Their Applications to Human Welfare*. H. Baillière, 45 (1855): 33.

Anonymous. "Gossip of the World." *Frank Leslie's Illustrated Newspaper*. July 3, 1858.

Barton, Russell, and Whitehead, J. A. "The Gas-Light Phenomenon." *The Lancet* 1, no. 7608 (1969): 1258–60.

Bennet, Catherine. "'Barking Mad' . . . How Dickens Led to Our Modern Gaslighting Men." *The Observer*. February 24, 2019. https://www.theguardian.com/commentisfree/2019/feb/24/barking-mad-how-dickens-led-to-our-modern-gaslighting-men-charities.

Bolivar, Robin. "The Madhouse Divorce: The Effect of Victorian Property, Lunacy and Divorce Laws and Their Portrayal in Popular Culture." *University of New Brunswick Law Journal* 63 (2012): 252–79.

Bowen, John. "Madness and the Dickens Marriage: A New Source." *The Dickensian* 115, no. 507 (2019): 5–20.

———. "Query about Cook Letters." Received by Katherine J. Kim, July 31, 2023.

Camus, Marian. *Gender and Madness in the Novels of Charles Dickens*. Edwin Mellen Press, 2004.

Conolly, John. Letter to George Combe. April 2, 1854. MS. 7340. The Combe Collection in the National Library of Scotland. Edinburgh, Scotland.

Crowe, Catherine. "Cruel Rumours about an Authoress." *The Daily News*. April 29, 1854.

———. *The Night-Side of Nature, or, Ghosts and Ghost Seers*. Henry T. Coates & Company, 1901.

Dickens, Charles. "Doubtfully Divine Missions." *All the Year Round: A Weekly Journal*. May 5, 1866.

———. *Hard Times*. Edited by Paul Schlicke. Oxford University Press, 1998.

———. *The Letters of Charles Dickens Volume 7: 1853–1855*. Edited by Graham Storey and Kathleen Tillotson. Clarendon, 1965.

———. *The Letters of Charles Dickens Volume 8: 1856–1858*. Edited by Graham Storey and Kathleen Tillotson. Clarendon, 1995.

———. "Personal." *Household Words*. June 7, 1858.

———. *The Pickwick Papers*. Edited by James Kinsley. Clarendon Press, 1986.

———. Review of Catherine Crowe's *The Night-Side of Nature. Examiner*. February 26, 1848.

———. "The Star of Bethlehem," *Household Words*. August 15, 1857.

Dickens, Charles, and William Henry Wills. "A Curious Dance Round a Curious Tree," *Household Words*. January 17, 1852.

Fielding, K. J. "Charles Dickens and His Wife. Fact or Forgery?" *Études Anglaises: Grande Bretagne, Etats-Unis* 8 (1955): 212–22.

Forster, John. *The Life of Charles Dickens*. E. P Dutton & Co., 1927.

Guiliano, Edward. "Complex Women Because of or Despite Dickens? An Introduction." In *Dickens & Women ReObserved*, edited by Edward Guiliano, 1–14. Edward Everett Root, 2020.

Heholt, Ruth. *Catherine Crowe: Gender, Genre, and Radical Politics*. Routledge, 2021.

Holbrook, David K. *Charles Dickens and the Image of Women*. New York University Press, 1993.

Hopkins, Annette B. "Dickens and Mrs. Gaskell." *Huntington Library Quarterly* 9, no. 4 (1946): 357–85.

Kim, Katherine J. "Catherine Crowe, Charles Dickens, and Perceptions of Female Insanity." *Dickens Quarterly* 38, no. 3 (2021): 276–96.

Larken, Geoffrey, et al. Catherine Crowe Collection, 1930–1981. Special Collections and Archives, Templeman Library, University of Kent, F191859.

McKnight, Natalie. *Idiots, Madmen, and Other Prisoners in Dickens*. St. Martin's Press, 1993.

Nayder, Lillian. *The Other Dickens: A Life of Catherine Hogarth*. Cornell University Press, 2012.

Schwieso, Joshua John. "'Religious Fanaticism' and Wrongful Confinement in Victorian England: The Affair of Louisa Nottidge." *The Society for the Social History of Medicine* 9, no. 2 (1996): 159–74.

Shankar, Kartikeya. "Lost in Time: The Forgotten Wife of Charles Dickens." *Times of India*. March 8, 2022. https://timesofindia.indiatimes.com/life-style/books/features/lost-in-time-the-forgotten-wife-of-charles-dickens/articleshow/90076146.cms.

Slater, Michael. *Dickens and Women*. Stanford University Press, 1983.

———. *The Great Charles Dickens Scandal*. Yale University Press, 2012.

Storey, Gladys. *Dickens and Daughter*. Frederick Muller, 1939.

Sussex, Lucy. "The Detective Maidservant: Catherine Crowe's *Susan Hopley*." In *Silent Voices: Forgotten Novels by Victorian Women Writers*, edited by Brenda Ayres, 57–66. Praeger, 2003.

Sutherland, John. *Victorian Fiction: Writers, Publishers, Readers*. Palgrave Macmillan, 2005.

Tambling, Jeremy. "'Why Should I Call You Mad?': Dickens and the Literature of Madness." *Cahiers victoriens &* édouardiens 56 (2002): 59–79.

Thulin, Lila. "Trove of Letters Reveal Charles Dickens Tried to Lock His Wife Away in an Asylum." *Smithsonian Magazine*. February 22, 2019. https://www.smithsonianmag.com/smart-news/newly-analyzed-trove-letters-charles-dickens-180971545/.

Wilson, Collin. Introduction. *The Night Side of Nature* by Catherine Crowe. Aquarian Press, 1986.

Wise, Sarah. *Inconvenient People: Lunacy, Liberty and the Mad-Doctors in England*. Random House, 2012.

7

"Lit by a fury and a thought"

Resistance to Marital Gaslighting in Elizabeth Barrett Browning's *Aurora Leigh* and Amy Levy's "Xantippe"

Sarah E. Kersh

As the opening credits to MGM's 1944 adaptation of *Gaslight* begin, we hear a soprano voice singing a light operatic melody; the music, however, abruptly turns sinister just as the film's title flashes on the screen, and the woman's lilting vocals are silenced and replaced by orchestral horns and strings. After a brief expositional scene in which we see a young Paula Alquist (played by Ingrid Bergman) being escorted out of the London townhome in which her aunt, "the famous prima donna" Alice Alquist, has just been murdered,[1] we cut to a new scene, the camera alighting on a sign that reads: "Maestro Guardi Teacher of Singing." Maestro Guardi (Emil Rameau) is Alice Alquist's former singing coach, who is now attempting to "make [Paula] into a great singer, as [her aunt] was." As the scene in Guardi's Italian teaching studio begins, another disembodied female voice, again singing opera, seems to call the camera in through the window, first to focus on the hands of a piano player, and then on Paula herself, who is revealed to be the one singing. Paula looks confident and secure as she sings, but soon Maestro Guardi interrupts and chastises her for not concentrating. He also accuses her of not having the emotional intelligence and sensitivity needed to be a great artist — "This opera is tragedy, signorina! You seem incapable of understanding!" (a rather ironic accusation, as he soon acknowledges, considering that "real tragedy has touched your life, and very deeply," in the form of Alice Alquist's murder). After being remonstrated in this way, Paula looks ashamed and asks if she may speak to him "seriously, very seriously." Once the piano accompanist leaves the room and they are alone, Maestro Guardi tells her, "Your heart is not in your singing anymore," and then leans in to ask, "Tell me, Paula, you are in love?" A surprised Paula breathlessly answers, "Yes. It's something that has never happened to me before." He urges her to follow her heart, saying, "Forget your singing for a while. Happiness is better than art." Paula thanks her teacher, gathers her things, and exits the studio, only to run into the arms of the man for whom she has decided to forsake her artistic and professional ambitions: the piano accompanist, Gregory Anton (played by Charles Boyer). By the end of the film, we learn that this same man (whose real name is revealed to be Sergius Bauer) had also worked as Alice Alquist's accompanist a decade prior — shortly before he was the one to murder her.

The MGM adaptation of Patrick Hamilton's 1938 play *Gas Light* is the only version of the story that includes this added frame connecting the husband, the wife, and the murder victim through performance and music. I argue that this additional backstory is more than a simple plot device. By establishing Paula and Alice Alquist as performers and musical artists, the film investigates a specific kind of gaslighting that hinders women from realizing their own artistic visions and restrains female voice and speech. While the idea of "gaslighting" in the play and the film adaptations is usually connected to the postmarital drama in which the husband goads the wife into questioning her own reasoning and memory, in the MGM version Paula's gaslighting actually begins in this opening scene with Maestro Guardi. Love and art are presented to Paula as being fundamentally at odds with one another, and Guardi's gaslighting (his suggestion that she is "incapable" of understanding "tragedy" when in fact she has already experienced intense tragedy) emphasizes that a woman's artistic ability inevitably disappears as soon as she experiences the "happiness" of being pursued by a male suitor. From our first aural encounter in the film — the soprano voice heard over the opening credits, until it suddenly stops — the film underscores the connection between gaslighting and silencing. Part of what makes Paula's experience so uniquely cruel, in other words, is that she is manipulated into believing not just that she has misplaced or hidden random household items, but that she needs to give up her intended career in opera — that she needs to give up her *voice* — in order to follow her heart.

In this chapter, I illuminate a form of gaslighting that is directly related to women's desires to pursue their own artistic, intellectual, and creative endeavors. The suggestion that women need to sacrifice such endeavors in favor of marriage and heteronormative "happiness" builds on a long genealogy of patriarchal acculturation whereby legal, ideological, and cultural fictions about womanhood are deployed to deny a woman's capacity for independent thought or art. I trace this genealogy back through works by Victorian women poets, particularly Elizabeth Barrett Browning (EBB) and Amy Levy, while drawing on Jeff Englehart's notion of "normative gaslighting." In their article titled "Some Reflections on Gaslighting and Language Games," Englehart argues for the ways in which "dominant conversational norms give speakers warrant to gaslight."[2] Normative gaslighting happens when "a speaker reports a systemic injustice, and others then raise unwarranted doubts about the report and/or the reporter"; in such cases, the speaker voicing resistance is systematically doubted by "multiple gaslighters."[3] In EBB's *Aurora Leigh* (1856) and Levy's "Xantippe" (1881), multiple gaslighters — Aurora's male suitor and her aunt, and Xantippe's husband and his friends — use normative assumptions about women and marriage to make Aurora and Xantippe doubt not only their own minds and feelings, but also their creative and intellectual visions. This essay shows how EBB's and Levy's poems expose normative marital gaslighting, while at the same time demonstrating that women's authorial voices — both real and imagined — are essential to fighting it.

Elizabeth Barrett Browning's *Aurora Leigh* and the Problem of Marriage

In her verse novel *Aurora Leigh*, Elizabeth Barrett Browning's titular character refuses the marriage proposal of her cousin, Romney Leigh, in favor of exploring her own potential as a poet. In the proposal scene, Romney approaches Aurora to wish her happy birthday and return her errant manuscript. He jests, saying he did not read the text because he "saw at once the thing had witchcraft in't, / Whereof the reading calls up dangerous spirits: / I rather bring it to the witch."[4] At this point the exchange is jocular; however, their lighthearted raillery soon turns, as Romney remarks that he prefers to see Aurora as "not too much / Witch, scholar, poet, dreamer, and the rest" but as "a woman" (II.85–87). His hope is that she will see her twentieth birthday as the moment to leave her childish writing behind and be serious: "The time is done for facile settings up" (II. 150). When she balks, however, he unleashes a stream of assertions about women's intellectual inferiority ("None of all these things, / Can women understand" [II.182–83]) and draws upon the conversational norm of rehearsing conventional misogynistic ideas. Women, he suggests, are too "personal and passionate" to understand the world and are fit only to serve as mothers and wives, not prophets or poets:

> Therefore, this same world
> Uncomprehended by you, must remain
> Uninfluenced by you. — Women as you are,
> Mere women, personal and passionate,
> You give us doting mothers, and perfect wives,
> Sublime Madonnas, and enduring saints!
> We get no Christ from you — and verily
> We shall not get a poet, in my mind. (II.218–25)

When Aurora tries to interject, Romney thwarts her speech with yet another ideological commonplace, likening women's art to child's play: "you, Aurora," he insists, "cannot condescend / To play at art, as children play at swords" (II.227–31). His denigration of her basic cognitive and creative capacities builds toward a marriage proposal that he articulates in and through this same normative mythology of male intellectual supremacy.

Romney's proposal functions as an act of gaslighting that, for Aurora, demands resistance even before he has finished posing the question. When she explains that her own interests differ but that she will gladly admire his "compassion" for Christian socialism, he wonders whether she will give him "No other help?" (II.340, 344). "What help?" Aurora replies, boldly rejecting the hypocrisy embedded in his question: "You'd scorn my help — as Nature's self, you say, / Has scorned to put her music in my mouth / Because a woman's. Do you now turn round / And ask for what a woman cannot give?" (II.344–49). In this moment, he requests "what she only can" give — the "love" and "bitter duties" of "wifehood" (II.350, 353–56). Reinforcing normative misogyny, this formulation renders the prospect of marrying him inextricable from his psychologically damaging dismissal of her independent moral and intellectual standing. Aurora interprets his proposal as an insult — an injustice — and reports the offense immediately:

> "Now," I said, "may God
> Be witness 'twixt us two!" and with the word,
> Meseemed I floated into a sudden light
> Above his stature, — "am I proved too weak
> To stand alone, yet strong enough to bear
> Such leaners on my shoulder? poor to think,
> Yet rich enough to sympathise with thought?
> Incompetent to sing, as blackbirds can,
> Yet competent to love, like HIM?" (II.356–64)

Romney responds to her challenge by gaslighting her. He combines an accusation of mental frailty ("you translate me ill") with a denial of wrongdoing ("I do not contradict my thought of you") (II.368–69). Then, after invalidating her critique, he doubles down on the "truth" of his claim that women cannot produce art, but he begins to contort his misogynistic attacks into a gesture of "courtship" in her "honour": "your sex is weak for art / (And I who said so, did but honour you / By using truth in courtship)" (II.371–75). Turning insults into ideals, Victorian marital norms — here maintained and opposed in a life-changing conversation — discount women's actual experiences, abilities, and desires, especially when prospective wives dare to expose the lies and contradictions underpinning those norms.

Following his failed proposal, Romney's gaslighting takes the form of an exaggerated affective position in which he claims to praise the nobility of women's superior "comprehension" of love, despite having just repeatedly insisted that women cannot understand the world in which they live, much less themselves or others. He feigns disbelief at how he misunderstands women, insinuating that Aurora is out of step with women's true "heroic duties":

> Then, must it be
> Indeed farewell? And was I so far wrong

In hope and in illusion, when I took
The woman to be nobler than the man,
Yourself the noblest woman, — in the use
And comprehension of what love is, — love,
That generates the likeness of itself
Through all heroic duties? (II.417–24)

Romney works to make Aurora feel ostracized in her thinking about marriage. Indeed, his feigned disbelief ("was I so far wrong / In hope and in illusion") discredits her stance and implies that his beliefs stem from a normative standard shared by many. Aurora heartily disagrees: "With quiet indignation I broke in. / 'You misconceive the question like a man, / Who sees a woman as the complement / Of his sex merely. You forget too much / That every creature, female as the male, / Stands single in responsible act and thought" (II.432–36). Pushing back against his rhetorical performance, as well as the Victorian assumption that women's greatest desire is to be loved by a man and asked if they would "love and work" with him, Aurora reminds Romney that she has her own mind. Here, she uses her voice to "break in" and dispel the attempted gaslighting that pushes her to give up her work to become a wife.

While philosophically Aurora demands to be seen in her own right, her argument challenges midcentury coverture laws and, therefore, the very norms upon which Romney's arguments rely. Women writers and artists, once married, legally forfeited their intellectual ownership to their husbands. Aurora's impassioned plea that she is responsible for her own actions and thoughts, and by extension her desire to be a writer, is directly threatened by the law if she marries Romney. Cheri Larsen Hoeckley explains: "If claims to ownership rested on self-possession and bodily labor, Victorian wives had no grounds from which to argue their right to literary property. . . . Under Victorian law, a writing wife's independent status in the literary marketplace was obviated by her prior dependent status in the family; she could not be independent anywhere."[5] Not only are the economic considerations complicated, but the metaphorical implications that a woman writer's work in fact belongs to her husband weigh heavily on Aurora's mind, as well as, perhaps, EBB's.[6] Hoeckley posits that, through the character of Aurora, EBB grappled with the difficulties of being a woman writer facing coverture laws as she entered into her own marriage with Robert Browning.

Implicit in Aurora Leigh's coming of age is the connection between speaking the truth in both her conversation and her art, so that she may resist her suitor's gaslighting-cum-proposal: "I, who spoke the truth then, stand upright, / Still worthy of having spoken out the truth" (II.520–21). Her reaction to Romney's implication that she does not know or understand her own mind is to hold tightly to her belief in women's art:

Perhaps I am not worthy, as you say,
Of work like this: perhaps a woman's soul

Aspires, and not creates: yet we aspire,
And yet I'll try out your perhapses, sir,
And if I fail . . . why, burn me up my straw
Like other false works–I'll not ask for grace;
Your scorn is better, cousin Romney. I
Who love my art, would never wish it lower
To suit my stature. I may love my art,
You'll grant that even a woman may love art,
Seeing that to waste true love on anything,
Is womanly, past question. (II.485–96)

Aurora resolves to pursue her art, despite Romney's "scorn" should she fail, and does her best to expose his false assumptions about her self-knowledge. Emphasizing the undermining of her thoughts and feelings through his use of the word "perhaps," Aurora turns his "perhaps" back on him, reframing it as not indicative of the fallibility of her own thinking, but instead insisting on the possibility of failure as an option for all people, while emphasizing her determination to try rather than to give up before she has even begun.

Aurora Leigh is shamed by Romney for refusing marriage and an opportunity to work for the greater social good; however, it is the entrance of her aunt about a hundred lines later that hones EBB's exploration and critique of normative marital gaslighting in the poem. Aurora's aunt repeatedly suggests that Aurora does not know what she is doing by refusing marriage and thereby suggests she cannot discern her own reality, her own desires, or even her own thoughts. When Aurora attempts to stand up for her future, her aunt responds chidingly that Aurora is no more than a baby in a dark room and indicates that she understands nothing about the family inheritance:

"But I am born," I said with firmness, "I,
To walk another way than his, dear aunt."
"You walk, you walk! A babe at thirteen months
Will walk as well as you," she cried in haste,
"Without a steadying finger. Why, you child,
God help you, you are groping in the dark,
For all this sunlight. You suppose, perhaps,
That you, sole offspring of an opulent man,
Are rich and free to choose a way to walk?" (II.579–87)

And then, "'You,' she cried, / 'Have got a fever'" (II.655–56). Aurora must be infantile or ill, according to her aunt, to have declined Romney's hand in marriage in favor of pursuing her own writing. At the heart of her aunt's normative gaslighting is an economic argument: Aurora cannot inherit her father's money even if she is the "sole offspring of an opulent man" (II.586). Like Romney's speech before, Aurora's aunt suggests that she cannot imagine a woman who chooses not to marry, thereby goading Aurora into questioning her own sanity and her own desires. The entrance of Aurora's aunt as another gaslighter solidifies the verse novel as an example of Englehart's "normative gaslighting," which, they argue, requires multiple gaslighters.[7] EBB's inclusion of women as agents of gaslighting reminds readers that the heteronormative expectation of nineteenth-century marriage is woven into the social fabric of the era, for Aurora's resistance to this expectation is met with disbelief from both women and men.

EBB uses Aurora's aunt to illustrate the manipulation of women by other women, but she also adds an element of racialized othering that furthers her argument that Aurora is not thinking soundly. Aurora's family estate legally excludes "offspring by a foreign wife" (II.612). Cruelly, the aunt suggests that:

> Your mother must have been a pretty thing,
> For all the coarse Italian blacks and browns,
> To make a good man, which my brother was,
> Unchary of the duties to his house;
> But so indeed it fell. (II.618–22)

She shames Aurora's mother, and through her shames Aurora, for a kind of sexual trickery that made her father choose her mother's beauty over familial "duties." By extension, she suggests that Aurora's inability to think clearly is inherited from her mother's "coarse," nonwhite blood. As the encounter comes to a close, Aurora attempts to explain her reasons, but the words are "passionate, / Too passionate perhaps" (II.720–21), and her aunt rebuffs her in disgust. Aurora's mental state, as described by her aunt, is directly tied to her racialized position, and her aunt questions her sanity based on both her gendered and her racialized status: "'We'll leave Italian manners, if you please. / I think you had an English father, child, / And ought to find it possible to speak / A quiet 'yes' or 'no,' like English girls, / Without convulsions" (II.727–30). Whereas Aurora manages to resist her cousin's gaslighting, it is her aunt who finally causes her voice to falter, suggesting that she cannot speak "without convulsions." Here, EBB's heroine succumbs to the pressures of multiple gaslighters within her family circle, and, for a short time, her voice is silenced: "The next week passed in silence, so the next, / And several after: Romney did not come, / Nor my aunt chide me. I lived on and on, / As if my heart were kept beneath a glass, / And everybody stood, all eyes and ears, / To see and hear it tick" (II.854–59). It is only the death of her aunt and a small inheritance that allows her to once again pursue her art.

As a *Künstlerroman*, *Aurora Leigh* follows our titular character on her journey to become the writer and artist she yearns to be. Aurora wants to make her poetry "living art, / Which thus presents, and thus records true life'" (V.220–21). She contrasts her own poetic desires with a monologue about art in Book V, where she maintains, "I will write no plays" (V.267). Interestingly, her reasoning is not that drama cannot represent "true life," but that:

> The growing drama has outgrown such toys
> Of simulated stature, face, and speech,
> It also, peradventure, may outgrow
> The simulation of the painted scene,
> Boards, actors, prompters, gaslight, and costume;
> And take for a worthier stage the soul itself,
> Its shifting fancies and celestial lights,
> With all its grand orchestral silences,
> To keep the pauses of the rhythmic sounds.
>
> Alas, I still see something to be done,
> And what I do falls short of what I see
> Though I waste myself on doing. (V.334–45)

Aurora wants to push past "simulation," which she perceives in drama. She does not want her art to pretend, conceal, or masquerade, but rather to represent. "Actors, prompters, gaslight, and costume" line up for the poem as part of a fiction-making production antithetical to Aurora's own realistic aesthetic vision. While only a coincidental mention of "gaslight," EBB's contrast between gaslight and the "celestial lights" of the "worthier stage the soul itself" reminds readers that actual gas lamps were "continuously linked with deception" and that gas lighting bears a "related association . . . with the superficial and the spectacular."[8] Gas lamps, for Aurora, are the kind of metaphorical illumination she seeks to avoid — they are a performative simulation of the real within the realm of theater, not truth. Instead, Aurora — her very name implicating a "clear light of dawn" — seeks to produce art that sees in new, nonnormative ways. Gas lighting as technology and gaslighting as manipulation align in EBB's verse novel; ultimately, Aurora's poetry becomes a tool for both undermining normative gaslighting and reviving her voice. Through artistic interventions, Aurora suggests, poets and poetry can simultaneously illustrate and resist gaslighting.

Aurora faces similar constraints to Paula of *Gaslight*; interestingly, the verse novel and the 1944 film adaptation are set in both Italy and England. EBB's *Aurora Leigh*, like *Gaslight*, juxtaposes marriage and art, suggesting that women cannot have both. *Aurora Leigh* illustrates how the ideological tension between marital expectations and creative endeavors gaslights Victorian women, but the poem also charts a path of resistance through artistic production — Aurora ends up marrying Romney, but only after she has established her own career as a writer. Figuratively, her writing solidifies her voice and banishes the ongoing normative gaslighting experienced in the first few books — until the end. In Book IX, when Aurora reveals her love for Romney, she admits her mistaken thinking: "'Art is much, but love is more. / O Art, my Art, thou'rt much, but love is more!'" (IX.656–57). Even EBB's famously protofeminist poem cannot envision a marriage in which a woman's art competes, unfavorably, with "love" for a man.[9]

Responding with Fury in Amy Levy's "Xantippe"

Aurora Leigh proposes the prospect of a husband-to-be reframing his understanding of women's work and intellectual capabilities, thereby creating a space for marriage to unite intellectual equals and exposing gaslighting as the insidious manipulation that it is. In Amy Levy's dramatic monologue "Xantippe" (1881), however, the poetic voice suggests that women experience gaslighting not only within the confines of the marriage market, but even long after matrimony and possibly until death. For Levy's Xantippe, marriage — to Socrates, or perhaps to any man — is revealed as antithetical to intellectual possibility and synonymous with gaslighting.[10] Across both poems we see representations of male authorities barring and belittling female creative agency and free expression under the guise of marital propriety. Unfortunately, for Xantippe, marriage stands as a relentless barrier to a wife's creative and intellectual possibilities.[11]

"Xantippe" voices the maligned hopes of the wife of the ancient Athenian philosopher Socrates. Here, our speaker, Xantippe, has chosen to marry Socrates in part because she thought that, in doing so, she would gain access to pursuits of the mind. Instead, she is denied access to intellectual dialogue based on her gender and imagines what life would have been like if Socrates had given her the chance to learn and think and speak for herself. While Socrates — "Pregnant with noble theories" — enjoys vibrant debates with his friends, Xantippe stands on the sidelines, a "shattered . . . vessel" fit for neither the domestic work of women nor the intellectual work of men.[12] The word "Pregnant" underscores where Xantippe sees fertility and fecundity — in the life of the mind — because it is she at the end of the passage who is "barren" in body and mind:

> 'Twas only that the high philosopher,
> Pregnant with noble theories and great thoughts,
> Deigned not to stoop to touch so slight a thing
> As the fine fabric of a woman's brain —
> So subtle as a passionate woman's soul.
> I think, if he had stooped a little, and cared,
> I might have risen nearer to his height,
> And not lain shattered, neither fit for use
> As goodly household vessel, nor for that
> Far finer thing which I had hoped to be . . .
> Death, holding high his retrospective lamp,
> Shows me those first, far years of wedded life,
> Ere I had learnt to grasp the barren shape
> Of what the Fates had destined for my life. (28)[13]

"That/Far finer thing" Xantippe had hoped to be was a philosopher in her own right. The verse suggests that she believed in "those first, far years of wedded life" during which she might learn with her husband, but the speaker of the lyric has grown older and wiser to the rigid limitations placed upon married women.

Levy's "Xantippe," as Linda Hughes suggests, is "not only a brilliant poetic choice of a mouthpiece perfectly suited to distill issues of social justice and feminism but also a performative act in the sense of a self-conscious rehearsal of and claim to the role of the learned woman."[14] Levy herself was the first Jewish student to be admitted to Newnham College, Cambridge, and she keenly felt the mark of otherness, both in terms of her gender and her religion. (In addition, Levy's intimate relationships with women, categorized as queer or lesbian by scholars, would have further distanced her from the ideal Victorian woman, devoted wife, and devout heterosexual.[15]) As Emily Harrington argues, "The poem's anger against men who refuse to take women's academic ambitions seriously would surely have struck a chord at Newnham College as well, which Levy attended when the poem was published in 1881 but also where women would not be allowed to take degrees until 1948."[16] Levy's turn to the dramatic monologue form and the voice of Xantippe recasts the ancient figures of Socrates and his wife in order to articulate a contemporary commentary on the position of women in the nineteenth century.[17] Socrates, like the men who discouraged Levy herself, is portrayed as a gaslighting husband who inhibits Xantippe's intellectual life by questioning her mental abilities based on her sex.

In Levy's poem, our speaker fights back against this intellectual gaslighting with all her might, first through "gentle words" suggesting a kind of seduction that ultimately fails to win her the grace of her husband:

> At first I fought my fate with gentle words,
> With high endeavours after greater things;
> Striving to win the soul of Sokrates,
> Like some slight bird, who sings her burning love
> To human master, till at length she finds
> Her tender language wholly misconceived,
> And that same hand whose kind caress she sought,
> With fingers flippant flings the careless corn . . . (28–29)

Here, the poem gestures toward the effects of gaslighting that it later explicitly explores, suggesting that Xantippe's efforts to access "greater things" are repeatedly rebuffed. Xantippe is made to think that she is incapable of learning and she is repeatedly denied access to education because she is a woman. Unlike *Aurora Leigh*, Levy's dramatic monologue does not give voice to the gaslighting man, instead filtering Socrates's manipulation through the lens of Xantippe's reflections and the analogy of a small bird striving to win her master's approval. The reader can imagine Xantippe repeatedly and earnestly pleading to be allowed to learn and think — expressing her "burning love" for a life of the mind — only to be ignored, dismissed, or told by Socrates that she is unfit and does not know what she wants or asks for. Linda Hughes points out that this allusion to a domesticated bird aligns Levy's work with "a recurring Victorian trope of women's confinement,"[18] seen perhaps most famously in Jane Eyre's defiant lines to Rochester: "I am no bird; and no net ensnares me: I am a free human being with an independent will; which I now exert to leave you."[19] In fact, Hughes compares Levy's fascination with the caged bird directly to a passage from *Aurora Leigh* in which Aurora's gaslighting aunt appears as the misunderstanding master. Aurora laments:

> I, alas,
> A wild bird scarcely fledged, was brought to her cage,
> And she was there to meet me. Very kind.
> Bring the clean water; give out the fresh seed. (I.309–12)[20]

In EBB's poem, it is Aurora's aunt who brings water and seed but does not understand the desires of the "wild bird," while in Levy's poem it is Socrates who cannot understand Xantippe's impassioned song. What both figurative portraits have in common is the normative expectation of marital submission and wifely obedience.

"Xantippe" reaches a climactic moment when she is called to bring her husband and his friends more wine. Standing in the shadows, she hears them speak of another woman whose mind they deem to be "of a strength beyond her race" (30). Enraged that another woman might be allowed the access she has been denied, and realizing that Socrates's denials have been nothing but gaslighting all along, Xantippe erupts with profound anger at finally seeing how she has been abused:

> Lit by a fury and a thought, I spake:
> "By all great powers around us! can it be
> That we poor women are empirical?
> That gods who fashioned us did strive to make
> Beings too fine, too subtly delicate,
> With sense that thrilled response to ev'ry touch
> Of nature's, and their task is not complete?
> That they have sent their half-completed work
> To bleed and quiver here upon the earth?
> To bleed and quiver, and to weep and weep,
> To beat its soul against the marble walls
> Of men's cold hearts, and then at last to sin!" (30)

Her impassioned speech is met with "cold contempt." Socrates taunts her:

> But Sokrates, all slow and solemnly,
> Raised, calm, his face to mine, and sudden spake:
> "I thank thee for the wisdom which thy lips
> Have thus let fall among us: prythee tell
> From what high source, from what philosophies
> Didst cull the sapient notion of thy words?"
> Then stood I straight and silent for a breath,
> Dumb, crushed with all that weight of cold contempt; (31)

Socrates belittles her with the implication that her words merely regurgitate ideas drawn from other male philosophers, thereby publicly humiliating her. The other men, specifically Plato and Alcibiades, smirk at her. In this moment, she is "flooded with all the flowing tide of hopes" that she once clung to, and the breaking moment of the poem shows how Xantippe's internalization of the years of gaslighting has caused tremendous emotional pain — she is silently "crushed." Her reaction is swift and metaphorically bloody. She throws the wine skin and it bursts, showering the men, and herself, in red:

> But swiftly in my bosom there uprose
> A sudden flame, a merciful fury sent
> To save me; with both angry hands I flung
> The skin upon the marble, where it lay
> Spouting red rills and fountains on the white;
> Then, all unheeding faces, voices, eyes,
> I fled across the threshold, hair unbound —
> White garment stained to redness — beating heart
> Flooded with all the flowing tide of hopes
> Which once had gushed out golden, now sent back
> Swift to their sources, never more to rise . . . (32)

The "blood" is a reminder of women who are "born to bleed and quiver." Her words, "To bleed and quiver, and to weep and weep, / To beat its soul against the marble walls / Of men's cold hearts," gesture toward menstruation and pregnancy, as well as the connection of women to emotion rather than intellect. She has been told that she cannot pursue the life of the mind simply because she is a woman, and yet she knows now that womanhood is not what keeps her from learning — it is the false ideology imposed by her husband and other male philosophers. Dousing the whole of the men in red not only marks them as willing participants in this ruse but also sullies their bodies with her alleged female "inferiority." Thinking about "Xantippe" through the lens of Levy's own personal experiences as a Jewish woman trying to survive and be heard in the Victorian higher education system allows us to see the poem's connection to normative gaslighting all the more strongly.

"Fling it wide": Poetics as Resistance

Both *Aurora Leigh* and "Xantippe" connect the women's normative gaslighting to imagery of light. Aurora hopes to write truthful poetry instead of the deceptive dramas of the gaslit theater, and in response to Romney's marriage proposal, she "darkened, as the lighthouse will / That turns upon the sea" (II.365–66). Levy opens "Xantippe" with two forms of light — the "rosy dawn" and the lamp:

WHAT, have I waked again? I never thought
To see the rosy dawn, or ev'n this grey,
Dull, solemn stillness, ere the dawn has come.
The lamp burns low; low burns the lamp of life:
The still morn lays expectant, and my soul,
All weighted with a passive wonderment,
Waiteth and watcheth, waiteth for the dawn. (23)

These sources of light are evocative of the state of Xantippe's mind, and the chiastic structure of line four equates the low-burning lamp with the dullness of her own life. The flame of the lamp is low, as is the flame of life in our speaker. This poem, obviously, does not depict lamps lit by gas, but the metonymical use of light to evoke Xantippe's closeness to death reminds readers of the ways in which lighting and domestic spaces function as tropes often used to reference women's own intellectual spaces and mental capabilities.[21]

In the film *Gaslight,* Paula's awareness of lighting is paramount to both her sense of self and, ultimately, her survival. The gas lamps in the house become the epistemological linchpin in the story: when Scotland Yard detective Brian Cameron notices the dimming flames, Paula asks him, "You saw that, too?"; this dialogic revelation represents both the first time someone has validated Paula in the observation she has been savvy enough to make all along and the moment when the detective exposes the mystery at the heart of the story — that Paula has been a mark in Gregory's plot to steal her late aunt's jewels. Light — the lighthouse for Aurora as well as her own name, the candle for Xantippe, and the gas lamp for Paula — becomes an indicator of the woman's self-knowledge and her understanding of her circumstances. It is both metaphor and domestic reality. At the end of "Xantippe," the dawn returns, but the speaker's frame of mind has shifted. No longer is the lamp light even part of her monologue. Instead, calling out for light and air, she tells her maids to open wide the window so that she may jump:

Ha! the dawn has come;
I see a rosy glimmer — nay! it grows dark;
Why stand ye so in silence? throw it wide,
The casement, quick; why tarry? — give me air —
O fling it wide, I say, and give me light! (34)

While Xantippe might be an articulation of Levy's frustration with restricted access to intellectual pursuits via her call to "fling it wide," it is also hard not to read the poetic voice as a broader version of Levy herself. Xantippe's suicide at the end of the poem sadly foreshadows Levy's eventual death just shy of her twenty-eighth birthday.[22] While the end of "Xantippe" does not have the same partial reclamation of voice and marriage that *Aurora Leigh* does, that Levy does end the poem with Xantippe's voice and commands ("O fling it wide, I say, and give me light") suggests a form of resistance. The poetic voice will not stay quiet; she will speak.

In the closing scene of *Gaslight*, Paula also basks in her newfound liberation and the realization that she is not mad after all. Having spent the bulk of the film losing her ability to articulate her thoughts and feelings more and more — gradually moving from singing, laughing, and easy talking to stammering, stuttering, and whispering — the closing scene shows her triumphantly regaining her voice. When Gregory, now captured and bound to a chair by the police, begs her to help him escape, she responds in a final monologue that crescendos in volume and confidence at one and the same time: "If I were not mad, I could have helped you. Whatever you had done, I could have pitied and protected you. But because I am mad, I hate you. Because I am mad, I have betrayed you. And because I am mad, I am rejoicing in my heart, without a shred of pity, without a shred of regret, watching you go with glory in my heart!" Here, Paula flips the narrative of gaslighting and uses it as her moment of resistance. With all the power of dramatic irony, her words echo yet repurpose the painful moments earlier in the film when Gregory's gaslighting crushed her hopes and manipulated her into thinking she would suffer the same fate as her mother.

After Gregory has been taken away, the film ends with Paula walking out onto the balcony of her London townhome, spires of other buildings visible in the distance and clouds billowing before the glowing moon. "This night will be a long night," Paula says. "But it will end," responds Brian, who has opened the doors to the balcony for her and joined her there. In this moment, away from the indoor, gaslit rooms, Paula is allowed hope for tomorrow, as she looks to the vastness of the night sky, moonlight reflecting in her eyes. It is important to note, too, that in the earlier, British National film adaptation of *Gaslight* from which the MGM film borrowed the idea to end with a scene on the balcony, the heroine — named, in that version, Bella — is the one who "flings" the casement "wide" *herself* and steps out onto the balcony alone, with no prospective love interest there to take her husband's place. There are, moreover, no hints of suicidal ideation in this balcony scene as there are at the end of "Xantippe"; in this version of *Gaslight*, to be released from the bonds of matrimony is to be free.

Writing about Victorian literature in the age of #MeToo, Ellen Stockstill and Jessica Mele argue that part of our work as scholars is the challenge of "resisting, for example, the tendency to treat Victorian women as an oppressed monolith, and reckoning with the complex and varied ways that race, class, ability, age, religion, and sexuality create vectors of oppression and complicate narratives of sexual violence."[23] It's hard not to read the biographical across these texts — from EBB's struggle with coverture laws as they applied to her own income from writing after her marriage to Robert Browning, to Amy Levy's own struggle with antisemitism and her eventual tragic suicide. Both poems highlight facets of systemic violence and the normative systems used to limit women's autonomy and voice, and both show us ways in which a woman's poetic voice can serve as a mode of resistance. "Reckoning" with the "vectors of oppression," perhaps these poems offer a new window, a new light in a dark room.

Notes

1. We learn about the murder of Alice Alquist in the opening scene via a brief shot of a newspaper article announcing it.
2. Englehart, "Some Reflections," 3–4.
3. Englehart, "Some Reflections," 3.
4. Barrett Browning, *Aurora Leigh*, II.78–80. Further references to the verse novel will appear parenthetically within the text.
5. Hoeckley, *Anomalous Ownership*, 142.
6. One has only to look at the cases of Caroline Norton and Charlotte Smith to see the painful realities of women writers and the financial effects of coverture laws.
7. Englehart, "Some Reflections," 3.
8. Milan, "Refracting the Gaselier," 95.
9. It is worth noting that Romney does make concessions at the end of the text that allow for Aurora to strive for both love and art. Therefore, we might read him as a sort of 'reformed' gaslighter. He calls her "O poet, O my love" (IX. 900) and confesses "*I* was too ambitious in my deed" (IX. 901). Nevertheless, I argue that his reform stems not from a new belief in the worth of women or women's desires, but because he has seen that art can do public good. He tells Aurora, "Art's a service, —" (IX. 915) and "The world waits/For help." (IX. 923–24).
10. Levy's poem offers no future in which Xantippe can escape or expose marital gaslighting since it ends with her suicide.
11. Note that by the early 1880s, laws and coverture implications were in flux, and the 1857 Matrimonial Causes Act allowed for easier access to divorce for women. By 1870, women were entitled to keep their wages earned while married, but it would not be until 1882 that women would be allowed to retain all property inherited or acquired.
12. Scholars have noted that Diotima's speech in Plato's *Symposium* argues that there is a kind of "male pregnancy," which E. E. Pender relates to the concept of spiritual pregnancy, in contrast to women's "mere" physical pregnancy ("Spiritual Pregnancy," 72).
13. Levy, *A Minor Poet and Other Verse*, 28. Further references will be cited parenthetically.
14. Hughes, "Discoursing of Xantippe," 260.
15. See Bernstein, "Introduction," 16–22.
16. Harrington, "Merciful Fury," 189.
17. Many scholars have noted that the mythology of Xantippe links the name to that of both a difficult woman and a devoted wife and mother. The name's subsequent synonymous meaning of "shrew" in the *OED* only further emphasizes Xantippe's symbolism as a metaphor for the Victorian woman—caught between two impossible versions of femininity as either shrewish or submissive. (See Hughes, "Discoursing of Xantippe," 259.)
18. Hughes, "Victorian Newspapers," 462.

19. Brontë, *Jane Eyre*, 253.
20. Hughes points out that "Levy knew her precursor's poetry well, having published a prize-winning essay on *Aurora Leigh* at age thirteen in *Kind Words* (1 Oct 1875: 318)" ("Reading Poet," 462). In addition, Susan David Bernstein includes an essay on Christina Rossetti's poems in her edited edition of Levy's novel *The Romance of a Shop* to illustrate "how Levy viewed the field of Victorian poetry by women" (203).
21. John Ruskin, in *Sesame and Lilies*, argues that women's place is in the home to look after the domestic interior, particularly the fire and light (152).
22. Sarah Parker, focusing on Levy's photographic representation, argues that "following her suicide in September 1889, a number of commentators set to work reanimating Levy in order to support their own ideas about female education, genius and 'madness,' degeneration, and Jewish identity." Parker, "Reframing Amy Levy," 53.
23. Stockstill and Mele, "#MeToo and Victorian Literature."

Bibliography

Barrett Browning, Elizabeth. *Selected Writings*. Edited by Josie Billington and Philip Davis. Oxford University Press, 2014.

Bernstein, Susan David. "Introduction." *The Romance of a Shop* by Amy Levy, 11–41. Broadview Press, 2006.

Brontë, Charlotte. *Jane Eyre*. Edited by Margaret Smith. Oxford University Press, 2000.

Cukor, George, dir. *Gaslight*. Metro-Goldwyn-Mayer, 1944.

Engelhardt, Jeff. "Some Reflections on Gaslighting and Language Games." *Feminist Philosophy Quarterly* 9, no. 3 (2023): 1–25.

Harrington, Emily. "'A Merciful Fury Sent to Save Me': Amy Levy's 'Xantippe' and Women's Conversations." *Victorian Studies* 62, no. 2 (2020): 188–93.

Hoeckley, Cheri Larsen. "Anomalous Ownership: Copyright, Coverture, and Aurora Leigh." *Victorian Poetry* 36, no. 2 (1998): 135–61.

Hughes, Linda K. "Discoursing of Xantippe: Amy Levy, Classical Scholarship, and Print Culture." *Philological Quarterly* 88, no. 3 (2009): 259–81.

———. *The Cambridge Companion to Victorian Women's Poetry*. Edited by Linda K. Hughes. Cambridge University Press, 2019.

——— "Reading Poet Amy Levy through Victorian Newspapers." In *Women, Periodicals and Print Culture in Britain, 1830s-1900s: The Victorian Period*, edited by Alexis Easley, Clare Gill, and Beth Rodgers, 456–69. Edinburgh University Press, 2019.

Levy, Amy. *A Minor Poet and Other Verse*. T. Fisher Unwin, 1884.

Milan, Sarah. "Refracting the Gaselier: Understanding Victorian Responses to Domestic Gas Lighting." In *Domestic Space: Reading the*

Nineteenth-Century Interior, edited by Inga Bryden and Janet Floyd, 84–102. Manchester University Press, 1999.

Moore, Grace. "Neo-Victorian and Pastiche." In *A Companion to Sensation Fiction*, edited by Pamela K. Gilbert, 627–38. Wiley and Sons, 2011.

Parker, Sarah. "Reframing Amy Levy: Photography, Celebrity, and Posthumous Representation." *Victoriographies: A Journal of Nineteenth-Century Writing, 1790–1914* 12, no. 1 (2022): 52–77.

Pender, E. E. "Spiritual Pregnancy in Plato's Symposium." *Classical Quarterly* 42, no. 1 (1992): 72–86.

Ruskin, John. *Sesame and Lilies*. W. L. Allison Co, 1890.

Stockstill, Ellen, and Jessica Mele. "#MeToo and Victorian Literature: Reading against Rape Culture in the Undergraduate Classroom." *Nineteenth-Century Gender Studies* 16, no. 2 (2020).

Part III

Case Studies in Institutional Gaslighting

The following essays examine instances of structural gaslighting made possible by powerful, male-dominated institutions: the coal-gas industry, the discipline of political economy, and the fundamentalist Puritan church. These case studies illuminate the tactics used by beneficiaries of these institutions to police communities or individuals who criticized, disobeyed, or simply sought inclusion within them. Such tactics ranged from misogynistic vitriol and public shaming to elaborate lies and baseless accusations, variously buttressed by established patriarchal networks of financial, political, and/or religious authority. Each analysis takes a closer look at acts of institutional gaslighting, sometimes by women pitted against other women, as well as acts of defiance, persistence, and solidarity.

8

"The thralldom of gas"

Capitalist Gaslighting and the Victorian Coal-Gas Industry

Grace Franklin

In 1829, an anonymous report authored by "A Water Drinker" (who was almost certainly also a coal-gas manufacturer) circulated publicly and within the House of Commons. Its language and rhetorical posture echoed those of recent pamphlets published by representatives of the emergent gas industry.[1] Opening at a sanctimonious pitch, this document discusses the ostensible dumping of toxic gasworks waste into the Thames — or, rather, it spends more than 100 pages mocking and belittling those who had brought forth this charge. News outlets are not immune from the author's criticism for printing "such absurd and ridiculous stories as have lately been told about *gas*, *fish*, and *Thames water*," but the report primarily has in sight gasworks neighbors and local fishermen, whose nuisance complaints had brought this issue to the attention of Parliament.[2]

In an extended analysis of minutes from ongoing hearings, the author works to undermine the epistemic standing of the witnesses. "All of the fishermen seemed to concur in ascribing the dreadful destruction of eels to *the gas*," he writes, "though probably not one of them . . . really knew anything about the properties of gas" (12). The pamphleteer often reminds readers that the gas industry, by contrast, relies on "modern science . . . to ascertain by actual experiment the *qualities* of both *air and water*" (6). When quoting from testimonies, he sows doubt about complainants' reliability by means of extensive editorializing. "Wonderfully 'intelligent' indeed!" he mocks before excoriating an eyewitness account (15). "Can such a ridiculous story . . . be really true?" the author asks again and again (9). Moreover, he accuses witnesses of "industriously" and "artfully" spreading "delusive and erroneous statements" about poisonous drinking water and dead animals in the river "to the detriment . . . of many worthy individuals" (iv). Blaming victims, undermining their credibility, questioning their knowledge — today we call this gaslighting, and in the 1820s it worked. A proposed bill to regulate coal-gas production did not pass, and portraying detractors in this fashion became characteristic of the industry for decades to come.[3]

The play on words here is not incidental. The term gaslighting, as discussed in the introduction to this collection, derived from Patrick Hamilton's melodrama *Gas Light* (1938). Elsewhere I argue that the debut production's flickering gas lamps were not merely a thrilling plot twist. Rather, Hamilton staged a critique of social relations that were premised on energy infrastructure, specifically on Britain's still-prominent coal-gas industry.[4] As this essay will demonstrate, the roots of the behavior that Hamilton dramatized reach back to the industry's inception. Britain's coal-gas utility, which supplied light and heat, was a pioneering fossil-fuel distribution network. It set precedents for later distribution systems, such as the electricity grid, as well as other fossil-fueled networks, including the railways. Developed at the firm of Boulton and Watt (of the Watt steam engine), the first large-scale gas-lighting apparatus was installed at a Manchester textile mill in 1805. A group of London-based entrepreneurs that became the Gas Light and Coke Company (GLCC) saw the potential of expanding this technology from self-contained factories into urban-scale infrastructure and of widening the coal-gas customer base accordingly. The formation of the GLCC, and of other gas companies on its heels, involved aggressive Parliamentary lobbying in pursuit of construction charters, along with what historian Leslie Tomory describes as "wildly exaggerated" advertisements, which appeared in London papers almost daily.[5] Via this two-pronged strategy, aimed at hastening legal processes and securing investors, the coal-gas network spread rapidly, lighting not only factories and streets but also the interiors of civic buildings, shops, and high-end homes as early as 1814.[6] By 1820, 300 miles of gasworks extended throughout London, and in 1832 the GLCC alone consumed more than 1.2 million pounds of coal in the process of supplying gas to consumers.[7]

However, the developmental pace and unprecedented nature of coal-gas infrastructure meant that its progress was also chaotic and its reception ambivalent, to say the least. Theaters burned regularly; the debut of gas lamps along Pall Mall involved an explosion; difficulty controlling supply use resulted in blackouts and leaks.[8] In addition to demonstrable hazards posed by fire and carbon monoxide poisoning, public relations challenges derived from the novelty of networked fuel. Turning a gas valve proved cleaner and more convenient than candles or oil lamps, but public reaction was not all wonder at the new technology's efficiency and aesthetics. Customers were wary of unnatural light from underground, of the security threat posed by central generating stations, and of piping the factory — its actual soot and its social ills — into the home.[9] This latter concern gained traction as the idea of the Victorian home became increasingly conflated with the moral character of its inhabitants. The gas industry responded to pushback with technological adjustments and trial-and-error approaches to managing user behavior.[10] Yet its success was also predicated on the strategies it honed for managing public perception.

This essay contends that tactics employed by the Victorian coal-gas industry to deflect attention from the full scope and harms of its activities constituted a form of institutional gaslighting, long before this mode of power abuse acquired its name. Gas companies adapted their responses toward critics, legal opponents, and concerned customers as needed over the course of the nineteenth century, successfully evading safety and environmental legislative checks until the late 1860s, but we see core traits of their "cast-blame," "concede-nothing" approach already at play in the Thames pollution affair.[11] As exemplified in the water drinker's report, gaslighting aims to undermine victims' faith in their own capacities to observe and interpret the world, a manipulation reinforced by persuading others that the victim's viewpoint cannot be trusted. Philosopher Cynthia Stark defines gaslighting, fundamentally, as a form of "testimonial injustice."[12] Recent scholarship on gaslighting has begun to conceive of it as a structural, rather than primarily or exclusively interpersonal, form of harm. In this ideation, gaslighting on the part of institutions or political entities mobilizes existent structural vulnerabilities, even as, Nora Berenstain explains, gaslighters "locate the cause of pervasive inequalities in flaws of oppressed groups themselves," thereby obscuring "the actual causes, mechanisms, and effects of oppression."[13] In this vein, the water drinker exploits class prejudice in order to shift focus from the waste-disposal practices of the gas industry and onto the nuisance-complaint filers themselves. Decrying their "attempts to *alarm* . . . wealthy and polished residents" with "pestiferous tales," he casts underclass witnesses as the "real" nuisance (vii, 6).

I explore this formative case study in institutional gaslighting first by turning to Charlotte Elizabeth Tonna's *The Wrongs of Woman* (1843–1844). This four-part fiction about women who work in garment manufacturing pointedly recalls the subtitle of *Maria: or, The Wrongs of Woman* (1798) in a nod to Mary Wollstonecraft's formative feminist critique of gaslighting that takes place in an asylum, a different kind of institutional setting.[14] I argue that gaslight, in Tonna's stories, functions as more than a marker of the real. Rather, invoking the physical properties of gas illumination and gas industry stratagems, Tonna uses gaslight to stress industrial capitalism's distortion of what was natural and, by her account, right. In doing so, she exposes what I am retrospectively calling capitalist gaslighting, a compound form of institutional manipulation that, in Tonna's dramatizations, combines medical, epistemic, and misogynistic modes of gaslighting. As coal gas powers inhumane workdays and more-than-human rates of production, Tonna's characters get pressured into believing that inability to persevere amounts to a personal failing. Broadly speaking, the author portrays a system in which workers are made to feel at once redundant, irrational, and individually culpable for structural injustices in the workplace and the market.

This essay's second section considers Britain's network of urban gas and its producers from the vantage point of the Victorian home. As the gas industry expanded to include middle-class residences, it began distributing household user manuals. These present as innocuous aids, but they read as a form of propaganda, advancing the industry's official narrative about itself and working to undercut contrary perspectives. In this context, capitalist gaslighting takes a subtler form, drawing on tropes of female fragility to subvert the housewife's faith in her perceptive instincts and rational capacities. I read these manuals against midcentury housekeeping guides written for and primarily authored by women, a genre that pushes back at user-manual rhetoric by refusing either to accept blame for gas utility mishaps or to concede that the technology's dangers have been imagined or overblown.

Collectively, the disparate texts gathered in this essay exhibit the aesthetic gasification of nineteenth-century print culture, a phrase I use to describe rhetoric that invokes the material properties of coal gas and the distorting communicative practices of its producers. All of these assorted materials demonstrate the process of capitalist gaslighting, even as each medium exposes the phenomenon from a different perspective: the water drinker's report offers insight into corporate-industrial legal tactics; Tonna's fiction dramatizes capitalist gaslighting as it transpired in the workplace; and housekeeping manuals illuminate propaganda deployed to gaslight consumers. Of course, capitalist gaslighting in the nineteenth century was not confined to the coal-gas industry. Nevertheless, the Victorian gas industry played a central role in propagating this complex form of manipulation, both by pioneering legal and public relations stratagems and by literally fueling other industries. Though the consequences of capitalist gaslighting in this sector impacted working-class victims across age and gender, as well as underclass citizens who were the primary sufferers of urban-environmental injustice, I have selected works that highlight interrelations between the coal-gas industry and female workers and consumers. These women were precursors to *Gas Light*'s Bella Manningham, who, in turn, prefigures contemporary women in the domestic space. I conclude by looking briefly at gas industries' continued practice of marking women as their primary targets of persuasion and manipulation.

Exploitation by Gaslight: Charlotte Tonna's *The Wrongs of Woman*

Charlotte Tonna published in numerous genres over the course of her life, but without fail she wrote in service of reform. The plight of factory workers was chief among her causes, and she is best known for her role in the Ten Hours Campaign, which advocated to reduce the working hours of women and children in textile production. As introductory remarks and didactic chapter conclusions make clear, Tonna intended *The Wrongs of Woman* to advance this movement. She began writing it on the heels of two searing labor investigations: Edwin Chadwick's *Report on the Sanitary Conditions of the Labouring Population* (1842) and Richard Grainger and Richard Henry Horne's *Second Report* (1843) on behalf of the Children's Employment Commission, which declared that "nothing so immediately concern[ed] the health and comfort of the whole manufacturing population" as unventilated gaslit rooms.[15] Tonna immersed herself in these reports, liberally transposing anecdotes, factory details, and testimony into her stories. Though Tonna's fiction had never wandered far from life, Joseph Kestner notes an "increasing reliance on documentary evidence" at this stage of the author's career.[16]

However, Tonna set out not only to expose grueling working conditions, but also to lay bare the moral contours of the industrial factory system. At the outset of her career, Tonna had experienced an ecstatic conversion to evangelical Christianity, a belief system that underpinned her conviction of the need for Biblically ordained, separate gendered spheres. Beyond prolonged work hours, a great evil of the factory system, by Tonna's account, was the fact that poor women had to leave their children and domestic duties at all. Guided by Tonna's pre-millenarian stance — a theology that understood the second coming as imminent — Ella Dzelzainis argues that the stakes of the Ten Hours Campaign, for Tonna, were urgent and outsized.[17] According to the author's worldview, disintegrating family structures would indicate a degenerate civilization at the time of Christ's return. Indeed, in the final passage of *The Wrongs of Woman*, Tonna denounces "the atrocious system" by which "the fair inheritance of England's Queen is becoming as a throne whose pillars rest on an awakening volcano."[18] Tonna, of course, did not know that fossil-fueled capitalism would, in fact, disorder the earth's rhythms, but she was keen to ways in which coal-powered industries had already "reversed the order of nature," a disruption she presents in both gendered and ecological terms (103).

In Tonna's effort to convey the physiological and psychological effects of a morally askew system, I find that her stories become less clinical and more imaginative. Since her reclamation from relative historical obscurity in the 1970s, scholarship on Tonna has primarily lauded her for the working-class content of her fiction rather than for its formal qualities.[19] From a craft perspective, Christian piety and legislative citations have hardly stood the test of time. More recently, however, Joanne Nystrom Janssen has posited Tonna as an inventive novelist, arguing that she created a "hybrid literary genre" in order to reach readers who were wary of fiction's corrupting influence.[20] My reading of gaslight in *The Wrongs of Woman* expands upon this view: I similarly interpret Tonna as lacing the factual with the figural in order to reveal truth and advance her cause. Beyond replicating the physical experience of work by gaslight, Tonna uses the technology as her premise for disrupting the initial steady rhythm of each story, as a catalyst for focalizing her characters' unsteady perception of their condition, and as the defining point of contrast between natural, healthful, rural life and the inverse world in which her protagonists find themselves. In doing so, she positions coal gas as the root of workplace manipulation that destabilizes the reality of its victims — or, capitalist gaslighting.

Tonna initially wrote "Milliners and Dressmakers" (1843) as a stand-alone piece for the *Christian Lady's Magazine*, but it was so successful in raising alarm that she followed it with three more stories over the course of the next year: "The Forsaken-Home," "The Little Pin-Headers," and "Lace-Runners." Each part tracks neighbors from a rural village who end up employed in different sectors of the garment industry. Though the characters and the type of work change, distinctive patterns and a formulaic structure recur in every narrative. Tonna's systemic critique works in part through accrual, each case at once distinctly horrific and seemingly a universal of factory life. I want to focus on two situations that exemplify the ways and means of capitalist gaslighting. The first concerns the fate of Ann King, the protagonist of Part I, whose story sets the stage for ensuing narratives. The second instance involves Mrs. Collins, whose grim experience of capitalist gaslighting par excellence serves as the collection's weighty finish.

Like her neighbors in later tales, Ann King leads an idyllic pastoral life until her father, a farmer, suffers financial losses and can no longer provide for her and her sister. He spends his remaining savings on indentured apprenticeships for his daughters, and we spend much of "Milliners and Dressmakers" with Ann in a section ironically titled "The Young Milliner's Debut," for Ann's entry into London connotes decline rather than flourishing womanhood. Worked to exhaustion and consumption, she meets an early death, a tragic yet (Tonna makes clear) preferable end to that of her sister, who falls into sex work, ultimately wearing out her days as a prison laborer.

Ann begins her first day of work filled with optimism and naiveté, mistaking her coworkers' wan appearances for a sign of sophistication. As the morning hours pass, Ann is surprised to discover that she receives no breaks, save fifteen minutes for lunch. Weary by afternoon and longing for fresh air, she pins her hopes on teatime and looks eagerly outside as that hour approaches:

> The sweet mellow twilight that everybody loves, but none so well as the dweller in a rural spot, was about to soften down some of the glaring tints that lay heaped upon the tables, and Ann would welcome it, as bringing to her mind pleasant pictures connected with that season of rest from the farmer's toil; but, behold! In a moment the blaze of gas-lights is shed upon every corner of the room, and with the increased heat comes the indescribable oppression, the giddiness, and nausea produced by the fumes of gas in a confined, low-roofed space. (33–34)

With the flare of gas, Ann's dimming hope gives way to despair. She learns that work will last until two in the morning and that it commences again at six each day, "by gas light, of course" (35). This news weighs heavily with Ann, who ordinarily would not mind rising early, "but to lose her natural rest . . . and to seek it without having taken fresh air . . . these are evils for which she was not prepared" (35). From this point on, Tonna's plodding narrative becomes disjointed. Midnight strikes, and "the scene is so strange to the newcomer that she regards it as a dream" (35). Suddenly, the morning, "a London morning by gaslight," revives "the scene of yesternight," as though Ann has only dozed at her work (41). The story then skips forward a year, and Ann, seated in a doctor's office, appears as a shadow of her former self. "The slim, bowed figure, and the tress of thin, loose, flossy hair bear little vestige of [her former] plump contour and bright rich curls," and "she breathes as though her slow progress along a level street had been a wild race to the summit of a mountain" (46).

The destabilizing effects of overwork by gaslight lay the groundwork for other, less tangible distortions of reality that plague Tonna's characters in their attempts to navigate the frontier of industrial capitalism. We first encounter the warped logic of capitalist gaslighting when it is articulated by Ann herself. A well-meaning physician has all but told her that she will die if she does not return home and adhere to the remedies he prescribes, to which Ann replies, "I will try it, sir, a little while where I am. Others are as badly off as me, but still keeping up for the sake of their families, and why should I be the first to give in?" (57). Her question turns an oppressive system into a personal failing: if she quits, it will be because she is weak. The doctor remains silent, and Ann, who has so internalized this mode of thinking that she uses it against herself, interprets his silence as tacit agreement. In fact, he contacts her father as soon as she departs.

Back at the millinery, we meet an instigator of this rhetoric in Ann's employer, Madame A., who watches for Ann "with looks portending a storm" and berates her upon entry (58). When Ann offers a doctor's note as an explanation for her absence, Madame A. "hints that the doctor's name is often made a pretext for other less creditable appointments" (58). Tonna leaves the reader to speculate about the specific meaning behind this aspersion — whether it implies an abortion or sex work. In either case, however, the author makes it clear that Madame A. cares about the duration of a "most unreasonably long" break from work rather than about Ann's moral or physical well-being (58). The employer engages in what we would now describe as medical gaslighting, insisting, in the days that follow, that Ann's health merits "no call for particular indulgence," even as our narrator reports "the returns of fainting fits, the rapidly increasing cough, the fever-flushed cheek, asthmatic gaspings, and other concomitants of disease" (59). Recent studies of gaslighting in institutional contexts find the primary goal to be "acquisition of a benefit through the intentional distortion of facts."[21] True to form, Madame A. does not prove to be simply mean-spirited or sadistic. Rather, we learn that a competing millinery has opened nearby, leading her to conclude that "if any opening should appear for getting rid of an exhausted sufferer, and, without even present diminution of gains, supplying the vacancy with a newer and more efficient workwoman — we had almost said machine — now is the time to profit by it" (60). Accordingly, when Mr. King arrives to inquire about his daughter's health, Madame A. seizes the opportunity to dismiss Ann under the pretense that she has "carried on a plot, privately, with a gentleman" (61). On the basis of this accusation, Madame A. replaces Ann with a more able-bodied worker without refunding the remaining cost of her indenture.

The protagonist of an upside-down story in which virtue garners her no reward, Ann returns home feeling that she has doubly failed her family. Her perseverance up to this point has been driven by not wanting "to be a burden upon [her] parents," "besides forfeiting the value of what they scraped together to pay a premium for [her]" (48, 55). In the end, Ann scarcely needs their support, as death swiftly follows her homecoming. Tonna concludes the tale by informing readers that, though the name of fictional Ann King does not appear on an actual gravestone, there are "not less than fifteen thousand young women . . . employed *in*, not merely working *for*, the millinery and dressmaking establishments" (94). Many of these establishments, Tonna reiterates, contain no source of natural light and so are "lighted night and day with gas" (100). She closes by exhorting readers to help curb the forces of capitalism "from bursting in, to bring ruin, destitution, and death to the hearths of England's cottages" (106).[22]

In "Milliners and Dressmakers" and Tonna's two succeeding stories, this threat of domestic destruction looms outside the frame of factory-centered narratives, but in "The Lace-Runners," the final portion of *The Wrongs of Woman*, Tonna brings readers into the intimacies of a collapsing working-class homelife. The story begins with adolescent Kate Clarke leaving her rural life to work for a family in one of England's lace-manufacturing districts. Kate provides our entry into the Collins household, where she assumes she will help with domestic tasks and minding children. However, on her first morning, Kate is surprised to find that Mrs. Collins does not want her to make the bed. Instead, the woman of the house "stuff[s] behind its frame all the clothes and other things that had been lying about, without the slightest attempt at folding them up, or any other idea, apparently, than of getting them out of the way" (27). Mrs. Collins takes care to wash her children's hands but not their faces before pulling out benches from under the dining table and assembling stands and frames for running lace. Kate realizes that, alongside Mrs. Collins and her children, her work will consist of running lace from dawn until long after dusk. She finds Mrs. Collins unfeeling and severe, and she becomes horrified when asked to administer a laudanum sedative to the family's newest infant so that he does not cry for milk and distract from the work at hand.

Mrs. Collins, however, does not remain a cipher set up for the easy judgment of Kate and, by proxy, Tonna's readers. When illness enters the home, the two women grow closer through their tandem efforts to care for ailing children while attempting, unsuccessfully, to keep up with lace orders sent over by the factory that employs Mrs. Collins. Kate begins to understand that every bit of meagerly paid lacework is essential to sustaining the poor family, and, on a harrowing evening when the infant teeters on the verge of death, she learns the family's sad history. Mrs. Collins explains that she and her husband began their life together optimistically, both eager and able to work during a time when "steam-machines were so expensive . . . [that] the labour of hands and feet [was] worth a deal more" (59). However, as wages fell to a state in which workers "c[ould]n't get half their toil's worth," she felt compelled to put her children to work as well, a decision that led to her oldest son getting paralyzed by a piece of machinery (61). Afterward, Mrs. Collins found herself unable to return to the factory and began working out of her home, a situation that, the reader has already begun to glean, is even more vexed than the plights of young factory workers detailed in Tonna's preceding stories. In order to complete work in this context, Mrs. Collins has been "forced to be cold-hearted like, even to [her] own flesh and blood" (55). As Mrs. Collins talks to Kate, Tonna establishes a terrible parallel between the embroidery thread in the mother's hand and "the yet more delicate thread" of the nearby baby's existence, both of which snap simultaneously (60). With a look of "unutterable desperation," Mrs. Collins "clenches her teeth, stamps her foot," and "groans from the depth of a mother's desolate heart" upon realizing that her baby has died (65). In earlier stories, Tonna prompted readers to have sympathy *for* the working-class heroine, a figure she arguably originated; by the close of this scene, she seems to almost dare them not to feel *with* Mrs. Collins.

The mother's unspeakable helplessness in this moment makes the following scene, in which blame leveled at Mrs. Collins reaches an apex, all the more affecting. Unable to afford a coffin, Mrs. Collins visits her employer's office on the morning after her baby's death in order to request a loan on the basis of her good character and ten years of employment. His response echoes criticisms she has encountered over the course of her economic decline: "Well, Mrs. So-and-so," he replies, "you ought not to have burdened yourself with a family of children. Marriages among those who have nothing to live upon but their chance earnings are the root of pauperism" (69). In deflecting attention away from the industrial manufacturing system by which he benefits and onto a purported character flaw in Mrs. Collins, the employer engages in textbook institutional gaslighting. He also discounts Mrs. Collins's status as an individual by reducing her to a generic female worker among many, a "Mrs. So-and-so." In both framing Mrs. Collins as personally at fault for her situation and erasing her selfhood, the employer enacts a defining paradox of capitalist gaslighting. As Mrs. Collins struggles to maintain her distinctiveness — "I never asked [for a loan] before" — the employer persists in dismissing her particularity: he cannot give hundreds of workers loans whenever they ask (71). He meets her specifics — "I am greatly distressed for a little help to bury my dead babe" — with statistical extrapolation: "By the last census, it appears . . . the chances [of death] are every way increased by the excess of children in a household. . . . Now, what inference do you draw from those facts?" (71–72, 74). The employer attempts to impress on Mrs. Collins not only that she is to blame for the horrific outcome of her child's death, but also the belief (previously internalized by Ann King) that her case is not worth pursing, because it amounts to a speck in the sands of industrial commerce.

If capitalist gaslighting "conceptually severs" a victim's experience from the corporate forces that gave rise to it, *The Wrongs of Woman* attempts a kind of suturing.[23] All four parts of the collection conclude with chapters titled "Consequences" that are addressed directly to readers. These chapters perform the opposite of victim-blaming, persistently reminding readers that "the evil resides in the system" (71). Without absolving individual managers of their gaslighting behavior, Tonna makes it clear that in order for the gears of industrial capitalism to grind forward, its pace and demands must be asserted as the natural way of things. By this logic, contrary perceptions of justice, fairness, or ordinariness must appear to be deluded. In calling readers to empathy and action, Tonna aims to restore what she understands to be natural order. Reading *The Wrongs of Woman* with close attention to its source texts and within the context of Britain's burgeoning coal-gas industry enables us to appreciate the role of gaslight in this endeavor — the ways in which Tonna treats it not only as a cause of ill health and material harm, but also as a crucial source of industrial capitalism's relentless imperatives.

Although Mrs. Collins's cries fall on deaf ears within the story, her tale's position at the conclusion of *The Wrongs of Woman* ensures that they ring in the ears of readers. We last see Mrs. Collins interminably at work in her home, with "that hated manufacture spread out on all sides," before Tonna begins her final exhortation (117). In this closing plea, she makes explicit not only her call to action — to purchase sparingly from the garment industry — but also her call to identification. Referencing the title, Tonna insists that wrongs "against woman in every rank and every class, perpetrated by the means which have been . . . sketched in these pages" are wrongs against all women (138). Tonna has worked to cultivate identification in part by drawing on, and then inverting, sentimental genres that would have been familiar to middle-class female readers. I am proposing that she also establishes fellow feeling by emphasizing the mutual experience, shared by women in divergent economic spheres, of gaslight indoors. Of course, the intensity of gaslit experiences was not equivalent. Middle-class women did not labor beneath numerous jets in unventilated spaces, but they were growing accustomed to the fumes, heat, brightness, and hissing of gas lamps in confined rooms. By implicitly encouraging her readers to recognize this parallel, Tonna both pushes for radical cross-class empathy and troubles the fiction of the sacrosanct middle-class home, secure from the perils of the outside world.

Domestic Vigilance: Gaslighting in Housekeeping Literature

In marketing efforts aimed at domestic consumers, gas companies were not keen to emphasize gaslight's origin as a factory technology. As the industry's response to Thames pollution accusations made evident, it was anxious not only about legislation but also about news coverage that drew wealthy customers' attention to the mal-effects of gaslight technology that plagued working-class residents of gasworks-adjacent slums. The water drinker's report that I cited at the start of this chapter had complained about publicity that "deeply affected the minds and depressed the spirits of delicate females," who, having swallowed "gilded pills" (sensational stories), found "their capacity for every domestic enjoyment utterly destroyed" (viii). This quote contains the seeds of strategic manipulation directed at the middle-class female gas consumer that began in the 1840s as the domestic gas utility expanded. Like physical encounters with gas, this capitalist gaslighting differed in degree, but not in kind, from that which was imposed on underclass detractors.

The success of the gas industry's counterstrategy in combating legal challenges during the 1820s meant more of the same. Representatives were quick to portray their industry as a victim, even as hundreds of miles of gasworks extended throughout Britain. Public outcry and formal legal suits died down to some extent until the formation of the Gas Consumers' Mutual Protection Agency in 1857, but we see gaslighting rhetoric still at play in the emergent genre of the gas user's manual. Samuel Clegg's *Practical Treatise on the Manufacture and Distribution of Coal-Gas* (1841), for example, devotes an entire section to the "strange prejudice" of those who "believe that coal-gas . . . gives off some highly deleterious agents."[24] I want to focus briefly on John W. Parker's *Hints to Gas-Consumers* (1840), which sold widely and established formal trends that later manuals follow.

Parker's manual begins, as Clegg's and others' do, with a history of the coal-gas industry that positions gaslight as both "one of the most important inventions of modern times" and a convenience that has "received a greater share of abuse than any other . . . modern improvement."[25] Calibrating his guide to the middle-class consumer, Parker confides that gas, as though coming up in polite society, was at first "merely tolerated, not cordially approved" in fashionable homes, due to prejudices that were "as absurd as they were unjust" (3). This version of events enables Parker to dismiss initial customer hesitation as snobbery, rather than justified wariness, while cultivating a sense of shared understanding with the middle-class homemaker on the up-and-up. Yet, a few pages later, in a tonal shift from confidante to something more imposing, Parker doubles down on his disparagement of skeptics. He makes it clear that "we," the gas manufacturers, "have no fellow-feeling with those who seem purposely to . . . [attach] an air of mystery to everything connected with gas operations," and "who live in continual apprehension of some unidentified danger . . . whether it be real or imaginary" (6). The user manual goes on to cover topics such as the "Relative Cost of Coal-gas" and "Utility, Convenience, and Safety" in sections that extol the benefits of gaslight while denying culpability for its harms. Whenever a hazard or drawback arises in the course of discussion, Parker becomes imperious. The conduct of a person who fails to notice a leak in her home is "reprehensible" (38). The customer who complains that gas has blackened ceilings in a rented house is "so perfectly regardless . . . of the commonest principles of honesty, that their object seems to be how they may destroy as much as possible of other people's property" (41). Parker acknowledges that he censures "in terms which to some may appear as unnecessarily severe," but he persists even so (47).

Throughout these censorious passages, Parker identifies women, specifically, as the consumers most responsible for mishaps and misrepresentation (for example, "In the minds of some persons, and especially of females, [gas] is associated with everything offensive and unwholesome" [32]). Females *"fancy* they are in danger of being suffocated the moment they detect the slightest odor of gas; but this is so palpably absurd that it hardly deserves a thought" (33). *Hints to Gas-Consumers*, like later guides, concludes with an appendix containing actual cases that expand upon and corroborate the manual's advice. "Note G." gets unsubtly to the point of what Parker has been suggesting about gender and gas all along. It begins with an effusive description of the vigorously healthy men who work in gas manufacturing where they regularly "inhale the carbureted gases" in order to contrast their condition with a "patient (a female)" who suffered from consumption (84). (Tonna's source texts and stories understand consumption to be a result of prolonged overexposure to coal gas.) According to the *Lancet*, a doctor cured this patient by requiring her "to inhale a mixture of . . . coal-gas and atmospheric air," a concoction that the doctor "very freely" breathed in himself (84–85). In the same vein as Ann King, women readers are supposed to deduce from these cases not only that fears of suffocation by gas are unfounded, but also that the sensation of actual physical symptoms does not accord with the (implicitly more reliable) experiences of sturdy working men or educated male physicians. Faulty interpretation must arise, then, from the mind of the female consumer.

In contrast to the female workers represented in Tonna's stories, however, readers of Parker's manual, and of similar guides that followed, had an avenue through which to combat the insidious strategies of persuasion employed against them. During the middle decades of the nineteenth century, the housewife's domestic manual emerged. Its contents appeared first in serial form and were then collected into volumes. As a result of Britain's industrializing economy, class mobility was increasingly in flux, in both directions, and so numerical income was not a stable marker of status. Andrea Kaston Tange has demonstrated that in light of this economic instability, the home itself became a critical indicator of middle-class identity. She means this both symbolically and literally, in that the "material object" of the house was viewed as having moral character.[26] "Housekeeping guides represented the role of the woman of the house as extending to the physical structure itself," she explains. "Her 'natural' moral sense and capacity for nurture were expected to ensure that the home she created was a private haven from the dangers of the public world."[27] As Tange's paraphrasing makes evident, housekeeping guides, like Tonna's writings, were deeply invested in the "natural" way of things, but whereas Tonna had provocatively sought to expose the nature of the nation gone wrong, the oft-stated purpose of these guides was to uphold the ideology of innate fireside virtue that, by extension, reflected the moral character of Britain.

Fascinatingly, however, housekeeping guides formally register something amiss when discussing the coal-gas utility. A defining trait of midcentury housekeeping guides was their shift away from the morally charged rhetoric and priorities of early Victorian conduct manuals. Earlier manuals had focused sentimentally on feminine character, but domestic advice literature was encyclopedic, offering a fastidious catalog of practical skills in a manner that professionalized the role of the housewife.[28] Strikingly, then, passages on gas read as a kind of rupture in which sensational language appears in the modernizing woman's handbook.

Spurred by, as Sarah Stickney Ellis put it in her proto-housekeeping guide, *The Women of England* (1839), "the darkest substance from the bowels of the earth, the very source of all this light," aesthetic gasification arises in the gothic manner of an uncontained past intruding on present circumstances.[29] "However convenient or pleasant gas-light may be," cautions the author of *Cassell's Household Guide* (1869),

> its use should always be adopted with a full knowledge of the serious evils which accompany it, evils which can only be guarded against by proper ventilation. In ill-ventilated rooms pains in the head, nausea, languor, and bronchial irritation are frequently experienced . . . The serious consequences of inhaling unburnt gas are too often forgotten, and there are thousands now burning it who never heard or read a word upon the subject. We should ill deserve the title Household Guide if we did not set up our warning here.[30]

In similar fashion, *A Manual for Domestic Economy* (1856) cautions the woman reader to guard herself and her home against a threat — "as far as possible . . . we ought to provide for the exclusion of this injurious gas from our rooms" — and, as many guides do, this text refers to gas as an "evil."[31] As late as 1887, after gas companies had incurred at least a modicum of regulation and decades into the professionalization of the housekeeping genre, otherwise pragmatic Jane Ellen Panton penned this unrestrained outburst: "I feel consumed with rage and anger to think that I was not born in an age when the electric light will be as much a matter of course as the present odious system of lighting by gas . . . but as we are still unemancipated to the thralldom of gas, we must try to . . . confine the enemy where it can do least harm."[32] Read against gas users' manuals, passages like the ones excerpted here attest to the manipulative gaslighting rhetoric employed against female consumers. Not coincidentally, in other words, Panton and her predecessors discuss the housewife in terms that parallel Tonna's descriptions of besieged working-class heroines. However, the passionate warnings expressed in housekeeping guides also function as a form of resistance, both in calling out the presence of a wrong and in meeting it with rigorous empiricism.

In a fitting response to the networked threat under discussion, the knowledge shared in these guides was dispersed throughout an increasingly accessible print network. The transition to coal-gas power entailed a loss of tangible interaction with one's fuel source — which had been visible, contained, self-tended — and consequent reliance on faceless, privatized suppliers. As historian Wolfgang Schivelbusch grimly puts it, "Once a house was connected to a central gas supply, its autonomy was over."[33] However, like *The Wrongs of Woman*, which tapped into the link between the housewife in her drawing room and the seamstress at the end of the pipe, housekeeping guides maximize the advantages of networked form. *Cassell's* guide actually invites readers to conceive of gas infrastructure as a form of communication. The anonymous author describes Britain's gasworks as "contrived after the manner of arteries or veins," and a section on in-home speaking tubes insists that "the ordinary iron gas-pipe answer[s] the purpose nearly as well as gutta percha," a latex material typically used for this device.[34] In contrast to Parker's gas manual, we can appreciate the significance of circulating information about how to arrange one's nursery so that "inflammable gas ascends to the top [of the room]," thereby mitigating "consequences" that are "often fatal."[35] This advice was published in *The Englishwoman's Domestic Magazine*, edited by Isabella Beeton, who later collected many of the magazine's columns into her *Book of Household Management* (1859). Contrary to Parker's presumed female customer, whom he describes as ignorant of gas properties and operations, Beeton's guide evinces, and propagates, an exhaustive understanding of coal gas from raw material through to distribution, including passages detailing the mineral composition of coal and where it appears in the earth's strata. In her book, Beeton goes further than recommending ways to prevent gas poisoning from occurring. Rather than rely on the authority of medical professionals, she empowers women via "a few rough rules" to respond to gas asphyxiation more swiftly than it would take a surgeon to arrive.[36] Her recommendations include taking the victim outside, offering smelling salts, and performing a rudimentary version of CPR involving a pair of bellows, actions which, she tells readers, "turn the balance between recovery and death."[37]

Bella Manningham, the heroine of Patrick Hamilton's *Gas Light*, had precedents, in other words — a genealogy of women who had made vigilance about gas lamps integral to their domestic practice. In writing to middle-class female readers, Tonna had acknowledged not only the commonality of their experience with that of working-class women, but also their contrastive agency, delimited though it may have been by the constraints of Victorian womanhood. Paradoxically, given her conservative stance on separate gendered spheres, Tonna viewed "female influence" as "the basis of . . . all commercial intercourse," and so she wrote in service of "rousing [her readers'] energies to a work which they alone [could] accomplish."[38] Interestingly, the strategies deployed in gas paraphernalia in order to influence the female consumer demonstrate that while gas companies marked her, on the one hand, as vulnerable to manipulation, they also recognized women as crucial to the industry's success. Parker actually describes his readers, somewhat flatteringly but not wholly inaccurately, as "those on whom the prosperity of gas establishments entirely depends" (6).

***

This dynamic between gas interests and female consumers has continued into the present day. In June 2022, a Harvard study titled "Home Is Where the Pipeline Ends" found that the volatile organic compounds (VOCs) in natural gas are more prone to leak during gas stove usage than had been previously thought. Methane, the predominate VOC present in natural gas, has been a primary contributor to rising global temperatures since the industrial revolution. A few months later, a leading environmental research journal published a study that demonstrated the extent to which gas stoves increase the risk of childhood asthma.[39] Summarizing the findings of both reports, a representative of the US Consumer Product Safety Commission (CPSC) described gas stoves as "a hidden hazard" and suggested that a future ban on production may be warranted.[40] These remarks led to an eruption of political debate over gas stoves, which became, seemingly overnight, "one of the most divisive issues in public health, as well as the fight over climate action," as the *New York Times* put it.[41] The CPSC itself was taken aback at the scale of the reaction from the political right to what was not new information about gas stoves, but rather newly confirmed degrees of pollutant severity and asthmatic correlation.

However, as NPR reported in an investigative piece, the American Gas Association has been engaged in "a lengthy campaign" to ensure the persistence of gas stoves since the 1970s, when research into negative effects of the appliance was first published.[42] As part of this effort, the American Gas Association conducted its own studies that highlighted uncertainties in scientific reports and, in turn, produced marketing campaigns targeted at female homemakers and aimed at sowing doubt about gas stove data. Internal reports reveal that the natural gas industry has long positioned the gas stove as its "gateway appliance" — the iconic household commodity that, if installed with the necessary gas utility hookups, makes consumers more likely to use other gas appliances such as driers, water heaters, and furnaces, which might otherwise have been electric.[43] The thrust of the natural gas industry's approach amid this most recent controversy was epitomized in the *Wall Street Journal* editorial "Biden Is Coming for Your Gas Stoves" (2023), which insisted that "the real hazard isn't gas stoves but how people use them." In other words, consumers who heat "oil, fat, and other ingredients, especially at high temperatures" or who use the stove hood improperly are to blame if any harmful health or environmental outcomes occur[44] — consumers who, even today, are implicitly presumed to be women.

Notes

1. See, for example, Matthews and Hedley, *Letter to the Right Honourable the Lord Mayor*.
2. Anonymous, *Water Question*, v. Further references will be cited parenthetically.
3. Tomory, "Environmental History," 44–46.
4. Franklin, "Gaslighting," 94.
5. Tomory, *Progressive Enlightenment*, 127.
6. Directors' Meetings, 415.
7. On mileage, see Nye, *American Illuminations*, 38; on coal consumption, see Binder, "Gas Light," 359.
8. Rees, *Theatre Lighting*, 20–23.
9. Fressoz, "Gas Lighting Controversy," 732–35.
10. Otter, *Victorian Eye*, 144–45.
11. On the 1860s Gas Acts, see Nead, *Victorian Babylon*, 90–96.
12. Stark, "Gaslighting, Misogyny," 221.
13. Berenstain, "White Feminist Gaslighting," 734.
14. For more on Wollstonecraft's *Wrongs of Woman*, see this collection's introduction.
15. Grainger and Horne, *Children's Employment*, 36.
16. Kestner, "Charlotte Elizabeth Tonna's *The Wrongs of Woman*," 196.
17. Dzelzainis, "Reason vs Revelation," 1–15.
18. Tonna, *Wrongs of Woman*, 138. Further references will be cited parenthetically.
19. See, for example, Kovacevic and Kanner, "Blue Book."
20. Janssen, "Embodying Facts," 329.
21. Roberts and Andrews, "Critical Race Analysis," 78.
22. Though Tonna does not use the term capitalism, she often discusses capital, asserting, for example, that "the only explanation that can be given of this system of inflicted and invited wrong is the fact that in the desperate spirit of speculation, commercial men will set no limits to the production of what they may possibly sell, to the farther increase of their growing capital" (23).
23. I borrow this phrase from philosopher Alison Bailey's formulation of epistemic gaslighting in institutional contexts. "On Gaslighting," 667.
24. Clegg, *Practical Treatise*, 90.
25. Parker, *Hints to Gas-Consumers*, 1, 32. Further references will be cited parenthetically.
26. Tange, *Architectural Identities*, 5–6.
27. Tange, *Architectural Identities*, 11.
28. See Langland, *Nobody's Angels*, 27, 74, 233.
29. Ellis, *Women of England*, 327.
30. *Cassell's*, 300.
31. Walsh, *Manual*, 106.

32. Panton, *From Kitchen to Garret*, 127.
33. Schivelbusch, *Disenchanted Night*, 28.
34. *Cassell's*, 181, 250.
35. Anonymous, "Sick-Room," 352.
36. Beeton, *Book of Household Management*, 2578.
37. Beeton, *Book of Household Management*, 2578.
38. First quote from Tonna, "Politics," 250; second quote from Tonna, *Wrongs of Woman,* 119.
39. See Gruenwald, "Population Attributable."
40. Anonymous, "How Gas Stoves."
41. Tabuchi, "In the Fight."
42. Brady, "How Gas Utilities."
43. Brady, "How Gas Utilities."
44. Editorial Board, "Biden Is Coming."

Bibliography

Anonymous. "How Gas Stoves Became Part of America's Culture Wars." *The Economist*. January 17, 2023. https://tinyurl.com/239ynvpf.

Anonymous. "Sick-Room and Nursery." *The Englishwoman's Domestic Magazine* 4, no. 370 (1855): 351–52.

Anonymous. *The Water Question. Animadversions of the Reports, Evidence, and Documents Relative to the Supply of Water to the Metropolis*. R. Hunter, 1829.

Bailey, Alison. "On Gaslighting and Epistemic Injustice: Editor's Introduction." *Hypatia* 35, no.4 (2020): 667–73.

Beeton, Mrs. Isabella. *The Book of Household Management.* S.O. Beeton, 1861.

Berenstain, Nora. "White Feminist Gaslighting." *Hypatia* 35, no. 4 (2020): 733–58.

Binder, Frederick Moore. "Gas Light." *Pennsylvania History: A Journal of Mid-Atlantic Studies* 22, no. 4 (1955): 359–73.

Brady, Jeff. "How Gas Utilities Used Tobacco Tactics to Avoid Gas Stove Regulations." *NPR*. October 17, 2023. https://www.npr.org/2023/10/17/1183551603/gas-stove-utility-tobacco.

Chadwick, Edwin. *Report on the Sanitary Condition of the Labouring Population of Great Britain*. W. Clowes & Sons, 1842.

Cassell's Household Guide: Being a Complete Encyclopedia of Domestic and Social Economy. Cassell, Petter, and Galpin, 1869–1871.

Clegg, Samuel. *A Practical Treatise on the Manufacture and Distribution of Coal-Gas: Its Introduction and Progressive Improvement*. 5th ed. D. Van Nostrand, 1868.

Directors' Meetings: Signed Minutes, June 1812–September 1814, B/GLCC/001, Chartered Gas Light and Coke Company. London Metropolitan Archives, London, UK.

Dzelzainis, Ella. "Reason vs Revelation: Feminism, Malthus, and the New Poor Law in Narratives by Harriet Martineau and Charlotte Elizabeth Tonna." *19: Interdisciplinary Studies in the Long Nineteenth Century* 2 (2006): 1–15.

Editorial Board. "Biden Is Coming for Your Gas Stoves." *The Wall Street Journal*. January10, 2023. https://www.wsj.com/articles/biden-is-coming-for-your-gas-stove-consumerproduct-safety-commission-richard-trumka-environmental-protection-agency11673303864.

Ellis, Sarah Stickney. *The Women of England, Their Social Duties, and Domestic Habits*. Fisher, Son, & Co., 1839.

Franklin, Grace. "Gaslighting: The Material History of a Metaphor." *Victorian Studies* 67, no. 1 (2024): 93–116.

Fressoz, Jean-Baptiste. "The Gas Lighting Controversy: Technological Risk, Expertise, and Regulation in Nineteenth-Century Paris and London." *Journal of Urban History* 33, no. 5 (2007): 729–55.

Grainger, Richard, and Richard Henry Horne. *Children's Employment Commission. Second Report of the Commissioners. Trades and Manufactures*. William Clowes and Sons, 1843.

Gruenwald, Taylor, et al. "Population Attributable Fraction of Gas Stoves and Childhood Asthma in the United States." *International Journal of Environmental Research and Public Health* 20, no. 1 (2023): 75.

Janssen, Joanne Nystrom. "'Embodying Facts': Anxiety about Fiction in *The Christian Lady's Magazine* and Charlotte Elizabeth Tonna's Social-Problem Novels." *Victorian Periodicals Review* 44, no. 4 (2011): 327–53.

Kestner, Joseph. "Charlotte Elizabeth Tonna's *The Wrongs of Woman*: Female Industrial Protest." *Tulsa Studies in Women's Literature* 2, no. 2 (1983): 193–214.

Kovacevic, Ivanka, and S. Barbara Kanner. "Blue Book into Novel: The Forgotten Industrial Fiction of Charlotte Elizabeth Tonna." *Nineteenth-Century Fiction* 25, no. 2 (1970): 152-73.

Langland, Elizabeth. *Nobody's Angels: Middle-Class Women and Domestic Ideology in Victorian Culture.* Cornell University Press, 1995.

Matthews, William, and Joseph Hedley. *A Letter to the Right Honourable the Lord Mayor of London . . . Upon the Delusive Nature of Many of the Projects for Gas-Lighting.* R. Hunter, 1828.

Michanowicz, Drew R., et al. "Home is Where the Pipeline Ends: Characterization of Volatile Organic Compounds Present in Natural Gas at the Point of the Residential End User." *Environmental Science Technology* 54, no. 14 (2022): 10258–68.

Nead, Lynda. *Victorian Babylon: People, Streets, and Images in Nineteenth-Century London*. Yale University Press, 2000.

Nye, David E. *American Illuminations: Urban Lighting, 1800–1920.* MIT Press, 2018.

Otter, Chris. *The Victorian Eye: A Political History of Light and Vision in Britain, 1800–1910*. University of Chicago Press, 2008.

Panton, Jane Ellen. *From Kitchen to Garret: Hints for Young Householders.* 1888. Cambridge University Press, 2012.

Parker, John W. *Hints to Gas-Consumers*. 2nd ed. John W. Parker, 1840.

Rees, Terence. *Theatre Lighting in the Age of Gas.* Entertainment Technology Press, 2004.

Roberts, Tuesda, and Dorinda J. Carter Andrews. "A Critical Race Analysis of Gaslighting Against African American Teachers." In *Contesting the Myth of a Post Racial Era: The Continued Significance of Race in U.S. Education*, edited by Dorinda J. Carter Andrews and Franklin Tuitt, 69–94. Peter Lang, 2013.

Schivelbusch, Wolfgang. *Disenchanted Night: The Industrialization of Light in the Nineteenth Century*. Translated by Angela Davies. University of California Press, 1995.

Stark, Cynthia A. "Gaslighting, Misogyny, and Psychological Oppression." *The Monist* 102, no. 2 (2019): 221–35.

Tabuchi, Hiroko. "In the Fight Over Gas Stoves, Meet the Industry's Go-To Scientist." *New York Times*. January 29, 2023. https://www.nytimes.com/2023/01/29/climate/gas-stovehealth.html.

Tange, Andrea Kaston. *Architectural Identities: Domesticity, Literature and the VictorianMiddle Class*. University of Toronto Press, 2010.

Tomory, Leslie. "The Environmental History of the Early British Gas Industry, 1812–1830." *Environmental History*" 17, no. 1 (2012): 29–54.

———. *Progressive Enlightenment: The Origins of the Gaslight Industry, 1780–1820*. MIT Press, 2012.

Tonna, Charlotte Elizabeth. *The Wrongs of Woman.* M. W. Dodd, 1845.

——— "Politics." *The Christian Lady's Magazine* (March 1, 1834): 249–56.

Walsh, J. H. *A Manual for Domestic Economy: Suited to Families Spending From £100 to £1000 a Year*. G. Routledge & Co., 1856.

9

Structural Scarcity

Women's Economic Writing and Epistemic Gaslighting

Lana L. Dalley

In the beginning of George Eliot's *Middlemarch* (1871–1872), the reader is made to understand that Dorothea Brooke is a young woman whose aspirations extend well beyond the domestic realm and into the realm of the economic. Dorothea wants to make a difference in the world and is "enamored of intensity and greatness" — qualities that, the narrator notes, will likely interfere with her marriage prospects.[1] In the first two chapters of the novel, political economy is named twice as an obstacle in the path of Dorothea's ambitions. First, the narrator refers to Dorothea as the kind of wife who "might awaken you some fine morning with a new scheme for the application of her income which would interfere with political economy and the keeping of saddle-horses: a man would naturally think twice before he risked himself in such fellowship."[2] And second, political economy is mentioned at a dinner conversation between Dorothea, her soon-to-be fiancé Casaubon, and her uncle Mr. Brooke when Dorothea shares her recently developed passion for improving the tenant buildings on her uncle's land. In doing so, "she spoke with more energy than is expected of so young a lady," which causes Casaubon to "turn[] his eyes very markedly" on her while she is speaking and "observe her newly."[3] In this moment, Mr. Brooke decides to shut Dorothea down by saying to Casaubon: "Young ladies don't understand political economy, you know. . . . I remember when we were all reading Adam Smith. *There* is a book now. I took in all the new ideas at one time — human perfectibility, now."[4] Mr. Brooke weaponizes his knowledge of political economy in order to undercut Dorothea's ambitions, using Adam Smith as a signifier of his knowledge, his masculinity, and his access to a discipline that "young ladies don't understand." The conspiratorial element of the exchange is underscored by the fact that Mr. Brooke is "smiling towards Mr. Casaubon" while making a dismissive comment about Dorothea, talking about her as though she is not also sitting at the table.

In this scene, Eliot draws the reader's attention to the common cultural assumption about women and economic knowledge — that they know nothing about the subject — while also critiquing that assumption by having Mr. Brooke, whose capacity for original thought and intellectual understanding is highly questionable, make the assertion in a rambling, incoherent way. In other words, no sensible reader believes that Brooke knows much about Adam Smith, and yet Brooke still manages, on the strength of his masculinity and confidence, to create a credibility deficit that silences Dorothea. The narrator concludes the scene by referring to political economy as "that never-explained science which was thrust as an extinguisher over all [Dorothea's] lights."[5] As it so often does, fiction here illuminates a phenomenon that remained shadowed in real life; namely, the epistemic gaslighting of Victorian women and the extent to which such gaslighting literally and figuratively kept them from having a voice at the table.

Veronica Ivy [Rachel McKinnon] defines epistemic gaslighting as a "form [of gaslighting], often unintentional, where a listener doesn't believe or expresses doubt about a speaker's testimony. In this epistemic form of gaslighting, the listener of testimony raises doubts about the speakers' reliability at perceiving events accurately."[6] The credibility deficit is the modus operandi of epistemic gaslighting; the curated exclusivity of political economy, as a discipline, in the nineteenth century renders it a rich case study for how the credibility deficit is wielded by those in power. Over the course of the century, political economy gained considerable clout, transforming itself from a humanistic field to a data-driven science.[7] As political economy amassed cultural authority, it also acquired a reputation for exclusivity; it was regarded as the difficult business of educated, wealthy men, something inaccessible to the majority of the population. Viewed through the lens of epistemic gaslighting, one might argue that political economy amassed cultural authority precisely because it was regarded as impenetrable, masculine knowledge. The procedures of the Political Economy Club provide a useful illustration of how such exclusivity was carefully curated. In 1821, a handful of prominent economists (including James Mill, David Ricardo, and Thomas Malthus) formed the club as a space to debate and settle the finer points of political economy and to promote that knowledge within society; the members of the club were, quite clearly, the gatekeepers of the discipline. The number of members was limited to thirty, and to be considered for membership, one had to be nominated by a current member of the club, debated on the floor of the meeting, and elected by secret ballot. Further evidence of the club's gatekeeping is the fact that minutes were not taken at meetings so the only people privy to the meeting debates — debates that were meant to decide key questions within the field — were members of the club. This was an intentional choice and one meant to limit the number of highly informed and influential economists to the thirty men sitting in the room. Unsurprisingly, there were no women elected to the Political Economy Club in the nineteenth century.

Political economy was represented as irrelevant to women because of the separate spheres ideology that confined them to the private sphere. In their written work, political economists rarely considered women as economic subjects, and within the discipline, women were not acknowledged as economists until well into the twentieth century. Economists use the term "structural scarcity" to describe a phenomenon wherein members of a population have unequal access to resources; in this essay, I propose that a similar phenomenon has occurred within the field of economics, wherein women have historically been denied equal access to the discipline, creating a structural scarcity of women economists within the field. Beginning with public responses to Harriet Martineau's *Illustrations of Political Economy* (1832), for example, there was a strain of visible backlash against women who wrote about economics in the nineteenth century; this hostility showed up in different places, including public forums like newspapers and journals and private spaces like letters and diaries. Importantly, the backlash carried over into institutional spaces, like publishing houses, universities, and academic societies; it also occasionally devolved into personal attacks, like critiques of a woman writer's physical appearance or accusations about her sexuality. Using epistemic gaslighting as a framework, I argue that such responses intended to trivialize and stereotype women's contributions to economic writing, creating a credibility deficit that made women writers (and their readers) doubt their ability to meaningfully engage with the discipline. In the case of economics, epistemic gaslighting often relied upon gender stereotypes to insist that while women might reasonably assume the title of fiction writer, they certainly could not claim the title of economist. Such gender bias simultaneously inspired doubt in women's scholarly capacity, downplayed or effaced their achievements within the field of economics, and reinforced broader myths about women's intellectual inferiority.

Gaslighting is a term most often used to describe "the mind-manipulating tactics of abusive people," and much of the literature about gaslighting focuses on gaslighting as a form of emotional intimate partner violence.[8] However, focusing solely on the psychological dimensions of gaslighting has, as sociologist Paige Sweet has noted, led many to "ignore the gender-based structural conditions that make gaslighting possible" and, by extension, to overlook other contexts where gaslighting is a harmful and common practice.[9] Gaslighting works when a perpetrator is able to cast the victim as crazy, irrational, and overly emotional, and labeling women in these ways has long been a way to silence them. The traditional association of women with irrationality makes them particularly vulnerable to gaslighting strategies that attempt to undermine and belittle them, making them question their sanity and, in institutional and disciplinary contexts, question their legitimacy. Within these contexts, gaslighting presents as a performance of knowledge that allows one, more powerful party to establish and/or maintain power over another, less powerful party. This performance of knowledge (or "knowledge") is a form of gendered gaslighting for two reasons: first, because it achieves its purpose of drawing boundaries around a particular body of knowledge and preventing women from crossing those boundaries by making them feel as though they are *fundamentally incapable* of understanding or contributing to the discipline because of traits they are presumed to possess as women; second, this gaslighting is enacted in order to reassert the dominance of the more powerful party by belittling the already disenfranchised group and making them question their intelligence and their sanity. Such gaslighting often masquerades as academic critique, as is evident in the *Middlemarch* example.

Ivy refers to this type of gaslighting as "epistemic injustice" — a phrase she borrows from Miranda Fricker — and uses the example of grammar "policing" to make her point: if, she argues, someone points out the use of imperfect grammar in order to "discredit the underlying message," then epistemic gaslighting is occurring. Ivy draws upon Kristie Dotson's understanding of "testimonial smothering and testimonial quieting" to articulate her theory. Testimonial smothering occurs when "typically, a marginalized person judges that their potential audience will respond to their testimony with such a severe credibility deficit that they might as well not speak in the first place."[10] Testimonial quieting, on the other hand, happens when a speaker, typically a marginalized person, suffers "such a severe credibility deficit that it's as if they didn't speak at all."[11] Kate Abramson explains that gaslighting is different from simply dismissing someone because gaslighting aims to convince "another not to take herself seriously as an interlocutor."[12] There's an unmooring of self that occurs here — a fundamental lack of confidence that can prevent someone from entering a conversation (as readers observe with Dorothea's silencing) or make them disavow their own competence (essentially beating the gaslighter to the punch). When being gaslit, women are accused of being crazy and paranoid; within epistemic gaslighting, women are accused of being incapable and illegitimate. Both sets of accusations are rooted in sexist stereotypes about women's behavior that aim to isolate and undermine them and, perhaps most importantly, to cause them to undermine themselves. Epistemic gaslighting occurs when those in power exploit existing structural inequalities to discredit and trivialize the contributions of less powerful members of the institution, ultimately creating a "credibility deficit" that isolates and silences those members, disallowing them full participation in the institution.[13] The insidious nature of the attacks, and the fact that they often masquerade as critique, can make them particularly difficult to recognize and combat.

Take, for example, the preface to Elizabeth Gaskell's industrial novel *Mary Barton* (1848). Near the end of the preface, after explaining to readers how she came to write the novel, Gaskell insists, "I know nothing of Political Economy, or the theories of trade. I have tried to write truthfully; and if my accounts agree or clash with any system, the agreement or disagreement is unintentional."[14] Rather, she suggests, her novel is simply a representation of what she has observed while living in Manchester. Gaskell aligns her writing with feminine sympathetic observation, rather than masculine economic theory; she would have been keenly aware, in writing a novel that addresses economic relations, that she was infringing upon the gendered boundaries of economic discourse, and her framing of the story offers an anticipatory mea culpa. In other words, Gaskell seems to expect that her credibility on economic matters will be challenged by her readers and, in response, preemptively disavows any claim to knowledge of the subject.

In truth, Gaskell did know something about political economy. Jane Marcet was a family friend, and, in her teens, Gaskell read Marcet's *Conversations on Political Economy* (1816).[15] Gaskell was also familiar with Harriet Martineau's *Illustrations of Political Economy* (1832) and likely based several aspects of *Mary Barton* on Martineau's story "A Manchester Strike." Gaskell also gathered knowledge about political economy from within her family. Her father, William Stevenson, wrote a series on political economy in *Blackwood's Edinburgh Magazine* in 1824 that aimed "to prove that Political Economy is neither so perfect as one party maintain, nor so completely out of human intellect, as the other party insinuate by their scepticism and ridicule."[16]

There is also evidence that Gaskell had a knowledge of canonical economic texts themselves. In a letter to her daughter, Marianne, written in April 1851, Gaskell writes:

> Before you fully make up your mind [on the subject of a Protectionist Ministry], read a paper in the Quarterly on the subject of Free Trade, (written by Mr. George Taylor) in (I think) the year 1839; and then when you come home I will read with you Mr. Cobden's speeches. But first I think we should read together Adam Smith on the Wealth of Nations. Not confining ourselves as we read to the limited meaning which he affixes to the word "wealth." Seriously, dear, you must not become a *partizan* in politics or in anything else, — you must have "a reason for the faith that is in you," — and not in three weeks suppose you can know enough to form an opinion about measures of state. That is one reason why so many people dislike that women should meddle with politics, they say it is a subject requiring long patient studies of many "branches of science," and a logical training which few women have had, — that women are apt to take up a thing without being even able to state their reasons clearly, and yet on that insufficient knowledge they take a more violent and bigoted stand than thoughtful *men* dare to do. Have as many and as large and varied interests as you can; but do not again have a decided opinion on a subject which you can at present know nothing.[17]

Gaskell's letter reveals a commitment to teaching her daughter about economic theory and practice; her willingness to challenge Smith's definition of wealth suggests a certain level of confidence in her own understanding of political economy and belies her claim in *Mary Barton* that she "know[s] nothing" of the subject. So why would Gaskell make a claim of total ignorance when she had knowledge of the subject, a knowledge that would presumably grant her greater authority with her readers? The answer can be found in epistemic gaslighting. Although Gaskell did indeed know something about political economy, she seemed to feel as if her claim to knowledge lacked credibility, and so she disavowed the knowledge altogether. Gaskell's letter to her daughter also makes clear the stakes for a woman's professed knowledge of a "masculine" subject and, in so doing, underscores Gaskell's hesitancy to claim a knowledge of political economy that, if proved incomplete or flawed, would provide further support for those who argue against women's "meddl[ing] with politics." The consequences of a perceived "credibility deficit" are intensified by the sense that a misstep will be a disservice to women everywhere. Epistemic gaslighting here creates a panoptic enforcement of disciplinary boundaries, wherein women are reticent to speak or write about disciplines that they are made to feel they cannot comprehend.

In her concerns about credibility, Gaskell was certainly not alone. To elucidate this point, I will turn to Harriet Martineau and the resistance to her participation in the field of economics, including one specific press campaign that is a clear instance of epistemic gaslighting. Throughout the nineteenth century, women's writing about political economy was primarily didactic. For writers like Martineau (and Jane Marcet and Millicent Garrett Fawcett, to name just a few), authorial access to the discipline of economics was achieved primarily through didactic fiction writing; limiting women's economic writing to didactic forms marked their participation in the discipline, from its very inception, as gendered.[18] Women were not to *be* economists, but they could *teach* economics. (One is reminded here of Aurora Leigh's comments about her early education: "I read a score of books on womanhood / To prove, if *women* do not *think* at all / They *may teach thinking*."[19]) And yet, as the campaign against Martineau's *Illustrations of Political Economy* makes clear, even that type of participation was often hard-won.

In her *Autobiography* — which she wrote in 1855 but did not allow to be published until after her death in 1877 — Martineau describes the project of writing *Illustrations* as "the strongest act of will that I ever committed myself to" and describes her anxiety about the project: "owing to the nature of some of the subjects to be treated, my effort would probably be fatal to my reputation; that the chances of failure in a scheme of such extent, begun without money or interest, were most formidable, and that failure would be ruin."[20] She recounts, in great detail, the difficulty she has in finding a publisher for her series, as publisher after publisher declares that the recent Reform Bill has rendered the reading public too volatile for such a work. Martineau finally strikes a deal with Charles Fox and *Illustrations* becomes her first commissioned work. Much to her dismay, though, Fox insists on a subscription model and stipulates that a subscription of 500 must be reached before publication can proceed. Martineau recounts two responses to her request for subscription, both of which demonstrate what she was up against:

> Suffice it that, at the very time when certain members of parliament were eagerly inquiring about the announced work, the wife of one of them, a rich lady of my acquaintance, to whom a prospectus had been sent, returned it, telling me that she "knew too well what she was about to buy a pig in a poke": and the

> husband of a cousin of mine, a literary man in his way, sent me, in return for the prospectus, a letter, enclosing two sovereigns, and a lecture against my rashness and presumption in supposing that I was adequate to such work as authorship, and offering the enclosed sum as his mite towards the subscription; but recommending rather a family subscription which might eke out my earnings by my needle.[21]

The subscription model of publication provides a particularly illustrative example of how women's scholarly ventures were often discouraged before they were even begun. The responses Martineau details here are clearly meant to undermine her project and make her question her ability to successfully complete it; her cousin's husband tells Martineau that she does not truly understand what she is getting into (she's being rash) and that she does not have the authority to write the text in the first place (she's being presumptuous). The rich parliament member's wife uses the metaphor of buying a "pig in a poke" to suggest that the quality of Martineau's prospective series is dubious and therefore a bad investment. All of these claims are clearly meant to weaken Martineau's credibility and her understanding of the task at hand. In her recounting, Martineau explains that while she can now look back on such instances with humor, at the time they made her feel as though "success was growing more and more questionable and difficult every day."[22] As publication looms closer, she begins getting "warnings from various quarters that some of my relations were doing me 'more harm by their tongues than they could ever do by their guineas.'"[23]

As she pursues *Illustrations*, she is continually met with misogynistic condescension and discouragement; again and again, she is made to question her ability to accomplish the project and offer something meaningful to the public. Shortly after receiving discouragement from her relatives, for example, Martineau visits her publisher to share some of the promotional material she has created only to find that he was in "a mood as gloomy as the day": "He had seen Mr. James Mill, who had assured him that my method of exemplification, — (the grand principle of the whole scheme) could not possibly succeed; and Mr. Fox now required of me to change my plan entirely, and issue my Political Economy in a didactic form! Of course, I refused. He started a multitude of objections, — feared every thing, and hoped nothing. I saw, with anguish and no little resentment, my last poor chance slipping from me."[24] Because of James Mill's clout in the field of political economy, one word of warning from him nearly shuts the project down. Martineau's publisher does not, though, give up on the project entirely but instead sets nearly impossible terms for its continuance: she must sell 1,000 copies in a fortnight, or the series will be canceled after two issues. Martineau describes walking away from Fox's office feeling "almost too ill to walk" and "too giddy to stand without support," noting that passersby mistake her for being drunk. As she recounts the rest of her miserable evening, she laments that James Mill, "the one person who had seemed best to understand the whole affair[,] now urged me to give up either the whole scheme, or, what was worse, its main principle!"[25] For Martineau, it is particularly painful that Mill doubts the project because he is an expert in the field and she feels he is best suited to understand her aims. While Martineau had smarted from previous discouragement, Mill's authority makes his dismissal an especially powerful trigger for Martineau to doubt her own.

In her *Autobiography*, Martineau recounts feeling that writing about political economy was a risk and she was putting her "reputation and prosperity" on the line. She writes:

> On five occasions in my life I have found myself obliged to write and publish what I entirely believed would be ruinous to my reputation and prosperity. In no one of the five cases has the result been what I anticipated. . . . But it may be considered to have been a narrow escape in the first instance [of writing *Illustrations*]; for everything was done that low-minded recklessness and malice could do to destroy my credit and influence by gross appeals to the prudery, timidity, and ignorance of the middle classes of England.[26]

Martineau here details how the attacks against her were meant to destroy her credibility and minimize her influence; as with Dorothea, political economy is described as getting in the way of Martineau's ambitions. The most striking examples of gaslighting in this context are the hostile press campaign by George Poulett Scrope in the *Quarterly Review* and by William Maginn in *Fraser's Magazine*. Martineau describes being at a party when she finds out that "the atrocious article in the *Quarterly Review* which was avowedly intended to 'destroy Miss Martineau,' was at that time actually printed."[27] The aim of the campaign was plainly to make readers mistrust Martineau and, to use Abramson's terms, to convince Martineau and her readers "not to take [Martineau] seriously as an interlocutor."[28] It is useful to analyze Maginn and Scrope's efforts "to destroy Miss Martineau" through the framework of epistemic gaslighting, where a speaker with more cultural power attempts to "discredit the underlying message" of the speaker with less cultural power. Acts of epistemic gaslighting work to police the boundaries of disciplines by making readers — and the writers themselves — question not only the interlocutor's expertise, but their capacity to even hold expertise in the first place. Such acts are especially insidious because they are often couched as legitimate disciplinary critique. In the examples I am considering, it is the gaslighter's reliance on misogynistic character defamation that tips the scales from critique to gaslighting. Good faith disciplinary critique invites participation, whereas epistemic gaslighting precludes it.

As part of its series "Gallery of Literary Characters," *Fraser's Magazine* published an article on Harriet Martineau in November 1833, at the height of popularity for *Illustrations*. The article, along with its accompanying illustration, is a sexist, vitriolic attack on Martineau's character and, specifically, her work on political economy. Early in the article, for example, Maginn suggests that Martineau's pro-Malthusian views are tied to the fact that she is unmarried: "after proper inspection, that it is no great wonder that the lady should be pro-Malthusian; and that not even the Irish beau, suggested to her by a Tory songster, is likely to attempt the seduction of the fair philosopher from the doctrines of no-population."[29] The most spiteful implication of this claim is that Martineau is a Malthusian because she is sexually undesirable — no male suitor in his right mind, the author claims, would try to seduce her. Thus, Martineau's claim to legitimate economic knowledge based on research and intellectual introspection is weakened, and her pro-Malthusian texts are represented as simply a response to her inability to attract a male suitor. The way Maginn makes his claim further juxtaposes his own expertise ("after proper inspection") with what he suggests is a commonsense interpretation of the lady Malthusian ("it is no great wonder").

Maginn continues his gender-based attack of Martineau's economic writing when he writes, "it was indeed a wonder that such themes should occupy the pen of any lady, old or young, without exciting disgust nearly approaching to horror."[30] It is, at this point, probably unnecessary to point out that there is nothing salacious in Martineau's *Illustrations* (no matter how much a modern reader slogging through the stories' Platonic dialogues on rent and taxation might wish there were!); the implication that there is something improper in the text suggests that a reputable woman cannot write about economics without losing her character. In other words, the very subject matter is off limits to women writers; readers, Maginn argues, will approach female-authored economic writing with disgust amounting to horror, a premise that undermines women's legitimacy within the discipline from the moment they lay pen to paper. After drawing an unfavorable comparison between Martineau and "Mother Wollstonecraft," Maginn states: "We wish that Miss Martineau would sit down in her study and calmly endeavour to depict to herself what is the precise and physical meaning of the words used by her school — what is preventive check — what is moral check — what it is they are intended to check — and then ask herself, if she is or is not properly qualified to write a commentary."[31] Here, again, Maginn criticizes Martineau's engagement with Malthusian theory, but it is the way he does so that warrants more attention. Maginn advises Martineau to "sit down in her study and calmly endeavour" to understand the meaning of words that she has written entire stories about; his use of the word "calmly" suggests that her writing was done in a fevered way, driven not by sound logic and intellect but rather by emotion. The implication here is that she does not know what she is *actually* writing about; that the expertise she claims is rather the product of a naive and confused mind. In other words, he tries to convince Martineau (and her readers) that she does not actually know what she claims to know; she may *think* she knows what "moral check" and "preventive check" mean, but, Maginn claims, a moment of "calm" thought about the terms would be enough to convince her that she is not qualified to offer commentary. It is worth noting that at no point does Maginn establish his own credibility as a critic of

Martineau or an expert on political economy; rather, his credibility seems to be taken for granted. After dismissing Wollstonecraft's work as "disgusting," he characterizes *Illustrations* as

> far less disgusting than when we find the more mystical topics of generation, its impulses and consequences — which the common consent of society, even the ordinary practice of language . . . has veiled with the decent covering of silence, or left to be examined only with philosophical abstraction — brought daily, weekly, monthly, before the public eye, as the leading subjects, the very foundation-thoughts of essays, articles, treatises, novels! Tales! Romances! –to be disseminated into all hands, to lie on the breakfast-tables of the young and the fair, and to afford them matter of meditation.[32]

The tenor of Maginn's comments is not unusual in the nineteenth century; there was certainly plenty of concern about what women were reading and writing, and there was an especially strong taboo against women openly discussing sex and reproduction. Rather than meaningfully engaging with Martineau's economic writing, though, he essentially accuses her of disseminating pornographic material that will damage its "young and fair" readers. Martineau's significant contribution to the discipline of political economy is dismissed as no such thing; instead, it is represented as dangerous drivel, a characterization that is clearly meant to make readers question Martineau's authority as an economic interlocutor.

In an earlier review of Martineau's tale "Cousin Marshall" in *Fraser's Magazine*, Maginn lodges a similar gender-based critique of Martineau's writing when he says that after reading her story "we" — the "we" here seems to represent the entirety of the *Fraser's Magazine* staff —

> could not help saying to ourselves — "What a frightful delusion is this, called by its admirers, Political Economy, which can lead a young lady to put forth a book like this! — and a book written by a *woman* against the *poor* — a book written by a *young lady* against *marriage*! And what is more, where a long tirade against all charity, and an elaborate defence of the closest selfishness, is received with acclamation by those who profess themselves the friends of the people and the advocates of the distressed."[33]

On the one hand, Maginn offers a fair critique of Malthusian political economy, specifically its position on charity and income inequality — an opinion many readers (then and now) may agree with; on the other hand, though, his claims seem to be far less concerned with political economy and far more concerned with the gender identity of the writer. Maginn is less interested, in other words, in offering his readers a thoughtful assessment of the views that Martineau asserts and more concerned with undermining her authority to assert them at all. The tone of the passage is one of shock and disbelief that a woman would even contemplate engaging with economic theories; the fact that Martineau did makes not only her writing suspect, but her person as well.

George Poulett Scrope wrote a similarly caustic review in *The Quarterly Review* in 1833; this is the review that, in her *Autobiography*, Martineau said was intended to destroy her career. Like Maginn, Scrope focuses on the Malthusian elements of Martineau's *Illustrations*, and his review quickly devolves into misogynist character defamation meant to destroy public confidence in Martineau. He begins by stating that it is "impossible not to laugh at the absurd trash which is seriously propounded by some of her characters, in dull didactic dialogues, introduced here and there in the most clumsy manner"; through its use of descriptive terms like "clumsy" and "absurd," Scrope here implies that Martineau does a poor job of representing political economy.[34] Similar to Maginn, Scrope suggests that Martineau's tales are both shocking and disgusting because they were authored by a woman: "it is quite impossible not to be shocked, nay disgusted, with many of the unfeminine and mischievous doctrines on the principles of social welfare, of which these tales are made the vehicle."[35] In reference to a passage about crop production and consumption from "Weal and Woe in Garveloch," Scrope states, "This is rare logic and arithmetic, and not a little curious as natural history. . . . But these are the discoveries of genius!" — a statement that, in its ironic tone, suggests that Martineau is anything but genius. He continues to try to convince his readers that she is both ignorant and unladylike, stating: "A little ignorance of these ticklish topics [reproduction and population growth] is perhaps not unbecoming a young unmarried lady. But before such a person undertook to write books in favour of 'the preventive check' [methods of contraception], she should have informed herself somewhat more accurately upon the laws of human propagation. Poor innocent! She has been puzzling over Mr. Malthus's arithmetical and geometrical rations, for knowledge which she should have obtained by a simple question or two of her mamma."[36] This comment paradoxically seems to suggest that Martineau both knows *too much* and *too little* about the subject on which she is writing; she knows too little to make her trustworthy and too much to make her a proper woman.

Later in the review, Scrope refers to Martineau as a "*female Malthusian*," which he defines as "a *woman* who thinks child-bearing a *crime against society*! An *unmarried woman* who declaims against marriage!! *A young woman* who deprecates charity and a provision for the *poor!!!*"[37] In a manner strikingly similar to Maginn's, Scrope uses anti-feminist myths to defame Martineau's character and to suggest that her *Illustrations* is not worth reading. The emphasis throughout is on her gender, her youth, and her marital status, a focus that reveals Scrope to be engaged not in good faith critique but in epistemic gaslighting. Similarly, a reviewer in the *Poor Man's Guardian* attacks Martineau's appearance, suggesting that her "repulsive" looks are evidence that her ideas are also "repulsive": "the anti-propagation lady, a single sight of whom would repel all fears of surplus population, her aspect [her physical appearance] being as repulsive as her doctrines."[38] The language used by this reviewer and by Maginn and Scrope is meant to belittle and demean Martineau, and to keep her from writing. Indeed, Scrope states that "the best advice we can give her [Martineau] is, to burn all the little books she has yet written"; the use of the word "little" functions to again denigrate her work.[39]

The negative reviews and responses documented here are clearly meant to diminish Martineau's accomplishments, to call into question her expertise, and to tarnish her character so that she loses authority with readers. In other words, they are designed to create a credibility deficit that will prevent Martineau from meaningfully contributing to the discipline of economics. The extreme anxiety and stress that resulted from this epistemic gaslighting nearly did just that; they not only made Martineau question her ability to complete *Illustrations*, but they also made her very physically ill, which could have prevented her from doing the work. Martineau describes the toll this hostility took on her physical health; she describes herself during the period as "thin," "yellow," "coughing with every breath," and "confined to . . . bed for a month": "I am confident that that serious illness [liver inflammation] began with the toils and anxieties, and long walks in fog and mud" during the stressful process of publication.[40] The physical effects are not dissimilar to what other victims of gaslighting have described; it is frequently represented as causing physical, emotional, and psychological damage. For Martineau, the anxiety caused by trying to enter a male-dominated field threatened not only her reputation, but also her life.

After the period of serious concern about the steep subscription numbers and apprehension about her authorship, Martineau's series far exceeded expectations. She details this success while recounting a letter from her publisher: "He sent with his letter a copy of my first number, desiring me to make with all speed any corrections I might wish to make, as he had scarcely any copies left. He added that the demand led him to propose that we should now print two thousand. A postscript informed me that since he wrote the above, he had found that we should want three thousand. A second postscript proposed four thousand, and a third five thousand."[41] *Illustrations of Political Economy* was a roaring success, going on to sell approximately 10,000 copies and to enjoy a readership of "about 144,000."[42] Elaine Freedgood points out that sales of *Illustrations* were "several times that of many of Dickens's novels, which at 2,000 or 3,000 per month were considered highly successful."[43] Positive reviews of *Illustrations* praise Martineau for the "beauty" and "power" of her descriptions, as well as the "useful direction" of her stories and their "truth of character."[44] The popularity of *Illustrations* was likely due, at least in part, to her readers' desire to know more about political economy, a fact acknowledged by one reviewer who referred to Martineau as a "national instructress, on the topics of the country's most essential interests."[45] While the popularity of *Illustrations* turned Martineau into a momentary literary celebrity, economists John Vint and Keiko Funaki note that she remained "largely ignored by the political economy profession from which she, as a woman, was excluded."[46] For example, in a private letter to Walter Couson in 1850, John Stuart Mill, another political economist with a great deal of authority, refers to Martineau as a "mere tyro": "Mr. Kingsley's notions must be a little less vague about my political economy than about my socialism when he couples my name with that of a mere tyro like Harriet Martineau."[47] Mill is clearly angry that his name, as an economist, has been paired with Martineau's, presumably because he feels that his authority far exceeds hers; he then undermines her authority by referring to her as a "mere tyro," an insult tantamount to calling her a trivial amateur.[48]

Harriet Martineau was a pioneer in the field of economics, but as such examples illustrate, she was rarely recognized as one; at a time when the field was amassing cultural authority, Martineau introduced a novel mode of articulating and disseminating economic information to the general public. While one might assume that the originality and terrific success of *Illustrations* would garner respect from men in the field, they continued to undermine her work, especially when it was placed in relation to their own. J. R. Shackleton explains that such exclusion continues today: "It is now largely forgotten that the two best-selling English economists of the first half of the nineteenth century were both women [Martineau and Jane Marcet]. Although they sometimes rate a footnote or two in modern texts on the history of economic thought, comments are usually dismissive."[49] The biases underlying the gaslighting highlighted in this essay — namely, Martineau's gender and her consequent lack of formal economic training — continue to cast doubt upon her legitimacy as an economic interlocutor. This is evidenced by the fact that, despite being the bestselling English economist of the nineteenth century, Martineau's economic writing is still not taken seriously. Epistemic gaslighting works to keep women out of male-dominated disciplines by convincing them (and their readers) that they are *incapable* of meaningful participation — by manipulating, like *Middlemarch*'s Mr. Brooke, them into believing that "young ladies don't [and can't] understand" a particular field of knowledge simply because they are women.[50] In the discipline of economics, such gaslighting has served to keep women at the margins of the field from the nineteenth century to the present day.

In the wake of the #MeToo movement, the discipline of economics came under fire for its long history of hostility toward women. In a 2019 *New York Times* article, Ben Casselman and Jim Tankersley explain that "the economics profession is facing a mounting crisis of sexual harassment, discrimination and bullying that women in the field say has pushed many of them to the sidelines — or out of the field entirely." Such harassment, discrimination, and bullying have undoubtedly contributed to the fact that "only about a third of economics doctorates go to women" and that women account "for about 23 percent of tenured and tenure-track faculty in the field."[51] Economist Victoria Bateman has argued that much of the sexism that continues to permeate the field of economics originated in the nineteenth century, when "economists created an artificial barrier between the public and the private sphere of life. The public sphere — life in the market and in politics — was deemed important enough for economists to study. By contrast, what went on in private — the home, the family and community — was deemed irrelevant; it was seen as too female and too soft."[52] She explains: "Gender bias is built into economics through its very choice of assumptions and approach."[53] Misogyny in economics, though, is not confined to subject matter but extends to who is sanctioned to be an "expert" in the field. In other words, the artificial division described by Bateman has worked to keep women outside the field of economics, as *economists*, as well. And, as this essay has demonstrated, that form of gender bias also has its origins in the nineteenth century. It would seem that Dorothea is not the only one who has experienced economics as an "extinguisher over all [her] lights."[54]

Notes

1. Eliot, *Middlemarch*, 8.
2. Eliot, *Middlemarch*, 9.
3. Eliot, *Middlemarch*, 17.
4. Eliot, *Middlemarch*, 17.
5. Eliot, *Middlemarch*, 18.
6. Ivy, "Allies Behaving Badly," 286.
7. See Gagnier, *The Insatiability of Human Wants*; Poovey, *Genres of the Credit Economy*; and Gallagher, *The Body Economic*.
8. Sweet, "Sociology of Gaslighting," 851.
9. Sweet, "Sociology of Gaslighting," 853.
10. Ivy, "Allies Behaving Badly," 289–90.
11. Ivy, "Allies Behaving Badly," 290.
12. Abramson, "Turning up the Lights," 2.
13. Ivy, "Allies Behaving Badly," 288.
14. Gaskell, *Mary Barton*, 4.
15. See Uglow, *Elizabeth Gaskell*, 61.
16. Stevenson, "The Political Economist," 525.
17. Gaskell, quoted in Chapple and Pollard, *Letters*, 148.
18. As political economy gained clout throughout the century, it increasingly became a mainstay of boy's education, but research suggests that the landscape was more complicated for girls. Political economy was largely viewed as irrelevant to women because of the separate spheres ideology that confined them to the private sphere. The informal educational segregation that prompts early didactic writing on political economy is also evidenced in later debates about women's education and, specifically, what should be on the curriculum. As Joan Burstyn has explained, the fact that men and women presumably had "different goals in life" meant that they should be "educated differently" (*Victorian Education*, 48). The 1870 Education Act and the establishment of Girton College in 1869 and Newnham College in 1871 intensified debate about what constituted a proper education for women, including debate about whether girls should be taught political economy in school. While political economy courses and examinations were eventually established for women at Newnham College, Cambridge, where Millicent Garrett Fawcett served as cofounder and occasional lecturer, women could not receive degrees in the field until well into the twentieth century.
19. Barrett Browning, *Aurora Leigh,* 12.
20. Martineau, *Autobiography*, 122.
21. Martineau, *Autobiography*, 128.
22. Martineau, *Autobiography*, 128.
23. Martineau, *Autobiography*, 131.
24. Martineau, *Autobiography*, 129.
25. Martineau, *Autobiography*, 129.

26. Martineau, *Autobiography*, 151.
27. Martineau, *Autobiography*, 155.
28. Abramson, "Turning up the Lights," 2.
29. Maginn, "Gallery," 576.
30. Maginn, "Gallery," 576.
31. Maginn, "Gallery," 576.
32. Maginn, "Gallery," 576.
33. Maginn, "On National Economy," 403.
34. Scrope, "Review," 136.
35. Scrope, "Review," 136.
36. Scrope, "Review," 136–37.
37. Scrope, "Review," 151.
38. Quoted in Vint and Funaki, "Harriet Martineau," 64.
39. Scrope, "Review," 151.
40. Martineau, *Autobiography*, 132.
41. Martineau, *Autobiography*, 136.
42. Logan, "Introduction," 34.
43. Freedgood, *Victorian Writing*, 213.
44. Lytton, "On Moral Fictions," 151; review of "Cousin Marshall," 418–19.
45. Review of "Weal and Woe in Garveloch," 414.
46. Vint and Funaki, "Harriet Martineau," 63.
47. Mill, quoted in Robbins, *Evolution*, 125.
48. This was not the only instance of John Stuart Mill actively calling a woman's economic writing and expertise into question; later in the century he also prevented Millicent Garrett Fawcett from entering the Political Economy Club when her name was forwarded for consideration. According to David Rubinstein, in 1871 Sir Charles Dilke wrote a letter to Mill "to recommend [Garrett Fawcett's] election to the club. He cited in her support her 'little book' (*Political Economy for Beginners*), many articles 'both signed and anonymous.' . . . Dilke pointed out that he was too junior a member to propose her and suggested that Mill might be willing to do so. Mill, who had been elected in 1836, lacked neither seniority nor prestige, but, on this occasion, courage and good will. Although acknowledging that 'Mrs Fawcett has far better claims to be a member of the Political Economy Club than many of its present members,' he refused to propose her, allegedly because he was known as an advocate of the rights of women. She was not elected, nor was any woman at least until after 1920" (*A Different World*, 31).
49. Shackleton, "Jane Marcet and Harriet Martineau," 283.
50. Eliot, *Middlemarch*, 17.
51. Casselman and Tankersley, "Female Economists."
52. Bateman, *Sex Factor*, 2.
53. Bateman, *Sex Factor*, 2; see also Ferber and Nelson, eds., *Beyond Economic Man*; and Marçal, *Who Cooked Adam Smith's Dinner*.
54. Eliot, *Middlemarch*, 18.

Bibliography

Abramson, Kate. "Turning up the Lights on Gaslighting." *Philosophical Perspectives* 28 (2014): 1–30.

Barrett Browning, Elizabeth. *Aurora Leigh and Other Poems*. Edited by John Robert Glorney Bolton and Julia Bolton Holloway. Penguin, 1995.

Bateman, Victoria. *The Sex Factor: How Women Made the West Rich*. Polity, 2019.

Berenstain, Nora. "White Feminist Gaslighting." *Hypatia* 35 (2020): 733–58.

Burstyn, Joan. *Victorian Education and the Ideal of Womanhood.* Rutgers University Press, 1984.

Casselman, Ben, and Jim Tankersley. "Female Economists Push Their Field Toward a #MeToo Reckoning." *New York Times*. January 10, 2019. https://www.nytimes.com/2019/01/10/business/economics-sexual-harassment-me-too.html.

Dotson, Kristie. "Tracking Epistemic Violence, Tracking Practices of Silencing." *Hypatia* 26, no. 2 (Spring 2011): 236–57.

Eliot, George. *Middlemarch.* Edited by Rosemary Ashton. Penguin, 2003.

Ferber, Marianne A., and Julie A. Nelson. *Beyond Economic Man: Feminist Theory and Economics*. University of Chicago Press, 2009.

Freedgood, Elaine. *Victorian Writing about Risk: Imagining a Safe England in a Dangerous World.* Cambridge University Press, 2000.

Fricker, Miranda. *Epistemic Injustice: Power and the Ethics of Knowing*. Oxford University Press, 2007.

Gagnier, Regenia. *The Insatiability of Human Wants: Economics and Aesthetics in Market Society*. University of Chicago Press, 2000.

Gallagher, Catherine. *The Body Economic: Life, Death, and Sensation in Political Economy and the Victorian Novel*. Princeton University Press, 2005.

Gaskell, Elizabeth. *The Letters of Mrs. Gaskell.* Edited by J. A. V. Chapple and Arthur Pollard. Manchester University Press, 1966.

———. *Mary Barton*. Edited by MacDonald Daly. Penguin, 1996.

Graves, Clint G., and Leland G. Spencer. "Rethinking the Rhetorical Epistemics of Gaslighting." *Communication Theory* 32 (2022): 48–67.

Ivy, Veronica [Rachel McKinnon]. "Allies Behaving Badly: Gaslighting as Epistemic Injustice." In *The Routledge Handbook of Epistemic Injustice*, edited by Ian James Kidd, José Medina, and Gaile Pohlhause Jr., 167–74. Routledge, 2017.

Logan, Deborah Anna. Introduction to *Illustrations of Political Economy: Selected Tales* by Harriet Martineau, 9–50. Edited by Deborah Anna Logan. Broadview, 2004.

Lytton, Edward Bulwer. "On Moral Fictions. Miss Martineau's *Illustrations of Political Economy*." *The New Monthly Magazine and Literary Journal* 37 (1833): 146–51.

[Maginn, William]. "Gallery of Literary Characters." *Fraser's Magazine* 8 (1833): 576–77.

——— "On National Economy: Review of Miss Martineau's 'Cousin Marshall.'" *Fraser's Magazine for Town and Country* 6 (November 1832): 403–13.

Marçal, Katrine. *Who Cooked Adam Smith's Dinner? A History of Women and Economics*. Pegasus Books, 2016.

Martineau, Harriet. *Autobiography*. James R. Osgood, 1877.

Poovey, Mary. *Genres of the Credit Economy: Mediating Value in Eighteenth- and Nineteenth-Century Britain*. University of Chicago Press, 2008.

———. Review of "Cousin Marshall." *The Spectator* (September 8, 1832). In *Illustrations of Political Economy: Selected Tales* by Harriet Martineau, edited by Deborah Anna Logan, 418–19. Broadview, 2004.

———. Review of "Weal and Woe in Garveloch." *The Spectator* (July 7, 1832). In *Illustrations of Political Economy: Selected Tales* by Harriet Martineau, edited by Deborah Anna Logan, 414. Broadview, 2004.

Robbins, Lord. *The Evolution of Modern Economic Theory and Other Papers on the History of Economic Thought*. Aldine Publishing Company, 1970.

Rubinstein, David. *A Different World for Women: The Life of Millicent Garrett Fawcett*. Ohio State University Press, 1991.

Sanders, Mike. "From 'Political' to 'Human' Economy: The Visions of Harriet Martineau and Frances Wright." *Women: A Cultural Review* 12, no. 2 (January 2001): 192–203.

Sanders, Valerie, and Gaby Weiner. "Introduction: The disciplines and Harriet Martineau." In *Harriet Martineau and the Birth of Disciplines: Nineteenth-Century Intellectual Powerhouse*, edited by Valerie Sanders and Gaby Weiner, 1–14. Routledge, 2019.

[Scrope, George Poulett]. "Review of *Illustrations of Political Economy*." *The Quarterly Review* 49 (1833): 136–52.

Shackleton, J. R. "Jane Marcet and Harriet Martineau: Pioneers of Economics Education." *History of Education* 19, no. 4 (1990): 283–97.

Stevenson, William. "The Political Economist: Essay I." *Blackwood's Edinburgh Magazine* XV (May 1824): 522–31.

Sweet, Paige. "The Sociology of Gaslighting." *American Sociological Review* 84, no. 5 (October 2019): 851–75.

Uglow, Jenny. *Elizabeth Gaskell: A Habit of Stories*. Faber and Faber, 1999.

Vint, John, and Keiko Funaki. "Harriet Martineau and Classical Political Economy." In *Harriet Martineau and the Birth of Disciplines: Nineteenth-Century Intellectual Powerhouse*, edited by Valerie Sanders and Gaby Weiner, 49–68. Routledge, 2019.

10

"When evidence takes a supernatural character"

Religious Gaslighting in Elizabeth Gaskell's "Lois the Witch"

Shalyn Claggett

In her 1861 gothic tale "Lois the Witch," Elizabeth Gaskell traces the religious gaslighting of a fictional young woman who becomes a victim of the Salem witchcraft trials. The orphaned daughter of an Anglican parson, Lois travels from England to America to seek shelter with the family of her father's estranged brother. After taking her in, the household becomes increasingly hostile toward her: her aunt Grace nurses a prejudice against Lois for her English heritage, and her cousin Faith becomes vindictive out of jealousy. In addition, her cousin Manasseh insists she consent to marry him against her wishes because their union was revealed to him as God's will. When a panic over witchcraft grips the Puritan community, the women in the family punish Lois by accusing her of witchcraft — a claim that Lois, under extreme psychological duress, is nearly gaslit into believing.

This story reveals something important about gaslighting's relationship to religion and patriarchy, not despite but *because* of the fact that women deploy it in this case. Crucially, Gaskell's fictionalized Salem narrative traces the cause of the trials back to an origin in social arrangements that fail women. More insidiously, her narrative shows why women turn against their own gender when they feel dissatisfied with the paltry compensations of patriarchal systems. This dynamic is perhaps most economically expressed when Lois shares her memory of the public stoning and drowning of old Hannah, a woman suspected of witchcraft in her father's parish. Lois recounts, "her eyes met mine as they were glaring with fury . . . she caught sight of me, and cried out, 'Parson's wench, parson's wench, yonder, in thy nurse's arms, thy dad that never tried for to save me, and none shall save thee when thou art brought up for a witch.'"[1] In this moment, Hannah looks beyond the townspeople who are actively trying to kill her to focus her wrath on an innocent female child. While she correctly identifies the parson as culpable for her plight, her rationale in targeting Lois can only be understood within a hierarchy of power. As a poor woman without the strength or status to oppose her attackers, she fixes her fury on the only individual both adjacent to the man who failed her and naive enough to be haunted by her words. These same dynamics play out twice more in the narrative, compounding Lois's innocence while also exposing the futility of women scapegoating women within a patriarchal society. Gaskell offers an alternative to women's misdirected rage in Lois, who spends her last night alive comforting Nattee, an Indigenous servant who is also falsely accused: "And in comforting her, Lois was comforted; in strengthening her, Lois was strengthened" (222).

Given that "Lois the Witch" is a work of historical fiction, it is perhaps unsurprising that most scholarship on the novella focuses on context, whether it is that of the story's 1690s setting or the Victorian concerns it reflects.[2] Yet, as much as the story says about the historical past and present, it is what Gaskell adds to the historical record — namely, a definitive explanation for the origin of the witchcraft panic and subsequent trials — that foregrounds the dark logic of retributive justice under systems of oppression. Understanding how religious gaslighting works in the story reveals how asymmetrical power arrangements create the conditions for psychological exploitation of the disempowered. In other words, it makes clear how and why gaslighting always punches down.

There are multiple instances of gaslighting in the story, but in all cases a patriarchal religion is the instrument through which individuals' moral agency is challenged and finally denied. As Rebecca Styler has observed, the Calvinist worldview portrayed in "Lois the Witch" sharply conflicts with Gaskell's own Unitarian beliefs. Whereas Unitarianism embraces universal benevolence, religious tolerance, and natural law, Puritans believed in predestination, religious exclusion, and the omnipresence of supernatural influence.[3] Because Puritan theology was both hierarchical and premised on a supernatural reality that controls the visible world, it could be conveniently tailored by those with power to reinforce male supremacy and police women through the threat of witchcraft accusations. From the fifteenth century on, the European tradition of witch-hunting made the connection between women and witches theologically explicit: following the pattern of Eve, all women were inherently evil and thus more liable to become witches. This Catholic view conflicted with the Puritan view, which sought to cast women as willing servants and helpmates of men, rather than insatiably carnal and inherently wicked daughters of Eve. As Carol F. Karlsen points out, the Puritans were just as rigidly devoted to hierarchy and authority as the Anglicans and Catholics, but they found that authority to be mislocated in the (external) church or state rather than within each individual. Male headship within the family regulated proper internalization of God's authority while reflecting the hierarchical arrangement of the church (minister to congregants). This system magnified men's power within the domestic sphere by making any challenge to a man's authority an implicit challenge to God's. In the Puritan interpretation of the Fall, Eve's sin was not due to inherent wickedness but rather pride and a failure to subordinate herself to Adam by strengthening his virtue, making her "the archetypal witch."[4]

To ensure women's willing submission to men's authority, Puritan ministers repeatedly emphasized the reversal of the sexual hierarchy as a perversion of nature and conflated it with the demonic and monstrous. It is little wonder, then, that women were far more likely than men to be accused of witchcraft, a fact made glaringly clear in the list of victims in Charles W. Upham's *Lectures on Witchcraft* (1831), Gaskell's principal source for the story. As Karlsen explains, the typical targets for witchcraft accusations were "disorderly women" who "posed a greater threat than disorderly men because the male/female relation provided the very model of and for all hierarchical relations, and because [Puritan leaders] hoped that the subordination of women to men would ensure men's stake in maintaining those relations."[5] Importantly for Gaskell's story, "disorderly" in the Puritan context simply means the failure of a woman to submit to male authority, even under the most untenable conditions and in response to completely illogical demands.

Puritan theology also primed women to suspect one another and even themselves of witchcraft — ideal conditions for religious gaslighting. As historian Elizabeth Reis points out, in addition to being executed more often than men, women were also more frequently accused, more likely to confess, and the principal accusers of other women. Reis traces this asymmetry to Puritan theology, which held that because Satan attacked the soul through the body, women's comparatively weaker bodies must render them more vulnerable to attack.[6] Further, the religion's pervasive emphasis on women's spiritual deficiencies led women to conflate acts of "ordinary sinning" with the "more egregious act of signing the devil's book," for they viewed the former as evidence of having unconsciously committed the latter sin.[7] As will be shown, similar dynamics structure Lois's victimization, leading her to doubt her own innocence, despite having no memory of signing Satan's book.

Even before this climactic scene, characters continually gaslight Lois by mobilizing the unassailable moral authority of patriarchal Puritanism. The first and most paradigmatic instance occurs in response to Lois's refusal to accept her cousin's offer of marriage. Although an unacknowledged sexual attraction motivates Manasseh's pursuit, Lois's repeated rejection prompts his recourse to divine revelation. He claims:

> It is borne in upon me — verily I see it as in a vision — that thou must be my spouse, and no other man's. Thou canst not escape what is foredoomed. Months ago, when I set myself to read the old godly books in which my soul used to delight until thy coming, I saw no letters of printers' ink marked on the page, but I saw a gold and ruddy type of some unknown language, the meaning whereof was whispered into my soul; it was, "Marry Lois! Marry Lois!" (170)

Manasseh perceives Lois as having power over him, as his lust distracts him from his spiritual studies, and yet Lois's rejection bars him from satisfying his desires through marriage. The right of refusal being one of the few freedoms women could legitimately exercise, his appeal to the supernatural reveals a strategy of control that negates the validity of even the possibility of refusal. According to Manasseh's logic, Lois is not simply making a bad decision but asserting the reality of a future that cannot possibly exist. As Kate Abramson explains, a gaslighter "aims to destroy the possibility of disagreement by so radically undermining another person that she has nowhere left to stand from which to disagree, no standpoint from which her words might constitute genuine disagreement."[8] And indeed, according to Manasseh, since Lois disagrees with the will of God, her position is both inconceivable and heretical. When she refuses him a third time, he responds, "God forgive thee thy blasphemy!" and warns her to "remember Hazael" whose "evil courses were fixed and appointed for him from before the foundation of the world" (171). Insofar as blasphemy is the act of treating the sacred as that which it is not (the profane), this escalation provisionally positions Lois outside Christian ontology, making her morally opposed to the will of God. Hazael, whose name in Hebrew means "God has seen," denies the prophet Elisha's prediction that he will brutally massacre the Israelites. When Hazael nevertheless commits the foretold atrocities, the act affirms the supremacy of God's omniscience over mortals' will.[9] Conveniently, Manasseh accords Elisha's abilities to himself and vouchsafes Lois a "godly" course as his wife in place of Hazael's "evil courses" (171). The most salient difference, however, is that whereas Elisha's prophecy causes him to weep for the impending fate of his people, Manasseh is both prophet and beneficiary of God's will. As the self-appointed prophet of the Puritan community, he can order reality according to his libido simply by appending the rationale of divine revelation.

The power of Manasseh's gaslighting, however, has less to do with God than with the patriarchal Puritanism that underwrites it. After his accusation of blasphemy, Lois feels "as if his words must come true, and that, struggle as she would, hate her doom as she would, she must become his wife" (171). Gaskell further explains that, under the same conditions, many girls would succumb to his insistent pursuit after having lived in the "monotonous routine of a family with one man for head, and this man esteemed a hero by most of those around him, simply because he was the only man in the family" (171). Manasseh's "hero" status derives merely from the early death of his father, which divinely installs him as the head of the household and the sole representative of God's authority within the domestic sphere. The consistent overvaluation of his status on the basis of gender is what begins to tip the balance in his favor. As will later be shown, the idea that women must subordinate themselves to men because Puritan headship requires it is central to understanding the reasoning that undergirds Lois's rapid transformation from innocent girl to witch in the eyes of the Puritan community.

The predicament in which Lois first finds herself with Manasseh offers a straightforward and recognizable form of gaslighting: psychological manipulation deployed by a man against a woman to get what he wants at the expense of her sense of reality. The ironically named Grace and Faith, however, deploy gaslighting differently by mobilizing the Salem community's spiritual worldview against Lois through an accusation of witchcraft. It is difficult to imagine a more extreme form of gaslighting than this charge, in which the accused must either assent to the asserted reality of the accuser, and thereby assume the identity of "witch," or be put to death. Both fates ensure the negation of the possibility of disagreement: the first by undermining the victim's standing in the community forever, and the second by eliminating the possibility of exercising agency at all.

In Gaskell's fictional account of the Salem trials, she pinpoints the actions of women as origin and cause, but she locates the motivations for these women's accusations in men's failures. Faith's disappointment arises from the romantic disinterest of Mr. Nolan, the younger of the community's two pastors. Temporarily dismissed from the church due to the jealousy of Pastor Tappau, he returns when the congregation's size and needs overtax the older churchman. Although the narrator never overtly confirms that the trials have their ultimate origin in Faith's desire for Mr. Nolan, the evidence provided in dialogue and through Faith's reactions is unambiguous. Briefly put, the implied subplot reveals that Faith has colluded with two Indigenous women — Nattee (the Hicksons' servant) and Hota (the Tappaus' servant) — to simulate a Satanic attack on the Tappaus' home and drive the family from town. Gaskell suggests this collusion early in the narrative when Nattee responds to Faith's despondency over Nolan's disinterest, explaining, "How can he [Nolan] build a nest, when the old bird [Tappau] has got all the moss and the feathers? Wait till the Indian has found means to send the old bird flying far away" (181). While the entire community reacts with fear to the reported supernatural occurrences and spiritual possession of Tappau's daughters, Faith remains conspicuously calm and, according to the narrator, would have revealed the truth to Lois had she not refused to be bound by a secret (188). Faith's indifference shifts to apprehension only when the Tappau children accuse Hota of bewitching them, leading to her arrest, torture, and conviction. On the morning of the execution, Faith asks Lois to carry a letter to Mr. Nolan that presumably reveals that the supernatural events were a hoax. When Nolan receives the letter, however, he unwittingly betrays his romantic interest in Lois, which Faith, who followed after, jealously observes.

At this point, Gaskell repeats the dynamics of displacement that had been illustrated in the story of old Hannah. Snatching back her letter, Faith states, "My mind is changed. Give me back my letter, sir; it was about a poor matter — an old woman's life. And what is that compared to a young girl's love?" (198). Here, as before, a man of God causes the curse, but the person who must pay is a disempowered woman. The comparison of "an old woman's life" to "a young girl's love" foregrounds the grossly incommensurate substitution of a life for a personal disappointment, while installing Lois as the instigating cause of Nolan's regard. Gaskell writes that Lois's dumbfounded expression of guileless innocence would have stopped Faith "had it not been that, at the same instant, the latter caught sight of the crimsoned and disturbed countenance of the pastor" (198). Nolan's blush is the actual offense that leads to Hota's death, but just like old Hannah, Faith shifts her target away from the man who hurt her to a blameless woman whom she can punish. Because the story is set in the seventeenth century, at a time when New England was a colonized space, Hota is even more institutionally vulnerable than Lois. In Faith's estimation, Hota is an expendable placeholder for Lois's future punishment: if the hoax were revealed, after all, Faith could not leverage the Puritan community's belief in the reality of witchcraft against Lois.

Faith gaslights Lois by mobilizing preexisting gendered stereotypes perpetuated by Puritan theology. Gaskell earlier implies Faith's intent to do so in the moment when she snatches away the letter and states, "Let [Hota] die, and let all other witches look to themselves; for there be many kinds of witchcraft abroad" (198–99). In fact, there were not "many kinds" of witchcraft in Puritanism, as witchcraft is specifically defined as the act of signing a pact with the devil to oppose God. Faith's comment, however, conflates Lois with the witch archetype of the carnally insatiable Eve, transforming her from oblivious object of Nolan's desire to active temptress, and Nolan from besotted lover to innocent victim. When they return home, Faith reifies the implied accusation by telling the highly suggestible Prudence that their cousin "has bought success in this world" and that to touch her belongings is to "meddle with a witch's things" (201). Consistent with the Puritan belief that Satan tempted his victims by promising worldly power in exchange for one's soul, Faith explicitly attributes Nolan's regard to demonic influence catalyzed by Lois's collusion with the devil.[10] Although Lois does not, at this point, doubt her sense of reality, Faith's accusation sets the stage for the mass gaslighting of the congregation that will similarly embrace the idea that Lois is a witch to preserve a preferred image of a godly man.

Whereas Faith's grudge against Lois stems from a romantic disappointment, Grace Hickson's prejudice rests in her husband's preexisting partiality for his English relatives. Native to New England, Grace "had a kind of jealous dislike to her husband's English relations, which had increased since of late years his weakened mind yearned after them, and he forgot the good reason he had had for his self-exile, and moaned over the decision which had led to it as the great mistake of his life" (155). This regret marks a double betrayal: first, because Grace perceives living in England under Charles II to be a tacit recognition of his legitimacy and allegiance to a popish religion. More intimately, however, Grace's husband wounds her by characterizing the life they built together as the result of a "great mistake." Unable to punish her husband, who remains the head of the household even in his enfeebled state, she transfers her rage to Lois by constantly mocking her country and religious beliefs. When Lois demurs from speaking of her past life, Grace feigns interest and sympathy to draw her out, only to "turn round upon her with some bitter sneer" (159). In her frequent harassment, Grace leverages her dominant position in the hierarchy established through settler colonialism, which in this case elevates colonial Puritans above newly arrived English settlers, and both above their Indigenous neighbors. This allows Grace to supplant a hierarchy in which she has little power with one in which she has comparatively more, because it is based on national and racial difference rather than gender. Although this sustained psychological abuse does not lead to the accusations of witchcraft that follow, it nevertheless establishes an atmosphere of constant hostility and marks Lois as a sanctioned target for victimization within the home.

When Ralph Hickson dies and Manasseh becomes the head of the household, his incipient madness threatens Grace's economic security and social standing. Gaslighting Lois into admitting that she is a witch thus emerges as a strategy for the maintenance of patriarchal power both within the family and within the Puritan community. Since Manasseh has been enclosing land and is the best hunter in Salem, Grace initially hopes to consolidate her financial security through a far more prosperous match. Perceiving Lois's ability to manage and sooth her son's depressive episodes, however, she accepts her son's choice "as a medicine for Manasseh, if his mind get disturbed again" (180). Thus, we see a downward negotiation in terms of Grace's social and economic aspirations through marriage, from a match that would secure or raise the family's class status to one that preserves the illusion of Manasseh's competence (upon which her own standing in the community largely depends). Lois's value to Grace transforms from "medicine" to scapegoat only when Manasseh exhibits his unmanaged madness in public, exposing the family to indelible shame.

Gaslighting thus becomes a recuperative strategy through which Grace and the Puritan congregation can instantly exchange one reality for another. After Manasseh reveals his madness through a fit of incoherent speech following Prudence's accusation of Lois, Gaskell explains:

> A solution of it all occurred to them. He was another victim. Great was the power of Satan! Through the arts of the devil, that white statue of a girl had mastered the soul of Manasseh Hickson. So the word spread from mouth to mouth. And Grace heard it. It seemed a healing balsam for her shame. . . . And over all reigned the idea that, if he were indeed suffering from being bewitched, he was not mad, and might again assume the honourable position he had held in the congregation and in the town, when the spell by which he was held was destroyed. (209–10)

Useful here is Paige L. Sweet's examination of gaslighting in its sociological aspect. She explains that "gaslighting tactics become consequential when abusers mobilize macro-level inequalities related to gender, sexuality, race, nationality, and class against an intimate other," a key strategy of which is "flipping the script"; that is, making the subject of gaslighting appear to be the aggressor.[11] In other words, the aggressor reverses the actual power dynamics by asserting a version of reality that accords power to the person in a subordinate position and posits the aggressor as a victim or potential victim of that power. Lois is subordinate by virtue of her gender, but by labeling her a witch the community provisionally attributes supernatural power to her in order to morally justify removing her agency entirely. As Sweet observes, the reason why women rarely perpetrate gaslighting is because they usually do not have the necessary social power to gaslight men.[12] This is certainly true, but in "Lois," it is precisely the Puritan belief that women should not have power over a man that Faith and Grace exploit to expose Lois's "power" as illegitimate, in essence leveraging patriarchy for their personal ends. While for Faith this end is retributive, Grace's gaslighting is more psychologically complex. As psychologists Victor Calef and Edward Weinshel argue, gaslighting often involves a "special kind of 'transfer' . . . of painful or potentially painful mental conflicts" to achieve "the removal of the attendant anxiety."[13] In this formulation, Grace projects the cause of her own disgrace onto Lois in a defensive maneuver that instantly becomes a "healing balsam for her shame." Similarly, the congregation shifts the source of its shame from a man to a woman, thereby preserving the coherence of the Puritan model of headship.

In doing so, the congregation deploys what Sweet identifies as one of the most common and effective gaslighting strategies: exploiting "women's institutional vulnerabilities," which often takes the form of the victimizer mobilizing the cultural force of gendered stereotypes to negate the target's right to agency.[14] As mentioned, the Puritan stereotype of the witch hailed directly from Eve after the fall; thus, by simply accusing Lois, the Hickson women associate her with insatiable carnality, pride, and a failure to submit to male authority. Gaskell underscores how accusations of witchcraft sanction violence against women in particular by choosing to limit her representation to the imprisonment, mistreatment, and execution of three female characters (Hota, Natee, and Lois). She also, however, highlights women's role in creating and perpetuating such violence, observing that, when it comes to the accusers, "it was most frequently a woman or girl that was the supposed subject" of being bewitched (185). By having the congregation ratify the accusation in the service of preserving one man's "honourable position," Gaskell clarifies how scapegoating Lois is really a tactic for temporarily obscuring the failure of Puritan gender ideology.

What gives gaslighting its teeth in "Lois," however, is how Puritanism as an institution recognizes spiritual reality as more legitimate than empirical reality. Puritans believed that God and Satan were engaged in a continual battle for control of God's kingdom, each actively recruiting human soldiers to serve in their respective armies. Satan was not an abstract or symbolic entity but an actual creature able to roam the land and invade one's home.[15] Possessing power second only to God's, Satan was central to Puritan theology; to deny the magnitude of his abilities was tantamount to heresy.[16] While anyone could temporarily fall under his influence through manipulation or moral weakness, Puritan doctrine defined a witch as someone who chose to make a pact with the devil and fight on his side in the ongoing battle against God.[17] In the moment when the Hickson women accuse Lois of witchcraft, the script that gets flipped is reality itself as they activate the congregation's alleged belief in the supremacy of a terrifying cosmology that supersedes the empirical world. From this point on, Lois must contend with what Gaile Pohlhaus Jr. calls "epistemic gaslighting," in which a dominant group's epistemic framework is assumed (by that group) to be aligned with reality in contrast with the experience of the gaslit individual. The legitimacy of the former in relation to the latter, however, has little to do with matching objective reality. Rather, it is fabricated through "interdependent epistemic pressures," which include "other [in-group] knowers, collective epistemic practices, and socially recognized epistemic institutions."[18] Insofar as Puritanism is the only recognized epistemology within the community, Lois's conflicting claims to a personally experienced truth have no value within the dominant framework.

But as Gaskell's narration makes clear, the true evil that underlies the confrontation is not Satanic but self-serving, collectively embraced to preemptively suture the rupture Manessah's madness would otherwise introduce to both his family and the community. Manasseh is not simply the head of his household but also revered as the most pious and theologically learned in the community. If the spiritually gifted man chosen by God to be the head of the household is insane, his insanity implicitly calls into question the efficacy of a society organized around the religious principles that legitimize his power. Gaslighting, then, emerges as a counterbalance to this destabilizing threat by displacing a man's patently obvious deficit onto a disposable woman whose collectively orchestrated expulsion reinforces the community's shared religious values — indeed, it allows them to rehearse and enact these values as public spectacle.

Religion's ability to justify the exchange of a rationally perceived reality for an unseen spiritual one is so powerful that even Lois begins to doubt the truth status of her conscious memories. The key moment at which religious gaslighting gains psychological purchase occurs after she has been dragged to jail and isolated in an eight-by-eight cell:

> Could she indeed be possessed by a demon and be indeed a witch, and yet till now have been unconscious of it? And her excited imagination recalled, with singular vividness, all she had ever heard on the subject — the horrible midnight sacrament, the very presence and power of Satan. Then remembering every angry thought against her neighbour . . . ; oh, could such evil thoughts have had devilish power given to them by the father of evil, and, all unconsciously to herself, have gone forth as active curses into the world? And so, on the ideas went careering wildly through the poor girl's brain — the girl thrown inward upon herself. At length, the sting of her imagination forced her to start up impatiently. What was this? A weight of iron on her legs — a weight stated afterwards, by the gaoler of Salem prison, to have been "not more than eight pounds". It was well for Lois it was a tangible ill, bringing her back from the wild illimitable desert in which her imagination was wandering. She took hold of the iron, and saw her torn stocking, — her bruised ankle, and began to cry pitifully, out of strange

> compassion with herself. They feared, then, that even in that cell she would find a way to escape. Why, the utter, ridiculous impossibility of the thing convinced her of her own innocence, and ignorance of all supernatural power; and the heavy iron brought her strangely round from the delusions that seemed to be gathering about her. (211–12)

In this powerful scene, Gaskell dramatizes the intense psychological struggle gaslighting incites in the mind of a victim. Primed by stories of supernatural attack she has heard since her arrival, Lois identifies her everyday sinful thoughts as likely conduits for Satan's control, potentially rendering her guilty of acts she does not consciously remember committing. Gaskell distinguishes between two epistemological paradigms that inform contradictory interpretations of the same situation. The first, aligned with the Hicksons and the elders who call for her confession, works on Lois's imagination and demands she accept that her conscious understanding of her own experience and memories is fundamentally incorrect. The second, aligned with the "weight of iron," is empirical and external to Lois, allowing her to reevaluate the claims of her gaslighters in light of sensory, rather than supernatural, evidence. Lois only resists gaslighting by moving her attention outside and beyond herself, and in so reorienting her perspective, she realizes that those who are truly delusional are her accusers.

The collective fury against Lois reaches a fever pitch when she refuses to confess, revealing another aspect of gaslighting: the abuser's "interpersonal need for assent."[19] Although Gaskell's narration has already revealed that the collective decision to scapegoat Lois is really a "solution" to the patriarchal and religious instability Mannaseh's madness would pose, the church elders double down on their investment in the supernatural reality they have invoked. Lois's refusal to willfully assume the identity of "witch" thus defies the ontological veracity of their asserted religious worldview. This explains why, when the elders fail to compel her confession, Pastor Tappau becomes "enraged at her resolution of not confessing" and is "scarcely able to keep himself from striking her," a curious reaction given that she will be more severely punished if she does not confess. What actually "enrages" him is her refusal to ratify his power to create and alter her reality at will — a reality he can conveniently reify with the imprimatur of God. Tappau's fury hyperbolically echoes Manessah's earlier claim that refusing to marry him constituted blasphemy. In both cases, the issue is not whether the spiritual world to which they claim privileged access is real; rather the issue is whether she complies with the version of reality her gaslighters endorse. In Lois's case, the cost of this refusal is death, the ultimate way to eliminate the possibility of protest. Although Lois manages to resist confessing, the tactics used to draw a confession from her — including isolation, bribery, and the threat of torture — *do* briefly part her from her right mind. As the jailor reports, she seemed to have "'gone silly'; for indeed, she did not seem to know him, but kept rocking herself to and fro, and whispering softly to herself, smiling a little from time to time" (221). This detail underscores the tremendous psychological trauma gaslighting inflicts on victims, particularly when reinforced with the considerable power of institutional mechanisms of control.

The only other victims Gaskell represents in the story are Hota and Nattee, two non-Christian Indigenous servants who also have the spiritual beliefs of others forcibly imposed upon them through religious gaslighting. Although we do not know Nattee's particular spiritual beliefs, Gaskell reveals that she is "not a christened woman" and that she periodically entertains the Hickson girls with "wild stories . . . of the wizards of her race" (160). With absolutely no institutional authority, after Nattee and Hota are accused, the Puritan community recategorizes their beliefs as not merely different, but Satanic. The rationalization for Hota's execution spectacularly demonstrates how the church elders mobilize the logic of settler colonialism to hold an Indigenous woman accountable for spiritual beliefs that are not even her own. Despite having promised to spare her life in exchange for a confession, the elders conclude that "it was well to make an example of the first-discovered witch, and it was also well that she was an Indian, a heathen, whose life would be no great loss to the community" (192). Connecting Hota's value to her racial, colonial, and religious difference demonstrates the ways in which gaslighters weaponize structural inequalities. Indeed, the compelled confession, conviction, and public execution of Hota and Nattee exhibit all the hallmarks of what Angelique M. Davis and Rose Ernst call "racial gaslighting," a "cultural process that perpetuates and normalizes a white supremacist reality through pathologizing those who resist" by staging "racial spectacles."[20] In this case, the trial operates as a way of publicly delegitimizing a competing set of Indigenous spiritual beliefs by using the full force of institutional power, thereby enshrining a single religious ideology as valid and marking all others as both dangerous and ripe for elimination.

In the story's conclusion, Gaskell contrasts the Salem community's use of religion to gaslight and condemn with Lois's more inclusive faith, potentially offering an alternative vision of spiritual practice in which women support other women. When the jailers throw the beaten and bruised Nattee into Lois's cell, Lois "held her in her arms, and softly wiped the old brown wrinkled face with her apron, crying over it, as she had hardly yet cried over her own sorrows" (222). In tending to the woman up to the moment of their simultaneous execution, Lois enacts sympathy and inclusion, qualities that are central to Gaskell's own Unitarian faith. Unlike the church elders and the Hicksons, who wield religion as an ideological cudgel to manipulate others or achieve their personal ends, Lois recounts the passion of Christ — "the marvelous and sorrowful story of one who died on the cross for us and for our sakes" — as a way of "comforting the helpless Indian woman with the sense of the presence of a Heavenly Friend" (222). However well intentioned, as a white colonist Lois is also in this moment implicitly imposing her own religious beliefs onto an Indigenous person, revealing that she, too, assumes the "correct" spiritual epistemology to be Protestant Christianity. From a gendered perspective, though, Nattee and Lois's mutual embrace on their walk to the gallows emblematizes a perspective on faith that encourages communion between women and across barriers of age, race, and religion. Further, this orientation is inimical to the hierarchy of patriarchal structures that underwrites and encourages the gaslighting of non-compliant women.

***

Gaskell was inspired to write "Lois the Witch" when, during a visit to a country magistrate, a missive arrived from a neighboring village urging him to counteract agitation to execute an old woman for being a witch. Gaskell echoes this event in Lois's story of her father's failure to intervene on Hannah's behalf, for which she is cursed in her father's place. Understandably, Gaskell was struck by the incident, occurring not in the distant seventeenth century but in a modern Victorian England supposedly far removed from superstition or belief in the reality of witchcraft. Yet, however enlightened a country may become, scapegoating women seems to be timeless — even scapegoating that explicitly deploys accusations of witchcraft. In Paige Sweet's aforementioned sociological exploration of gaslighting from 2019, for example, she cites the case of a woman whose husband "insisted she was a witch who had hired a shaman to keep him trapped in their marriage, although it was *he* who was following her and keeping her trapped in the home."[21] What "Lois the Witch" so penetratingly shows is that appeals to the supernatural often conceal a legacy of patriarchal systems and internalized misogyny that continues to fail and doom women to this day.

Remarkably, while writing this chapter I discovered that my own family's history had been shaped by the same form of religious gaslighting that Gaskell fictionalized. A file inherited from my maternal grandfather revealed that I am a direct descendant of Ann Alcock Foster, a woman who was convicted of witchcraft during the Salem trials and who died in prison on December 3, 1692. At the time of her arrest, Foster was a seventy-two-year-old widow, accused by her neighbor Joseph Ballard of bewitching his wife with fever. Ballard also accused Ann's daughter and granddaughter of witchcraft, although they were subsequently acquitted.[22] Foster's investigation and trial initiated a second wave of witch-hunting in the nearby town of Andover, eventually resulting in forty-six accusations — more than in Salem Town and Salem Village combined.[23] Although the official historical records do not offer any reason as to why Foster was accused, the family record suggests that she had repeatedly refused to sell her land to Ballard, who then took advantage of the ongoing trials to cast suspicion on her.[24] In this expedient way, he sought to enrich himself by removing the impediment of a woman's will through her execution.

In making this discovery, I was even more forcefully struck by how the specter of patriarchal Puritanism continues to be used to gaslight women today. As critics of the US Supreme Court's 2022 decision to overturn *Roe v. Wade* were quick to point out, Justice Alito's opinion cites the work of Matthew Hale, an English jurist who sentenced two women to death for witchcraft and wrote a treatise in support of the marital rape exemption.[25] Further, Hale's *Tryal of Witches* (1662), which detailed his handling of the witchcraft case, significantly informed the juridical process of the Salem trials. Hale's claim (which Alito cites) that abortion qualifies as homicide is inextricable from his view of women through the lens of patriarchal Puritanism. In this way, Alito resurrects and reinforces a seventeenth-century religious ideology in order to deny women their bodily autonomy in the twenty-first century.[26] Following the US Supreme Court's decision, judges in a number of states have become increasingly brazen in their use of Christian doctrine to support rolling back reproductive rights. As recently as February 16, 2024, for example, the Supreme Court of Alabama ruled that stored embryos be afforded the same protections as children, exposing medical professionals who perform in vitro fertilization to legal action. In his concurring decision on the ruling, Chief Justice Tom Parker marshalled the support of the Ten Commandments, the Book of Genesis, and the biblical commentary of John Calvin to argue that "the theologically based view of the sanctity of life adopted by the People of Alabama" insists that "life cannot be wrongfully destroyed without incurring the wrath of a holy God."[27] The Alabama case demonstrates the rupture between two incompatible worldviews: the scientific worldview that holds an embryo before implantation to be a cluster of cells, and the theological worldview that holds an embryo to be a child. By invoking Christian scripture and Calvinist doctrine in support of a legal decision that directly impacts women's control of their own fertility, Parker's opinion deploys the same gaslighting strategy as Manasseh and Joseph Ballard — one that delegitimizes women's freedom by claiming that it defies God's will.

Religion has long been a useful tool in the arsenal of misogyny, linked as it is to a community's most deeply held beliefs, while also often being connected to the institutional machinery that determines and organizes the community members' lives. Insofar as its reach is both psychological and social, gaslighting lends itself to the most insidious applications of religion: to coerce a woman into marriage, to sanction the theft of a woman's land, to deny a woman's rights to reproductive freedom and bodily autonomy (to name just a few examples among many). What better instrument than religious gaslighting to accomplish, at a stroke, a reversal of fortune in one's favor by changing the rules of reality itself? As Gaskell's narrator in "Lois the Witch" observes, "Where evidence takes a supernatural character, there is no disproving it" (186). Although Ann Foster and Lois ultimately met grim ends, historical retrospection and the psychological insight of Gaskell's fiction reveal that witches are often martyrs, and true devils wear a human face.

Notes

1. Gaskell, "Lois the Witch," 150. Further references will be cited parenthetically.
2. For instance, Deborah Wynne reads the tale as a commentary on the challenges faced by women in midcentury Britain, Louise Henson explores its connections to contemporary mental science, and both Rebecca Styler and Suzy Holstein examine the work's connection to Victorian Unitarianism. Among those focusing on the historical setting, Deborah Denholtz Morse examines the legacy of the English Civil War in the story, whereas Louisa Jane Foster traces the role of Gaskell's transatlantic source material for the witchcraft trials. For a recent examination of how gaslighting works in another story by Gaskell, see Kathleen Gentle's "Gaslighting and Mental Cruelty in Elizabeth Gaskell's 'The Grey Woman.'"
3. Styler, "Lois the Witch," 73–76.
4. Karlsen, *Devil*, 177.
5. Karlsen, *Devil*, 181.
6. Reis, *Damned Women*, 3.
7. Reis, *Damned Women*, 2.
8. Abramson, "Turning Up the Lights," 10.
9. 2 Kings 8:7–14, NIV.
10. Reis, *Damned Women*, 57–60.
11. Sweet, "Sociology of Gaslighting," 852, 853.
12. Sweet, "Sociology of Gaslighting," 852.
13. Calef and Weinshel, "Some Clinical Consequences," 53.
14. Sweet, "Sociology of Gaslighting," 865.
15. Reis, *Damned Women*, 65–66.
16. Reis, *Damned Women*, 87–88.
17. Reis, *Damned Women*, 80.
18. Pohlhaus, "Gaslighting and Echoing," 681.
19. Abramson, "Turning Up the Lights," 12.
20. Davis and Ernst, "Racial Gaslighting," 763.
21. Sweet, "Sociology of Gaslighting," 866.
22. Ray, *Satan and Salem*, 107.
23. Ray, *Satan and Salem*, 105.
24. Historian Benjamin C. Ray provides the most robust account of Ann Foster's case. Although he concludes that there's no apparent reason for why Ann was selected, "it is clear that Joseph Ballard . . . initiated Andover's massive witch-hunt." Ray, *Satan and Salem*, 107.
25. See, for example, Field, "How the Legal History of Witches Impacts Abortion"; Levin, "Samuel Alito's Antiabortion Inspiration: A Seventeenth-Century Jurist Who Supported Marital Rape and Had Women Executed"; and Armstrong, "Draft Overturning Roe v. Wade Quotes Infamous Witch Trial Judge with Long-Discredited Ideas on Rape."

26. See *Dobbs v. Jackson's Women's Health Organization.*
27. LePage v. Center for Reproductive Medicine, 37–38.

Bibliography

Abramson, Kate. "Turning Up the Lights on Gaslighting." *Philosophical Perspectives* 28, no. 1 (2014): 1–30.

Armstrong, Ken. "Draft Overturning Roe v. Wade Quotes Infamous Witch Trial Judge with Long-Discredited Ideas on Rape." *ProPublica*. May 6, 2022. https://www.propublica.org/article/abortion-roe-wade-alito-scotus-hale.

Calef, Victor, and Edward Weinshel. "Some Clinical Consequences of Introjection: Gaslighting." *Psychoanalytic Quarterly* 50 (1981): 44–66.

Davis, Angelique M., and Rose Ernst. "Racial Gaslighting." *Politics, Groups, and Identities* 7, no. 4 (2019): 761–74.

Dobbs v. Jackson's Women's Health Organization, 597 U.S. 18 (2022).

Field, Robert I. "How the Legal History of Witches Impacts Abortion." *Philadelphia Inquirer*. August 1, 2022.

Foster, Louisa Jayne. "The Monstrous Transatlantic Witchcraft Narrative: Elizabeth Gaskell's 'Lois the Witch.'" In *Transatlantic Traffic and (Mis) Translations*, edited by Robin Peel and Daniel Maudlin, 63–83. University of New Hampshire Press, 2013.

Gaskell, Elizabeth. "Lois the Witch." In *Gothic Tales*, edited by Laura Kransler, 139–226. Penguin, 2004.

Gentle, Kathleen. "Gaslighting and Mental Cruelty in Elizabeth Gaskell's 'The Grey Woman.'" *Gaskell Journal* 37 (2023): 23–42.

Henson, Louise. "'Half Believing, Half Incredulous': Elizabeth Gaskell, Superstition and the Victorian Mind." *Nineteenth-Century Contexts* 24, no. 3 (2002): 251–69.

Holstein, Suzy Clarkson. "In Harm's Way: Tolerating Intolerance in Elizabeth Gaskell's Fiction." *Gaskell Journal* 12 (1998): 46–50.

Karlsen, Carol F. *The Devil in the Shape of a Woman: Witchcraft in Colonial New England*. Norton, 1998.

LePage v. Center for Reproductive Medicine. SC-2022-0515 (2024).

Levin, Bess. "Samuel Alito's Antiabortion Inspiration: A Seventeenth-Century Jurist Who Supported Marital Rape and Had Women Executed." *Vanity Fair*. May 3, 2022. https://www.vanityfair.com/news/2022/05/samuel-alito-roe-v-wade-abortion-draft.

Morse, Deborah Denholtz. "Haunting Memories of the English Civil War in Elizabeth Gaskell's 'Morton Hall' and 'Lois the Witch.'" *Gaskell Journal* 24 (2010): 85–99.

Pohlhaus, Gaile. "Gaslighting and Echoing, or Why Collective, Epistemic Resistance is Not a 'Witch Hunt.'" *Hypatia* 35 (2020): 647–86.

Ray, Benjamin C. *Satan and Salem: The Witch-Hunt Crisis of 1692*. University of Virginia Press, 2015.

Reis, Elizabeth. *Damned Women: Sinners and Witches in Puritan New England.* Cornell University Press, 1997.
Styler, Rebecca. "'Lois the Witch': A Unitarian Tale." *The Gaskell Society Journal* 21 (2007): 73–85.
Sweet, Paige L. "The Sociology of Gaslighting." *American Sociological Review* 84, no. 5 (2019): 851–75.
Wynne, Deborah. "Hysteria Repeating Itself: Elizabeth Gaskell's 'Lois the Witch.'" *Women's Writing* 12, no. 1 (2005): 85–97.

Part Four

Rape Culture and Rhetorical Control

This section traces fundamental connections between gaslighting and rape culture; that is, the cultural practices that normalize men's sexual violence against women and shame, scapegoat, or silence victims, thereby denying the reality of their lived experiences. The essays gathered here explore how such intersections operated in texts from three very different reform movements: the abolitionist movement, the Church Reform movement, and the aesthetic movement. Some nineteenth-century writers who claimed to support the progressive ideals associated with these movements nevertheless perpetuated rape myths and social injunctions against women speaking openly about sex. These chapters illustrate how difficult resistance can be when an entrenched culture of rape infiltrates even those groups and discourses thought to be fighting for a more just society.

Part Four

11

A Matter of Practicality

Mary Prince and Abolitionist Gaslighting

Doreen Thierauf

Introduction: Mary Prince in the Cage

In or around 1820, *The History of Mary Prince, A West Indian Slave; Related by Herself* (1831) informs the reader, the thirty-two-year-old enslaved protagonist appeared before an Antiguan magistrate regarding "a quarrel" with another enslaved woman over "a pig" at her enslavers', the Woods', behest.[1] Prince was "put in the Cage" overnight and flogged on her "naked back" the next morning (*MP* 80). While the episode effectively illustrates Prince's enslavers' cruelty and the violent arbitrariness of the colonial judicial system, the *History*'s paratexts tell another, more complex story. Ten months after the *History*'s publication, James Macqueen, a former plantation manager and a defender of colonial slavery, ran a twenty-page slander in *Blackwood's Magazine* in which he accused Thomas Pringle, the coeditor of Prince's pamphlet, of having fabricated Prince's story.[2] Macqueen's source, the Woods' biracial servant, Martha Wilcox, claims that Prince appeared before magistrate Dyett because another enslaved woman, Phibba, found Prince in bed with a white Captain William. Wilcox's report culminates by half-hiding, half-publicizing the unspeakable: "She took in washing and made money by it. She also made money *many*, *many* other ways by her badness; I mean, by allowing men to visit her, and by selling ***** to worthless men."[3] The same incident was reported on March 1, 1833, when the *Times* ran a summary of *Wood v. Pringle*, a libel suit brought on by Prince's enslaver against Pringle. In the *Times* account of the seventeen-hour trial, the actors are reversed: Prince allegedly found a Captain Abbott in bed with another enslaved woman and flogged her. The *Times* notes that Prince "told all this to Miss Strickland [Pringle's coeditor] when that lady took down her narrative"; however, "these statements were not in the narrative published by the defendant."[4] The *Times* report records three instances of the court's boisterous laughter during Prince's examination, indicating that the assembly viewed Prince's reminiscences as entertaining, low-brow bawdy.

While the *Times* and *Blackwood's* paratexts are not more authentic than the *History*'s main narrative, they are both complementary and productively contradictory to it. Enslaved women were crucial to the "war of representation" between abolitionist and pro-slavery media campaigns, each claiming that their respective depictions accurately reflected the circumstances of British Caribbean slavery.[5] Mary Prince's understanding of her actions as they relate to her sexual experiences is almost entirely disregarded in the *History* and across the paratexts. Disregard for Mary Prince's sexual agency — for how she encountered, conceptualized, and negotiated the demands upon her body and in her mandatory reminiscences — permeates the surviving materials.

Here I argue that readers' encounters with these texts are shaped by a rhetorical structure I term abolitionist gaslighting, a specific type of racialized testimonial injustice produced by the competing yet interlocking ideological imperatives of abolitionist and pro-slavery discourses. I build upon Veronica Ivy's [Rachel McKinnon's] formulation of an "epistemic form of gaslighting" in which the recipients of someone's personal testimony, including ostensible allies, raise doubts regarding "the speaker's reliability at perceiving events accurately."[6] Where Ivy shows that "gaslighting involves expressing doubts that the harm or injustice that the speaker is testifying to really happened as the speaker claims," I will show that abolitionist gaslighting, in addition to expressing such doubts both verbally and generically, is largely uninterested in figuring some of the speaker's experiences — specifically as they relate to sexuality — as potentially harmful or morally unjust while continuously expressing solidarity with the speaker's situation.[7] Saidiya Hartman famously posits that any sexual exchange between white men and enslaved women constitutes rape, and this conception underlies my use of the term colonial rape culture.[8] The workings of that rape culture are a distinguishing factor in the rhetorical structure I identify: abolitionists *did* acknowledge unjust treatment based on race, yet they reinforced nineteenth-century rape culture by distorting, and sometimes denying, the realities of sexual violence and sex work under slavery.[9] All three tellings of Prince's imprisonment in "the Cage" silence Prince's potential not only to challenge how her story is told, but also to protest the conditions of her enslavement that enlist her sexuality as a site of mandatory contention. Kate Abramson, outlining gaslighting's effects, argues that "aiming at the obliteration of another person's independent perspective and moral standing constitutes one of the deepest kinds of moral wrongs," and my essay is part of the ongoing scholarly pursuit to secure Prince's place in the critical canon and do justice to her legacy.[10] Uncovering what's not in the *History* is part of that task.

To understand the workings of abolitionist gaslighting, it is necessary to remember that, in the texts at hand, the living, breathing Mary Prince as she historically existed is superseded by abolitionist and antislavery avatars bearing her name, and that these avatars, even where they are narrators, are barred from challenging the everyday sexual violence in the colonies.[11] This gives the impression that Prince had mostly internalized the sexual codes of her day, which, in turn, perpetuates the white, middle-class, patriarchal status quo after

British colonial slavery's abolition.[12] The maintenance of white and patriarchal supremacy, including rape culture, *is the long-term political effect, if not purpose, of these texts.*

In what follows, I trace the relationship between slavery's culture of non-optional sexual vulnerability for Black women and various modes of discourse control at work in nineteenth-century abolitionism as guided by simultaneously operating linguistic, religio-moral, colonial, and political agendas. Reading Caribbean slavery historically, I then suggest that Prince might have been part of the widespread Antiguan concubinage system since the *History* and its paratexts contain traces of her complex negotiation of and resistance to conflicting, yet equally oppressive, colonial and metropolitan sexual norms. My conclusion will sketch how abolitionism's success, depending on white evangelical women's political mobilization, naturalized this form of gaslighting for the Victorian era, rendering all women's negotiations of sexual exploitation illegible to the British public.

Abolitionist Gaslighting at Work: Authenticating and Falsifying, Pruning and Adding

Veronica Ivy posits that, often, self-proclaimed "allies" of people of marginalized identities, "when listening to a person's testimony, privilege their own first-hand experience over the testimony of the person they're supposed to be supporting," thereby denying the person providing the testimony the capacity for objectivity or appropriate epistemic situatedness.[13] Yet, those receiving the testimony are morally obliged to grant narrative authority to the person reporting, especially when that person is socially disadvantaged. The *History* is a prime example of epistemic gaslighting, since Thomas Pringle and Susanna Strickland, neither of whom had set foot in the Caribbean, fail to honor the "epistemic weight" of Prince's first-person authority.[14] They subordinate Prince's account to abolitionism's political aims, and the result is a "willful hermeneutical ignorance" that shapes the *History*'s (mis)representation of colonial slavery and figures Prince as acquiescent to metropolitan sexual ideology.[15] This section illustrates how the generic boundaries of the slave narrative enabled the gaslighting committed by the editors of Prince's testimony.

Female abolitionists like Susanna Strickland focused their energy on drawing public attention to those aspects of slavery that violated domestic ideology, successfully reframing them — women's flogging and fieldwork, the separation of families, enslaved women's split loyalty between enslavers and husbands, and enslaved mothers' inability to spend their pregnancies in seclusion and care for their children — as slavery's essential crimes, without regard for enslaved women's own cultural memory, everyday living conditions, future aspirations, or current strategies of survival.[16] The formulaic representation of enslaved women "both verbally and visually as the ultimate passive victim," according to Clare Midgley, occurred because female abolitionists preferred figuring them as incapable of self-assertion — and, in the ways of print culture, they were — and without male protection.[17] The brief glimpses of Mary Prince's lived experience make the *History* important to scholars; owing to Strickland and Pringle's mediation, however, it is impossible to tease apart individual points of view.

As John Thurston observes, "the shaping of *Mary Prince* into an intelligible, linear, grammatically correct narrative has taken this text away from [her]. It is a corporate text . . . that finally only the Anti-Slavery Society could be said to author."[18] Rather than constituting a collaborative endeavor, the *History*, like many slave narratives, was a business venture, and most of its production occurred outside of Prince's sphere of influence. Prince was disadvantaged by her illiteracy, her likely total ignorance of the British abolitionist literary circuit, and her inability to contact Black abolitionists in London.[19] Her material dependence on Pringle influenced the *History*'s gestation and permitted its white editors to discount the epistemic weight of Prince's experience.[20] While it appears that Prince was incapable of physical labor by 1830, she was obliged to carry out domestic tasks in Pringle's home, including caring for Pringle's ailing wife. Her continued residence was contingent on her ability to work: Prince left the Pringles' service in June 1832, perhaps because her rheumatism and worsening eyesight left her unable to labor, or because the allowance of ten or twelve shillings per week she received from Pringle was sufficient to maintain her (*MP* 29).[21] Prince had to submit to the political and economic incentives that led to the composition of her testimony.

In the prefatory remarks to the *History*, dated January 25, 1831, Pringle states that Prince's testimony was initially

> written out fully, with all the narrator's repetitions and prolixities, and afterwards pruned into its present shape; retaining, as far as was practicable, Mary's exact expressions and peculiar phraseology. No fact of importance has been omitted, and not a single circumstance or sentiment has been added. It is essentially her own, without any material alteration farther than was requisite to exclude redundancies and gross grammatical errors, so as to render it clearly intelligible. (*MP* 55)

Pringle assures readers thrice that alterations to Prince's words were guided by considerations of practicality, relevance, and correctness, implying that information the editors thought would deviate from their target audience's cultural comprehension was excised. The pamphlet was to foster readers' sympathy with an enslaved woman who, insufficiently empowered to achieve her own liberation, conveyed her experiences via a morally reliable first-person narrator.[22] By framing the editing undertaken by Pringle and Strickland as the generic work of abolitionist gaslighting, I underscore these self-appointed antislavery advocates' moral failure to accurately report slavery's atrocities and their creation of a narrative voice that ventriloquizes metropolitan views and is likely not Prince's own.

As later legal documents suggest, Pringle and Strickland filtered certain "redundancies," many of them pertaining to Prince's complex sexual history, a history that domestic ideology would have branded as that of a sex worker. Pringle and Strickland morally purified and selectively replotted aspects of Prince's testimony for rhetorical effectiveness and marketability, weakening the narrative's historical accuracy and erasing Prince's claim to dictate the terms of how she was represented.[23] The extant pamphlet enfolds Prince's memories in a semantic web of Christian moral principles and preserves her account only "as far as was practicable" for the Society's purposes because the media "war" between proslavery and abolitionist writers was fully responsive to, and contingent on, metropolitan discourses governing women's sexuality (*MP* 55). The *History*'s goal was to formulate a respectable "character" for Prince, and so Prince's editors largely excised her sexual experiences, intimate life, and possible complicity in the culture of colonial violence at which the *Times* hinted with its report of Prince allegedly flogging another enslaved woman.

James Macqueen, Pringle's proslavery adversary, ridiculed Pringle's depiction of Prince's chastity and, in his long *Blackwood's* invective, insinuated that Prince, Anti-Slavery Society's "despicable tool," was Pringle's prostitute.[24] While Macqueen's shrillness is a good indicator of the *History*'s power in strengthening public support for abolition, Pringle was pressured to authenticate details of Prince's story that Macqueen and others had cast into doubt.[25] Hence, subsequent editions' page count swelled as Pringle inserted long footnotes into the main text and appended supplementary letters, legal documents, quasi-forensic statements, eyewitness accounts, and unrelated testimonies to prove that the *History*'s representation of Prince's experience was accurate.[26] The result is the present "concatenation of mutually validating and interlinked documents," as Sara Salih notes.[27] The mass of verifying documents — which also include present-day scholarly texts that confirm almost all the names, dates, and locations mentioned in the *History* — is itself a symptom of abolitionist gaslighting. Pringle's preface insists that the *History*'s main text is "essentially her own" when, obviously, the existence of the preface as well as the sprawling textual apparatus and appendices belie that assertion. The aim of the *History* was to give Mary Prince "character" — to convert her from a maximally degraded enslaved person to a plucky, semiautonomous agent within slavery, and afterward to a paid servant and respectable working-class recipient of philanthropic monies, thereby gaslighting both Prince and the reader. Abolitionist gaslighting is thus at once individual and collective, interpersonal and rhetorical: it is an overtly political form of epistemic violence that manipulates the testimonial agent and the testimony's target audience.[28]

Gillian Whitlock observes that "an overwhelming sense of readership, of audience, pervades the *History*": the text's political commitments as well as its cultural intentions complicate notions of Prince's status as the primary autobiographical subject.[29] I would argue that the first-person narrator of Mary Prince produced by the *History* is a white, middle-class fantasy. As Laura Ann Stoler memorably writes, "discourses of sexuality do more than define the distinction of the bourgeois self; in identifying marginal members of the body politic, they have mapped the moral parameters of European nations."[30] By casting Mary Prince's sexual experiences under slavery as marginally representable, by *pretending* to excise all references to sexuality, the *History*, with its massive public response and subsequent proliferation of authenticating-yet-obfuscating appendices and footnotes, creates "Mary Prince" as Black-and-poor-and-hypersexual subject and, in ever finer detail, calibrates that subject's ability to demand public recognition, self-ownership, property rights, and, crucially, public relief money.

In the end, Prince's disappearance from the historical archive after 1834 — the fact that all storytelling, data-gathering, and activism surrounding Prince's case ceases at that point — confirms that this subject has been eliminated after and due to abolition. The archive fails to reveal how Prince herself might have wanted to reimagine the world. Nationhood, whiteness, and middle-class morality are the *History*'s, and abolition's, true offspring. The editors' invention of Prince as a literary subject without claims to a biological or archival afterlife — their theft of Prince's epistemic authority — is the necessary underside of abolition's victory, even when allowing for the possibility that Prince successfully attempted "to evade the archive and its strategies of surveillance, to elude the threat of capture and classification that official archives represent," as Gabeba Baderoon has speculated.[31]

Pretending Not to Tell: Gaslighting and Colonial Rape Culture

By circulating ideologically palatable representations of enslaved people's suffering, the Anti-Slavery Society's publishing outlet, the *Anti-Slavery Reporter* — for which Thomas Pringle served as editor in 1832 — had won attention among mostly female evangelical readers in England and Scotland. Its accounts of slavery employed coded yet, for publishers and audiences' tastes, maximally frank language that imagined slavery in terms of saintly martyrdom undergone by chaste women of color. Sexual experiences under slavery — whether consensual or enforced — were largely censored because "Christian purity, for those abolitionists, overrode regard for truth," as Moira Ferguson writes.[32] Despite willingness to display enslaved women's bodies in states of agony, candid representations and the naming of morally degrading experiences, including sexual assault and rape, were taboo.[33] The muting or excision of such experiences forestalls the recording of enslaved women's own framing, while creating an alternative narrative — what Angelique M. Davis and Rose Ernst refer to as a "racial spectacle" — that leaves the reader to assume enslaved women's compliance with white ideological preferences while "obfuscate[ing] the existence of a white supremacist state power structure," of which colonial rape was an integral part.[34]

The greatest logical gap in the *History* is its silence about Mary Prince's reproductive experience. Moira Ferguson notes that the *History* "enciphers motherhood obliquely, [Prince's] strange silence [being] an egregiously conspicuous omission in near-Victorian, family-conscious England."[35] If scholars understand the *History* as part of a longer tradition of ritualized inquest targeting unmarried mothers among the working poor to determine the allocation of welfare aid — noting, for example, that philanthropic organizations and governments "often demanded a [written] story in exchange for [their] dole" — the absence of Mary Prince's child in the *History*, Pringle's appended documents, and surviving archival paratexts are neither a contradiction nor a coincidence.[36] The *History*'s narrow emplotment in the service of abolitionism's tenets not only delimits the narrator's agency but also enfolds whatever agency is left within the strictures of evangelical emancipation. Prince's possible pregnancy or maternity are unrepresentable outside domestic ideology, while the *History*'s manipulation of the meaning of Prince's sexual life is, on the other hand, *constitutive* of white domestic ideology and indicative of the epistemic form of gaslighting I have outlined above.[37] Prince's body, the experiential site of degradation and terror, cannot be mobilized as pregnant or maternal; yet, it is hinted to be sexually active and fully enmeshed in colonial rape culture.

The *History* contains multiple scenes that figure sexuality and corporeal punishment as part of the same disciplinary apparatus. For instance, it describes regular humiliating violations that Prince experienced while living with the Inghams at the age of twelve: "To strip me naked — to hang me up by the wrists and lay my flesh open with the cow-skin, was an ordinary punishment for even the slightest offence" (*MP* 66). The description is repeated nearly verbatim when the narrator recounts her years on Turks Island: "Mr. D— has often stripped me naked, hung me up by the wrists, and beat me with the cow-skin, with his own hand, till my body was raw with gashes" (*MP* 72–73).[38] A washing scene provides another clue to the immensity of the narrative's elisions regarding Robert Darrell's sexual exploitation of Prince:

> He had an ugly fashion of stripping himself quite naked and ordering me then to wash him in a tub of water. This was worse to me than all the licks. Sometimes when he called me to wash him I would not come, my eyes were so full of shame. . . . I then told him I would not live longer with him, for he was a very indecent man — very spiteful, and too indecent; with no shame for his servants, no shame for his own flesh. (*MP* 77–78)

These passages are characterized by linguistic struggle as the *History*'s narrator strives to relate what (supposedly) cannot be told. The final sentence stumbles in its attempt to create meaning; its staccato echo risks tautology as it appeals to the reader to understand while pretending that nothing is to be understood. Only two words, "shame" and "indecent," are available to express what is occurring. Paul-Mikhail Catapang Podosky, when articulating a definition of "second-order gaslighting," writes: "the subject of gaslighting comes to doubt her ability to judge whether sexual harassment has occurred *because she doubts that she has the right concept to pick it out*."[39] Judgment is stymied and the language turns repetitive, fettered, and narrow. Symbolically speaking, the disruption, even mutilation, of syntactical and semantic flow match the mutilations that Prince's tormenters unleashed on her body.[40] "Washing" functions as an inverted rhetorical substitute for and concentration point of the implied sexual activity with the enslaver, besmirching speaker and enslaver. Such passages witness an epistemological breakdown that prevents the *History*'s narrator from developing her own concept of, much less language for, the sexual trauma she experiences, though the historical Mary Prince may have indeed possessed such language and concepts.

While the *History* contains other such scenes of voyeuristic spectacle, its most violent episode concerns Hetty, a pregnant woman enslaved by the Inghams. Abolitionist tales often prefaced the narrator's own abuse with an eyewitness account of another enslaved person's beating to prepare readers for the narrator's martyrdom. Hetty's experience anticipates Prince's own, and since the *History*'s narrator cannot tell her sexual abuse, the narrative employs Hetty as Prince's double.[41] Hetty embodies innocent femininity punished for following women's primary duty, motherhood, a stock motif employed by abolitionists to demand an end to the flogging of pregnant women.[42] Prince's entry to the Inghams' home begins with an auditory account of Hetty's flogging that, considering Captain Ingham's state of undress and the mentioning of "his bed," could also involve a rape (*MP* 65). Since Hetty is already pregnant, the scene doubly announces her status as Ingham's chattel. After miscarrying the child — an outcome Ingham perhaps intended — Hetty's body continues to swell until it ejects edematous fluid upon the kitchen floor. Slavery's rape culture results in enslaved women's painfully aborted maternity and finds its climax in spilling into the space where the system nourishes its laboring bodies. Prince is the next body to be inserted into this atrocity-producing economy, as the girl inherits "all [Hetty's] labours," suggesting a convergence of productive and reproductive work.[43]

A scene of extreme corporal punishment occurs right after Hetty's story, creating a causal chain between Prince and her adopted "Aunt" (*MP* 67). When ordered to "empty a large earthen jar" with a long crack running through it, Prince feels the jar coming apart in her hands. "Dreadfully frightened," she reports the "accident" (nevertheless "my fault") to her mistress, who beats her and denounces her to Ingham. He then ties her "up upon a ladder, and [gives her] a hundred lashes." When he catches his breath, a "heavy squall of wind and rain" arises before "a dreadful earthquake" shakes the house, destroys the roof, and enables the girl's escape. Prince, "all blood and bruises," hides under the porch (*MP* 68–69). Brought near the brink of death, Prince's body, her earthen jar, and earth itself break open: all three vessels signify femininity as irreparably damaged. I would suggest that the jar scene signals Prince's absent maternity as terrifyingly violent metaphorical haunting because a literal description would be "too, too bad to speak in England" (*MP* 68). The twelve-year-old child's experience of physical and sexual violence materializes as a broken jar, "part[ing] in my hand," and the abuse finds its catastrophic culmination — the last rung of the ladder to which the slave girl is tied — in a literal natural cataclysm. Perhaps, on the day the jar breaks, Prince is raped by Captain Ingham, maybe not for the first time, since the jar bears the mark of an "old deep crack" (*MP* 68). Yet, the event might break her "vessel": the earth's opening and the jar's destruction could indicate Prince's miscarriage or sterilization, metaphorizing the slave woman's impossible motherhood as gothic violence.

The jar episode, with its atmospheric stage directions and causal determinism, enacts colonial rape culture as gothic melodrama, implicating the reader in the quasi-pornographic racial spectacle through a barrage of erotic signifiers: the white mistress flogging with irrational fury; the sadistic male punisher getting "hot" and "exhausted" from whipping the girl; the Inghams' voyeuristic son, Benjy, standing by to count the lashes; the earth "groaning and shaking"; and, finally, Prince's body, first "trembling," then "all blood and bruises . . . moaning piteously" (*MP* 68–69). Subsequently, Prince mentions that Mrs. Ingham reminds her of the broken jar, possibly encoding accusations that Prince had seduced Captain Ingham and that there had been a pregnancy. The very next sentence relates that the cow had freed itself again, just when the girl is "milking" it (*MP* 69). Two pages prior, Hetty's brutal beating and resulting miscarriage had occurred for the same reason. Prince has inherited Hetty's place, and the two women's associations with a runaway milk cow might not be coincidental. Captain Ingham notices the cow's (or Prince's) flight and brutally beats Prince's lower back with his boot, inducing the girl to run to her mother (*MP* 69–70). The violence of slavery's (re)productive labor leads to bovine and human escape — both valuable, lactating commodities. Abolitionist gaslighting restricts meaning in these scenes to a densely loquacious symbolic domain with embattled maternity at its center. Ensuring the plausible deniability of everyone involved, these passages leave the *History*'s narrator without an "independent standpoint from which to issue a challenge," to return to Abramson's phrasing: only metaphors and gothic ambiance tell the tale, a sign of gaslighting's metalinguistic deprivations.[44] Ultimately, the testimony's main target — its readership — is gaslit by such obfuscating rhetorical devices.

What's Not in *The History*: Caribbean Concubinage

Prince's interactions with her female enslavers are in line with slave narratives' usual representation of white Caribbean women as cruel and violent. Nevertheless, white women were rare in the Caribbean, and most white men of authority — overseers, ship captains, bookkeepers — kept Black or mixed-race mistresses, although some of these men were married to white women present on the island. As Joseph Phillips, a longtime acquaintance of the Woods who was married to a Black woman, mentions in a letter to Pringle, sexual relations between white men and women of color were a fundamental part of the social structure, often accompanied by exploitation and violence (*MP* 111). Enslaved women who refused to submit were generally subjected to severe violence, and the many instances of horrific violence in the *History* might obliquely refer to punishments for sexual noncompliance. If white metropolitan discourse perceived enslaved women's reputations to be tainted by prostitution, many of them, in fact, sold their bodies, sometimes to one man for an extended period and sometimes in rapid succession and to many men from all social strata at once.[45] Enslavers often declared that enslaved women sold sex voluntarily and, given that slavery legally erased enslaved women's consent, it is impossible to speculate about the percentage of voluntary forms of prostitution compared to those that were forced. It was obviously convenient for enslavers to suggest that enslaved women benefited from casual rape.

In order to understand the extent of abolitionist gaslighting at work in the *History*, the historical reality of Black women's non-optional self-prostitution, along with the "high incidence of miscegenous unions in the West Indies" that Adrienne Davis has noted, must be kept in mind.[46] The motives of enslaved women were manifold and justified, even if they were frowned upon by some segments of the heterogeneous enslaved community. Historical evidence suggests that many non-enslaving white men came through urban centers, harbors, and non-agrarian trading posts — such as Antigua's towns — which fostered a formalized system of Black sex work.[47] Sex workers likely sought to improve their own and their children's living conditions and hoped for eventual manumission as well as protection from other men's advances, exploitation, or violence. It was further normal for enslavers to "hire out" enslaved women as "housekeepers" to white acquaintances, guests, or enslaved Black people in overseer positions without consideration for women's willingness or preparedness for sexual intercourse. Such trafficking, often more profitable than the sale of enslaved women, likely caused anger and resistance among members of enslaved communities in some places, while it was unremarkable in others.[48] Some enslavers allowed enslaved women a share or the total of the profits to stymy such resistance. For many enslaved women, freedom, if only of a temporary and precarious kind, was best attained through intimacy with European men.

Mary Prince's remarks that she "took in washing" and sold provisions to ships' captains when her enslavers were absent — personal liberties that included independent travel and the maintenance of a social network — should be understood in the context of the general assumption that hired labor by enslaved women, especially domestic tasks, included sexual access. The narrator's assurance that she strove to earn cash "by all honest means" refutes the possibility of self-prostitution, an automatic expectation for any reader who had visited the Caribbean (*MP* 81).[49] This affirmation can be considered an instance of "existential silencing," a pernicious element of abolitionist gaslighting wherein the *History*'s narrator parrots metropolitan morality.[50] However, labor power and sexual services in the British colonial Caribbean were conflated, and most men with whom Prince interacted likely perceived her with this reality in mind. The many male advocates mentioned by Prince — Captain Abbott; Captain William; the Black cooper, Adam White; the freedman, Oyskman; Mr.

Burchell — should give readers pause, since they are reported to have either promised to help Prince with her manumission or to have cohabited with her (*MP* 81, 85).[51] Enslaved women, especially in urban areas, often earned manumission funds through sex work and asked their clients to support them in appeals to their enslavers.[52] At times, white enslavers manumitted their own mixed-race children and their children's mothers, which turned sexual relationships into important tools of social mobility for enslaved women.[53] Yet, not a single record of a Bermudan enslaver manumitting Black or mixed-race children exists.[54] Since the extended family that traded Mary Prince among its members had been originally based in Bermuda, John Adams Wood's adherence to the Bermudan culture of non-manumission ought to be considered when speculating on Prince's sexual agency. Manumission on Antigua was similarly rare, although not unheard of. Less than one percent of Antiguan enslaved people were manumitted annually (with numbers increasing as Emancipation drew closer), and chances improved for urban enslaved persons who were domestics or artisans and who had saved up enough money.[55] Prince's determination to collect money is understandable even when considering her enslavers' rigid stance and the steady increase of manumission prices before emancipation. Her enforced or voluntary self-prostitution probably did not lead to a fundamental improvement of her situation, though accommodation to and within slavery's sexual regimes should not be equated with absolute powerlessness.[56]

It is possible that freedman Daniel James, a carpenter and cooper, had an arrangement with Prince that included concubinage and culminated in a marriage encouraged by the Moravians. Missionaries on Antigua regulated Black couples' sexual relations or those of congregants who were nonmonogamous, although it was illegal for ministers to marry freedpersons and enslaved people without the enslaver's consent. What the *History* fails to note is that the Moravians excluded enslaved women from congregations and church-run schools if they resisted marriage or committed adultery.[57] In case Mary Prince saw literacy and Moravianism as possible avenues to freedom — despite the Moravians' preaching of European gender hierarchies and the sexual double standard — her marriage might not have been solely a spiritual matter. Prince might have utilized the many strategies toward manumission available to her, including income-generating activities such as sex work, domestic work, and marketing, as well as increasing her respectability and economic leverage through conversion and marriage.[58]

By embracing Christianity, the *History*'s narrator enters the ideological universe of the *History*'s target readers and makes visible the influence of Western marital models and notions of status, respectability, and civilization in Antigua. Prince reports that she only learns of fornication's sinfulness when she joins the Moravians: "I never knew rightly I had much sin till I went there" (*MP* 83).[59] This is another instance of Podosky's "second-order gaslighting": the narrator's reliable assessment of her own reality is shown to be impaired after joining the Moravians. Christian morality induces Prince to form "negative attitudes about [her] attitude-forming mechanisms," gaslighting her to believe that Caribbean enslaved women's survival tactics are, in fact, producing "sin."[60] The narrator does not trust herself to formulate the concepts necessary to describe her own life and comes to accept the hegemonic metropolitan ones — which render her permanently "fallen."

Historically, the Moravian encouragement of monogamy and Christian courtship was probably closely tied to planters' belief that promiscuity led to infertility as well as to the visibility of respectable, free Black women who had joined the Anglican Church after 1816. As the *History* illustrates, by the third decade of the nineteenth century, the church wedding had become established as a cultural ideal among Antiguan enslaved people, denoting "civility, education, financial stability, enduring love, and religious salvation."[61] Many enslaved people followed the model outlined by the *History* in which initial, sometimes decades-long experimentation with multiple partners and occasional polygamy was followed by long-term monogamy, not necessarily accompanied by cohabitation.[62] The *History* hints that Prince and James maintained a visiting relationship because the Woods forbade James to live on their property — and, perhaps, because the couple preferred it that way. Visiting relationships were the most common form of romantic relationships among the enslaved, and husbands were generally free to take further wives if they could afford it to increase their status.[63]

Considering that Captain Abbott oversaw one of John Wood's vessels, it is further possible that Wood encouraged Prince's cohabitation with Abbott.[64] In urban coastal areas, it was common for enslavers to "lease" enslaved women to nautical crews. This would also account for the Woods' anger about Prince's unapproved marriage to James and for Prince's keeping it a secret for several months — Prince reports she was whipped by Wood when he found out — since, in case Prince actually began to live monogamously, the Woods would not only have lost an important source of profit but also incurred financial obligations due to Prince's marriage.[65] Social pressure on enslavers to encourage enslaved people's morality might have prevented Wood from flat-out denying Prince the right to stay married. Still, enslavers believed they were entitled to full sexual access to domestic enslaved people and housekeepers. Even if unlikely, it cannot be ruled out that Prince and John Adams Wood's domestic intimacy included a sexual dimension that was interrupted or complicated by Prince's marriage.[66]

In light of the historical circumstances recounted here — some of which are spelled out in the *History*'s later editions and exist in strenuous tension with the *History*'s narrator's testimony only a few pages apart — the extent of the abolitionist gaslighting that the testimony performs upon its narrator (and perhaps upon the historical Mary Prince) becomes apparent. Enslaved women, as epistemic subjects, did not simply perceive the world they encountered but rather "actively contribute[d] to the pool of epistemic resources shared by members of a community" in the Caribbean, both Black and white.[67] However, the situated sexual knowledge of enslaved women — their survival strategies, their negotiations, their pains and pleasures — are taken seriously almost nowhere in the *History*'s main text. The story told by the *History*'s narrator is a deeply epistemically unjust masquerade *whose own framing materials* provide ample evidence to discredit its veracity. As Podosky warns, "the decision as to which epistemic resources a diverse community of thinkers and speakers ought to possess isn't something that should be in the hands of a privileged few."[68] Finally, by denying epistemic agency to the enslaved women who experienced the realities narrated in the *History*, the text also distorts readers' understanding of the realities of rape under slavery.

Conclusion: The Story of a Disappearance

On March 6, 1833, a week after losing the libel suit Wood had brought against him, Thomas Pringle wrote, "slavery will be extinguished throughout the British dominions before January 1835 — and Mary Prince shall go back to her husband . . . in spite of the spiteful Mr Wood."[69] Archival traces of the legal and personal conflict between Pringle and Wood end here, and Prince, the discursive conduit between two colonial men equally defending their respective ideological and economic commitments, disappears from the archive. Pringle's prophecy about the abolition of slavery being correct, it stands to hope that the prediction regarding Prince's return to Antigua, contingent on her health and ability to raise money for her passage, was also realized. Unlike most parts of the British Caribbean, neither Antigua nor Bermuda transitioned from slavery to a repressive apprenticeship system, and after August 1, 1834, Prince would have set foot on either island as a free woman. In the wake of emancipation, John Adams Wood returned to England and was awarded £10,575 in compensation monies by the British government.[70] He died in London in 1836, fourteen months after Pringle had passed away from tuberculosis.

Proslavery and abolitionist writers agreed that enslaved women's sexual conduct in the colonies — regardless of their consent — disqualified them from discursive participation in the political struggle to end slavery. Abolitionist materials depicted sexually exploited enslaved women as soon-to-be-"redeemed" sex workers deserving of affective and pecuniary charity, whereas proslavery accounts took advantage of centuries-old stereotypes of Black licentiousness. Regardless of whether Prince was enfolded within abolitionism's melodramatic gothic regime or within proslavery's discourse of African sexual "barbarity," Prince's possible nonmonogamy excludes her from epistemic authority and, at least textually, forestalls her reproductive legacy. The *History* judges Prince's capability to report slavery's atrocities by the impossible standards of liberal selfhood and white female domesticity, an act of rhetorical contortion I have dubbed abolitionist gaslighting. For all that is known about Mary Prince, this kind of domestic morality might have been completely alien to her, even if she might have realized it as a vehicle for attaining increased respectability — which, in the colonies, was accompanied by greater safety from physical violence and, in rare cases, by freedom.

What remains in the Eurocentric archive are Mary Prince's "performative remains," fragments of body parts and testimonies, reorganized to fit historical as well as recent trajectories of epistemological desire.[71] It is difficult, if not impossible, to locate the historical person's agency in such contexts. Scholars should be wary of the impulse to identify with Prince's political and social position because such identification will continue to silence, victimize, or sanctify her, perpetuating the idea that Prince's life matters solely because of her sexual and racial alterity. Inattention to the social and material conditions of the *History*'s production risks involuntary compliance with Pringle and Strickland's ambition to make slavery palatable to their target metropolitan audiences, and neutralizes, rather than unpacks, the fabulation they created in her name. Prince's own experiences of slavery are likely forever closed off to history and we should, in the words of Siphiwe Gloria Ndlovu, cultivate "a way of knowing that respects the 'opaqueness' of the body, a way of knowing that is comfortable with the unknown, the forgotten, and the silenced: a way of knowing that allows us to realize the limits of the archive."[72] When studying abolitionist gaslighting and its attendant epistemic violations, it is best to pursue careful historical contextualization to highlight known realities balanced by a tolerance for the many historical gaps that remain.

While Mary Prince's own views on her enslavement are lost, the mode of abolitionist gaslighting underpinning the *History* (and, of course, other antislavery texts) reverberates through the nineteenth century, both ideologically and formally. The nineteenth century incompletely processed slavery, culturally speaking, because the eighteenth-century literary tradition that emerged alongside abolitionism was so successful in producing politically explosive affect that it never queried its form's inherent ethical contradictions, particularly its purposefully imperfect concealment of slavery's atrocities and its refusal to grant Black subjects epistemic authority. Abolitionist gaslighting achieved its goal of figuring Black British women as "object[s] of treatment and management, rather than [as] member[s] of the moral community," thereby disallowing their independent reasoning and moral standing.[73] Alongside other grand-scale processes, abolition helped sustain the nineteenth-century sexual double standard, depriving women of their ability to publicly name the mechanisms of their sexual subordination and leaving them unable to determine the assailant's culpability when targeted for sexual violence. The kind of editorial mediation and silencing of sexually coercive social structures I have traced in the *History* continued for much of the century, and, exacerbated by the passing of the 1857 Obscene Publications Act, stripped publications of the language — and left readers without the epistemic gauge — to describe and resist Victorian rape culture.

Notes

1. Prince, *History of Mary Prince*, 88. Instances hereafter are quoted parenthetically as *MP*.
2. Thomas, "Pringle v. Cadell," 117.
3. Macqueen, "The Colonial Empire," 749.
4. "Wood vs. Pringle," 7.
5. Hall, *Civilising Subjects*, 107.
6. Ivy [McKinnon], "Allies Behaving Badly," 181. Since her essay's initial publication in 2017, Ivy has sharpened her terms, preferring "accomplice" over "ally." See "Preface to the Original Essay," 177–79. On gaslighting as epistemic injustice, see also Podosky, "Gaslighting," 218.
7. Ivy, "Allies Behaving Badly," 181; see also Davis and Ernst, "Racial Gaslighting," 762.
8. Hartman, *Scenes of Subjection*, 83.
9. This distinguishes abolitionist gaslighting from racial gaslighting (that is, the denial of racist structures), as defined by Davis and Ernst, "Racial Gaslighting," 771.
10. Abramson, "Turning up the Lights," 12.
11. Feuerstein, "*History*," pars. 5–6.
12. Abramson, "Turning up the Lights," 3.
13. Ivy, "Allies Behaving Badly," 183.
14. Ivy, "Allies Behaving Badly," 184.
15. Ivy, "Allies Behaving Badly," 184.
16. Midgley, *Women against Slavery*, 2; Beckles, *Natural Rebels*, 38.
17. Midgley, *Women against Slavery*, 102.
18. Thurston, *The Work of Words*, 61.
19. Midgley, *Women against Slavery*, 90.
20. For further discussion of this question, see Peterman, *Susanna Moodie*, 46; Rauwerda, "Naming," 400; Schroeder, "Narrat[ing]," 273; Whitlock, "Silent Scribe," 251.
21. Thomas, *Telling West Indian Lives*, 121.
22. Sharpe, *Ghosts of Slavery*, 120.
23. See Whitlock, "Silent Scribe," 252; Peterman, *Susanna Moodie*, 46–47; Woodard, *African-British Writings*, 144; and Schroeder, "Narrat[ing]," 272–73, for discussions of Pringle and Strickland's editorial interventions.
24. Macqueen, "Colonial Empire," 750–51.
25. Vigne, *Thomas Pringle*, 218.
26. For provenances of the *History*'s supplements, see Salih, "*The History of Mary Prince*."
27. Salih, "*The History of Mary Prince*," 132.
28. See Ivy's "Preface to the Original Essay" for the provenance of her use of "epistemic violence" instead of "epistemic injustice" (Ivy, "Allies Behaving Badly," 177–79).
29. Whitlock, "Silent Scribe," 252.

30. Stoler, *Education of Desire*, 7.
31. Baderoon, "Baartman and the Private," 73.
32. Ferguson, "Introduction," 4.
33. Sharpe, *Ghosts of Slavery*, 121.
34. Davis and Ernst, "Racial Gaslighting," 763.
35. Ferguson, *Subject to Others*, 289.
36. Steedman, *Dust*, 48. Prince's living and working conditions allow for a variety of scenarios, including sterility, contraception, miscarriage, self-induced abortion, politically motivated infanticide, forced neglect, and childhood death. If Prince had given birth, her pregnancy might have been a difficult one, owing to decades of hard labor, severe malnutrition, inadequate clothing, physical abuse, and likely rape. Her child might have been born weakly and suffering from nutrient deficiencies that were virtually universal among Caribbean newborns. See Turner, *Contested Bodies*, 179–80.
37. It warrants repeating here that "Mary Prince," the *History*'s narrator and object of its many intertexts, is an editorial, critical, and, above all, literary construct. This designation functions as a placeholder and does not denote the historical person unless explicitly referenced.
38. Ferguson had already identified "Mr. I—" as John Ingham (or Ingraham) of Spanish Point, Bermuda (*Subject to Others*, 376n25). Maddison-MacFadyen, "Toiling in the Salt Ponds," suggests that the sadistic "Mr. D—" and his son, "Master Dicky," are Robert and Richard Darrell, respectively.
39. Podosky, "Gaslighting," 217.
40. See Hartman, *Scenes of Subjection*, 108.
41. Hetty, like Prince, is also "stripped quite naked" and "tied up" (*MP* 67). See Thomas, *Telling West Indian Lives*, 127; Sharpe, *Ghosts of Slavery*, 130; Feuerstein, "*History*," par. 13.
42. Flogging was cited as the primary cause for the British Caribbean's lack of natural increase among enslaved populations since it frequently led to miscarriage (Altink, *Representations*, 135). Ferguson considers sterilization a possible result of the many beatings Prince endured (*Subject to Others*, 289).
43. Later in the narrative, Prince's body "dreadfully swell[s]" due to rheumatism (*MP* 86). Hetty's ghost is present.
44. Abramson, "Turning up the Lights," 10; Podosky, "Gaslighting," 219.
45. Beckles, *Natural Rebels*, 142.
46. Davis, "Sexual Economy," 116.
47. Morrissey, *Slave Women*, 69.
48. Altink, *Representations*, 67–69.
49. Altink, *Representations*, 75.
50. Abramson, "Turning up the Lights," 18.
51. "Wood vs. Pringle," 7.
52. Beckles, *Natural Rebels*, 149.

53. Morrissey, *Slave Women*, 4.
54. Morrissey, *Slave Women*, 66.
55. Lazarus-Black, *Legitimate Acts*, 98.
56. Rauwerda, "Naming," 409n14; see Sharpe, *Ghosts of Slavery*, 150.
57. Lazarus-Black, *Legitimate Acts*, 68, 81, 91–92.
58. Prince reports that she would only marry James after his conversion to Moravianism (*MP* 84). See Cooper, "Tracing the Route," 202.
59. Sharpe suggests that the *History*'s conversion chronology is likely wrong, as Prince was already a member of the Moravian society when she started cohabiting with Captain Abbott (*Ghosts of Slavery*, 142). Thomas's spectacular finding regarding Captain Samuel Abbott's conviction of manslaughter in 1827 as well as the 1833 *Times* report, according to which Prince had lived with Abbott "seven years before," suggest that Prince and Abbott separated in 1826, three or four years after she joined the Moravians and in the year she married James (Thomas, *Telling West Indian Lives*, 208n100; "Wood vs. Pringle," 7). For other takes on Prince's relationship with Abbott, see Salih, "Introduction," xxix–xxx; Maddison-MacFadyen, "Mary Prince," 658, 661n15; Feuerstein, "*History*," pars. 21–23.
60. Podosky, "Gaslighting," 208.
61. Lazarus-Black, *Legitimate Acts*, 93.
62. Lazarus-Black, *Legitimate Acts*, 85–87.
63. Beckles, *Natural Rebels*, 121.
64. According to the cross-examination report printed by the *Times*, Prince "slept with" Abbott "in another hut she had, in addition to her room in [Wood's] yard" ("Wood vs. Pringle," 7). The hut might have been provided by John Wood, who perhaps wanted to avoid that Prince's sexual transactions occurred on his property. In his letter to Pringle, Wood claims that he "induced" Prince "to take a husband" (*MP* 100). Wood might have also encouraged Prince to end her pregnancies as they would have been an inconvenience to the household and interruptions to "business." According to Wood's registers, no child was born on his property between 1817 and 1832, although he enslaved (and sold) women of childbearing age.
65. "Wood vs. Pringle," 7.
66. See Altink, *Representations*, 94.
67. Podosky, "Gaslighting," 218.
68. Podosky, "Gaslighting," 218.
69. Vigne, *Additional Letters*, 23.
70. Thomas, *Telling West Indian Lives*, 164. About $1.7 million in 2024 currency.
71. Ndlovu, "'Body' of Evidence," 29.
72. Ndlovu, "'Body' of Evidence," 27.
73. Abramson, "Turning up the Lights," 13.

Bibliography

Abramson, Kate. "Turning up the Lights on Gaslighting." *Philosophical Perspectives* 28 (2014): 1–30.

Aljoe, Nicole N. *Creole Testimonies: Slave Narratives from the British West Indies, 1709–1838*. Palgrave Macmillan, 2012.

Altink, Henrice. *Representations of Slave Women in Discourses on Slavery and Abolition, 1780–1838*. Routledge, 2007.

Baderoon, Gabeba. "Baartman and the Private: How Can We Look at a Figure that Has Been Looked at Too Much?" In *Representation and Black Womanhood: The Legacy of Sarah Baartman*, edited by Natasha Gordon-Chipembere, 65–83. Palgrave Macmillan, 2011.

Beckles, Hilary. *Natural Rebels: A Social History of Enslaved Black Women in Barbados*. Rutgers University Press, 1989.

Cooper, Helen M. "'Tracing the Route to England': Nineteenth-Century Caribbean Interventions into English Debates on Race and Slavery." *The Victorians and Race*, edited by Shearer West, 194–212. Scolar Press, 1996.

Davis, Adrienne. "'Don't Let Nobody Bother Yo' Principle': The Sexual Economy of American Slavery." In *Sister Circle: Black Women and Work*, edited by S. Harley, 103–27. Rutgers University Press, 2002.

Davis, Angelique, and Rose Ernst. "Racial Gaslighting." *Politics, Groups, and Identities* 7, no. 4 (2019): 761–74.

Ferguson, Moira. "Introduction to the Revised Edition." In *The History of Mary Prince, A West Indian Slave. Related by Herself*, edited by Moira Ferguson, 1–51. University of Michigan Press, 1997.

———. *Subject to Others: British Women Writers and Colonial Slavery, 1670–1834*. Routledge, 1992.

Feuerstein, Anna. "*The History of Mary Prince* and the Racial Formation of Rape Culture." *Nineteenth-Century Gender Studies* 16, no. 2 (2020).

Hall, Catherine. *Civilising Subjects: Metropole and Colony in the English Imagination, 1830–1867*. University of Chicago Press, 2002.

Hartman, Saidiya V. *Scenes of Subjection: Terror, Slavery, and Self-Making in Nineteenth-Century America.* Oxford University Press, 1997.

Ivy, Veronica [Rachel McKinnon]. "Allies Behaving Badly: Gaslighting as Epistemic Injustice." In *Gaslighting: Philosophical Approaches*, edited by Kelly Oliver, Hanna Kiri Gunn, and Holly Longair, 177–91. SUNY Press, 2025.

Lazarus-Black, Mindie. *Legitimate Acts and Illegal Encounters: Law and Society in Antigua and Barbuda*. Smithsonian Institution Press, 1994.

Macqueen, James. "The Anti-Slavery Society and the West-India Colonists." *Glasgow Courier* (July 26, 1831): 1.

———. "The Colonial Empire of Great Britain: Letter to Earl Grey, First Lord of the Treasury, &c &c." *Blackwood's Magazine* 30, no. 187 (November 1831): 744–64.

Maddison-MacFadyen, Margot. "Mary Prince, Grand Turk, and Antigua." *Slavery & Abolition* 34, no. 4 (2013): 653–62.

———. "Toiling in the Salt Ponds." *The Times of the Island: Sampling the Soul of the Turks & Caicos Islands* (2008). https://www.timespub.tc/2008/09/toiling-in-the-salt-ponds/.

Midgley, Clare. *Women against Slavery: The British Campaigns, 1780–1870.* Routledge, 1992.

Morrissey, Marietta. *Slave Women in the New World: Gender Stratification in the Caribbean.* University Press of Kansas, 1989.

Ndlovu, Siphiwe Gloria. "'Body' of Evidence: Saartjie Baartman and the Archive." In *Representation and Black Womanhood: The Legacy of Sarah Baartman*, edited by Natasha Gordon-Chipembere, 17–30. Palgrave Macmillan, 2011.

Peterman, Michael. *Susanna Moodie: A Life.* ECW Press, 1999.

Podosky, Paul-Mikhail Catapang. "Gaslighting, First- and Second-Order." *Hypatia* 36, no. 1 (2021): 207–27.

Prince, Mary. *The History of Mary Prince, A West Indian Slave. Related by Herself*, edited by Moira Ferguson. University of Michigan Press, 1997.

Rauwerda, Antje M. "Naming, Agency, and 'A Tissue of Falsehoods' in *The History of Mary Prince*." *Victorian Literature and Culture* 29, no. 2 (2001): 397–411.

Salih, Sara. "*The History of Mary Prince*, the Black Subject, and the Black Canon." In *Discourses of Slavery and Abolition: Britain and Its Colonies, 1769–1838*, edited by Brycchan Carey, Markman Ellis, and Sara Salih, 123–38. Palgrave Macmillan, 2004.

———. Introduction to *The History of Mary Prince*, by Mary Prince, vii–xliii. Penguin, 2004.

Schroeder, Janice. "'Narrat[ing] Some Poor Little Fable': Evidence of Bodily Pain in *The History of Mary Prince* and 'Wife-Torture in England.'" *Tulsa Studies in Women's Literature* 23, no. 2 (2004): 261–81.

Sharpe, Jenny. *Ghosts of Slavery: A Literary Archeology of Black Women's Lives.* University of Minnesota Press, 2002.

Steedman, Carolyn. *Dust: The Archive and Cultural History.* Rutgers University Press, 2002.

Stoler, Ann Laura. *Race and the Education of Desire: Foucault's* History of Sexuality *and the Colonial Order of Things.* Duke University Press, 1995.

Thomas, Sue. "Pringle v. Cadell and Wood v. Pringle: The Libel Cases over *The History of Mary Prince*." *The Journal of Commonwealth Literature* 40, no. 1 (2005): 113–35.

———. *Telling West Indian Lives: Life Narrative and the Reform of Plantation Slavery Cultures 1804–1834.* Palgrave, 2014.

Thurston, John. *The Work of Words: The Writing of Susanna Strickland Moodie.* McGill-Queen's University Press, 1996.

Turner, Sasha. *Contested Bodies: Pregnancy, Childrearing, and Slavery in Jamaica.* University of Pennsylvania Press, 2017.

Vigne, Randolph. *Thomas Pringle: South African Pioneer, Poet, and Abolitionist*. James Currey, 2012.

———. *Additional Letters to* The South African Letters of Thomas Pringle. Van Riebeeck Society, 2011.

Whitlock, Gillian. *Intimate Empire: Reading Women's Autobiography*. Continuum, 2000.

———. "The Silent Scribe: Susanna and 'Black Mary.'" *International Journal of Canadian Studies* 11 (1995): 249–59.

Woodard, Helena. *African-British Writings in the Eighteenth Century: The Politics of Race and Reason*. Greenwood Press, 1999.

["Wood vs. Pringle."] *Times* (March 1, 1833): 6–7.

12

"Old Ladies, Male and Female"

Gaslighting the Reader in Margaret Oliphant's *The Perpetual Curate*

Elizabeth Coggin Womack

In Margaret Oliphant's 1864 novel, *The Perpetual Curate*, a parochial community holds a minister accountable for allegedly "seducing" a teenager.[1] The establishment figures in the town of Carlingford are surprisingly quick to assume that Reverend Frank Wentworth, the novel's protagonist, must be guilty of this "seduction," which would more accurately be termed rape. His fellow clergy, his father, his aunts, his landlady, and even his true love Lucy all suspect him, and he faces a diocesan inquiry. Wentworth turns out to be innocent, and like any enthralled reader, I find myself rooting for his acquittal. And yet, reading this novel in 2025, there is something refreshing about the ability of these characters to believe that he *might* be guilty. Contrary to centuries of institutionalized sympathy ("himpathy," as Kate Manne terms it) for accused rapists, their suspicion reflects an epistemology in which sexual assault is taken seriously and well-connected men of the cloth can and should be held accountable.[2] Yet the novel's resolution undermines this epistemology. Oliphant's omniscient narrator frames those who suspect Wentworth as ridiculous, even comedic. The victim, Rosa, reappears at the end, termed the "cause of all the commotion" (275). And finally, Wentworth's defense centers not on his innocence, but on his standing in the community; a man of his position and reputation, he argues, should not have to defend himself against accusations of sexual violence.

The Perpetual Curate was published just after Margaret Oliphant's most popular novel, *Salem Chapel* (1863), which also dealt with the professional struggles of a minister; while both novels were widely read in the 1860s, they are less well known today. *The Perpetual Curate* is comprised of three overlapping plots. The central plot is the career arc of Frank Wentworth, who is the perpetual curate of St. Roque's. Perpetual curacies were funded by stipends rather than tithes, and they were often lower paid and of lesser status. In Wentworth's case, the title also captures his circumstances early in the novel: he lacks opportunities to advance and the money to marry; he seems likely to remain a curate perpetually. His high-church ministry style alienates the evangelical aunts who might otherwise grant him a desirable living; meanwhile, he has deeply offended the new rector of Carlingford, who is lying in wait for revenge. The second plot concerns the stability of Wentworth's true love, Lucy Wodehouse. Lucy's ne'er-do-well brother, believed to be dead, appears in disguise to claim the property of their father, who dies intestate; Lucy is left penniless. The third plot is the fall of Rosa Elsworthy, a girl said to be "going wrong as fast as she can," who naively pursues Wentworth before she disappears for several days (88). Wentworth is accused of seducing and hiding her, but the true villain is Lucy's brother, Tom Wodehouse. Wentworth faces an inquiry for Rosa's abduction, uniting the three plots of the novel. Rosa's testimony against Tom Wodehouse vanquishes both Wodehouse and the Rector of Carlingford, and they both leave Carlingford. Lucy regains her portion of her father's fortune. Wentworth improbably becomes the new rector, which allows him to marry Lucy. It is implied that Wodehouse and Rosa also marry, which readers are encouraged to see as positive, in a manner analogous to the conclusion of Samuel Richardson's *Pamela; or Virtue Rewarded* (1740). Everyone in Carlingford agrees that running off with a middle-aged criminal is "the best thing Rosa could have done" (340).

In (falsely) blaming Wentworth for Rosa's disappearance, the well-intentioned townspeople of Carlingford share a general awareness that clerical abuse does indeed happen. By incorporating the framework of Diocesan Commissions of Inquiry, Oliphant signals her expectation that her readers are also familiar with stories of clergy who harm their parishioners — stories that appeared in major newspapers including the *Times*, the preferred news source of many residents of fictitious Carlingford. Yet even as her novel obliquely references such well-publicized clerical misdeeds, Oliphant's comedic characterization and plotting deemphasize the potentially abusive power dynamics of church communities. She immediately and omnisciently establishes Wentworth's innocence; she uses humor to dismiss any characters willing to consider Wentworth's possible guilt as gossiping "old ladies . . . , male and female" (167); she caricatures the young victim as an airheaded "hussy" (340) and the true villain as a repulsive monster; and she depicts the investigation as a witch hunt. She focalizes the novel's dominant institution, the Anglican Church, through the lens of this falsely accused, handsome young man, while she denigrates victims of religious abuse and their sympathizers as anxious and unreasonable. In doing so, she masks the actual power dynamics of religious and sexual abuse. These and other strategies from the rape-culture playbook lure readers into the complacency of rape mythology — to fall, in the words of Pierre Bourdieu, for a "semblance of reality which allows the reader to ignore the real state of things, to refuse to see things as they really are."[3]

The Perpetual Curate responded to the 1840 Church Discipline Act, which expedited the removal of miscreant clergy from the Established Church.[4] The law was first and most publicly applied in the case of Frederick Smyth Monckton, a perpetual curate accused in 1845 of fornication with his servants.[5] These reports, like many narratives of alleged sexual assault, do not lend themselves to tidy interpretation. The witnesses questioned in Monckton's case offered a number of conflicting viewpoints: that he impregnated a willing servant; that he undressed an unwilling one; that he offered employment to women in need; that he sang too loud and drank too much; that he was the victim of a conspiracy by, in his words, "a parcel of d — d old women."[6] Neither the inquiry nor the newspapers that reported it could offer concrete proof of what Monckton did or did not do. But the inquiry itself, and other inquiries that followed in the coming decades, revealed the Church's struggles to police its own ranks and maintain credibility. It is this credibility that Oliphant's novel attempts to shore up. While parallels indicate that Monckton's inquiry or others like it inspired Oliphant, it is her changes to Monckton's story that reveal the novel's misleading rhetoric on ecclesiastical accountability. In conceiving of her clergyman as fully innocent and deriding those who nurse suspicions as foolish "old ladies," Oliphant undermines her readers' sense that any layperson is fit to question clergymen about the realities of sexual abuse. In short, Oliphant is gaslighting us.

Epistemic gaslighting, according to Gaile Pohlhaus Jr., "occurs when a person, practice, image, or institution exerts unwarranted pressure on epistemic agents to doubt their own perceptions."[7] Pohlhaus observes that the target of epistemic gaslighting might be more a social category than a person since it operates more diffusively at an institutional or communal level. The consequences of epistemic gaslighting are not the "psychological breakdown" of a particular individual, but rather to undermine or eliminate a "particular way of understanding the world."[8] One way of understanding the world is to see the problem of delinquent priests and the harms they cause as a serious issue to be resolved by structural changes to an institution. Oliphant's narrative undermines this view by (1) questioning the severity of harm, (2) insinuating the culpability of victims, (3) questioning whether scandal or controversy is the greater harm, and (4) speculating whether institutions truly need to change in response to aberrant or external threats. Oliphant's gaslighting strategy corresponds to well-known rape myths: "Rape is a trivial event"; "She asked for it"; "She lied"; and, finally, "Rape is a deviant event."[9] Kate Harding calls this last a foundational rape myth: the thinking goes, in Harding's words, that "*rape hardly ever happens, and it's only committed by mentally ill monsters, not people who resemble — or are — my friends, coworkers, and family members*."[10] This particular rape myth is the one that appears most critical to Oliphant's narrative strategy. On the one hand, her novel's plot enacts the myth on its own terms: the abduction is the work of a criminal deviant, not the local clergyman. Yet, on the other hand, the novel also radically inverts the script, because the "old ladies" in town are so quick to suspect Wentworth: their friend, coworker, and family member. This temporary inversion allows Oliphant to double down on the myth in her conclusion, demonstrating the terrible wrongness of anyone who had suspected the perpetual curate. Oliphant does not merely show that these "old ladies" are incorrect. She renders women's and readers' knowledge of rape and clerical abuse both untenable and laughable.

Another insidious aspect of Oliphant's gaslighting is the way Wentworth's struggle to clear his name in a professional (rather than a criminal) inquiry eclipses the story of a victimized young woman. Few Victorian novels feature a formal investigation of a protagonist accused of a sexual assault as this one does, but what Erin Spampinato calls "adjudicative" readings are common in criticism of novels that represent rape.[11] The problem with adjudicative reading — or, in Oliphant's case, adjudicative narrative framing — is that it prioritizes the guilt, innocence, or intentions of the accused rapist over the harm experienced by the victim.[12] In this novel, the primary plot of Wentworth's career arc, threatened by a false accusation, poses a direct obstacle to our sympathies for the novel's rape victim. Ultimately, the novel frames the abduction of Rosa as something that happens *to* Wentworth; Rosa carries blame for this outcome, even as she testifies on Wentworth's behalf.

In what follows, I first lay groundwork for what Oliphant and her readers had every opportunity to know: the stories of sexual abuse by the clergy that sparked the church discipline debate in which *The Perpetual Curate* intervenes. I then turn to the novel itself, highlighting the ways in which the novel inverts rape culture tropes to help readers forget the actual power dynamics revealed by the church discipline debate. Specifically, I show how the character of Wodehouse functions to reinforce the myth that rape emerges from deviance, rather than from reliable institutions staffed by men with good reputations. Lastly, I consider the underlying current of women's anxiety in the text, particularly the ambiguous character of Wentworth's aunt Dora, whose momentary fear of rape, played for laughs, represents an eruption of *knowing* in a text that otherwise tries quite hard to undermine what everyone seems to know.

The Church Discipline Debate

The need for ecclesiastical discipline in the established church was well publicized in the decades that preceded Oliphant's *Chronicles of Carlingford*. While Oliphant does not engage specifically in the nuts and bolts of ecclesiastical law, her novel is informed by the public discourse around church discipline, and her frequent references to the *Times* as the paper of record for her *Carlingford* readers implies that her contemporary readers share an awareness of this ongoing debate. Together with more didactic novels such as John Ashworth's *The Young Curate; or the Quicksands of Life* (1859), Oliphant's novel incorporates procedures codified in the Church Discipline Act of 1840. Ashworth's novel, which features a similar plot, was in fact advertised in the *Times* as a "new Work of Fiction" that reveals "the peculiar temptations to which this class are exposed, and the measure which is dealt by Ecclesiastical Law to clerical delinquents."[13] Not only were Ashworth's readers expected to know about these scandals, but they were invited to read fiction as a way to engage in the discourse about them.

Prior to the Church Discipline Act, ecclesiastical discipline was expensive and ineffective. According to Frances Knight, "the Church's structure, and in particular the strength of the parson's freehold" made it quite difficult to police its ranks.[14] The publicity surrounding clerical misdeeds sparked "an urgent desire that appropriate measures be swiftly introduced in order to combat cases of clerical irregularity."[15] Some of this urgency came from especially egregious cases, such as that of Edward Drax Free, who was accused of selling lead from the church roof, letting pigs root up the graves, and extorting money for burials. He also physically (and one assumes sexually) assaulted several servants and took little responsibility for the children he fathered.[16] Proceedings against Free, chiefly motivated by his attempts at extortion, cost the bishop over £1,500 and lasted 17 years.[17] The difficulty and expense deterred other bishops from similar cases, and throughout the 1830s Free served as an example of the need for ecclesiastical discipline reforms, which eventually resulted in the Church Discipline Act. Clergy charged with violating ecclesiastical law or inciting scandal were subject to an inquiry by a commission of five persons named by their bishop.[18]

The first public Diocesan Commission of Inquiry took place in 1845 and featured a defendant who resembles Oliphant's Wentworth: Frederick Smyth Monckton, the third son of the fifth Viscount Galway and a perpetual curate of St. Peter's Church in West Hackney.[19] Like Wentworth, Monckton was around thirty years old, popular, and good at his job. Also like Wentworth, Monckton was not a rector or vicar, but a perpetual curate. Monckton was the well-connected son of a viscount with many children, while Wentworth was the well-connected son of a wealthy squire with many children. The proceedings against both were ignited by a personal grudge that inflamed local gossip. Like Wentworth, Monckton resented the proceedings against him and chose to stand his ground publicly rather than make any effort to diffuse the scandal. Whether or not Monckton inspired Oliphant's fiction, he certainly offers a case study for anyone seeking evidence that a community of feminized gossips might take down a promising young man, as well as a model for how centering a man's professional crisis might destroy the prospects of the woman he may or may not have abused.

The complaint against Monckton began not with a victim of assault, but with the schoolmaster and his wife, whom Monckton accused of failing to turn over accounts from the church school. When Monckton confronted the couple, they retaliated with complaints about his sexual conduct. Monckton was pressured to dismiss his servants and take a few weeks of leave until the scandal died down, but he refused on the grounds that it would confirm his guilt. The inquiry — the first of its kind — was conducted across four days between March 14 and March 29, 1845, and was self-consciously experimental as participants interpreted and argued about the new law and its procedures. Thirty witnesses offered testimony. The *Times* devoted multiple columns to each day of the inquiry and published various updates and letters to the editor regarding Monckton's case.

Certain facts of Monckton's case were undisputed. He, a bachelor of thirty-four, kept three young women servants at his parsonage, all between the ages of twenty and twenty-three.[20] No other servants — significantly, no older housekeeper — lived on the premises. Monckton was generally well liked but was sometimes said to be too "frolicksome" or "unguarded" in his manner.[21] His three servants enjoyed more autonomy, higher wages, and fancier dresses in his household than they might have found elsewhere. Monckton was particularly solicitous of the well-being of Sarah Huggins, who became pregnant during her time at the parsonage. When Monckton dismissed Huggins on grounds of impropriety, she traveled to Gravesend to give birth to seven-month's twins in September 1844.[22] The infants died the next day, and Monckton visited to console her; he eventually allowed her to come back to work at the parsonage.[23]

More salacious details were provided by the schoolmaster's wife, Mary Ann Williams, and a disgruntled former servant, Fanny Froude. Williams claimed that Monckton spent much of his time in the kitchen with his servants, smoking, singing, and taking the women on his lap; she alleged he also slept with Huggins several nights per week. Froude claimed that Monckton and his other servants poured water upon her and forcibly undressed her in her bedroom, with Monckton himself working at her laces. The committee dismissed Froude's testimony, but left with the fact of Huggins's pregnancy and Monckton's unwillingness to "liberate himself from the suspicions," they agreed that his actions had "diminish[ed] and destroy[ed] his utility in the parish," "creat[ing] great scandal to the church."[24] In June 1845, the Bishop of London sentenced Monckton to a one-year suspension.[25] Monckton's case continued to set the terms of church discipline inquiries for over a decade; he was referenced in the *Times* as late as 1859, when a case of attempted bigamy by a clergyman led to a fresh round of articles on delinquent clergy.[26] One editorial commented, "When a witness is able to cause loud laughter by the flippant remark that 'in the present state of The Church of England I don't care to acknowledge the acquaintance of a clergyman,' it is high time to throw aside all false delicacy in alluding to this subject."[27]

One striking difference between Monckton's and Wentworth's cases is that while Oliphant's protagonist is fully exonerated, Monckton's case ended ambiguously at best. Perhaps he did not father Huggins's child, precipitating her tragic loss and public notoriety; yet some of Monckton's decisions clearly escalated tensions in his community that worsened her situation. This partial culpability features in Ashworth's *The Young Curate*; the protagonist is innocent of "seduction" — in fact, no woman is sexually harmed in the novel. However, the curate is impulsive and unwise, and he ultimately inflames the scandal that harms the woman he is falsely accused of "seducing." Oliphant, however, paints Wentworth as virtually blameless. By removing the gray area from stories of clerical abuse, Oliphant comes to perpetuate the binary thinking that undergirds one of the chief myths of rape culture: specifically, that men are either upstanding community members who transcend suspicion, or monsters who deserve it.

Gaslighting the Reader

The primary plot of *The Perpetual Curate* is not about the abduction of Rosa Elsworthy. Rather, it is about the degree of success to which Wentworth is entitled given his high birth, unimpeachable conduct, and personal attractions. Wentworth's troubles begin with this entitlement, specifically his willfully intrusive missionary work in the district belonging to the new rector of Carlingford. The offended rector is thus primed to act against Wentworth on any pretext; Rosa's disappearance offers this pretext. She serves as a useful tool for the rector's professional jealousies, an obstacle for Wentworth, and a frequent butt of jokes.

As a narrative tool, Rosa walks a fine line. She must be naive enough that we care about what happens to her, but not appealing enough that we care too much. The crime against her must be bad enough to generate a narrative foil for the protagonist; Wentworth cannot be altogether innocent of sexual indiscretion unless someone else — namely, Wodehouse — is altogether guilty. Yet Rosa's experience must not be so bad that tragedy overwhelms the primary plot about Wentworth's career. The result is a series of contradictions: Rosa is both slutty and childlike, and the offense against her is bad, but not "too bad" — scandalous and predatory, but not, from the narrator's perspective, quite tragic. When the novel concludes, the false charge against Wentworth is dismissed, and Wentworth is rewarded for all that he has endured. The Rector of Carlingford is so embarrassed that he resigns his living and improbably arranges for Wentworth to have it in his stead. Critically, Rosa plays a central role in this chain of causality. Even as the novel begins, then, Rosa's rape is organized around the needs of Wentworth's plot.

Humor at Rosa's expense is a consistent part of her characterization throughout the novel, both before and after her abduction. Early in the novel, she is often depicted as an "incautious little coquette" (88), hanging out the front window of her uncle's shop, flirting with passers-by; her portrayal is consistent with the core rape myth that women are always "asking for it." The omniscient narrator, privy to her thoughts, exposes her delusions of grandeur, specifically her expectation, inspired by novels, that her good looks will lead to an advantageous marriage; she "knew that it was quite usual for gentlemen to fall in love with pretty little girls who were not of their own station; — why not with her?" (70). She is too pretty, too conceited, and too loud for her own good; accordingly, Rosa is flagged as a character whom readers need not take seriously. This humor is especially jarring because she is so profoundly vulnerable. While technically of consenting age at seventeen years old, Rosa is referred to as a "young girl" twenty-three times in the novel, and her aunt and uncle are alternately indulgent and verbally abusive.[28] While Oliphant implies that Rosa is all too welcoming of sexual interest, I argue that the novel's characterization of Rosa as immature undermines any sense that she can offer knowing consent; therefore, I read what Wodehouse does to her as rape.

In the context of Wentworth's inquiry, it does not matter whether Rosa is seduced or raped in this novel, since even sex outside of marriage would result in a judgment against him in a commission of inquiry. Yet Oliphant carefully demonstrates that even though Rosa is not worthy of the reader's empathy, she is victimized just enough to make Wodehouse an obvious predator. During her absence, public opinion labels Wentworth her "seducer and a villain" (197); Wentworth speculates that Wodehouse has "carried her away, and hidden her somewhere close at hand," although we never learn how or where Wodehouse kept her (239). In contrast to the omniscience that exposes Rosa's innermost and ostentatiously inappropriate desires early in the novel, none of her experiences during this period are described, allowing the narrative to focus on the supposedly greater victimhood of Wentworth. When Rosa reappears at Wentworth's trial, she claims that Wodehouse promised to marry her, and Wodehouse claims unconvincingly that he "never touched her" (278–79). Yet Oliphant implies that sex has occurred; Rosa appears physically transformed by what she has experienced, hinting at lost virginity: "Passion and shame had set their marks upon the child's forehead — lightly, it is true, but still the traces were there" (276). While the novel does not specify a sexual encounter between Wodehouse and Rosa, Oliphant's previous novel, *Salem Chapel*, features a similar abduction of a young woman. In that novel, Oliphant carefully removes all suspicion from the victim, who is confirmed to be "spotless — without . . . speck upon her good fame."[29] No such disclaimer appears for Rosa. The language used to describe Rosa's degree of consent is similarly vague. She is simultaneously the "cause of all the commotion" and acknowledged to be incapable of consent. One of the men at the inquiry, Dr. Marjoribanks, declares that she is not "a responsible moral agent," meaning that he does not believe Rosa is mature enough to make choices for herself (279). Wodehouse's actions against this "young girl" disgust everyone in Carlingford, which forces him to leave and surrender his ill-won inheritance.

As the novel approaches its resolution with Wentworth's promotion and marriage, the plot of Rosa's rape is resolved through comedy rather than tragedy. Rosa is condescendingly termed a "poor little pretty wretch" by the narrator, and her ungrammatical wailing becomes a ludicrous spectacle: "I wish I was dead! — and nobody wouldn't care!" (299). Her cries prompt mischievous errand boys to plot her escape, and her exasperated aunt seems to hope Rosa will die by suicide. Instead, Rosa flees, leaving behind a note that reads: "them as has took charge of me has promised to make a lady of me" (340). Her narrative comes to an end with the statement, "The neighbours, on the whole, were inclined to believe it was the best thing Rosa could have done; and the Elsworthys, husband and wife, were concluded to be of the same opinion" (340).

Rosa's importance to the narrative, then, is not as a subject but rather as a particularly indeterminate, defiled female object: one that poses a danger to men by potentially marking one of them as a rapist. In the novel's logic, Wentworth is either so good as to be above all reproach, or he is a rapist. This binary thinking is reinforced by the limited housing stock in Carlingford; Wentworth and Wodehouse, the actual rapist, live in the same boarding house, and Wentworth is already tainted by association with this "strange lodger" (51). Wodehouse appears at first only synecdochally as a pair of poorly mended boots that contrast strangely with Mr. Wentworth's "handsome pair," or as a disembodied voice in the lodging house that speaks in "growl[s]" (51, 71). Hiding in anticipation of his father's death, Wodehouse appears only at night and shows a "clandestine skulking instinct" (194). Wentworth's aunt Dora first encounters him as a "terrible apparition" and a "monster" in a scene that plays the elderly woman's fear of rape for laughs; when he approaches Dora at twilight, she screams and "stagger[s] backwards, thinking the worst horrors she had dreamed of were about to be realized" (56). Yet perversely it is Wentworth, not Wodehouse, who is immediately suspected of Rosa's abduction.

The dichotomy between Wentworth (the suspected rapist) and Wodehouse (the actual one) reinforces the myth of the deviant rapist. Kate Manne recasts this myth as a binary between "the golden boy" and "the rapist as monster"; as she argues in *Down Girl: The Logic of Misogyny*, this binary is rooted in pervasive falsehoods "about what rapists must be like."[30] Manne explains that "what is frightening about rapists" is partly that they cannot be identified as such on sight, and they might be anyone at all; "the idea of rapists as monsters exonerates by caricature."[31] In other words, Wentworth's purity and innocence are enhanced by Wodehouse's overtly seedy and repugnant appearance, which marks him to the reader as the actual rapist. The contrast further marks Wentworth's false accusers as not only wrong, but also lacking in common sense. Wentworth's innocence ultimately recenters falsely accused young men as the true victims of rape, in that they are vulnerable to, among other things, church commissions of inquiry.

It is unremarkable, of course, that Wentworth possesses all the attributes of Manne's "golden boy" and Wodehouse embodies the "rapist as monster."[32] We might expect Oliphant, or any popular nineteenth-century novelist for that matter, to uphold what are now thought to be common rape myths and a sexist status quo. What marks the novel's strategy as gaslighting is, first, how accurately Oliphant describes the stereotypical language communities use to defend a beloved figure accused of something unthinkable; and second, how thoroughly Oliphant inverts this language and all reasonable critiques of it to exasperating and comic effect. Put simply, all defenders of Wentworth's innocence are unattractive characters whom Wentworth distrusts; all those who suspect Wentworth are characters whom he loves. These counterintuitive suspicions read as shockingly disloyal and — when combined with the overtly menacing presence of Wodehouse — comically obtuse, even "insane." The rhetorical effect of this inversion is epistemic breakdown; the reader comes to associate reasoned suspicion of a clergyman with disloyalty, anxiety, and a lack of common sense. This is how the novel, in Pohlhaus's words, undermines a "particular way of understanding the world."[33]

The "golden boy" exculpatory logic outlined by Manne pervades the novel and is most clearly evident in Wentworth's defense of himself:

> "I could not believe it possible that I, being tolerably well known in Carlingford as I have always supposed, could be suspected by any rational being of such an insane piece of wickedness as has been laid to my charge; and consequently it did not occur to me to vindicate myself, as I perhaps ought to have done, at the beginning. I have been careless all along of vindicating myself. I had an idea," said the young man, with involuntary disdain, "that I might trust, if not to the regard, at least to the common-sense of my friends." (274)

Of course, Wentworth *is* innocent, but his justification, based on his reputation rather than on evidence, bears striking resemblance to Monckton's resentment of any need to "liberate himself from . . . suspicions."[34] Wentworth appeals not to evidence but to "common sense," which is another way of appealing to his own entitlement and a sexist status quo. It also anticipates testimony of the kind given by friends of convicted rapist Brock Turner in 2015: "I know for a fact that Brock is not one of these people."[35] As Manne puts it, "virtually no one will seem like 'that person' to people who know them."[36]

Yet none of Wentworth's friends support him. Only Wentworth's enemies — the rector's wife, the aunt most determined to blight his professional prospects, and his criminal older brother — assume Wentworth's innocence. These less likeable characters each recite Manne's halo-effect playbook in Wentworth's defense: his fine connections and good manners prove that Wentworth is too nice to rape anybody. The rector's wife notes that he is "so gentlemanly and nice — and of a very good family, too" (9). She is shocked and disgusted that "everybody is just as ready to believe that he is guilty as if he were a stranger or a bad character" (208).

While these "common sense" defenses are to be expected, we expect them to come from friends and allies. Yet, in this novel, Wentworth's closest friends, family, and allies are the ones who most fully embrace the possibility of his guilt. They frame their concerns in terms that seem purposefully written to critique the logic of the golden boy: "Why should people trust him?" says Lucy's father (unaware that his criminal son is alive); "I don't understand trusting a man in all sorts of equivocal circumstances, because he's got dark eyes, &c., and a handsome face — which seems *your* code of morality" (83). Wentworth's own father, the squire, who had once "sworn by Frank," develops "a terrible shadow of distrust in his mind" and spends most of the novel in suspense, expecting to learn the worst of his favorite son (264). Wentworth's loving and feckless aunt Dora has "scarcely a doubt in *her* mind that Frank was guilty" (194). Mr. Proctor, Wentworth's friend and a fellow of All Soul's, admits that Wentworth's "'consistent life' [does] not go for much" when one considers his probable temptation (208).

The character who best articulates her suspicions of Wentworth is his landlady — also the landlady of the monstrous Wodehouse. Literally shaken by Wentworth's fretful pacing, she faces the possibility that her nice young tenant has done something dreadful, all the while forgetting the proximity of Wodehouse, a man she personally abhors:

> As she stood putting on her cap, his footsteps vibrated along the flooring, which thrilled under her feet almost as much as under his own. Mrs. Hadwin . . . could not but wonder to herself what could make Mr. Wentworth walk about the room in such an agitated way. . . . And then the old lady thought of that report about little Rosa Elsworthy, which she had never believed, and grew troubled, as old ladies are not unapt to do under such circumstances, with all that lively faith in the seductions of "an artful girl," and all that contemptuous pity for a "poor young man," which seems to come natural to a woman. All the old ladies in Carlingford, male and female, were but too likely to entertain the same sentiments, which at least, if they did nothing else, showed a wonderful faith in the power of love and folly common to human nature. It did not occur to Mrs. Hadwin any more than it did to Miss Dora, that Mr. Wentworth's good sense and pride, and superior cultivation, were sufficient defences against little Rosa's dimpled cheeks and bright eyes; and with some few exceptions, such was likely to be the opinion of the little world of Carlingford. (166–67)

While the story of a man of thirty tempting a teenage girl into a sexual liaison is here euphemized as "the power of love and folly common to human nature" and the victim takes the lion's share of the blame, the threat of the handsome, single young clergyman is nonetheless rendered explicit: What if the minister has ruined his "artful" young parishioner? And while scandal erupts, the circumstances are taken as a matter of course; no one but Wentworth himself appears much surprised that someone in his position might be guilty. The suspense of the novel's climax is generated by the reader's frustration that the dimwitted citizens of Carlingford are incapable of either personal bias or criminal profiling, either of which might lead them to suspect the stranger in the bushes whom they have gossiped about for three months. Our frustration with Wentworth's friends at these moments masks Oliphant's narrative misdirection; rape accusations against beloved men are not typically accepted so readily.

Nor are their suspicions the product of lies or malice. *The Perpetual Curate* depicts instead a series of disquieting moments, as Wentworth's intimates confront a horrifying possibility. The measured and reflective responses of these gentle characters who love Wentworth are treated by the narrator as ridiculous — as a failure to consider what is most likely, what is right before their faces.

Yet, to a twenty-first-century reader, one aware of the #MeToo movement, their responses seem nuanced, judicious, even well informed.

What Old Ladies Know

One of the most compellingly specific similarities between Monckton's inquiry and Oliphant's novel is the dismissal of a community of accusers as "old ladies." This term is a common insult, a pithy combination of ageism and sexism. Old ladies, the logic goes, have too much time on their hands. They are stuck in the past. They gossip. They don't understand the world of men. Oliphant uses this term in a derogatory way in a number of her novels; most notably, it appears in *Salem Chapel*, where the dissenting minister is hounded out of his role by congregational malcontents termed "a parcel of old women."[37] But old ladies also carry the social history of communities; the reason they are empowered to gossip is because they have been around long enough to know things.

The most central and most anxious of the "old ladies in Carlingford, male and female" is Wentworth's aunt, Dora Wentworth, who encounters Wodehouse early in the novel and immediately believes that she is about to be raped. Throughout the novel, Dora is discredited because her chronic anxiety is so extreme that she generates conflict where none previously existed; she even signs her letters, "your loving and anxious Aunt Dora" (23). As with earlier and more mundane manifestations of Dora's anxiety, the near-rape scene is portrayed as a comic misunderstanding. Dora's reaction is framed as characteristically excessive, yet the scene reads quite differently once the reader knows that Wodehouse is, indeed, a rapist.

> Nothing happened in the quiet road, where there were scarcely any passengers, and the poor lady arrived with a trembling sense of escape from unknown perils at Mrs. Hadwin's garden-door. For Miss Dora was of opinion, like some few other ladies, that to walk alone down the quietest of streets was to lay herself open to unheard-of dangers. She put out her trembling hand to ring the bell, thinking her perils over — for of course Frank would walk home with her — when the door suddenly opened, and a terrible apparition, quite unconscious of anybody standing there, marched straight out upon Miss Dora, who gave a little scream, and staggered backwards, thinking the worst horrors she had dreamed of were about to be realised. (56)

When readers first encounter this scene, they do not yet know that this "terrible apparition" — Wodehouse — will prey upon Rosa, abducting her from this very spot. Without that context, which is only evident upon rereading, this scene is grotesquely played for laughs. How ridiculous, the narrator winks, that this undesirable old woman would be afraid of rape! Yet Dora's fears will later prove valid: Wodehouse is, in fact, a sexual predator.

Somehow Oliphant is having it both ways in this scene, which works as a rape joke: the implied unlikelihood of the rape of Dora prefigures the unlikelihood that Wentworth could be a rapist. At the same time, Dora's fears foreshadow the identity of the actual culprit. Heightening this seeming opposition is the misogynistic humor, which even for Oliphant is particularly dark. Oliphant is more than capable of black humor; in one of the novel's funnier moments, the outraged wife of a clergyman ousted from a profitable living contemplates the poisonous laburnum berries at her erstwhile rectory "in connection with [the new rector's] problematical children" (267). But even given Oliphant's occasional bitter edge, the mockery of Dora's fright in this near-rape scene is too cruel for me not to read it as double-voiced. Yes, Dora's fears are ridiculous. And also, no, they are not. Seen in this light, perpetually anxious Dora appears not so much delusional as a victim of gaslighting herself: the victim of her own creator. Oliphant discursively undermines the legitimacy of Aunt Dora's fears even as she plots the justifications of those fears. It is this scene that prompted my entire reading of the novel. In no other moment can we be so certain of the opposition between what Oliphant's narrator "knows" is going to happen and her discursive attempts to manipulate both the character's and the reader's perceptions of what will happen.

The current of anxiety that surges throughout Carlingford, as Wentworth's community turns on him and his aunt startles from strangers in the dark, suggests more awareness of the threat of rape than the novel's tidy resolution can fully assuage. It also serves to reinforce the link between anxiety and gaslighting. Gaslighters are motivated by a need for control, yes, but this need can be accompanied by anxieties of their own; one of the reasons why rape myths endure is because they promise that reasonable precautions deter rape. In believing that rape victims are "asking for it" and that rapists are "monsters," we seek to reassure ourselves that avoiding rape is easy. These beliefs do not necessarily coexist with feelings of security for the gaslighter, although they may be maladaptive attempts to generate security through control. Meanwhile, victims of gaslighting may say, as Kate Abramson puts it, that they feel "carved up," "nobody"; they use "language that speaks to a sense of having lost one's independent standing as deliberator and moral agent."[38] Dora's seemingly fragile mental state in the novel is played for laughs, but her nerves also signal her struggle — and perhaps her author's failure or unwillingness — to reconcile the myths that (purport to) make us feel safe in communities plagued by ongoing harm.

Oliphant's writing has long been dismissed as domestic and conservative rather than incisive or visionary, and thus her body of work is often considered less important than more canonical novels by her peers. Yet, as *The Perpetual Curate* demonstrates, that very conservatism, expressed in popular domestic fiction, can function as a rhetorically complex reinforcement of rape culture that rewards close critical attention. Indeed, while the concept of gaslighting is especially illuminating in the case of this novel, it may also offer a useful category for understanding other novels with highly individuated omniscient narrators, particularly those embedded in controversial issues. Neither gaslighters nor narrators need to outright deny a conflicting interpretation of events, motive, or causality; instead, they can shape our perceptions and guide our judgments, tailoring evidence to suit predetermined ends, perhaps glossing over or denying some of the painful complexities of reality. As Bourdieu has argued,

> Literary fiction is undoubtedly, for the author and his reader, a way of making known that which one does not wish to know. It is in this light that one should consider all those fictional conventions of the novel as a game which defines what we call *realism*. The appearance of reality which satisfies the need to know is in fact achieved by that semblance of reality which allows the reader to ignore the real state of things, to refuse to see things as they really are.[39]

Bourdieu posits a shared denial of reality between author and reader — a denial that makes itself felt in ways unique to but universal within literature. Bourdieu notes that these patterns of negation in literature — anxious denials of what is known but repressed — offer a more comprehensive representation of disagreeable truths than nonfiction ever could.[40] Bourdieu's framing, however, allows us to read this shared denial as a form of pleasure, or at least a mutually embraced cognitive dissonance. To read for narrative gaslighting is to reject such mutuality and tease out an anxious and perhaps unspoken power differential between the author and the informed reader as potentially conflicting epistemic agents. The gaslighting author does not merely argue that she is right and that others are wrong; rather, she strategically manipulates narrative and character to eradicate her opposition's ways of knowing. She creates a version of realism that seeks to unmake reality.

Notes

1. Public opinion labels Wentworth a "seducer and a villain" (Oliphant, *Perpetual Curate*, 197). Hereafter, references to the novel will appear parenthetically within the text.
2. Manne, *Down Girl*, 23.
3. Bourdieu, "Is the Structure?" 158. On rape myths, such as the myth that "she wanted it" or that "rape is deviant," see Harding, *Asking for It*, 22.
4. Joanne Shattock notes that Oliphant reviewed Frederick William Robinson's three church novels — *High Church* (1860), *No Church* (1861), and *Church and Chapel* (1863) — and she seems to borrow certain themes from that series ("Introduction," xvi–xviii); however, with its plot of false accusation or sexual entrapment and the staging of an inquiry, Oliphant's novel shares more plot elements with Ashworth's novel.
5. "Diocesan Commission of Inquiry," March 15, 1845, 7.
6. "Diocesan Commission of Inquiry," 7.
7. Pohlhaus, "Gaslighting and Echoing," 679.
8. Pohlhaus, Gaslighting and Echoing," 677.
9. Harding, *Asking for It*, 22.
10. Harding, *Asking for It*, 25.
11. Spampinato, "Rereading Rape," 124.
12. Spampinato, "Rereading Rape," 137.
13. "The Young Curate," 13.
14. Knight, "Ministering to the Ministers," 357.
15. Knight, "Ministering to the Ministers," 357.
16. Patterson, *Ecclesiastical Law*, 28.
17. Patterson, *Ecclesiastical Law*, 28, 29.
18. Patterson, *Ecclesiastical Law*, 30.
19. "Diocesan Commission of Inquiry," March 15, 1845, 7.
20. "Diocesan Commission of Inquiry," March 31, 1845, 6; "Diocesan Commission of Inquiry," March 15, 1845, 7.
21. "Diocesan Commission of Inquiry," March 28, 1845, 3.
22. "Diocesan Commission of Inquiry," March 15, 1845, 7; "Diocesan Commission of Inquiry," March 29, 1845, 7.
23. "Diocesan Commission of Inquiry," March 29, 1845, 7.
24. "Diocesan Commission of Inquiry," March 31, 1845, 6.
25. "The Hon. and Rev. Mr. Monckton," June 2, 1845, 5.
26. "It Is Difficult to Conceive Anything More Scandalous," Dec. 17, 1859, 6.
27. "The Rev. Mr. Bonwell's Case." Dec. 17, 1859, 4.
28. For example, Mrs. Elsworthy is loud in her dislike of Rosa: "I'd have— murdered her, ma'am, though it ain't proper to say so, afore we'd have gone and raised a talk like this" (90). She locks Rosa in the back room and threatens to disown her (88, 237). She mutters about Rosa's possible

suicide (340). Elsworthy, meanwhile, rarely interferes with Rosa's behavior.

29. Oliphant, *Salem Chapel*, 214.
30. Manne, *Down Girl*, 198.
31. Manne, *Down Girl*, 199.
32. Manne, *Down Girl*, 199.
33. Pohlhaus, "Gaslighting and Echoing," 677.
34. "Diocesan Commission of Inquiry," March 31, 1845, 6.
35. Manne, *Down Girl*, 211.
36. Manne, *Down Girl*, 211.
37. Oliphant, *Salem Chapel*, 257.
38. Abramson, "Turning Up the Lights on Gaslighting," 8.
39. Bourdieu, "Is the Structure?", 158.
40. Bourdieu, "Is the Structure?", 159.

Bibliography

Abramson, Kate. "Turning Up the Lights on Gaslighting." *Philosophical Perspectives* 28 (2014): 1–30.

Ashworth, John. *The Young Curate; or the Quicksands of Life*. Routledge, 1859.

Bourdieu, Pierre. "Is the Structure of *Sentimental Education* an Instance of Social Self-Analysis?" In *The Field of Cultural Production*, edited by Randal Johnson, 145–60. Columbia University Press, 1993.

"Diocesan Commission of Inquiry." *Times*, March 15, 1845, 7. The Times Digital Archive 1785–1985.

"Diocesan Commission of Inquiry." *Times*, March 28, 1845, 3. The Times Digital Archive 1785–1985.

"Diocesan Commission of Inquiry." *Times*, 29 March 29, 1845, 7. The Times Digital Archive 1785–1985.

"Diocesan Commission of Inquiry." *Times*, March 31, 1845, 6. The Times Digital Archive 1785–1985.

"Diocesan Commission of Inquiry." *Times*, April 9, 1845, 7. The Times Digital Archive 1785–1985.

Harding, Kate. *Asking for It: The Alarming Rise of Rape Culture — and What We Can Do about It*. Da Capo Press, 2015.

"The Hon. and Rev. F. S. Monckton." *Times*, April 30, 1845, 6. The Times Digital Archive 1785–1985.

"The Hon. and Rev. Mr. Monckton." *Times*, June 2, 1845, 5. The Times Digital Archive 1785–1985.

"It is Difficult to Conceive of Anything More Scandalous." *Times*, December 17, 1859, 6. The Times Digital Archive 1785–1985.

Knight, Frances. "Ministering to the Ministers: The Discipline of the Recalcitrant Clergy in the Diocese of Lincoln, 1830–1845." *Studies in Church History* 26 (1989): 357–66.

Manne, Kate. *Down Girl: The Logic of Misogyny*. Oxford University Press, 2018.

Oliphant, Margaret. *The Perpetual Curate*. Edited by Joanne Shattock. Pickering and Chatto, 2014.

———. *Salem Chapel*. Edited by Lyn Pykett. Pickering and Chatto, 2011.

Patterson, Neal. *Ecclesiastical Law, Clergy and the Laity: A History of Legal Discipline and the Anglican Church*. Routledge, 2019.

Pohlhaus, Gaile, Jr. "Gaslighting and Echoing, or Why Collective Epistemic Resistance is not a "Witch Hunt." *Hypatia* 35, no. 4 (2020): 674–86.

"The Rev. Mr. Bonwell's Case." *Times*, Dec. 17, 1859, 4. The Times Digital Archive 1785–1985.

Shattock, Joanne. Introduction to *The Perpetual Curate*, by Margaret Oliphant, xiii–xxiii. Edited by Joanne Shattock. Pickering and Chatto, 2014.

Spampinato, Erin. "Rereading Rape in the Critical Canon: Adjudicative Criticism and the Capacious Conception of Rape." *Differences* 32, no. 2 (September 2021): 122–60.

Stevenson, Kim. "Crimes of Moral Outrage: Victorian Encryptions of Sexual Violence." In *Criminal Conversations: Victorian Crimes, Social Panic, and Moral Outrage*, edited by Judith Rowbotham and Kim Stevenson, 232–46. Ohio State University Press, 2005.

Tange, Andrea Kaston. "Redesigning Femininity: Miss Marjoribank's Drawing-Room of Opportunity." *Victorian Literature and Culture* 36, no. 1 (2008): 163–86.

"The Young Curate." Advertisement. *Times*. Jan. 12, 1860. 13. The Times Digital Archive 1785–1985.

13

Gaslighting Vernon Lee

Hysteria, Rape Culture, and the Lesbian Intellectual

Diana Bellonby

On December 31, 1884, twenty-eight-year-old art critic Vernon Lee (born Violet Paget) ruminated in her journal:

> Perhaps all those people are right, perhaps the British public is right; perhaps I have no right to argue on the matter, because I may be colour blind about the data. Here I am accused of having, in simplicity of heart, written, with a view to moralise the world, an immoral book, accused of having done more mischief by setting my readers' imagination[s] hunting up evil, than I could possibly do good by calling on their sympathies to hate that mischief.[1]

Suddenly, after several years of professional success, she doubted her moral sense, her interpretive ability, and her right to debate a controversial issue: how London's avant-garde artists treat young women. "May this be true?" she asked herself. "May I be indulging a mere depraved appetite"?[2] Was *she* the real problem? Lee stood accused of having published a sexually corrupting story, despite having written it to challenge sexist corruption. The story in question — her debut novel, *Miss Brown* (1884) — satirizes members of the so-called Pre-Raphaelite Brotherhood (PRB), a countercultural clique of male artists who banded together in 1848 to call for a return to the styles of the late Middle Ages and Renaissance; that is, before Raphael. Pre-Raphaelite painters and poets influenced Britain's aesthetic movement, a celebration of beauty over didacticism — of "art for art's sake" — that reached its peak during the 1880s. This movement created new avenues of expression and experimentation for queer Victorians, most famously Oscar Wilde. Lee, a queer aesthete who came, as Dustin Friedman puts it, "as close to fulfilling the modern definition of lesbian identity as any late nineteenth-century woman could," aspired to make substantial intellectual contributions to the movement.[3] She wanted to reform its sexual ethics in the process.

Miss Brown tells the story of an English artist named Walter Hamlin who attempts to transform Anne Brown — an orphaned, half-Italian nursemaid who looks "half-Jewish, and almost half-Ethiopian" — into his personal muse and celebrity wife (174). Walter devises a Pygmalion plan to turn Anne into a lady by becoming her legal guardian, paying for her education, and housing her in London before courting her as his wife. Here Lee was fictionalizing a socially sanctioned abuse of power she had observed in the real lives of aristocratic male artists: preying upon working-class girls hired as models. Dante Gabriel Rossetti, William Morris, Ford Madox Brown, Frederick Shields, G. F. Watts, and many other Victorian men married young women under these circumstances.[4] Anne agrees to Walter's scheme in the hopes of becoming a teacher, only to find herself psychologically and physically sickened by the man with legal custody of her, the relentless sexualization of girls and women by his circle of friends, and her growing sense of isolation. The story's resolution hinges on a "hysterical" woman, Walter's cousin Sacha Elaguine, whom Anne at first interprets as a pitiable victim of childhood trauma. In the end, Sacha reveals herself to be a pathological liar and theatrical seductress tempting Walter into a drug-addled downfall. Anne's fate has become so intertwined with Walter's that she feels compelled to rescue him from Sacha by marrying him, despite loathing the sight of him.

Scholars overwhelmingly interpret this roman à clef as an embarrassingly tactless failure. Lee's caricatures of living artists offended most members of Britain's aesthetic set, some of whom never forgave her.[5] But social tensions did not cause Lee's crisis of self-doubt. Upon returning to London in June 1885, she smoothed over most of these tensions.[6] Rather, her conviction crumbled because reviewers gaslit her by accusing her of being obsessed with sex. The author of an unsigned review in the *Spectator* began, "We cannot review this book at the length its power would justify, the subject and treatment being too repulsive."[7] "It takes a great poet," this critic goes on, "to describe minutely satyrs and she-apes without exciting disgust; and Vernon Lee is not a poet, but only a strong writer overloaded with knowledge, who exaggerates the area of the sexual question in life."[8] The problem with *Miss Brown* was its author's perverted mind — her sordid exaggerations, overabundance of knowledge about sex, and lack of poetic talent — not the exploitative culture it was designed to condemn.

This chapter tells the story of how Vernon Lee, a child prodigy and leading late-Victorian intellectual, fell from a zenith of self-confidence and emotional support to a nadir of self-doubt and social isolation. Her psychological distress was fueled by reviewers who shamed her for being sex-crazed when she dared to imply that renowned British artists had committed sexual abuse. I read *Miss Brown* as Lee's protest against rape culture in London's art world, and I examine the personal crises she suffered in its wake as a valuable window into late-Victorian hysteria panics and the forms of gaslighting endured by queer intellectuals like Lee and Wilde. Crucially, Lee wrote *Miss Brown* during a turning point in hysteria discourse — shortly *after* leading neurologists and psychiatrists had advanced ostensibly progressive theories, but shortly *before* fears of social "degeneration" sparked newly discriminatory applications of the word.

Originating in the ancient Greek *hystéra* ("womb"), hysteria refers to a feminine disease supposedly caused by a "wandering womb," a uterus that refused to stay in its proper place. Nearly 2,300 years after Hippocrates had asserted that the "womb is the origin of all diseases," the late nineteenth century saw the heyday of hysteria — a period when popular images, formal studies, and diagnoses surged across Europe.[9] It was "the illness of the age," as one French journalist put it.[10] Most antiquated myths attached to this catch-all concept remained authoritative, making treatments for female patients as ineffectual or injurious as ever. For example, "the steadfast hold on marriage as a cure for hysteria," notes Melissa Rampelli, "managed to persist in medical treatises" from 350 BCE to the end of the nineteenth century.[11] In the late 1870s, however, French neurologist Jean-Martin Charcot authoritatively declared that men, too, could be hysterics. This condition, he argued, was a universal, hereditary disease of the nervous system, not the uterus. Charcot's medical breakthrough may have seemed to finally wrest the misogynistic stigma away from hysteria, rendering it less damagingly tied to patriarchal fictions about women's reproductive bodies, marriage, and what would later be termed heterosexuality. Not so. Just a few years after Lee published her novel, a blockbuster work of pseudoscientific cultural criticism signaled a new, epochal threat targeting the very men and women *Miss Brown* satirizes: In *Degeneration* (1892), German physician Max Nordau pathologized British aesthetes, including the Pre-Raphaelites, but especially Oscar Wilde, diagnosing them with a combination of "hysteria" and "degeneracy."[12] Lee found herself caught in a cultural-medical-intellectual bind, suddenly vulnerable to both the relentless misogyny *and* nascent homophobia tied to the notion of hysteria.

In what follows, I chronicle Lee's self-assured approach to writing her novel, the deeply researched critique she wove into it, and the destabilizing attacks she sustained after its publication. Her letters, journals, and later writings testify to the psychological harm caused by two readers in particular: the *Spectator* reviewer and her mentor, Henry James, who echoed and spread critical condemnations of her book. I then look more closely at Lee's and Wilde's different experiences with gaslighting. Their responses to public accusations of moral depravity and/or sexual madness — charges that variously intertwined moral, sexual, epistemic, and medical forms of gaslighting — help us better understand the challenges faced by queer artists, especially lesbian intellectuals.[13] I conclude by considering Lee's legacy and why her works were more radical than we realize.

Calling Out Rape Culture: The Case of *Miss Brown*

Vernon Lee enjoyed a healthy sense of confidence while composing her debut novel, having received high praise for her first three books: *Studies of the Eighteenth Century in Italy* (1880), *Belcaro* (1881), and *Euphorion* (1884). These collections of essays on art and literature announced her identification with aestheticism and her serious ambition to serve as a leading voice in the movement.[14] Founding English aesthete and personal mentor, Walter Pater, whom Lee visited in Oxford and London, lauded *Belcaro* as a "very rare" union of "extensive knowledge and imaginative power."[15] Encouraged, she dedicated *Euphorion* to him, and he heaped even greater praise upon it. Meanwhile, she impressed Henry James so much during his visits to Florence that he insisted to Edmund Gosse, the "only intelligent person in the place is Violet Paget [Lee]—who is so, however, with a vengeance. She has one of the best minds I know."[16] She relished in having secured his support, proudly telling her mother that "he takes a most paternal *interest* in me as a novelist, says that *Miss Brown* is a very good title, and that he will do all in his power to push it."[17]

When she began writing her novel, Lee was not only prolific, critically acclaimed, and well connected; she was also in love. She immersed herself in London's aesthetic scene through lengthy stays at the home of the woman she wanted to marry, poet A. Mary F. Robinson, herself a rising star among the aesthetes.[18] Robinson's family afforded Lee access to Fitzroy Square high society, and the pair developed deep intellectual and emotional bonds, sharing a drive to reform the movement of "art for art's sake." As Emily Harrington explains, the "passionate relationship between Robinson and Lee became a crucible for their bold attempt to establish an ethical aesthetics."[19] They exchanged drafts, debated new views on art and beauty, and even wrote their first novels nearly simultaneously. In the process, they reread Samuel Richardson's *Clarissa* (1748), England's most famous rape story. Lee affirmed the influence of Richardson's heroine on her own, telling Robinson that English novelist "Ouida has secretly expressed her anxiety to read *Miss Brown*. . . . If she were to say that Anne is a cousin of the heroine of *Moths* [Ouida's 1880 novel about marital violence], & both descendants (the *pas commode* silent virtue) from Clarissa Harlowe, she wouldn't perhaps be so far wrong."[20] Lee determined to write her own rape novel, but, unlike Richardson's or Ouida's, hers would rebuke a specific group of people: the Pre-Raphaelites.

Lee based Walter's character on PRB cofounder Dante Gabriel Rossetti, a painter-poet who notoriously fetishized his first muse and mistress, Pre-Raphaelite supermodel Elizabeth ("Lizzie") Siddal. Rossetti's PRB comrade, Walter Deverell, had plucked nineteen-year-old Siddal from a milliner's shop, and Rossetti soon insisted that she model only for him. He worshipped her pale, emaciated, deathlike countenance. Yet, for eight years, Rossetti refused to marry Siddal, conducting affair after affair (often with teenage models) until she was dying from her addiction to laudanum. Siddal became famous after modeling for John Everett Millais's celebrated portrait of Shakespeare's

Ophelia — arguably English culture's best-known female hysteric — floating dead in the water. Siddal died by suicide in 1862. Physically, the hysterical Sacha Elaguine character resembles slender, pale, sickly Siddal, whereas formidable Anne Brown resembles tall, strong, dark-haired Jane Morris, who, despite being married to William Morris, replaced Siddal after her death as Rossetti's chief model, muse, and (for a time) lover. Lee likely felt safe satirizing Rossetti and his treatment of women because he had died in 1882, and critical disapproval had swirled around him since 1871 when Scottish critic Robert Buchanan inveighed against Rossetti's "fleshly school" of poetry.[21] Also, by the early 1880s, parodies of the aesthetes had become common fare in magazines and theaters.[22] Lee herself was mocked in an 1882 *Belgravia* article that lists her as the only woman in a lineage of male elites striving "to make a little esoteric kingdom of culture."[23] Not only did British aesthetes seem to find satire acceptable, sometimes even sought-after, but also Lee could count herself among them. Or so she thought.

Anticipating public outrage, a senior editor at *Blackwood's Magazine* advised Lee to change her novel's ending. The editor's (prophetic) concerns focused on her heroine's misery-inducing consent to a marriage portrayed as a self-sacrificial prostitution. The unwanted kisses Walter forces upon Anne during the proposal scene make it clear that this union will involve marital rape. In July 1884, Lee confidently responded to Blackwood, requesting the freedom to keep her story's ending as she wished. "*Miss Brown*," she wrote,

> is the apple of my eye, and I am willing to run the risk of staking my reputation upon it, for it is a bold thing for an art-essayist suddenly to appear as a highly realistic novelist. But I feel that if *Miss Brown* is to have the degree of success as my other books, it must be the same sort of success: a success due to thorough independence & outspokenness, a success mingled with doubt & disapproval of the methods, but the main element of which is a sense of the writer's honesty & fearlessness.[24]

Even at the age of twenty-eight, Lee did have a reputation at stake. And she rightly emphasized her "fearlessness" alongside her hopes of achieving the "same sort of success" with *Miss Brown*, for by combining art criticism with a "highly realistic" story about sexual exploitation, she was courageously broadcasting an art-historical argument about rape culture.

Miss Brown uses psychological realism to present a searing ideological exposé according to which the Pre-Raphaelites' Rossetti-influenced vision of art is grounded in a rape fantasy: the ancient Roman myth of Pygmalion. Ovid's original poem in the *Metamorphoses* (8 CE) tells the tale of a sculptor named Pygmalion who hates women, having seen those condemned by Venus to be the first sex workers, so he carves his own perfect beauty out of stone. He courts the statue as if it were alive, lavishing his "ivory girl" with gifts and caresses, before begging Venus to enliven it. In the climactic moment of metamorphosis,

Pygmalion's own sexual force animates the blushing statue-woman. Put simply, his rape brings her to life. Lee realized that this fantasy was neither romantic nor benign, that it contradicted the PRB's supposed pursuit of moral virtue through truth to nature, and that it functioned as a driving force in their works and lives: D. G. Rossetti launched the Brotherhood with an erotic, Pygmalion-esque manifesto, "Hand and Soul" (1850), about a man who finds himself in the image of a beautiful woman, and later Morris published "Pygmalion and the Image" in his *Earthly Paradise* (1868–1870), for which Edward Burne-Jones painted a triptych, *Pygmalion and Galatea* (1875–1878).[25] This popular strain of Pre-Raphaelitism helped Ovid's rape romance, already a core element of the European canon since the twelfth century, maintain its status as a master narrative of creativity — a classic scene of male artistic genius symbolized by the acts of ogling, judging, and sexually possessing a beautiful white woman.[26] In *Miss Brown*, Walter aspires to achieve mastery in precisely this way.

Upon first meeting Anne, he stares at her as if she were a sculpture, "imagin[ing], as she sat motionless at the head of the table, that this was no living creature, but some sort of strange statue — cheek and chin and forehead of Parian marble" (18). Walter's letters reveal "the mental attitude of an artist before a beautiful model. . . . There was not much perception of the reality of Anne Brown's personality, nor indeed of her having any personality at all, being a thing with feelings, thoughts, hopes, interests of her own" (222). Lee describes what it feels like to be scrutinized by a coterie of elite men. As soon as he has moved her to London, Walter designs a dress for Anne to wear to a party at which he will display her "strange" beauty to his friends: "there was in her a moment's humiliation at being so completely Hamlin's property as to warrant this" (148). He forces her to wear this tight-fitting, off-white, silk garment, which creates a sculptural, near-nude effect. Mortified, "she could not help shrinking back in dismay" (148); she feels "almost terrified at the figure that met her" in the mirror (149). Everyone at the party stares at her, making her feel "horribly alone, numb, unreal" (157). When asked his opinion of Walter's new model, the Oscar Wilde caricature Mr. Posthlethwaite quips, "''Tis the body of a goddess; we must give it the soul of a woman'" (156). By night's end, Anne collapses in tears. This humiliating, alienating, sexually objectifying life is beginning to make her ill.

With unprecedented breadth and depth, Lee portrays rape culture — a phenomenon that would remain unnamed until 1975 — as a complex social crisis whereby patterns of speech and cultural representation (not just bodily attacks) cause physical and psychological harm, ranging from nauseous repulsion, to shortness of breath, to a sense of suffocation, to incapacitating paralysis.[27] Forbidden from using explicit language thanks to the 1857 Obscene Publications Act, Lee relies on the vocabulary available to her (for example, "sin," "baseness," or "shamefulness") to signify unwanted sex acts and deploys context to make her meaning clear. She anatomizes the effects of sexualization on girls by describing their emotions and bodily responses. Lee begins with a look at formative cultural messaging. When Walter first meets the children under teenage Anne's care, we learn how his poetry influences their concept of love: "Mamma told us you were the great poet, and she read us a poem of yours," says the oldest daughter, age eleven; "I liked all about where he kisses the lady so much, . . . and then about Love, where he comes and takes her by the throat, and chokes her, and makes her feel like a furnace. Mamma says it's just like love" (16). Later, when one of Walter's predatory artist friends shows nude sketches to the daughters of a local vicar, we learn that "Anne had caught the surprised, vacant expression of the two girls, had seen the flush in their face, and understood the silence" (215). *Miss Brown* thematizes the difficulty for girls of speaking about sex at all, along with the shame and self-loathing they feel when merely *understanding* sexual references. In scene after scene, Anne refuses to stay silent when men casually harass children or herself, but she, too, succumbs to psychological destabilization at their words and pictures.

One night, Walter gives Anne the proofs of his new book: "These sonnets," he declares, "are not merely my verses; they are myself — and many of them, you will see, are about you" (190). She first feels shame and insecurity about her moral judgment, then embarrassment about her sexual knowledge:

> She felt half ashamed of herself, wondering whether all the impure poetry which she had lately been reading, . . . might not be making her imagine things which were not meant; and Anne blushed at the thought — blushed at her knowing so many things, having learned so many things, in her half education as an Italian servant, in her culture as an aesthetic personage, which perhaps other girls of her age would not dream of. It was probably only her own morbid fancy. (191)

Rape culture makes a woman doubt her mental acumen (was she "imagin[ing] things"?) and blame herself ("it was probably only her own morbid fancy") *even without a person doubting or blaming her*. Then Anne encounters a set of twelve sonnets that "put an end to her doubts. She felt giddy and sick as she read them" (191). The graphic content of these lyrical "longings after untold shameful things" stifles her breath: "She seemed to be smothering for want of air" (191). Anne begs Walter not to publish these poems. "Perhaps you think it strange of me to speak so openly; but, of course, I understand what those sonnets allude to, and, of course, so will every grown-up reader" (193–94). Enraged, Walter gaslights her, retorting "brutally, as if to bring home to Anne the unreliableness of her judgment" (196). He publishes them anyway.

While invested in unmasking the violence of Ovid's myth, Lee's art-critical analysis does not limit rape culture's operations to verbal and visual art. *Miss Brown* overtly connects Walter's sexual exploitation of Anne to his slave-owning ancestors and to the broader institution of British Caribbean slavery. During her visit to Walter's family home, Wotton Hall, Anne realizes that his ancestors made their money from enslaving Jamaicans, and that some were notoriously cruel agents of racial violence: "Sir Thomas Hamlin," Walter says, pointing to a family portrait, "they used to call the bad Sir Thomas, because he amused himself practicing pistol-shooting on black people, whom he had put all round his yard" (174). Miss Brown's "half-Jewish, and almost half-Ethiopian" appearance — her last name a symbol of her racialized otherness — aligns her character with these victims of generational sadism down the Hamlin line. That Walter "should have been brought up surrounded by vice and violence," Anne thinks, "explained so much" (211). Yet, when Walter's aunt, Mrs. Macgregor, tells her about the "hysterical" mother of Walter's cousin Sacha, Lee's consistent condemnation of British slavery slips into a racist, misogynistic rant: Mrs. Macgregor complains to Anne that Sacha's mother "was an odious woman herself, the regular slave-driving type of the Hamlins"; she "was violent, and overbearing, and tyrannical, and lazy, and hysterical, like a regular Jamaica woman" (205).

The threads of Lee's political critique come together in a turning point that involves Walter's property ownership and Anne's role as a would-be reformer brave enough to speak about sexual abuse. Anne's friend Marjory rushes into the room in "hysterics" and, "all blushing and stammering, and in a hesitating, roundabout way," informs Anne that children living at Cold Fremley, a hamlet owned by Walter, endure many forms of premature sexual experience, including "brutish sin" (presumably rape) and teen pregnancy, in part, because the houses are so cramped (226, 223). Struggling to speak, Marjory cries, "there's no hope of remedying things unless the miserable creatures be removed into more decent dwellings" (223). Anne determines to get the houses rebuilt by speaking to Walter. Marjory is aghast: "You wouldn't venture to mention such a thing to a man." Her sister Mary echoes the point: "Oh, Annie, dear, you'll find that you can't! . . . You'll find it impossible" (226, 227). When Anne finds a way to share these facts with Walter, he gaslights her again. First, he doubts her report ("there's a great deal of exaggeration about it"), then he insists that she cannot understand this kind of thing: "Of course *you*, who are pure and upright, who cannot conceive the reality of lust and the fascination of evil — *you* can never understand" (246, 248). Walter does nothing to improve the houses. Instead, he romanticizes child rape in a revised poem called "The Ballad of the Fens" about the "grand and tragic" horrors at Cold Fremley (249). Here, the interlocking forces of hysteria, rape culture, and gaslighting thwart a woman who tries to resist.

Once we finally learn about the upbringing of Walter's hysterical cousin Sacha, we cannot help but compare her to the children at Cold Fremley. Sacha was a neglected child raised by the French servants with whom her father was conducting sexual affairs. At seventeen, she was married off to a man twice her age, who turned out to be a cruel womanizer. In a scene that reads like a therapy session, Sacha confesses to Anne, "I was too young to care for my children, who were babies, and I was a baby myself" (286). To Anne, it seems "so frightful that a girl, a child, a victim, just because she was a victim, should have such a weight of guilt thrown upon her" (205). To drive home the point of Sacha's illness, Lee introduces a doctor character who casually diagnoses her from afar, explaining to Anne that hysteria does not refer to fits or spells, but rather to an inherited disease of nervous excitability. Memories "of all she had heard of Sacha's horrible profligate old Russian father, of her violent and weak and constantly ailing mother, flashed across Anne['s]" mind (268). With this new information, she feels *more* sympathy toward Sacha. Indeed, for much of the story, Lee suggests that Sacha's hysteria results from a combination of hereditary tendencies and childhood traumas, *not* her untamed sexuality. At this point, in other words, Lee's portrayal of this disease supports her radical feminist critique of normalized sexual violence against women and girls.

So sickening is this world of disturbed women, vulnerable children, and predatory yet indifferent men, and so strong is Anne's desire to escape by studying to become a teacher that she falls ill with "brain fever." Doctors diagnose her with "nervous prostration from overwork," but readers know better, for we have watched the devastating psychological effects of Walter's Pygmalion bargain and the patriarchal constraints tightening their grip on her life (378). Anne's delirium underscores the contrast between her reality and the fantasies Walter projects onto her. Feverish Anne raves only about her childhood and hoped-for future studying political economy at Girton College, but Walter assumes that his affair with Sacha has caused her illness: "It is I who am killing Anne" he screams at Sacha, ripping up a portrait he has painted of her, "and it is you — you — who are forcing me to do it" (378). In fact, Anne recovers partly because she thinks she might be free of Walter thanks to his affair with Sacha. She hopes the two will marry and leave her alone.

Meanwhile, Anne's own cousin, Richard Brown, proposes to her — again. She rejects him again, reinforcing the novel's political point that its heroine does not want marriage *or* a man. All along, we have been reading a queer novel that, instead of portraying a woman's love for another woman, portrays marriage to a lecherous man as the most soul-crushing fate of all. In the end, Lee aligns Anne's sexual independence with her rationality: we are meant to perceive the queer heroine who seeks freedom from men as the reasonable one, and the woman who jealously pursues an unworthy man as the "mad" one. At the same time, however, Lee undercuts her polemical exposé of Victorian rape culture by depicting Sacha's hysteria *not* as the result of a lifetime of patriarchal violence but as the performance of a scheming, lying villain. Indeed, as queer and feminist as it is, *Miss Brown* ends by drawing our attention to a timelessly misogynistic, heteronormative binary: the battle between Eves and Madonnas, evil sluts and chaste martyrs, Sacha and Anne — the hysterical mistress and the sane wife.

Backlash: Lee's Private and Public Gaslighters

Lee predicted controversy after the publication of *Miss Brown*, but she did not expect the career-upending backlash she faced.[28] Numerous women writers — her partner Mary Robinson, the novelist Ouida, and women's rights activist

Frances Power Cobbe — loved her novel, but their praise could not outweigh the hostility of her detractors. "The storm has astounded me beyond words," she lamented to P. W. Bunting; "I hear," she went on, "of no end of enemies which this book has made me."[29] One response disturbed Lee's mental health more than any other: the anonymous December 13 *Spectator* review. In this critic's estimation, Anne Brown was a repulsive monster: her "final act is revolting, and shows an utter perversity in the author's conception of nobility . . . a[n] Una who prostitutes herself is a monstrosity."[30] Blending epistemic and moral modes of gaslighting, the *Spectator* reviewer acknowledges "the vilenesses of the London fleshly school" but quickly undercuts this qualification by denouncing Lee's lack of talent and prurient exaggerations about sex. Rather than acknowledging the "vile" social harms Lee had painstakingly enumerated, this author branded *her* the social problem.

By maligning Lee's moral integrity, critics found the perfect means to undermine her mental health, for she was deeply concerned about the ethics of art. She recorded her moral self-doubts in her journal, where she named yet another person, historian Alfred Benn, who had accused her of sexual obsession: "May there not, at the bottom of this seemingly scientific, philanthropic, idealising, decidedly noble-looking nature of mine, lie something base, dangerous, disgraceful that is cozening me? Benn says that I am *obsessed* by the sense of the impurity of the world. . . . May this be true?"[31] Was Lee's own mind tricking her? "I have never felt so roused, so grieved, angry, frantic as I do," she admitted to Robinson; "I have never been checkmated in all my career; and the success of *Euphorion* had made me feel as if I could never be. I had no notion how weak I was; it is a thing to know, but the knowing it is bitter."[32] Again: the "worst of this confounded business of *Miss Brown*," she told her lover, "is that it has made me lose my head."[33]

Lee might have recovered her emotional well-being more swiftly had Henry James not privately reinforced the harshest judgments of her public gaslighters, while gossiping widely about *Miss Brown* as a "serious mistake."[34] James was not just any respondent; he was the contemporary novelist whom Lee admired above all others, the mentor who had encouraged her to write the novel in the first place, and its carefully chosen dedicatee. His egregiously belated response — a letter sent nearly five months after publication — echoed the *Spectator* critic's argument, but in a different vein. Rather than highlighting the moral repugnance and mediocre caliber of her writing, James adopted a "you can't take a joke" approach: "It will probably already have been repeated to you to satiety that you take the aesthetic business too seriously, too tragically, and above all with too great an implication of sexual motives. There is a certain want of perspective and proportion . . . you have impregnated all those people too much with the sexual, the basely erotic preoccupation: your hand was over violent, the touch of life is lighter."[35] The fault lay with Lee, who "impregnated" Pre-Raphaelite artists with sexual violence that, he implies, does not exist outside her imagination. *She* is the one wielding an "over violent" "hand" with her too-serious, too-tragic views about sex. James implied that there was no rape culture among the aesthetes; she was being too sensitive. The ad hominem attacks of Lee's critics exemplify how gaslighting can function seamlessly as a facet of rape culture: a woman is accused of being sexually perverse or overly sensitive for protesting sexual abuse.

Among the aftershocks Lee suffered following her book's disastrous reception was the financial blow of losing her shot at a career as a novelist. "I hope to goodness *Miss Brown* may succeed," she had confided to Robinson in September 1884; "this horse business [that is, the costly death of a horse at her family's home in Florence] makes me all the more anxious to get some more money."[36] For a young lesbian without family wealth, novel-writing presented a game-changing prospect, so her book's critical failure meant a financial failure and, as she phrased it, "a consequent return to the old article-grinding."[37] She grieved to her partner, "I feel as if I had suddenly lost something. I was not aware I had counted on Miss B so."[38] She was anxious about mentioning her sense of the novel's failure to her own loved ones for fear that doing so would further damage her career: "I feel I ought scarcely to have mentioned it to you," she worried, because "the people who would like my book to fail will somehow find out my belief, & make use of it."[39] Within five months, Lee went from confidently negotiating for intellectual freedom with one of the most prominent publishers in Europe to feeling afraid to speak openly about her own book to her own lover. Gaslighting, her story shows, intimately influences a person's speech, thought, sense of self — and, with them, her livelihood.

Spurned by the British press, Lee was forced to find new publishers and a new audience in France.[40] She managed to cultivate ties with an Anglo-French network of female editors and writers, foster a French translation of *Miss Brown*, and fictionalize her experience being gaslit by James in a new story called "Lady Tal" (1889). Her hard-won recovery faltered, however, when Dr. Max Nordau's *Entartung* (1892) appeared in English as *Degeneration* (1895) and became an instant bestseller. In this tour de force, the respected German physician diagnosed Pre-Raphaelites, aesthetes, and decadents — the very people Lee had criticized and with whom she still identified — with the disease of "hysterical degeneracy." Suddenly, the thorny matter she had satirized in *Miss Brown* resurfaced as a medicalized crisis on an international scale. These artists, Nordau argued, were all certifiably hysterical.

Nordau applied a combination of French psychiatrist Bénédict Morel's concept of "degeneration" and French neurologist Jean-Martin Charcot's definition of hysteria to leading European artists and their admirers, transferring medical theories from asylums and hospitals to the literary avant-garde. The "physician," he writes, "recognises at a glance, in the *fin-de-siècle* disposition, in the tendencies of contemporary art and poetry," the "confluence of two well-defined conditions of disease, with which he is quite familiar, viz. degeneration (degeneracy) and hysteria."[41] Like Charcot, Nordau believed that men were just as susceptible to hysteria as women. Unlike Charcot, he overwhelmingly targeted men. Nordau argued that acclaimed male artists from D. G. Rossetti to Henrik Ibsen, who purported to advance civilization with their progressive cultural movements, were actually corrupting whole nations with a regressive morbidity rooted in their diseased minds. These hybrid creatures joined the excessive "emotionalism" of the hysteric with the atavism of the degenerate, exhibiting a dizzying array of symptoms from narcissism to sexual deviance to pathological lying.[42]

A form of structural gaslighting, Nordau's pathologizing attack was designed to discredit his targets by weaponizing the institutional authority of medical science. His sweeping diagnoses mixed multiple types of manipulation into one heady stew of epistemic, moral, sexual, and medical gaslighting. His motivational psychology helps illuminate the ways in which deep-seated misogyny and antisemitism shaped nineteenth-century accusations of hysteria. Nordau's *Degeneration* resulted, according to Hans-Peter Söder, from the Jewish doctor's "struggle not to be perceived to be part of an 'effeminate' and 'degenerate' race."[43] Jews, as Nora Gilbert explains in her chapter in this volume, were widely believed to be more vulnerable to nervous conditions. Anxious about the double impact of sexism and racism on male Jews like himself, Nordau projected these labels onto male gentiles of the European avant-garde.

His rhetorical strategy worked, causing measurable harm to writers within Lee's milieu. Emile Zola, for example, "submitted to medical checkups in order to produce scientific proof of his normalcy."[44] *Degeneration* wielded the most devastating effect on Oscar Wilde, whose 1895 criminal trials for "gross indecency" coincided with the book's English translation. The English prosecutor in Wilde's case, employing Nordau's technique of blending medical jargon with cultural criticism, cited lines from Wilde's literature as evidence of his deviancy.[45] Wilde was found guilty and sentenced to two years of hard labor in Reading Gaol, a catastrophic trauma that precipitated his early death. Nordau's accusation carried such powerful cultural force that Wilde cited *Degeneration* in his attempt to secure early release: after over thirteen months of hard labor and solitary confinement, he wrote to the Home Secretary to plead that his "offenses are forms of sexual madness . . . to be cured by a physician, rather than crimes to be punished by a judge," noting that "Professor Nordau in his book on 'Degenerescence' [*sic*] published in 1894 [had] devoted an entire chapter to the petitioner."[46]

Even though Nordau did not name Lee, the debate about *Degeneration*, as Richard Dellamora observes, "posed significant dangers for Lee, a leading aesthetician and a prominent literary decadent in her own right."[47] Obsessing about sex ranked as a primary symptom of hysterical degeneracy, and she had already been accused of this very thing. Also, she dressed in masculine clothing, never married, maintained romantic partnerships with other women, and used a masculine pen name in public *and* private — in short, she lived an openly queer life. On top of her sudden vulnerability to allegations of mental illness, her novel took on new, unintended meanings. She had devoted hundreds of pages of *Miss Brown* to decrying the sickening — "false, emasculate, diseased" (189) — poetry of the aesthetes. Now that a neurologist had diagnosed these poets as *literally* sick, her fictional words morphed into indirect support for a pseudoscientific theory that threatened her own safety as much as that of her peers.

The differences between Wilde's and Lee's cases of gaslighting are striking. Whereas the English court system brutally disgraced, imprisoned, and arguably killed Wilde, its attempt to gaslight him failed. When the prosecution cross-examining Wilde asked him, "What is the 'Love that dare not speak its name?'" he responded with a now-immortal lesson in the ancient, biblical, and early modern authorities who sanctioned pederasty: "'The Love that dare not speak its name' in this century is such a great affection of an elder for a younger man as there was between David and Jonathan, such as Plato made the very basis of his philosophy, and such as you find in the sonnets of Michelangelo and Shakespeare. It is that deep, spiritual affection that is as pure as it is perfect."[48] Wilde's eloquent answer reflects precisely the measure of psychological self-possession that is lost in a victim of effective gaslighting. The final words of Justice Wills after the jury delivered its guilty verdict suggest disappointment at Wilde's *lack* of visible emotional effects, whether in the form of self-doubt or self-disgust: "It is no use for me to address you," Wills said. "People who can do these things must be dead to all sense of shame, and one cannot hope to produce any effect upon them."[49] Wills gave up, in other words, on altering Wilde's state of mind. Later, in a letter to Robbie Ross, the disgraced author wrote, "To have altered my life would have been to have admitted that Uranian [that is, homosexual] love is ignoble. I hold it to be noble — more noble than other forms."[50] Although Wilde was inhumanely shamed and fatally punished, he was not *gaslit*, for the ancient, culturally rich, intergenerational reality of same-sex male love bolstered his sense of self as a thinker, a writer, a man, and a lover.

Lee had no such framework to rely upon for her sense of self. As a lesbian intellectual, she was more vulnerable to gaslighting because of the intersecting cultural, political, and epistemic forces working against her: the nonexistence of an authoritative language of same-sex love between women, the constant challenges to her authority as an "amateur" woman writer in a field run by Oxford-educated men, and misogynistic attacks against her for publishing — even thinking — candidly and deeply about sexual relationships. As she later lamented in her 1908 feminist manifesto, "we do not really know what women *are*. Women, so to speak, as a natural product, as distinguished from women as a creation of men; for women, hitherto, have been as much a creation of men as the grafted fruit tree [or] the milch cow."[51] Instead of having a classical tradition with which to validate her sexual self-conception, much less her womanhood, Lee had to keep battling ancient patriarchal myths — that of Pygmalion and that of hysteria — with their ubiquitous fantasies of male creative supremacy and female irrationality. She had to build her own community, create her own foundation upon which to define, justify, and believe herself.

Despite the personal risk she faced, Lee reviewed *Degeneration* in June 1896. In this essay, she confesses her fear of the kind of epistemic violence — what she calls "intellectual injustice" — committed by the German doctor: "Nordau's book has inspired me with a salutary terror" both of degeneration and "of the deterioration of the soul's faculties and habits, which is the inevitable result of all intellectual injustice."[52] Today, we could substitute the word "gaslighting" for the kind of soul-crushing, alienating, debilitating self-doubt Lee captures with her titular phrase: "Deterioration of Soul." She goes on to obliquely defend Wilde by encouraging reasonable reflection on laws and to lament the loneliness felt by artists with unconventional ideas. Divergent voices, she implores her readers, must not be silenced: "we require to hear every one, to allow every variety of human being to express itself."[53] She kept voicing her own ideas for the rest of her life, but she never enjoyed freedom from regret. As late as 1920, she remarked, "What a pity I didn't put off writing *Miss Brown* for thirty years!"[54]

The Legacy of Vernon Lee

Lee never achieved recognition for her work during her lifetime, and the charge of hysteria haunted her critical reception. Modern scholars have called her everything from hysterical, humorless, and militantly Puritan to neurotic, naive, and tactless. The twentieth-century critics who resurrected her literature from oblivion reinforced, rather than questioned, the judgments of her Victorian gaslighters. In 1970, for example, Léonee Ormond blamed the failure of *Miss Brown* on Lee's "neurotic attitude" toward sex and "the hysteria of her approach."[55] Her story's progression toward a darker denunciation of aestheticism, Ormond argues, "was entirely the result of her own peculiar psychological make-up, and her inability to remain intellectually dispassionate."[56] These remarks come from the same scholar who — in the same article — underscored "the acuteness and clarity of Vernon Lee's observation[s]" about aestheticism, going so far as to describe *Miss Brown* as "perhaps the best short introduction to the aesthetic movement ever written."[57]

Since the 1970s, both misogyny and homophobia have shaped Lee's legacy. In 1987, Burdett Gardner published *The Lesbian Imagination (Victorian Style): A Psychological and Critical Study of 'Vernon Lee'*, which defines Lee's lesbianism as a "neurosis" and claims to trace the influence of her homosexuality on her writing.[58] Gardner's pathologizing study simultaneously evokes hysteria's diagnosis of insanity in women who shun sex with men *and* Nordau's idea of "sexual madness" in artists who depict same-sex love. Jo Briggs has argued that, in the wake of Gardner's study, Lee's works have been read narrowly "as examples of sexual dissidence," whereas the writings of her peers, such as art historian Bernard Berenson, have been analyzed for the full breadth of their cultural significance.[59] One thing is clear: the gaslighting of Vernon Lee continued into the twenty-first century. In 2003, Vineta Colby echoed Ormond's verdict: "Ormond detects precisely the fatal weakness of the novel: 'Vernon Lee was not a prude of the conventional type. She was personally repelled and obsessed by the whole idea of the love relationship, . . . and this distaste colored her whole attitude to life and art.'"[60] Based on evaluations like this, one might think there's no such thing as a woman who doesn't want sex with a man, or sexual violence in the art world. It's all in her head! Only in a world where readers possess a basic awareness of women's and LGBTQIA people's diversely constrained sexual lives in a rape culture can *Miss Brown* be interpreted as the fearless critique of an insightful activist, not the embarrassing failure of a neurotic prude.[61]

To grasp Lee's radicalism and what it means for readers today, consider how the late-Victorian histories of hysteria, rape culture, and gaslighting traced in this chapter intersect and reinforce one another. The myth at the core of rape culture — the fallacy that women are always "asking for it" — is also embedded in the medical mythology surrounding hysteria, according to which a menstruating girl or woman naturally wants sex with a man such that her body malfunctions, even becoming diseased, when she doesn't get it. In this way, the logic of hysteria turns rape into cure, harm into healing. Meanwhile, the language of rape culture mirrors that of gaslighting. Phrases that exemplify classic instances of the latter double as conventional responses to a woman who shares her story of sexual abuse: "*Don't be so sensitive*"; "*That's all in you*"; "*That never happened*"; "*It didn't happen like that*"; "*Don't you dare suggest that!*"; "*You're overreacting.*"[62] In addition to navigating a culture of rape, Victorian women had to contend with a disabling law of decorum: conventional injunctions against speaking about sex. This confluence of fabrication and silencing around real sexual experiences meant that some of the most profound events of a woman's life — as well as her sense of self — could exist outside socially recognized reality. Literally, beyond credibility.

A woman who dared to describe her own or another person's sexual trauma not only defied Victorian codes of propriety but also contradicted the false ideology of female sexuality underpinning both hysteria discourse and rape culture. To tell this kind of story — a story like *Miss Brown* — no matter how real and evidenced, was to risk being simultaneously discredited, blamed, and possibly institutionalized by a medical system that wielded the power to cast freshly destabilizing layers of doubt and shame. Vernon Lee defied a social world without safe spaces for girls and women to teach, learn, or speak about sex; without commonly recognized concepts of sexual harm; and rife with pseudoscientific nonsense about women's innately disorderly bodies. Perhaps most impressively, she tried to expose the simple, causal, physiological link between patriarchal heterosexuality and psychological suffering. Her stories themselves — those she wrote and those she experienced — help us strip away the distortions incurred by critical assaults on her moral and emotional compass, while also giving us a powerful model for finding one's truths against all odds.

Notes

1. Quoted in Gunn, *Vernon Lee*, 105–6.
2. Gunn, *Vernon Lee*, 105–6.
3. Friedman, *Before Queer Theory*, 117. In my title and throughout this essay, I use the anachronistic term "lesbian" because I think this word best captures Vernon Lee's sexual self-conception, to the extent that we can discern it from her writings. Notably, late Victorian critic John Addington Symonds suggested Lee's relationship with A. Mary F. Robinson to sexologist Havelock Ellis as a case study in lesbianism for their coauthored book, *Sexual Inversion* (1897), the first English medical textbook on homosexuality. Generally, I use the capacious if equally anachronistic term "queer" to signal the nonnormative sexual lives and works of Victorian aesthetes who lived shortly before the word "homosexual" emerged.
4. "The only distinction between Hamlin and these actual painters," notes Leonée Ormond, is that Lee's villain tries "to 'improve' his fiancée before and not after marriage" ("Vernon Lee," 148).
5. Among those displeased to find caricatures of themselves in *Miss Brown* were Oscar Wilde, Jane Morris, William and Lucy Rossetti, the Humphrey Wards, Watts Dunton, Marie Spartali, and Mathilde Blind. Jane and William Morris never forgave Lee for the unmistakable likeness between Jane and Anne.
6. Lee wrote to her mother, "I am very glad I have come"; "I have got the better of any intention to give me the cold shoulder" (quoted in Colby, *Vernon Lee*, 107).
7. Anonymous, "Miss Brown."
8. Anonymous, "Miss Brown."
9. Hippocrates, quoted in Comen, *All in Her Head*, 288. Egyptian papyruses dating back to the second millennium BCE describe the dangerous mental effects of a womb on the move, but it was Hippocrates who first used the term "hysteron" in the fifth century BCE.
10. Jules Arsène Arnaud Claretie, quoted in Hustvedt, *Medical Muses*, 27.
11. Rampelli, *Narratives*, 197. Similarly, so-called smelling salts given to Victorian women who fainted marked the relentless endurance of classical medical practices grounded in patriarchal fictions about women's bodies: ancient doctors believed that placing nasty scents under a woman's nose would lure her disobedient uterus back into place.
12. Nordau, *Degeneration*, 15.
13. For an overview of these and other types of gaslighting, see the introduction to this volume.
14. Lee boasted to Blackwood in July 1884, "I am myself surprised at the success of *Euphorion*; and I think I may say, although it may sound conceited, that a new book of mine, especially a novel . . . must be received with considerable curiosity" (Lee, *Selected Letters*, 566).
15. Pater, *Letters*, 42.

16. James, *Complete Letters*, 114.
17. Quoted in Colby, *Vernon Lee*, 97.
18. "Lee even suggested in a letter in 1881 that, had she been a man, she would have asked Robinson to marry her" (Harrington, "The Strain of Sympathy," 74).
19. Harrington, "The Strain of Sympathy," 71–72.
20. Lee, *Selected Letters*, 594. Lee's debut novel was also indebted to Ouida's *Ariadnê: The Story of a Dream* (1877), a source she does not seem to have acknowledged. See note 25.
21. According to Jay D. Sloan, Buchanan's blistering 1871 review of Rossetti's first published *Poems* (1870) launched the "Rossetti mythology," a public perception of the poet-painter "as a reclusive and eccentric painter of sensual dream-women and as a writer of overwrought and indecently 'fleshly' poetry" (Sloan, "Attempting 'Spheral Change,'" 7). While Sloan underscores the accusations of effeminacy that dogged Rossetti for embracing "grand moments of passionate freedom," his analysis does not mention Siddal, the patriarchal order of Rossetti's erotic visions, or the unequal stakes of "passionate freedom" for the poet and his "dream-women" (Sloan, 10).
22. W. H. Mallock's novel *The New Republic* (1877) established a tradition of satirizing the aesthetes, which Gilbert and Sullivan embraced in *Patience; Or, Bunthorne's Bride* (1881), a comic opera that dramatizes the kinds of celebrity caricatures illustrated in countless *Punch* cartoons. Wilde openly courted the attention brought to him by *Punch* cartoons and *Patience*, even advertising the play during his 1882 American lecture tour.
23. Anonymous, "The Philistine Turns," 166. Notably, this anonymous satirist places Lee's name alongside Rossetti's: "Our aesthetes and our Saturday reviewers want to bottle up the artistic revival as something special for themselves and their particular aesthetic friends. They want to make a little esoteric kingdom of culture. . . . They will fill its libraries with no books save Mr. Symonds's, Mr. Rossetti's, and Vernon Lee's" (166).
24. Lee, *Selected Letters*, 568.
25. The Pre-Raphaelite Brotherhood may have supplied the principal fodder for *Miss Brown*, but, formally and thematically, Lee was also influenced by Ouida's Pygmalion novel, *Ariadnê* (1877). See Sondeep Kandola's compelling analysis of how both stories "reconfigure the Pygmalion myth" in defiance of its patriarchal organization (Kandola, "Ouida," 95).
26. For more on Ovid's central role in the making of Western rape culture, see Bellonby, "Rape Culture, A Literary History from Ovid to Shakespeare."
27. Critics usually credit Margaret Lazarus's documentary, *Rape Culture* (Cambridge Documentary Films, 1975), with coining the term.
28. Lee had recently courted debate with "The Responsibilities of Unbelief" (1883), a *Contemporary Review* article that caused a minor uproar with its arguments against traditional religion.

29. Lee, *Selected Letters*, 2: 24. These enemies included friends, such as critic W. C. Monkhouse, who privately scolded Lee for writing a "very nasty" book (quoted in Gunn, *Vernon Lee*, 102). Charles Mudie's Select Library pulled the novel from circulation. And George Moore planned to include excerpts from it in his censorship pamphlet, *Literature at Nurse* (1885), until Robinson intervened on Lee's behalf.
30. Anonymous, "Miss Brown."
31. Quoted in Gunn, *Vernon Lee*, 105–6.
32. Lee, *Selected Letters*, 612, 614.
33. Lee, *Selected Letters*, 614.
34. To his American friend Grace Norton, he wrote, "*Miss Brown* is a rather serious mistake (I think) . . . with an awful want of taste" (James, *Letters*, 3: 66).
35. Quoted in Ormond, "Vernon Lee," 152.
36. Lee, *Selected Letters*, 582.
37. Lee, *Selected Letters*, 611.
38. Lee, *Selected Letters*, 615.
39. Lee, *Selected Letters*, 614.
40. For an illuminating study of Lee's savvy social networking in France and of her multilingual, transnational, queer relations more broadly, see Valentine, "Vernon Lee."
41. Nordau, *Degeneration*, 15.
42. Nordau, *Degeneration*, 15.
43. Nordau, *Degeneration*, 478.
44. Söder, "Disease and Health," 476.
45. Significantly, the prosecutor highlighted passages from *The Picture of Dorian Gray*, Wilde's radical take on Ovid's Pygmalion, calling it a "sodomitical book." Whereas, in *Miss Brown*, Lee had shown how Ovid's myth romanticizes rape in ways that still harm women, in *Dorian Gray*, Wilde had challenged Pygmalion's heterosexual order by replacing the female muse with a beautiful male dandy.
46. In this July 1896 letter, Wilde writes, "In the works of eminent men of science such as Lombroso and Nordau, to take merely two instances out of many, this is specially insisted on with reference to the intimate connection between madness and the literary and artistic temperament" (Wilde, *Complete Letters*, 656).
47. Dellamora, "Productive Decadence," 532.
48. Wilde, *The Trials of Oscar Wilde*, 201–2.
49. Wilde, *The Trials of Oscar Wilde*, 339.
50. Quoted in Holland, *The Real Trial*, xxxvi.
51. Lee, "The Economic Parasitism of Women," 54.
52. Lee, "Deterioration of Soul," 928.
53. Lee, Deterioration of Soul," 943.
54. Quoted in Gunn, *Vernon Lee*, 107.
55. Ormond, "Vernon Lee," 138, 151.

56. Ormond, "Vernon Lee," 151.
57. Ormond, "Vernon Lee," 140.
58. Gardner, *The Lesbian Imagination*, 28.
59. Briggs, "Plural Anomalies," 160.
60. Colby, *Vernon Lee*, 102.
61. More recently, feminist and queer studies scholars, including Dennis Denisoff, Dustin Friedman, Linda Hughes, Sondeep Kandola, Kristin Mahoney, Diana Maltz, and Colton Valentine, have turned the tide toward nuanced readings of Lee's life and literature.
62. Abramson, *On Gaslighting*, 1.

Bibliography

Abramson, Kate. *On Gaslighting*. Princeton University Press, 2024.

Anonymous. "Miss Brown." *The Spectator*, December 13, 1884.

Anonymous. "The Philistine Turns." *Belgravia* 49 (1882): 155–67.

Bellonby, Diana. "Rape Culture, A Literary History from Ovid to Shakespeare." In *New Rape Studies: Humanistic Interventions*. Edited by Michael Dango, Erin Spampinato, and Doreen Thierauf. SUNY Press, forthcoming.

Briggs, Jo. "Plural Anomalies: Gender and Sexuality in Bio-Critical Readings of Vernon Lee." In *Vernon Lee: Decadence, Ethics, Aesthetics*, edited by Catherine Maxwell and Patricia Pulham, 160–73. Palgrave Macmillan, 2006.

Colby, Vineta. *Vernon Lee, A Literary Biography*. University of Virginia Press, 2003.

Comen, Elizabeth. *All In Her Head: The Truth and Lies Early Medicine Taught Us About Women's Bodies and Why It Matters Today*. Harper Wave, 2024.

Cox, Devon. *The Street of Wonderful Possibilities: Whistler, Wilde and Sargent in Tite Street*. Aurum, 2022.

Dellamora, Richard. "Productive Decadence: 'The Queer Comradeship of Outlawed Thought': Vernon Lee, Max Nordau, and Oscar Wilde." *New Literary History* 35 (2005): 529–46.

Evangelista, Stefano. *British Aestheticism and Ancient Greece: Hellenism, Reception, Gods in Exile*. Palgrave Macmillan, 2009.

Friedman, Dustin. *Before Queer Theory: Victorian Aestheticism and the Self*. Johns Hopkins University Press, 2019.

Gardner, Burdett. *The Lesbian Imagination (Victorian Style): A Psychological and Critical Study of "Vernon Lee*." Garland Publishing, 1987.

Gunn, Peter. *Vernon Lee: Violet Paget, 1856–1935*. Oxford University Press, 1964.

Harrington, Emily. "The Strain of Sympathy: A. Mary F. Robinson, *The New Arcadia*, and Vernon Lee." *Nineteenth-Century Literature* 61, no. 1 (2006): 66–98.

Holland, Merlin. *The Real Trial of Oscar Wilde: The First Uncensored Transcript of The Trial of Oscar Wilde Vs. John Douglas (Marquess of Queensberry), 1895*. Fourth Estate, 2003.

Hustvedt, Asti. *Medical Muses: Hysteria in Nineteenth-Century Paris*. Bloomsbury, 2011.

James, Henry. *Letters of Henry James, Volume III: 1883–1895*. Edited by Leon Edel. Harvard University Press, 1980.

———. *The Complete Letters of Henry James: 1887–1888*, Vol. I. Edited by Michael Anesko and Greg W. Zacharias. University of Nebraska Press, 2022.

Kandola, Sondeep. "Ouida, Vernon Lee and the Aesthetic Novel." In *Ouida and Victorian Popular Culture*, edited by Andrew King and Jane Jordan, 93–108. Routledge, 2013.

Lee, Vernon. "Deterioration of Soul." *Fortnightly Review* 59, no. 354 (1896): 928–43.

———. *Miss Brown*. Wildside Press, 1884.

———. *Selected Letters of Vernon Lee, 1856-1935*. Vol. I: 1865–1884. Edited by Amanda Gagel. Routledge, 2017.

———. "The Economic Parasitism of Women." In *A Feminist Reader: Feminist Thought from Sappho to Satrapi*, Vol. III, edited by Sharon M. Harris and Linda K. Hughes, 32–56. Cambridge University Press, 2013.

Nordau, Max. *Degeneration*. D. Appleton, 1895. Kessinger Legacy Reprints, 2010.

Ormond, Léonee. "Vernon Lee as a Critic of Aestheticism in *Miss Brown*." *Colby Library Quarterly* 9, no. 3 (1970): 131–54.

Pater, Walter. *Letters of Walter Pater*. Edited by Lawrence Evans. Oxford University Press, 1970.

Rampelli, Melissa. *Narratives of Women's Health and Hysteria in the Nineteenth-Century Novel*. Palgrave Macmillan, 2023.

Showalter, Elaine. *The Female Malady: Women, Madness, and English Culture, 1830–1980*. Virago Press, 1987.

Sloan, Jay D. "Attempting 'Spheral Change': D. G. Rossetti, Victorian Masculinity, and the Failure of Passion." *The Journal of Pre-Raphaelite Studies* 13 (2004): 5–20.

Söder, Hans-Peter. "Disease and Health as Contexts of Modernity: Max Nordau as a Critic of Fin-de-Siècle Modernism." *German Studies Review* 14, no. 3 (1991): 473–87.

Tasca, Cecilia, Mariangela Rapetti, Mauro Giovanni Carta, and Bianca Fadda. "Women and Hysteria in the History of Mental Health." *Clinical Practice & Epidemiology in Mental Health* 8 (2012): 110–19.

Valentine, Colton. "Vernon Lee, Queer Relations, and a New Guard of Victorianist Multilingualism." *Victorian Studies* 64, no. 1 (2021): 62–87.

Wilde, Oscar. *Complete Letters of Oscar Wilde*. Fourth Estate, 2000.

———. *The Trials of Oscar Wilde*. Edited by H. Montgomery Hyde. William Hodge, 1948.

Contributors

Diana Bellonby is a Philadelphia-based writer who holds a PhD in English from Vanderbilt University. In 2014, she cofounded The Fringe Foundation for Social Justice and devoted ten years to codirecting its grantmaking operations while continuing her scholarship on Victorian literature, visual culture, and histories of gender and sexuality. Her essays have appeared in such venues as *Public Books*, *Criticism: A Quarterly for Literature and the Arts*, *The Microgenre: A Quick Look at Small Culture*, and *New Rape Studies: Humanistic Interventions*. She is currently working on a memoir that interweaves her own story of sexual trauma with a literary history of rape culture.

Shalyn Claggett is a Professor of English at Mississippi State University. She is the author of *Equal Natures: Popular Brain Science and Victorian Women's Writing* (SUNY Press, 2023) and coeditor of *Strange Science: Investigating the Limits of Knowledge in the Victorian Age* (University of Michigan Press, 2017). She is currently at work on a book titled *The Victorian Screen: Magic Lantern Shows and the British Imagination*, which examines mass-produced narrative magic lantern shows in the context of Victorian literature and visual culture. Her essays have appeared in such journals as *Nineteenth-Century Contexts*, *SEL*, *Victorian Literature and Culture*, *Prose Studies*, and the *Journal of Narrative Theory*.

Lana L. Dalley is Professor of English at California State University, Fullerton. She is the editor of the four-volume *Women's Economic Writing in the Nineteenth Century* and coeditor of *Economic Women: Essays on Desire and Dispossession in Nineteenth-Century British Culture*. Her work has appeared in *Victorian Literature and Culture*, *Women's Writing*, *Victorians Institute Journal*, *Victorian Poetry*, *Nineteenth-Century Gender Studies*, and *The Routledge Companion to Literature and Economics*, among others.

Grace Franklin is a PhD candidate in English at the University of Southern California. Her work has been published in *Victorian Studies* and *Power Shift: Keywords for a New Politics of Energy* (West Virginia University Press, 2025), and she coedited a special issue of *Nineteenth-Century Contexts*. Her dissertation project explores interrelations between coal-gas power and literary form.

Nora Gilbert is a University Distinguished Teaching Professor at the University of North Texas, where she co-specializes in Victorian literature and early Hollywood film. She is the author of *Better Left Unsaid: Victorian Novels, Hays Code Films, and the Benefits of Censorship* (Stanford University Press, 2013); *Gone Girls, 1684–1901: Flights of Feminist Resistance in the Eighteenth- and Nineteenth-Century British Novel* (Oxford University Press, 2023); and articles and book chapters that have appeared in such venues as *PMLA*, *Screen*,

Nineteenth-Century Literature, *Film & History*, *Victorian Review*, *Avidly*, and *Public Books*. She has served as the editor of the journal *Studies in the Novel* since 2017.

Narin Hassan is Associate Professor in the School of Literature, Media, and Communication (LMC) at Georgia Tech. Her research and teaching interests include Victorian literature and culture, gender studies, postcolonial studies, health humanities, and critical yoga studies. Her publications include the book *Diagnosing Empire: Women, Medical Knowledge and Colonial Mobility* (Ashgate/Routledge); articles in journals including *Nineteenth-Century Gender Studies*, *Mosaic*, *Race and Yoga*, and *WSQ*; and coedited special issues in *Nineteenth-Century Contexts* and *Medical Humanities.* She is currently working on a book project that traces the gendered cultures and histories of yoga. She has served as Vice President and President of Interdisciplinary Nineteenth-Century Studies (INCS).

Sarah E. Kersh is Associate Professor of English at Dickinson College, where she teaches courses on Victorian literature and culture, queer studies, and digital humanities. Her work has been published in *Nineteenth-Century Contexts* and *Digital Humanities Quarterly*, as well as in collections on the poet Michael Field, including *Michael Field, Decadent Moderns*. She is currently working on a book project investigating poetic form, disability studies, and aestheticism in late-Victorian literature.

Katherine J. Kim is an Associate Professor of English at Molloy University, where she teaches composition and British and American literature from *Beowulf* to the twenty-first century. She earned her AB (in English and Psychology) and AM (in Humanities) from the University of Chicago and a PhD in English from Boston College. Kim conceived of and co-organized the Edgar Allan Poe Bicentennial Celebration, which led to a Boston Public Library exhibit and the installation of a permanent statue of the author in Boston in 2014. Among other projects, she has written book chapters and articles on Poe, Charles Dickens, Charlotte Brontë, Joseph Sheridan LeFanu, folklore, fairy tales, and trauma.

Tara MacDonald is Professor of English and Women's and Gender Studies and Director of the Centre for Feminist Research at the University of Lethbridge. She is the author of *Narrative, Affect, and Victorian Sensation: Wilful Bodies* (Edinburgh University Press, 2023) and *The New Man, Masculinity, and Marriage in the Victorian Novel* (Routledge, 2015), as well as numerous articles on nineteenth-century literature, gender, and feminism. She recently coedited a special issue of *Studies in the Novel* entitled "Strange Temporalities: Gender, Time, and the Novel" and she is coeditor of the forthcoming *Routledge Companion to Sensation Fiction.*

Jill Rappoport is Professor of English at the University of Kentucky, where she teaches nineteenth-century British literature and culture. Her most recent book is *Imagining Women's Property in Victorian Fiction* (Oxford University Press, 2023); she is also the author of *Giving Women: Alliance and Exchange in Victorian Culture* (Oxford University Press, 2012), coeditor of *Economic Women: Desire and Dispossession in Nineteenth-Century British Culture* (Ohio State University Press, 2013), and Associate Editor of the University of Virginia's Victorian Literature and Culture book series. Her articles have appeared in journals such as *Victorian Poetry*, *Victorian Studies*, *SEL*, *Victorian Literature and Culture*, and *Nineteenth-Century Literature*, as well as in numerous book collections. She is grateful for the opportunity to add her voice to this volume's work against interpersonal and systemic gaslighting.

Doreen Thierauf is Associate Professor of English at North Carolina Wesleyan University, where she teaches Anglophone literature from 1800 to the present. Her scholarship on nineteenth-century sexuality, reproduction, and gender-based violence has appeared in *Victorian Studies*, *Victorian Review*, *Victorian Literature and Culture*, *Nineteenth-Century Gender Studies*, *Women's Writing*, and other venues. With Erin Spampinato and Michael Dango, she has edited the collection *New Rape Studies: Humanistic Interventions* (SUNY Press, 2026).

Elizabeth Coggin Womack is Associate Professor of English at Penn State Brandywine, where she teaches a variety of literature and writing courses. She has published work on Victorian literature, material culture, and urban poverty in journals including *Victorian Literature and Culture*, *Nineteenth-Century Contexts*, and *Victorian Periodicals Review*.

Rosetta Young is Senior Lecturer in the Writing Program at Dartmouth College. Her current book project focuses on the relationship between the novel and the development of the upper middle class as a sociocultural group in the transatlantic nineteenth century. Her articles have appeared in *Nineteenth-Century Literature*, *Nineteenth-Century Contexts*, and *Studies in the Novel*, among other venues.

Index

Page number(s) in *italics* refer to tables and figures.